MW01258097

THE
IDENTITY AND ATTRIBUTES
OF GOD

THE
IDENTITY AND ATTRIBUTES
OF GOD

Terry L. Johnson

THE BANNER OF TRUTH TRUST

THE BANNER OF TRUTH TRUST

Head Office
3 Murrayfield Road
Edinburgh
EH12 6EL
UK

North America Office
PO Box 621
Carlisle
PA 17013
USA

banneroftruth.org

© Terry L. Johnson 2019
First published 2019

Reprinted 2019

*

ISBN
Print: 978 1 84871 854 8
Epub: 978 1 84871 855 5
Kindle: 978 1 84871 856 2

*

Typeset in 10.5/13.5 Adobe Garamond Pro
at The Banner of Truth Trust, Edinburgh

Printed in the USA by
Versa Press Inc.,
East Peoria, IL.

Dedicated to three seventeenth-century giants

Stephen Charnock
(1628–80)

George Swinnock
(1627–73)

William Gurnall
(1617–79)

of whom the world was not worthy

HEBREWS 11:38

Contents

Preface

THE research for these studies began in the summer of 1979 for a summer Bible study of the youth group of the Community Presbyterian Church of Danville, CA. My research was renewed thirty-four years later in the fall of 2013 for what I planned to be ten sermons on the attributes of God. Before I stopped, the series had grown into eighty-two sermons. These messages expanded primarily because of the richness of the reading which lay behind them. The more I read of the classics of Reformed Protestantism, the more I felt compelled to share the insights to which I was being exposed. This book is published with the same compulsion, that others might profit from the deep insights into the 'identity and attributes of God' from the best authors of the Reformed faith, recast in light of the issues we face today.

I must thank Karen Hansill for her tireless efforts at deciphering my handwriting and turning it into type; Suzanne Mitchell for editing the manuscript, and the trustees and staff of the Banner of Truth Trust for agreeing to publish it; the congregation of the Independent Presbyterian Church for receiving my preaching with grace and mercy; and for my wife Emily for her loyal support of my ministry over the course of over thirty years of marriage.

TERRY L. JOHNSON
Savannah, Georgia
November 2018

Introduction

SINCLAIR B. Ferguson says that on reading John Owen's classic work *On the Mortification of Sin*, 'most contemporary Christians are left feeling they *have never read anything like it*'.[1] His sense of things is verified by the publishing in recent years of at least seven different versions of Owen's original work, reprints, updated language abridgements, study versions, and so on, as Owen's disciples eagerly attempt to re-present his powerful work to modern readers.[2]

Yet Owen's is just one of the many works of the Puritans that are worthy of equal accolades. The following studies have involved this author in delving deeply into the writings of Reformed Protestantism on the subject of God's attributes, and what he has found has been nothing less than astonishing.

Earl Radmacher (1931–2014), former President of Western Theological Seminary, challenged an auditorium full of college students in 1975 (of whom I was one) to read Stephen Charnock's *Existence and Attributes of God*. I read several chapters while in seminary. Returning to his work for these studies, I found it to be extraordinary. Discourse XII, 'On the Goodness of God', is in its subject matter the equal

---

[1] Sinclair B. Ferguson, *The Trinitarian Devotion of John Owen: A Long Line of Godly Men Profiled* (Sanford, FL: Reformation Trust, 2014), p. 12 (my emphasis).

[2] For example, John Owen, *The Mortification of Sin: Abridged and Made Easy to Read*, ed. Richard Rushing (Edinburgh: Banner of Truth Trust, 2004); *The Mortification of Sin; with Forward and Introduction by J. I. Packer* (Fearn, Ross-shire: Christian Focus, 1996); Kris Lundgaard, *The Enemy Within: Straight Talk about the Power and Defeat of Sin* (Phillipsburg, NJ: P&R, 1998); John Owen, *What Every Christian Needs to Know …: An Abridgment and Rewrite of Two Works by John Owen*, ed. Andrew Swanson (London: Grace Publications Trust, 1998); John Owen, *Sin and Temptation: The Challenge to Personal Godliness*, abridged and edited by James M. Houston (Portland, OR: Multnomah, 1983); and of course *The Works of John Owen*, Vol. VI (Edinburgh: Banner of Truth Trust, 1966).

of Owen in his. Charnock's work is fully 1,132 pages (not counting indices) of small type in my two-volume edition. I have found myself digesting only three to four pages at a time, underlining sentence after sentence and starring paragraph after paragraph. The insight, wisdom, thoroughness, and power of his writing is remarkable.

Yet there is also George Swinnock's *The Incomparableness of God*, which might well serve as a concise introduction to Charnock, covering 135 pages in the fourth volume of his collected *Works*. The same soul-searching power, the same profound insights, are in Swinnock as were found in Owen and Charnock, page after page after page.

Then, again, there is Richard Baxter's *A Divine Life*. Remarkable. Stirring. Challenging. Thomas Brooks' *An Ark for All God's Noahs* begins with a wonderful exposition of God's attributes covering nearly 40 pages. William Gurnall's *A Christian in Complete Armour* is a gold mine of insight, challenge, and inspiration. We find the same profundity in Jonathan Edwards' sermons and treatises. We may also turn to the exegetically insightful and devotionally rich whole Bible commentaries of Matthew Poole (1624–79), John Trapp (1601–69), and the incomparable Matthew Henry (1662–1714). Further, we may turn to the many collections of sermons and commentaries such as Owen on Hebrews (all seven massive volumes!), Thomas Manton (1620–77) on James and Jude, David Dickson (1583–1663) on Matthew, Psalms, and Hebrews, Alexander Nisbet (*c.* 1623–69) on 1 and 2 Peter, William Greenhill (1591–1671) on Ezekiel, John Davenant (*c.* 1576–1641) on Colossians, William Jenkyn (1613–85) on Jude, George Hutcheson (1626–74) on John's Gospel, Jeremiah Burroughs (1599–1646) on Hosea, and John Cotton (1584–1652) on 1 John. Space will fail me if I go on to speak of Thomas Boston (1676–1732), John Flavel (1627–91), Thomas Watson (1620–86), Lewis Bayly (d. 1631), John Howe (1630–1705), Thomas Goodwin (1600–80), Richard Sibbes (1577–1635), and Wilhelmus à Brakel (1635–1711).

When we move back to the sixteenth-century Reformers, we find insight and excellence; when we move forward to the eighteenth-through twenty-first-century Reformed writers, we find accuracy and faithfulness. Yet we do not find quite the same spirit in them as we find in the seventeenth-century Puritans. Their insight into the challenges and joys of the Christian life is unmatched. Their ability to look at a subject comprehensively, viewing it from every conceivable perspective, bringing God's truth to bear upon it, is unrivalled. There were giants in the land in those days, the equal of which have not been seen since.

Hughes Oliphant Old has likened the task of Reformed ministers and theologians to that of a homeowner going to the attic to retrieve forgotten antiques. We dust them off, repair the upholstery, sand and varnish the wood, and re-present them for use today. This has been the burden of much of my ministry. There are treasures in the attic. The equal of English Puritans has not been seen, before or since. Yet the rest of the Reformed church has much to say as well. The Reformers, especially Calvin, and their eighteenth- to twenty-first-century successors, such as Isaac Watts (1674–1748), John Gill (1697–1771), Charles Hodge (1797–1878), James Henley Thornwell (1812–62), Hugh Martin (1822–85), B. B. Warfield (1851–1921), J. G. Machen (1881–1937), John Murray (1898–1975), and J. I. Packer (b. 1926), have much to contribute to our understanding of God and his gospel.

I submit this work to the public with the hope that it will demonstrate continuity across the centuries in an understanding of both the nature of God and the practical lessons to be drawn from what we know. I aspire to motivate my readers to join the feast that is the heritage of Reformed Protestantism. 'Oh, taste and see that the LORD is good!' the psalmist invites us (Psa. 34:8). Henry describes the believer's life as one 'of complacency in God, in his being, his attributes, and relations to us'.[1] He speaks of the 'constant pleasure' the believer enjoys:

> To think that here is a God; that he is such a one as the Scripture has revealed him to be, and being infinitely wise and powerful, holy, just and good; that this God governs the world, and gives law to all creatures; that he is our owner and ruler; that in his hand our breath is; in his hand our times, our hearts, and all our ways are ... happy they that can please themselves with these thoughts.[2]

It is to promote these *happy thoughts* that this book has been written.

---

[1] Matthew Henry, *The Pleasantness of a Religious Life* (Fearn, Ross-shire: Christian Focus, 1998), p. 58.
[2] *Ibid.*

ONE

The Study of God

And this is eternal life, that they know you the only true God,
and Jesus Christ whom you have sent.—John 17:3.

J. I. Packer (b. 1926) began his twentieth-century classic, *Knowing God*, with this quotation from a sermon by the great nineteenth-century English preacher C. H. Spurgeon (1834–92), then but twenty years of age:

> It has been said by someone that 'the proper study of mankind is man'. I will not oppose the idea, but I believe it is equally true that the proper study of God's elect is God; the proper study of a Christian is the Godhead. The highest science, the loftiest speculation, the mightiest philosophy, which can ever engage the attention of a child of God, is the name, the nature, the person, the work, the doings, and the existence of the great God whom he calls his Father.
>
> There is something exceedingly *improving to the mind* in a contemplation of the Divinity. It is a subject so vast, that all our thoughts are lost in its immensity; so deep, that our pride is drowned in its infinity .... No subject of contemplation will tend more to humble the mind, than thoughts of God ....
>
> But while the subject *humbles* the mind, it also *expands* it. He who often thinks of God, will have a larger mind than the man who simply plods around this narrow globe .... The most excellent study for expanding the soul, is the science of Christ, and him crucified, and the knowledge of the Godhead in the glorious Trinity. Nothing will so enlarge the intellect, nothing so

magnify the whole soul of man, as a devout, earnest, continued investigation of the great subject of the Deity.

And, whilst humbling and expanding, this subject is eminently *consolatory*. Oh, there is, in contemplating Christ, a balm for every wound; in musing on the Father, there is a quietus for every grief; and in the influence of the Holy Ghost, there is a balsam for every sore. Would you lose your sorrow? Would you drown your cares? Then go, plunge yourself in the Godhead's deepest sea; be lost in his immensity; and you shall come forth as from a couch of rest, refreshed and invigorated. I know nothing which can so comfort the soul; so calm the swelling billows of sorrow and grief; so speak peace to the winds of trial, as a devout musing upon the subject of the Godhead. It is to that subject that I invite you this morning.[1]

We begin with this quote from *Knowing God* because there is a sense in which we could do nothing more valuable than read and re-read Packer's great work. Knowing God is the end for which we were made. Knowing God is the great task of life. To know God, Jesus says, is eternal life (John 17:3). This eternal life, says Matthew Henry (1662–1714), is 'To know him as our Creator and to love him, obey him, submit to him, and trust in him as our owner, ruler and benefactor,—to devote ourselves to him as our sovereign Lord, depend upon him as our chief good, and direct all to his praise as our highest end,—this is life eternal.'[2]

As nothing is more important than securing eternal life, so nothing can be more important, more vital, than knowing God.

The apostle Paul identifies the fundamental problem of humanity as ignorance of God. Truth is 'suppressed' and 'exchanged' for a lie. Thinking has become 'futile' and 'dark', the mind 'debased', passions 'dishonourable', relationships 'contrary to nature', and behaviour 'shameless' (Rom. 1:18-32). Why? Because of false notions of God. This is at the root of human depravity. The want of divine knowledge,

---

[1] J. I. Packer, *Knowing God* (Downers Grove, IL: InterVarsity Press, 1973), 13-14; Spurgeon's words are from the first sermon in the first volume of the New Park Street Pulpit collection of Spurgeon's sermons (1855).

[2] Matthew Henry, *Matthew Henry's Commentary on the Whole Bible*, Vols. 1-6 (1708–10; Old Tappan, NJ: Fleming H. Revell Co., n.d.), comments on John 17:3.

says Old Princeton's Charles Hodge (1797–1878), the greatest of the nineteenth-century American Presbyterian theologians, 'is both the effect and cause of moral depravity'.[3]

The prophet Hosea identifies this as the essential problem in ancient Israel: 'There is … *no knowledge of God* in the land' (Hos. 4:1). 'This is a heavy charge indeed,' says Jeremiah Burroughs (1599–1646) in his exposition of Hosea.[4] The prophet laments, 'My people are destroyed for *lack of knowledge*' (Hos. 4:6). Again, 'They *know not the* LORD' (5:4), that is, says Burroughs, 'they know not my greatness, my holiness, they know not what a jealous God I am'.[5] God declares, 'For I desire steadfast love and not sacrifice, *the knowledge of God* rather than burnt offerings' (6:6). 'Where there is no knowledge of God,' says Calvin (1509–64), 'there is no religion, piety is extinct and faith destroyed.'[6]

This basic problem has continued to plague the people of God across the centuries. The writer to the Hebrews is severe in his rebuke of his readers' failure to progress spiritually. He has much to say to them about Christ's high priesthood (Heb. 5:1-10), but cannot say it because they have become 'dull of hearing' (5:11). 'For though by this time you ought to be teachers, you need someone to teach you again the basic principles of the oracles of God. You need milk, not solid food' (5:12). They ought to have progressed from student to teacher, from infant to adult food, but they had not. Milk is sufficient for a child but not for the mature. For adults still to be 'bottle-fed' is a tragedy. They ought to be teachers by now. Instead, they must still be taught 'basic principles'. The writer to the Hebrews urges them (and us), 'Therefore let us leave the elementary doctrine of Christ and go on to maturity, not laying again a foundation of repentance from dead works and of faith toward God' (6:1). 'Leave the elementary doctrine of Christ,' he says. 'Go on to maturity.' Clearly he is alarmed by the failure to progress in knowledge and maturity, and he issues in this context the sternest of warnings (6:4-7).

---

[3] Charles Hodge, *A Commentary on Romans* (1864; Edinburgh: Banner of Truth Trust, 1972), p. 39.

[4] Jeremiah Burroughs, *An Exposition of the Prophecy of Hosea* (1643, 1863; Beaver Falls, PA: Soli Deo Gloria, n.d.), p. 210.

[5] *Ibid.*, p. 274.

[6] John Calvin, *Commentaries on the Twelve Minor Prophttets: Hosea*, tr. John Owen (1849; Grand Rapids: Baker, 1979), I:233.

We find the same complaint directed by the apostle Paul against the Corinthian congregation. 'But I, brothers, could not address you as spiritual people,' he complains. Why not? Because they had not matured. Instead he had to deal with them 'as people of the flesh, as infants in Christ' (1 Cor. 3:1)—'not yet past the spoon', as John Trapp (1601–69) puts it.[7] They had failed to grow in knowledge and maturity. They could not eat meat. They still were not ready for adult spiritual food long after they should have been. 'I fed you with milk, not solid food,' Paul complains, 'for you were not ready for it' (1 Cor 3:2). They should have been ready for it, but they were not. 'And even now you are not yet ready, for you are still of the flesh' (3:2-3). The meat he wishes to feed them is doctrine. They need solid, meaty doctrine.

Knowing God is the all-encompassing, all-determining factor in understanding who we are and the purpose of our existence. 'Nearly all the wisdom we possess,' says John Calvin in the opening lines of his famous *Institutes of the Christian Religion* (1559), 'consists of two parts: the knowledge of God and of ourselves.' 'Man,' he continues, 'never achieves a clear knowledge of himself *unless he has first looked upon God's face, and then descends from contemplating him to scrutinize himself.*'[8] The English Puritan George Swinnock (1627–73), in his treatise *The Incomparableness of God*, echoes Calvin in saying, 'Man never comes to a right knowledge of himself, what a pitiful, abominable wretch he is, till he comes to a right knowledge of God, what an excellent incomparable majesty he is.'[9]

Only on the basis of the knowledge of God can we ever realize even the basic outline of our identity: *who* we are, *why* we are here, *how* we are to live, *what* are our basic needs, and *where* we are going. Why for so many is life empty, meaningless, and pointless? Why are so many lost, wandering about aimlessly? Why are they unable to discern any purpose for anything; why is nihilism the predominant philosophy of the day? Because we cannot know ourselves unless we know God.

[7] John Trapp, *A Commentary on the Old and New Testaments* (1647, 1865–68; Eureka, CA: Tansky Publications, 1997), V:523.

[8] John Calvin, *Institutes of the Christian Religion*, Vols. 1 & 2, in John T. McNeill (ed.), *The Library of Christian Classics*, Vol. XXI (Philadelphia, PA: Westminster Press, 1960), I.i.1, p. 35; I.i.2, p. 37 (emphasis added).

[9] George Swinnock, *The Incomparableness of God*, in *The Works of George Swinnock* (1868; Edinburgh: Banner of Truth Trust, 1992), IV:474.

Knowledge is central to what the apostle Paul seeks in his prayers for the churches. He prays that God might give to the Ephesians 'a spirit of *wisdom* and of *revelation* in the *knowledge* of him, having the eyes of [their] hearts *enlightened*, that [they] may *know*' (Eph. 1:17-18). Similarly, he prays for the Colossians that they might 'be filled with the *knowledge* of his will in all spiritual *wisdom* and *understanding* … increasing in the *knowledge* of God' (Col. 1:9-10). His prayer for the Philippians is that 'your love may abound more and more, with *knowledge* and all *discernment*' (Phil. 1:9). 'This is eternal life,' Jesus said, 'that they know you the only true God, and Jesus Christ whom you have sent' (John 17:3). 'The end of Christ's sacrifice and inter-cession is to reconcile God and man,' said English Puritan Richard Baxter (1615–91). 'The end of his doctrine is *to teach us to know God*.'[10]

Need

Why do we need to study about God, rather than intuit the truth? We need to study because thoughts about God are inescapable, and errant thoughts about God are inevitable. We are all theologians. We all con-ceive of God as a particular sort of being who stands in a certain kind of relation to the world. This is true for all people, Christian and non-Christian, Protestant and Roman Catholic, Presbyterian and Baptist. Our conceptions may be deliberate and conscious, or subconscious and accidental, yet we all surely have them. Everyone has opinions about God. The question is, will our concepts of God be correct or erroneous? Will they be true or false?

Because of the effects of sin, our natural common-sense thoughts of God are predictably wrong. Since the fall, the human race has been worshipping a god of its own imagination and creation, not the God who is there. 'In the beginning man created God in his own image', the rock group Jethro Tull cynically claimed on the cover of its 1971 album *Aqualung*, speaking as it did so for an entire generational demographic. We have 'exchanged the glory of the incorruptible God for a god in the form of corruptible man and creatures' (Rom. 1:23 NASB). The things of the Spirit of God are 'foolishness' (NASB) to the natural man and he

---

[10] Richard Baxter, *The Divine Life*, in *The Practical Works of Richard Baxter* (Ligonier, PA: Soli Deo Gloria, 1990), III:764 (emphasis added).

cannot understand them (1 Cor. 2:14). 'Man's nature,' says Calvin, 'is a perpetual factory of idols.'[11]

Reliable thoughts of God are to be found only in the Scriptures. The Bible is God's own textbook for the study of God. 'God has spoken' through the Hebrew prophets and through Jesus Christ (Heb. 1:1-2). After establishing the identity of Christ as the Son of God and superior to the angels, supporting his argument with numerous citations from the Psalms and other Old Testament passages, the author of the letter to the Hebrews writes, 'Therefore we must pay much closer attention to what we have heard, lest we drift away from it' (2:1). Close attention to the biblical witness ('what we have heard') is necessary 'lest we drift away from it'. Infrequent study will not do. Haphazard engagement with the Bible is totally insufficient. What is necessary is 'much closer attention'—focused, systematic, serious study. We are to 'give heed with an attentive and intent mind', says Matthew Poole (1624–79) of this verse in his three-volume commentary on the whole Bible.[12] The godly meditate on God's word 'day and night' (Psa. 1:2; cf. 119:15, 97). They thrive, not on the basis of random encounters with Scripture, but through regular, sustained study and contemplation of God's self-revelation through his word.

If we are not careful to fill our minds with correct notions about God, our minds will surely be filled with incorrect ones. Nature abhors a vacuum. Our concepts will be either right or wrong. They will either accord with the knowledge of the true God as revealed in Jesus Christ and Scripture, or they will be idolatrous. Today's widespread ignorance of God can be traced in large part to a failure to submit ourselves to God's self-revelation in Scripture.

Neglect

Given its importance, why has the study of God been neglected? What factors have clouded our vision and undermined our pursuit of this knowledge? What have been the barriers to the pursuit of the true knowledge of God?

---

[11] Calvin, *Institutes*, I.xi.8, p. 108.
[12] Matthew Poole, *A Commentary on the Holy Bible* (1683–85; Edinburgh: Banner of Truth Trust, 1963), III:812.

Presumption

The first barrier to the study of God is presumption. Many of us bring to the table the assumption that God is like us. He shares our interests and our desires, our attitudes and our opinions. Consequently, careful study is thought to be unnecessary. Like the gods of ancient Greece and Rome, he is merely a bigger version of ourselves. 'You thought that I was one like yourself', God says, rebuking the morally indulgent and idolatrous (Psa. 50:21). His point is that he is not! 'Your God is too small', said J. B. Phillips (1906–82) a generation ago.[13] 'Your thoughts of God are too human', Martin Luther told Erasmus (1466–1536).[14] 'My thoughts are *not* your thoughts, neither are your ways my ways', declares the Lord through Isaiah (55:8). We are far too quick to think God's views and goals are identical with our own. It is a mistake to think that, because God is a person, he must be a person like us. 'Today, vast stress is laid on the thought that God is *personal*,' says Packer, 'but this truth is so stated as to leave the impression that God is the same sort as we are—weak, inadequate, ineffective, a little pathetic.' 'But,' he continues, 'this is not the God of the Bible.'[15]

God is 'wholly other', said Karl Barth (1886–1968).[16] He is above us and he is beyond us. Barth told the liberals of his day, 'You cannot find God by shouting Man with a loud voice.' *Finitum non capax infiniti*: The finite cannot comprehend the infinite. Should we fail to understand his 'otherness', we will end up positing a God who is as indifferent towards truth, as fickle and as compromising as we are. Such a God is not worthy of our worship, and perhaps that is why he inspires so little worship today. A god who is merely humanity writ large will never motivate reverent worship.

'Can you find out the deep things of God? Can you find out the limit of the Almighty?' Zophar asked Job (Job 11:7). The implied answer is, no, we cannot. 'Oh, the depth of the riches and wisdom and knowledge of God! How unsearchable are his judgments and how

---

[13] J. B. Phillips, *Your God Is Too Small* (1952; New York: Macmillan, 1953).
[14] Cited in A. W. Pink, *The Attributes of God* (Grand Rapids, MI: Baker, 2008), p. 35.
[15] Packer, *Knowing God*, p. 74.
[16] Karl Barth, in his famous *Epistle to the Romans* (1922; New York: Bloomsbury T&T Clark, 2016).

inscrutable his ways! "For who has known the mind of the Lord, or who has been his counsellor?"' (Rom. 11:33-34). God is beyond our reach. He is 'inscrutable'. We cannot know his mind, explore his 'deep things', or 'find out' his 'limits'. The deep rivers of God's mysteries (e.g. 1 Tim. 3:16) are 'not fordable by our short-legged understanding', says William Gurnall (1617–79) in his Puritan classic *The Christian in Complete Armour*.[17]

Even in Scripture God but 'lisps' to us.[18] 'He condescends to our littleness and narrowness,' says Charnock (1628–80), 'to our contracted and tethered capacities.'[19] We know him, Calvin maintains, 'not as he is in himself, but as he is toward us'.[20] We can know God truly, but never comprehensively. 'He hath given us a true representation of himself,' John Howe (1630–1705) explains of Exodus 33:18ff., 'not a full: such as will secure our apprehensions … from error, not from ignorance.' At our best, 'we have still but low, defective conceptions of each [attribute].'[21] 'Our thoughts' of God, he says, 'are empty and languid, straight and narrow, such as diminish and limit the Holy One.'[22] Wilhelmus à Brakel (1635–1711), whose Dutch classic *The Christian's Reasonable Service* was only translated into English in 1992, reminds us that at best 'we can only perceive the uttermost fringes of his being'. 'Can a small bottle contain an entire ocean?' he asks.[23] God communicates himself to us, says the English Puritan Thomas Watson (1620–86), 'according to the bigness of our vessel, but not the immenseness of his nature'.[24] At all points, there is more to be said, more to be understood, more to be carefully expressed. John Owen (1616–83), the greatest of the English

---

[17] William Gurnall, *The Christian in Complete Armour* (1662, 1665; Edinburgh: Banner of Truth Trust, 1964).

[18] Calvin, *Institutes*, I.xiii.1, p. 121.

[19] Stephen Charnock, *The Existence and Attributes of God* (1681–82; 1864; Edinburgh: Banner of Truth Trust, 2010), I:278.

[20] Calvin, *Institutes*, I.x.2, p. 97.

[21] John Howe, *The Blessedness of the Righteous*, in *The Works of Rev. John Howe* (1848; Ligonier, PA: Soli Deo Gloria, 1990), II:38.

[22] *Ibid*., p. 36.

[23] Wilhelmus à Brakel, *The Christian's Reasonable Service* (1701; Grand Rapids, MI: Reformation Heritage Books, 1992), I:88, 137.

[24] Thomas Watson, *A Body of Divinity* (1692; London: Banner of Truth Trust, 1958), p. 54.

Puritan theologians, warns us in his extraordinary treatise *The Mortifi-cation of Sin* of the paucity of our knowledge of God: 'We may suppose that we have here attained great knowledge, clear and high thoughts of God, but, alas! When he shall bring us into his presence we shall cry out, "We never knew him as he is; the thousandth part of his glory, and perfection, and blessedness, never entered into our hearts."'[25]

Only by the aggressive pursuit of the true knowledge of God can we overcome our vast ignorance.

Anti-intellectualism

A second barrier to the study of God is anti-intellectualism. A legacy of the Fundamentalist/Modernist controversies of the early twentieth century has been an understandable fear of serious study. Academia since the late nineteenth century has been dominated by theological scepticism. Once faithful old-line Christian institutions (like the Ivy League universities) are now overwhelmingly hostile to biblical Chris-tianity. Too much deep thought, some of the faithful have concluded, freezes the heart. Did not Luther call reason 'the devil's whore'?[26] Stick to the 'old, old story', the basic gospel facts, and leave deep theology for liberals and heretics. The simple gospel, not complex theology, is our need. Another trend has been to emphasize the need of love and to see doctrine as a divisive distraction.

A generation ago John Stott (1921–2011) found it necessary to write a booklet entitled *Your Mind Matters.*[27] God has given us minds. He expects us to use them. The warnings against anti-intel-lectualism continue to be sounded. 'The scandal of the evangelical mind,' says Mark Noll, 'is that there is not much of an evangelical mind.' Evangelical Christians are exemplary in their evangelistic and missionary endeavours, their generosity to the needy, and their supportive communities. They are excellent organizers, managers, marketers, and mobilizers, as evidenced by their hosts of mega-churches,

[25] John Owen, *On the Mortification of Sin*, in *The Works of John Owen*, ed. William H. Goold (1850–53; Edinburgh: Banner of Truth Trust, 1966), VI:65.

[26] Gurnall calls unaided reason a 'beautiful serpent' and a 'heathen judge' used by the devil to undermine faith (*Christian in Complete Armour*, II:111).

[27] John R. W. Stott, *Your Mind Matters* (Downers Grove, IL: InterVarsity Press, 1972).

colleges, seminaries, and para-church organizations, and by the variety of their ministries. Yet 'American evangelicals are not exemplary for their thinking,' Noll maintains, 'and they have not been so for several generations.'[28]

Noll quotes Os Guinness: 'most evangelicals simply don't think'; and Lebanese diplomat Charles Malik, who in his address at the opening of the Billy Graham Center at Wheaton College said, 'The greatest danger besetting American Evangelical Christianity is the danger of anti-intellectualism.'[29]

Among the many distinctives of Christianity is that Christians do theology. Adherents of Eastern religions do not. Taoists, Buddhists, and Hindus meditate. They contemplate mysteries. Yet religion is not for them a realm in which reason is interactive. They do not 'do theology' and they do not develop theologians. They may have mystics and gurus and wise men. Yet these are not theologians in any serious sense. They do not study God's works, the realm of nature, and draw conclusions about God on the basis of what they observe. They do not study their holy books and draw conclusions about God, which 'by good and necessary consequence may be deduced from Scripture' (Westminster Confession of Faith I.6). For them, God is unknowable. God is impersonal. He lacks consciousness. Even Muslims refrain from theological study because making statements about Allah would limit a deity whose will has no boundaries. For most non-Christian religions, religious instruction is limited to ethics, ritual, and spiritual disciplines.

Compare this outlook with that of B. B. Warfield (1851–1921) writing in 1903: 'It is the distinction of Christianity that it has come into the world clothed with the mission to *reason* its way to its dominion.'[30] We are to love God with all our hearts and with all our *minds* (Matt. 22:37; Mark 12:30; Luke 10:27). God himself invites us, saying, 'Come now, let us reason together' (Isa. 1:18). Regularly we find the apostle Paul 'reason[ing] with them from the Scriptures, explaining and proving …' (Acts 17:2-3; cf. 17:17; 18:4; 19:8).

[28] Mark A. Noll, *The Scandal of the Evangelical Mind* (Grand Rapids, MI: Eerdmans, 1994), p. 3.

[29] *Ibid.*, pp. 23, 26.

[30] B. B. Warfield, *Selected Shorter Writings*, ed. John E. Meeter (Phillipsburg, NJ: Presbyterian & Reformed, 1973), II:99.

One way to understand the sin problem is to see it as a knowledge problem, as the apostle Paul largely does in Ephesians 4. The problem with the pagan Gentiles is that they walk 'in the futility of their *minds*'; their *'understanding'* is 'darkened'; they are alienated from God because of 'the *ignorance* that is in them', leading to the practice of 'every kind of impurity' (Eph. 4:17-19). By contrast, believers, through the exercise of the word gifts of pastors and teachers, have attained 'the unity of *the faith* and of the *knowledge* of the Son of God'. No longer are they deceived by 'every wind of *doctrine*'. Now they '[speak] the *truth* in love' (Eph. 4:11-15). They have '*learned* Christ' and his way. They *'heard* about him and were *taught* in him, as the *truth* is in Jesus' (4:20, 21). Believers put off the old self and put on the new as they are 'renewed in the spirit of [their] *minds*' (4:22-24). The apostle's emphasis is unmistakable: our minds matter. Thinking matters. Doctrine matters. Truth matters. We are 'transformed by the renewal of [our] *mind[s]* (Rom. 12:2). 'Knowledge doth not make a heart good,' says William Gurnall, 'but it is impossible that without knowledge it should be good.'[31]

God addresses our minds. He expects us to think. Alone among the creatures we are able to offer to God intelligent praise. All creation praises God (Psa. 19:1ff.; 148–150). Humanity alone does so with reflection. Yet to do so we must study God's word to know of what that praise should consist. Only through careful study can we know with accuracy what it is in God that makes him praiseworthy.

Super-spirituality

Similarly, a third barrier is an imagined antithesis between study and spiritual knowledge. 'God speaks to me directly. I don't consult the opinions of others. I don't read human authors. I don't listen to man, but only to what God says in his word', some will say, with no small measure of spiritual pride. Francis Schaeffer (1912–84) published the booklet *The New Super-Spirituality* the same year as Stott published *Your Mind Matters*, addressing many of the same issues.[32] He lamented that the great gifted teachers of the church, such as Augustine,

---

[31] Gurnall, *Christian in Complete Armour*, I:161.
[32] Francis A. Schaeffer, *The New Super-Spirituality* (Downers Grove, IL: Inter-Varsity Press, 1972).

Aquinas, Calvin, and Hodge, were neglected, to the impoverishment of our thinking.

Yet should one trust one's own thinking? Gerald R. McDermott, co-author of a mammoth study of the theology of Jonathan Edwards (1703–58), the greatest of the American Puritans, writes about this very problem in an article whose title makes the point: 'Guided by the Great Cloud: Why Tradition Is Vital for Understanding Scripture'.[33] We need the guidance of the 'great Tradition', the creeds (e.g. Apostles', Nicene, Athanasian), the early church councils (e.g. Nicea I, Constantinople I, Ephesus I, Chalcedon), and the early fathers (e.g. Athanasius, the Cappadocians, Chrysostom, Augustine), and the Protestant Confessions when interpreting the Bible. We call upon the great 'cloud of witnesses' (Heb. 12:1), the Reformers (e.g. Luther, Calvin, Knox), the Puritans and Protestant 'Scholastics' (e.g. Perkins, Bunyan, Owen, Charnock, Turretin, Henry), and the nineteenth- and twentieth-century American evangelicals (e.g. Edwards, Hodge, Dabney, Thornwell, Warfield, Machen, Murray). We need the help of them all, and to get that help requires study.

Right thoughts about God do not come to us naturally, even as believers. Even regenerate minds must be applied to gain wisdom and seek understanding (Prov. 5:1-2). Even those filled with the Holy Spirit are urged to study and to show themselves approved (2 Tim. 2:15).

Our aim as Christians is to think God's thoughts after him (another of Calvin's phrases), and that happens not automatically upon conversion, but only as we work at replacing worldly with biblical thoughts. Doing so requires that we distrust even our own thoughts (which, of course, are 'man's thoughts') and consult the formulations of the outstanding theologians, creeds, and councils of the church— views of Christian doctrine that have been thoroughly vetted and which have stood the test of time.

---

[33] Gerald R. McDermott, 'Guided by the Great Cloud: Why Tradition Is Vital for Understanding Scripture', in *Christianity Today*, Vol. 58, No. 9 (Nov. 2014), pp. 54-57.

Impracticality

Some maintain that the study of God is not practical. This is our fourth and final barrier to the knowledge of God to consider, and perhaps it is the most widespread. Modern people are thoroughly pragmatic. We want teaching that will be helpful to us. Teach us the 'how-tos', we say, of personal finance, child-rearing, marriage; give us the keys to psychological or emotional health, even the 'biblical' principles of weight loss. A study of the attributes of God is too abstract, too theoretical, and therefore unappealing.

We see two problems with this perspective. First, right thinking about God is, in and of itself, glorifying to God. He has not revealed himself in order that we should know him wrongly and attribute false characteristics to him. He is no more pleased with wrong attribution than we are. Rather, God has spoken so that we might know him as he is revealed and bless him by praising him as he is revealed. We are a chosen people whose calling is to 'proclaim [his] excellencies' (1 Pet. 2:9). For us to do so, we must know what those excellencies are. What are his virtues? What are his attributes?

Second, the study of God's attributes is eminently practical, addressing all the basic questions of life. The 'knowledge of the truth', the apostle Paul tells Titus, 'accords with godliness' (Titus 1:1). There are those who 'profess to know God' but lack the practical impact that the truth, properly grasped, always makes. Hence: 'but they deny him by their works' (1:16). Titus is to teach the practical implications of gospel truth, that is, 'teach what accords with sound doctrine' (2:1). Good behaviour, like that which the apostle commends to Titus, leaves 'nothing evil to say' about believers and 'adorn[s] the doctrine of God our Saviour' (2:7-10).

In his classic *The Practice of Piety* the Puritan Lewis Bayly (d. 1631) begins not with the practical, the theme of his book, but with the theological.[34] Twenty-seven pages are spent on the essence and attributes of God, followed by eighteen pages on the misery of man and thirty-nine pages on redemption in Christ. Only then, Bayly understood, would his readers be ready to move on to the practical.

---

[34] Lewis Bayly, *The Practice of Piety: Directing a Christian How to Walk That He May Please God* (1611, 1842; Morgan, PA: Soli Deo Gloria, n.d.).

Only when the foundational knowledge of God and of ourselves had been laid could the practical be properly discussed. This is typical of the Puritan and Reformed tradition.

The connection between knowledge and practice clearly is visible in the apostle Paul's prayers. His prayer for the Colossians to be filled with knowledge is so that they might 'walk in a manner worthy of the Lord, fully pleasing to him, bearing fruit in every good work' (Col. 1:10). His prayer for the Philippians to grow in love and knowledge is 'so that you may approve what is excellent, and so be pure and blameless for the day of Christ, filled with the fruit of righteousness that comes through Jesus Christ' (Phil. 1:10-11). One's 'walk', the fruit of one's life, is clearly in view as he prays for knowledge, wisdom, understanding, and discernment. When there is a 'true and lively sense of God's attributes', says Bayly, 'there is bred in a man's heart a love, awe, and confidence in God'. Moreover, 'so far … as we imitate God in his goodness, love, justice, mercy, patience, and other attributes, so far do we know him'.[35]

The Reformed tradition defines theology as 'the science of living blessedly forever' (William Perkins) or 'the science of living to God' (William Ames). The practical is always in view. Jonathan Edwards refined this common definition to 'the doctrine of living to God by Christ', claiming that 'There is no one doctrine, no promise, no rule, but what some way or other relates to the Christian and divine life, or our living to God by Christ.'[36] After reviewing several passages in which we are urged to follow the example of Christ, such as John 13:15 (washing the disciples' feet), the call to servanthood in Mark 10:44 (giving his life as a 'ransom for many'), the call to suffering in 1 Peter 2:21 ('follow in his steps'), and the call to humble selfless servitude in Philippians 2:5 ('have this mind among yourselves, which is in Christ Jesus'), John Murray (1898–1975), late Professor of Systematic Theology at the Westminster Theological Seminary in Philadelphia, admires how in the New Testament the high doctrines of Christology (such as incarnation and atonement) are 'brought to bear upon the concrete

---

[35] Bayly, *The Practice of Piety*, p. 26.

[36] Jonathan Edwards, *Christian Knowledge: or, The Importance and Advantage of a Thorough Knowledge of Divine Truth*, in *The Works of Jonathan Edwards* (1834; Edinburgh: Banner of Truth Trust, 1974), II:158.

details of practical life'. His point: theology is practical. 'The most transcendent truths of the gospel,' he says, 'have a direct bearing upon how the life of the believer is to be lived.'[37] Knowing God lays the foundation for life. Yet theological heavy lifting is required to understand how this is so. We may be tempted to take a shortcut, the easy road, and do what is expedient rather than truly labouring to know God and understand from *who* he is *what* he would have us do.

Theology creates a world view and determines how we will serve God and live life. Our concept of God will determine the hymns we sing, the way we worship, and our moral notions. 'Different god, different mountain top', said one of the Cambridge professors in the film *Chariots of Fire*. The key is, who is God? What has he said to us? What are the duties, priorities, obligations, and objectives which he has given to us? 'We have a distorted conception of the relation of doctrine to life,' Murray continues, 'if we think that the most transcendent truths of the faith are impractical in their bearing upon the most menial tasks of our vocation.'[38] One pastor reports a slip of the tongue made by a lay leader of his church when he (the pastor) suggested a sermon series on God's attributes: 'We're not very interested in God.' Indeed!

'It is one of the defining marks of our time that God is now weightless,' says David F. Wells. 'I do not mean by this that he is ethereal but rather that he has become unimportant. He rests upon the world so inconsequently as not to be noticeable. He has lost his saliency for human life.'[39] These are the obstacles we face, the forces arrayed against the study of God that might persuade us to divert our attention to lesser endeavours. Add to these the persistent problems of worldliness, carnality, a culture of amusement, and an ethos of fun, and one can see that there is much there to distract us. We have our

---

[37] John Murray, *Collected Writings of John Murray* (Edinburgh: Banner of Truth Trust, 1977), II:308-9.

[38] *Ibid.*, II:308-9.

[39] David F. Wells, *God in the Wasteland* (Grand Rapids, MI: Eerdmans, 1994), p. 88. Wells continues, 'Those who assure the pollsters of their belief in God's existence may nonetheless consider him less interesting than television, his commands less authoritative than their appetites for affluence and influence, his judgment no more awe-inspiring than the evening news, and his truth less compelling than the advertisers' sweet fog of flattery and lies. That is weightlessness.'

work cut out for us. But let us now move on to the importance of persevering in such a study.

Important principles

We conclude our introduction to the study of God with several important principles to guide our pursuit of the knowledge of God.

Primary vocation

First, knowing God is the primary vocation of God's people. Listen to Jesus, the apostle Paul, and the prophet Jeremiah.

'And this is eternal life, that they know you, the only true God, and Jesus Christ whom you have sent' (John 17:3). Jesus provides us with a summary of his mission. He came that we might have eternal life. What is eternal life? It is to know God. Salvation from sin is a means to an end. The end is relational. We are *forgiven* our sins that we might be *reconciled* to God. We are *reconciled* to God that we might *know* God. His mission is not to confer 'merely conscious, unending existence', says the Scot David Brown (1803–97), 'but a life whose most distinguishing characteristic is acquaintance with the Father of our Lord Jesus Christ, and with Jesus himself'.[40]

Again the apostle says, 'I count everything as loss because of the surpassing worth of knowing Christ Jesus my Lord. For his sake I have suffered the loss of all things and count them as rubbish, in order that I may gain Christ' (Phil. 3:8). The apostle Paul reduces the whole Christian religion to one indispensable thing. What must he keep though he lose all else? In comparison with what does he count all things as 'rubbish'? It is the 'surpassing worth' of the *knowledge* of Christ Jesus our Lord.

The same essential truth was taught by the prophet Jeremiah:

> Thus says the LORD: 'Let not the wise man boast in his wisdom, let not the mighty man boast in his might, let not the rich man boast in his riches, but let him who boasts boast in this, that he understands and knows me, that I am the LORD who practises

---

[40] David Brown, *The Four Gospels: A Commentary, Critical, Experimental and Practical* (1863; London: Banner of Truth Trust, 1970), p. 450.

steadfast love, justice, and righteousness in the earth. For in these things I delight, declares the LORD' (Jer. 9:23-24).

What is the one thing about which we must boast? What is the one thing in all of life that surpasses wisdom, power, and riches? It is knowing and understanding God. The ultimate priority for the people of God is that we might know God.

As Spurgeon urged so eloquently in the quote at the start of this chapter, nothing is so fulfilling, nothing so humbling, nothing so comforting, as the knowledge of the Almighty. There are inexhaustible spiritual, emotional, psychological, and intellectual benefits to be had in plumbing the depths of God.

Knowing and knowing about

Second, it is important that we distinguish between knowing about God and knowing God.

To know God we must know *about* God. But knowledge alone is not enough. 'It is not, indeed, the bare knowing of truths of the gospel [that] saves', says Gurnall, yet 'the gross ignorance of them, to be sure, will damn souls'.[41] There is no replacement for studying the Bible, with the aid of the blessed teachers and theologians whom God has given to the church over the centuries, if we are to know the truth about God. Subtle distinctions are necessary if one is to understand the Holy Trinity or the incommunicable attributes of God, such as his infinity, immensity, and immutability. What do we mean when we say that the three are one and the one is three? What do we mean when we say that God never changes and yet Scripture speaks of God repenting? Considerable thought goes into figuring out how higher mathematical equations work. Similarly, comprehending the incomprehensible God—even the beginnings of such comprehension—requires study, careful thought, meditation, and careful articulation. 'The attributes of God are his royal diadem' which the believer is privileged to place on his head through his worship and praise, says William Gurnall.[42] The more we know of his 'being, wisdom, power, holiness, justice, goodness, and truth', and the more we delight in his

[41] Gurnall, *Christian in Complete Armour*, I:170.
[42] *Ibid.*, II:319.

infinity, eternality, and immutability, the more we are able to crown him in a manner suitable to his perfections. Knowing God begins with knowing about God.

Knowing God, however, is much more than merely knowing about God. Knowing about God is indispensable. Yet mere knowledge, theoretical knowledge, speculative knowledge, mental data, is inadequate. Our goal is experiential knowledge, personal knowledge. The eternal life Jesus promises in John 17:3 is more than an infinite extension of years. 'Eternal' (Gk *aiōnion*) suggests not mere longevity, not mere quantity of existence, but quality as well. 'Abundant life' (Gk *perissos*), which Jesus came to give us (John 10:10), probably should be seen as a synonym for 'eternal life', and vice versa. 'This is eternal life'—that is, the ultimate life for humanity, the highest good, the greatest joy—to 'know you the only true God' (John 17:3).

The knowledge of God is profoundly experiential. Henry speaks of the pleasure we derive from the knowledge of God in Christ:

> To know the perfections of the divine nature, the unsearchable riches of divine grace, to be led into the mystery of our redemption and reconciliation by Christ, this is food; such knowledge as this is a feast to the soul; it is meat indeed, and drink indeed; it is knowledge of that which the angels desire to look into (1 Pet. 1:12).[43]

To know God is to know that his nearness is our good, and to desire nothing else beyond him (Psa. 73:28). It is to taste and see, that is, to know by first-hand experience, that he is good (34:8). It is to know that his lovingkindness is better than life itself, even that to depart and be with Christ is far better than continuing in this world (63:3; Phil. 1:23). It is to know the fullness of joy that accompanies his presence (Psa. 16:11). It is to seek one thing above all else: to dwell in the house of the Lord all the days of our lives and behold his beauty (27:4). It is to know that God is the buried treasure and the pearl of great price for which we sell all that we have in order to obtain it, so dear, so valuable, so precious, is the knowledge of God to us (Matt. 13:44-46).

---

[43] Henry, *Pleasantness of a Religious Life*, p. 50.

Knowing Christ

Third, the attributes of God are most clearly seen in the person and work of Christ, when God became flesh and dwelt among us (John 1:1, 14). The true knowledge of God is to be found only in Christ. He is the true light that enlightens everyone (1:9). Though 'no one has ever seen God', Christ 'has made him known' (1:18; cf. 1 Tim. 6:16). To see Jesus is to see the Father (John 14:9). Again, the apostle John writes, 'And we know that the Son of God has come and has given us understanding, so that we may know him who is true' (1 John 5:20).

How do we 'know him who is true'? Not through natural revelation, but through 'the Son of God' who 'has come and has given us understanding'. On the basis of these and other verses, Owen concludes, 'There is no acquaintance with God, as love, and full of kindness, patience, grace, and pardoning mercy (on which knowledge of him alone we can walk with him), but only in Christ.'[44]

As we read Scripture, we can see various ways in which God's attributes are taught. The older theologians spoke of the *via causalitatis*, the way of causality, the causes and effects of creation. Because God made the heavens, 'the heavens declare the glory of God' (Psa. 19:1). In every creature, says Charnock, we find 'a footstep of divine wisdom'.[45] They spoke of the *via eminentiae*, the way of eminence: God as the perfection of all earthly virtues and powers. God is our Father, fatherhood being a human relation, and we understand his Fatherhood as the perfected virtues of the best of fathers. Thus Jesus helps us learn about prayer through the analogy of bad fathers giving good gifts (Matt. 7:11). They spoke as well of the *via negativa*, a way of negation: God as the opposite of all that is finite, mutable, and corrupt. As we observe the grass that withers and the flower that fades, we gain a glimpse, by way of contrast, of the word of God and the God of the word who stands forever (Isa. 40:6-8). Using these categories—not as did the Scholastic theologians, who started with creation and humanity apart from Scripture, but rather in conjunction with Scripture—we can enhance our understanding of the God who 'did not leave himself

---

[44] John Owen, *Of Communion with God the Father, Son, and Holy Ghost* in *Works of John Owen* (Edinburgh: Banner of Truth Trust, 1965), II:109.
[45] Charnock, *Existence and Attributes*, II:21.

without witness' (Acts 14:17), but whose 'invisible attributes, namely, his eternal power and divine nature' are 'clearly perceived ... in the things that have been made' (Rom. 1:20).[46] Citing Psalm 94:9 ('He who planted the ear, does he not hear? He who formed the eye, does he not see?'), Charnock affirms of God, 'He hath in himself eminently the beauty, perfection, life and vigour of all creatures; he created nothing contrary to himself, but everything *with some footsteps of himself in them*.'[47]

Still, the attributes are seen in their clarity, with comprehensibility and finality, only in Christ. Owen is right when he says that 'all true and solid knowledge is laid up in, and is only to be obtained by, the Lord Jesus Christ'.[48] 'Jesus Christ was set forth to display every attribute of the Godhead', says Robert Haldane (1764–1842) in his superb exposition of Romans.[49] Jesus is Immanuel, 'God with us' (Isa. 7:14). He is the image of the invisible God (Col. 1:15; 2 Cor. 4:4). He is 'the radiance of the glory of God and the exact imprint of his nature' (Heb. 1:3). 'All the fullness of God' dwells in him (Col. 1:19; 2:9). 'All the attributes of God illustriously shine forth in the face of Jesus Christ', says Jonathan Edwards from 2 Corinthians 4:6.[50] Commenting on the same passage, Charnock says of the attributes, 'They all centred in him, and shone forth from him in all their brightness, and in a full combination set off one another's lustre.'[51]

---

[46] See Louis Berkhof, *Systematic Theology* (1939; Edinburgh: Banner of Truth Trust, 1958), pp. 32-33 for a critique of the Scholastics' utilization of these categories.

[47] Charnock, *Existence and Attributes*, I:498 (emphasis added).

[48] Owen, *Communion with God*, *Works*, II:79. Among recent works, Clark and Johnson state that Christ's 'incarnate humanity is where the attributes of God are definitively displayed and properly understood'. Again, 'the fullest and clearest manifestation of God's nature and character is distinctly Christ-given and Christ-shaped, which is to say that God's attributes are definitively displayed in the incarnate Christ' (John C. Clark and Marcus Peter Johnson, *The Incarnation of God: The Mystery of the Gospel as the Foundation of Evangelical Theology* [Wheaton, IL: Crossway, 2015], p. 73).

[49] Robert Haldane, *Exposition of the Epistle to the Romans; with Remarks* (Edinburgh: William Oliphant & Co., 1874), p. 153.

[50] Jonathan Edwards, *Our Great and Glorious God*, compiled and edited by Don Kistler (Morgan, PA: Soli Deo Gloria, 2003), p. 33.

[51] Stephen Charnock, 'The Voluntariness of Christ's Death', in *Christ Crucified* (Fearn, Ross-shire: Christian Focus, 1996), p. 210.

His attributes come into particular focus at the cross. All that we might say about providence, holiness, judgment, love, grace, and mercy leaves the realm of theories and concepts when the Word becomes flesh, and in particular when the Word goes to the cross. 'Not only in his incarnation,' says Charnock of Christ revealing the glory of God's attributes, 'but also, and that chiefly in his sacrifice.' He continues:

> Mercy could not be glorified, unless *justice* had been satisfied; and *justice* had not been evident, if the tokens of divine *wrath* had not been upon him. *Grace* had not sailed to us, but in the streams of his blood: 'without blood there is no remission'. *Justice* had not been so fully known in the eternal groans of a world of creatures, nor could sin have appeared so odious to the *holiness* of God by eternal scars upon devils and men, as by the deluge of blood from the heart of this sacrifice. *Wisdom* in the contrivance had not been evident without the execution. *The glory of the divine perfections had lain in the cabinet of the divine nature without the discovery of their full beams*; and though they were active in designing it, yet they had not been declared to men or angels without the bringing Christ to the altar. *By the stroke upon his soul all the glories of God flashed out to the view of the creature.* When Judas went out from his company to prepare the way for his oblation, 'Now,' saith he, 'is the Son of man glorified, and God is glorified in him' (John 13:31).[52]

The apostle Paul told the Corinthians, 'I decided to know nothing among you except Jesus Christ and him crucified' (1 Cor. 2:2). What does he mean by 'nothing … except'? Is that all? Does that mean that all the sermons he preached were simple gospel sermons? Did he repeatedly harp on a few basic gospel facts in isolation from the whole biblical revelation? Not at all. What he means is that all he taught and preached found its ultimate expression at the cross. The cross is the focal point, the point at which all that is true about God is integrated and clarified. Some of the proud people at Corinth were embarrassed by the cross. They thought it was foolish. God on a cross? Ridiculous. They thought the doctrine of the atonement was philosophically crude. They urged the apostle Paul to tone down the cross talk, yet he tells them, I know nothing else but the cross, because it is the centrepiece,

---

[52] Charnock, 'Voluntariness of Christ's Death', in *Christ Crucified*, p. 210.

the stumbling block which is also the cornerstone of our faith. The grace of God, the mercy of God, the patience of God, the sovereignty of God, and the righteousness of God are all most clearly seen in the cross of Christ. Redemption, says Thomas Goodwin, is God's 'masterpiece, wherein he means to bring all his attributes upon the stage'.[53] His *wisdom* and *power* are seen in his devising and implementing the means of conquering death and the devil. 'His *justice*,' says Edwards, is seen 'in punishing the sins of men upon his own dear Son rather than let [them] go unpunished; but ... in his grace, that sweet attribute, he has magnified his mercy above all his names.'[54]

The 'knowledge of the glory of God [shines] in the face of Jesus Christ' (2 Cor. 4:6). There we see God's virtues with the greatest clarity. 'All the perfections of his nature are delineated in [his] saving sacrifice', Charnock explains.[55] The 'fullness of deity dwells bodily' in Christ, not merely in a body as it represents human nature, but in a body prepared for sacrifice (Col. 2:9). In Christ, particularly in the cross of Christ, the holiness, justice, righteousness, mercy, and grace of God all appear in their brightest colours. There 'the seat of justice is turned into a throne of grace'. That seat 'puts on the quality of an advocate instead of that of an accuser, uttering absolutions instead of condemnations'.[56]

As we have hinted already, the Christian life is largely an imitation of the communicable attributes of God, most clearly seen in Christ. The apostle Paul urges, 'Therefore be imitators of God, as beloved children. And walk in love, as Christ loved us and gave himself up for us, a fragrant offering and sacrifice to God' (Eph. 5:1-2). We are to 'follow in his [Jesus'] steps' (1 Pet. 2:21). We are to have the 'attitude' of humility and selflessness that was in Christ Jesus (Phil. 2:5ff. NASB.). The love of God, manifested in his sending his Son as a propitiation for our sins, is the pattern for our own love (1 John 4:8-9).

The whole Christian life may be regarded as a contemplation of the attributes of God and the realization of their meaning in the life

---

[53] Goodwin, *Christ the Mediator*, in *Works*, 5:16; cited in Joel R. Beeke and Mark Jones, *A Puritan Theology: Doctrine for Life* (Grand Rapids, MI: Reformation Heritage Books, 2012), p. 72.

[54] Edwards, *Great and Glorious God*, p. 33.

[55] Charnock, 'Voluntariness of Christ's Death', pp. 163-64.

[56] *Ibid.*, p. 164.

of the believer. What is right or wrong; what we should or should not do; how we should or should not live are all rooted in the nature of God, Father, Son, and Holy Spirit. God's nature is ultimate reality. His nature is eternal and unchanging. All approved conduct may be defined as that which is consistent with the nature of God, and all disapproved as that which is inconsistent with his nature. 'Blessed, and for ever blessed,' says Baxter, 'are those souls, that have the true and likely image of this God, and all his attributes, imprinted on them.'[57]

Calvin speaks of the believing mind being 'aroused to taste the divine goodness' and of 'that abundant sweetness which God has stored up for those who fear him', even of being 'utterly ravish[ed]' by it.[58] Through Jesus Christ this taste of the divine is realized. Jesus is the bread of life (John 6:35). He satisfies the deepest hunger and quenches the deepest thirst of the soul. Bernard of Clairvaux (1090–1153) captures the experiential dimension:

> Jesus, the very thought of thee
> With sweetness fills my breast;
> But sweeter far thy face to see,
> And in thy presence rest.[59]

The eleventh-century hymn-writer says much the same in another of his hymns:

> We taste thee, O thou living bread,
> And long to feast upon thee still;
> We drink of thee, the fountain head,
> And thirst our souls from thee to fill.
>
> Our restless spirits yearn for thee,
> Where'er our changeful lot is cast;
> Glad, when thy gracious smile we see,
> Blest, when our faith can hold thee fast.[60]

'God is infinitely excellent and desirable,' says Charnock, citing Zechariah 9:17 ('How great is his goodness, and how great his beauty!').

---

[57] Baxter, *The Divine Life*, *Works*, III:811.
[58] Calvin, *Institutes*, III.ii.41, p. 589.
[59] Bernard of Clairvaux (attr.), 'Jesus, The Very Thought Of Thee'.
[60] Bernard of Clairvaux (attr.), 'Jesus, Thou Joy Of Loving Hearts'.

'He hath … no defects or shadow of evil; there is infinite excellency to charm us, and infinite goodness to allure us. … He is the most lovely object.'[61] Charnock speaks of the 'loveliness in his nature', 'sweetness in his ways', and his 'desirable excellency above all other things'.[62] His conclusion: 'God is therefore to be studied, therefore to be honoured, therefore to be followed.'[63]

Let us then give ourselves to the study of this great God, Father, Son, and Holy Spirit. Let us do so 'in a godly frame of mind', counsels à Brakel, 'emptied of sinful desires and world conformity, for "the secret of the LORD is with them that fear him" (Psa. 25:14)'.[64] It is the pure in heart who shall see God (Matt. 5:8). Indeed, Jesus promises, 'he who loves me will be loved by my Father, and I will love him and manifest myself to him'. Indeed, 'we will come to him and make our home with him' (John 14:21, 23).

---

[61] Charnock, *Existence and Attributes*, I:253.
[62] *Ibid.*, I:255, 256.
[63] *Ibid*. I:253.
[64] à Brakel, *Christian's Reasonable Service*, I:138.

TWO

'Our Triune God'

*Go therefore and make disciples of all nations, baptizing them
in the name of the Father and of the Son and of the Holy Spirit,
teaching them to observe all that I have commanded you. And
behold, I am with you always, to the end of the age.*

—Matthew 28:19-20

IN his 'Great Commission' Jesus commanded his disciples to 'make
disciples of all nations', and to baptize them 'in the name of the
Father and of the Son and of the Holy Spirit' (Matt. 28:19). We
notice that 'the name' is both singular and preceded by the definite
article. Jesus speaks of *the* name, not a name, and the *name*, not names.
The sense is, 'the one and only name'.

Name, in Scripture, is no mere label, but speaks of the essential
nature of the person. The name *is* the person. Jesus is emphatically
speaking of the singularity of God. There is but one name, one God,
and there is no other. This is the foundational creed of the Hebrew
people, the *Shema*: 'Hear, O Israel: The LORD our God, the LORD is
one' (Deut. 6:4)

Yet *the* name, the singular name, is followed by three names, those
of Father, Son, and Holy Spirit. Each of these has its own definite
article: *the* Father, *the* Son, and *the* Holy Spirit. Jesus speaks of one
God, and yet three distinct entities or persons, 'who all unite in some
profound sense in the common participation of the one name', says the
great Princeton theologian B. B. Warfield.[1] One name means one God;

---

[1] B. B. Warfield, 'The Biblical Doctrine of the Trinity', in *Biblical and Theological
Studies*, ed. Samuel G. Craig (Philadelphia: Presbyterian & Reformed, 1968), p. 42.

three names mean three distinct persons. 'What else is this,' Calvin asks of the baptismal formula of Matthew 28:19, 'than to testify clearly that Father, Son, and Spirit are one God.'[2] Jesus taught his disciples that God was now to be known by a new name, a threefold name. Again we cite Warfield:

> When, therefore, our Lord commanded his disciples to baptize those whom they brought to his obedience 'into the name of …' he was using language charged to them with high meaning. He could not have been understood otherwise than as substituting for the name of Jehovah this other name 'of the Father, and of the Son, and of the Holy Ghost'; and this could not possibly have meant to his disciples anything else than that Jehovah was now to be known to them by the new name, of the Father, and the Son, and the Holy Ghost. The only alternative would have been that, for the community which he was founding, Jesus was supplanting Jehovah by a new God; and this alternative is no less than monstrous. There is no alternative, therefore, to understanding Jesus here to be giving for his community a new name to Jehovah and that new name to be the threefold name of 'the Father, and the Son, and the Holy Ghost'.[3]

Vital

Warfield's exposition of the Great Commission, following the church fathers, the Reformers, and the Westminster divines, is profound and crucial. It is the fundamental and indispensable Christian doctrine. It separates the orthodox from the heterodox, the church from the cult, the disciple from the heretic. It is the defining doctrine of the Christian religion. 'It is only when we contemplate this trinity that we know who and what God is', insists the great contemporary of Warfield, the brilliant Dutch theologian Herman Bavinck (1854–1921).[4]

The doctrine of the Trinity is a *distinctively Christian doctrine*. Others have had divine triads. The ancient Egyptians worshiped Osiris, Isis, and Horus. The Hindus venerate Brahma, Vishnu, and

---

[2] Calvin, *Institutes*, I.xiii.16, p. 141.
[3] Warfield, 'Biblical Doctrine of the Trinity', p. 44.
[4] Herman Bavinck, *Our Reasonable Faith* (1907; Grand Rapids, MI: Baker, 1977), p. 143.

Shiva. But three gods, a triad of deities who otherwise have little in common, is not the Holy Trinity. Knowledge of the Trinity does not come to us by nature or natural religion. It is 'purely a revealed doctrine', says Warfield, embodying 'a truth which has never been discovered, and is indiscoverable, by natural reason'.[5] Though there are analogies in nature (the lover, the loved, and love itself [Augustine] and the thinker, the one thought about, and thought itself), yet we know of the Trinity only because God has told us of himself in his word.

The doctrine of the Trinity is also *vital*. Bavinck points out that whenever God is conceived of apart from the Trinity, there is an inevitable diminishing of God as a personal being who is loving, self-conscious, and volitional. This happens in two directions. On the one hand, non-Trinitarian theism may tend to drift towards impersonal absolute transcendence. God becomes so separate, so remote, as to be unreachable. He becomes more a power than a person. Deism results.

On the other hand, non-Trinitarian theism may tend to drift towards absolute immanence. God becomes so near as to be indistinguishable from creation. God is confused with the creation, resulting in the equally impersonal deity of pantheism.

The former problem can be seen in the remote, transcendent deity of Islam and Judaism. The latter problem can be seen in the immanent deity of the New England transcendentalists (who despite the name of their movement were actually immanentist), such as Emerson and Thoreau, in the German philosopher Hegel, the German Romantics, and among more recent theological progressives.[6] A non-personal, 'God beyond God', as imagined by Tillich (1886–1965), far from marking an advance in our understanding of God, is rather, says Packer, 'a grotesque and barren freak from which Christian teachers of all schools of thought now take pains to disassociate themselves'.[7] Indeed, we can say that the doctrine of the Trinity is the key to the

---

[5] Warfield, 'Biblical Doctrine of the Trinity', p. 22.

[6] Their name derives from the organization founded by Ralph Waldo Emerson, among others, which they called 'The Transcendental Club'. They emphasized the soul's participation in the deity, the 'Over-soul', their name for the transcendent. Their concept of the deity was thoroughly pantheistic and heavily influenced by Hinduism. Hence, the transcendentalists were actually immanentists.

[7] J. I. Packer, 'Theism for Our Time', in *God Who Is Rich in Mercy*, ed. Peter T. O'Brien and David G. Pearson (Grand Rapids, MI: Baker, 1977), p. 10.

Christian understanding of God as transcendent, immanent, and personal. Bavinck calls it 'the heart and core of our confession, the differentiating earmark of our religion, and the praise and comfort of all true believers of Christ'.[8]

Biblical

There can be no denying that the Trinity is a difficult doctrine. 'The verbal expression of the Trinity is the most difficult job man has had to do', says Packer.[9] The difficulty of getting it right, Packer suggests, surpasses the difficulty of putting a man on the moon, formulating the theory of relativity, or creating the Internet.

No small part of the difficulty can be found in the fact that the doctrine of the Trinity is never explicitly elaborated in Scripture. Our understanding of the Trinity is more an outgrowth of our experience of redemption, of a Father who made and chose us, a Son who redeems us, and a Spirit who sanctifies us. It is 'not so much heard as overheard', says Warfield. Allusions to it throughout Scripture are 'frequent, cursory, easy, and confident', he explains.[10] Yet there is no deliberate setting forth of the doctrine in any specific place in Scripture.

How, then, does the Bible teach it? Do we have an answer when the cults point out that the word 'Trinity' is nowhere to be found in the Bible? Indeed we do. We point out that the sense of Scripture is Scripture. Muslims will not allow the Koran to be translated because the words themselves are inviolable. In contrast, Christians understand that it is the truth of Scripture that is crucial, not the words *per se*. The particular words through which God chooses to reveal himself are important *as conveyors of meaning*. The words themselves are not expendable or alterable; but, in the end, understanding the meaning is vital. Regarding the Trinity, the crucial thing is not whether this or that word can be found, but what Scripture actually teaches. Though unassembled, though scattered throughout the whole, the Bible teaches the doctrine that the one God is a Trinity of persons. How does it do so?

---

[8] Bavinck, *Our Reasonable Faith*, p. 145.
[9] J. I. Packer, Class notes, Trinity College, Bristol, England, Fall 1977.
[10] Warfield, 'Biblical Doctrine of the Trinity', p. 32.

- The Bible teaches that there is but one God.

- The Bible teaches that the Father, the Son, and the Spirit are each God.

- The Bible teaches that the Father, the Son, and the Spirit are each distinct persons.

Therefore the church, 'by good and necessary consequence', as the Westminster Confession of Faith puts it (I.6), has deduced that there is one God in three persons, who are 'the same in substance, equal in power and glory (Shorter Catechism, Q. 6). Warfield insists, 'When we have said these three things, then—that there is but one God, that the Father and the Son and the Spirit is each God, that the Father and the Son and the Spirit is each a distinct person—we have enunciated the doctrine of the Trinity in its completeness.'[11]

Let us examine the scriptural testimony.

Old Testament

The Old Testament teaches the Trinity slowly and cumulatively. On the one hand, repeatedly and emphatically the Old Testament teaches us that there is but one creator God (Gen. 1:1), who is God Almighty (Gen. 17:1; Exod. 6:3), and that there is no other (Exod. 20:2; Deut. 6:4-5; Isa. 45:5; etc.). On the other hand, there are hints of plurality in the Godhead:

- The divine name *elohim* is a plural noun (Gen. 1:1). Plural pronouns are used, as in 'Let *us* make man in *our* image ... So God created man in his *own* image' (Gen. 1:26-27; cf. 3:22; 9:7; 11:7; Isa. 6:8), as well as plural verbs (Gen. 20:13; 35:7).

- The 'one' (*echad*) of Deuteronomy 6:4 ('the LORD is one') is a one of unity not isolation, not of a stark, singular entity. It can be used of the 'one flesh' of Genesis 2:24 in which can be found two persons, the man and the woman. A bunch of grapes is a plurality within singularity, a multiplicity of grapes, not one grape.

- Various passages distinguish God from God (Psa. 45:6-7; 110:1; Hos. 1:7). That is, God speaks of God when not referring to himself.

---

[11] Warfield, 'Biblical Doctrine of the Trinity', p. 36.

- Threefold liturgical formulas are used (e.g. 'The LORD … the LORD … the LORD' [Num. 6:24-26]; 'Holy, holy, holy' [Isa. 6:3]).

- The angel of the Lord is at times identified as God (e.g. Gen. 16:7-13; 32:24-32; 48:15-16; Exod. 3:2-5; Judg. 13:22; Mal. 3:1; etc.).

- The Word (or Wisdom) and Spirit are at times distinguished from God and personalized (see especially Prov. 8:22-31 regarding Wisdom; and see Gen. 1:2; Psa. 143:10; Isa. 63:10; Ezek. 36:26-27; etc.).

- A Messiah is promised who will come in the name of God and yet be God. He is called 'Immanuel', God with us (Isa. 7:14), 'the LORD is our righteousness' (Jer. 23:5-6), Mighty God, and Eternal Father (Isa. 9:6).

If the Trinity is not revealed in the Old Testament, it is clear that God is not an abstract unity, a simple, solitary being. He instead is revealed as 'the living, true God, who in the fullness of his life embraces the highest variety', says Bavinck.[12] We find in the Old Testament, adds Warfield, 'at least the germ of the distinctions in the Godhead afterward fully made known in the Christian revelation'.[13]

New Testament
The New Testament *elaborates on* that which the Old Testament *introduced*; it makes *patent* what previously was *latent*. We cite Warfield again:

> The Old Testament may be likened to a chamber richly furnished but dimly lighted; the introduction of light brings into it nothing which was not in it before; but it brings out into clearer view much of what is in it but was only dimly or even not at all perceived before. The mystery of the Trinity is not revealed in the Old Testament; but the mystery of the Trinity underlies the Old Testament revelation, and here and there almost comes into view. Thus the Old Testament revelation of God is not corrected by the fuller revelation which follows it, but only perfected, extended and enlarged.[14]

---

[12] Bavinck, cited by Warfield, 'Biblical Doctrine of the Trinity', p. 30.
[13] Warfield, 'Biblical Doctrine of the Trinity', p. 30.
[14] *Ibid.*, pp. 30-31.

The New Testament writers show no awareness of innovation as they write in Trinitarian terms. They too stress the unity of God: that there is but one God. Jesus speaks of 'the only true God' (John 17:3), and the apostle Paul says, 'There is no God but one' (1 Cor. 8:4; cf. Rom. 3:30; 16:27; Gal. 3:20; Eph. 4:6; 1 Tim. 1:17; 1 Tim. 2:5; James 2:19).

Distinctive redemptive roles

Yet they also describe redemption in Trinitarian terms. Above all, it is in the work of salvation that the Trinity is revealed. 'The revelation of the Trinity,' says Warfield, 'was ... the inevitable effect of the accomplishment of redemption.'[15] Each divine person is attributed a role in redemption. The apostles teach us that we are saved by the Father's *electing and planning* love: 'God [the Father] so loved the world that he gave ...' (John 3:16; 6:38). Yet we are saved by the Son's *sacrificing and accomplishing* love: 'The Son of God ... loved me and gave himself for me' (Gal. 2:20; Phil. 2:6ff.). Yet again we are saved by the Holy Spirit's *applying and enabling love*: Jesus said we must be 'born of the Spirit' (John 3:5, 8), and the apostle Paul speaks of the love of God being shed abroad in our hearts by the Spirit (Rom. 5:5; cf. 1 Cor. 3:16). Our experience of redemption is Trinitarian. The apostle Paul brings this Trinitarian redemption together in Titus 3:4-7:

> But when the goodness and loving kindness of God our Saviour appeared, he saved us, not because of works done by us in righteousness, but according to his own mercy, by the washing of regeneration and renewal of the Holy Spirit, whom he poured out on us richly through Jesus Christ our Saviour, so that being justified by his grace we might become heirs according to the hope of eternal life.

Redemption's source is the 'goodness and loving kindness of God' (the Father) who is our 'Saviour'. 'He [the Father] saved us ... according to his own mercy.' Yet he did so 'by the washing of regeneration and renewal of the Holy Spirit', who is the agent of application. Yet again, what the Holy Spirit *applies* is that which the Son *accomplished*: 'whom

---

[15] Warfield, 'Biblical Doctrine of the Trinity', p. 33.

he poured out on us richly through Jesus Christ our Saviour'. The result is believers who are 'justified by his grace' and become 'heirs according to the hope of eternal life'. 'The whole Trinity appears here as concurring in the blessed work of our salvation,' says the nineteenth-century Scot Patrick Fairbairn (1805–74). They are 'co-ordinate agents in the work of salvation'.[16] John Owen (1616–83), whose pastoral application of the doctrine of the Trinity in his treatise *Of Communion with God the Father, Son, and Holy Ghost* is a spiritual classic, summarizes: 'The emanation of divine love to us begins with the Father, is carried on with the Son, *and* then [is] communicated the Spirit, the Father *designing*, the Son *purchasing*, the Spirit *effectually working*.'[17]

Stephen Charnock (1628–80), writing in another Puritan spiritual classic, *The Existence and Attributes of God*, summarizes the contribution of each person of the Trinity: 'The Father makes the promise of redemption, the Son seals it with his blood, and the Spirit applies it; the Father *adopts* us to be his children, the Son *redeems* us to be his members, and the Spirit *renews* us to be his temples.'[18]

When we celebrate redemption we may sing, 'How deep the *Father's* love for us', using the words of Stuart Townend, and rejoice in the wonder of our adoption. We may also sing of the grace of God the Son:

> Was it for sins that I had done
> He groaned upon the tree?
> Amazing pity! grace unknown!
> And love beyond degree![19]

Yet we may also sing,

> Come, Holy Spirit, heav'nly Dove,
> With all thy quick'ning pow'rs;

[16] Patrick Fairbairn, *The Pastoral Epistles* (1874; Minneapolis, MN: James and Klock, 1976), p. 298.

[17] Owen, *Communion with God*, *Works*, II:180; cited in Kelly M. Kapic, *Communion with God: The Divine and the Human in the Theology of John Owen* (Grand Rapids, MI: Baker Academic, 2007), p. 187 (emphasis added). Owen says elsewhere, 'Our participation is first by the work of the Spirit, to an actual interest in the blood of the Son; whence we have acceptation with the Father'; cited in Kapic, *Communion with God*, p. 88.

[18] Charnock, *Existence and Attributes*, II:319.

[19] Isaac Watts, 'Alas! And Did My Saviour Bleed'.

Kindle a flame of sacred love
In these cold hearts of ours.[20]

We pray to the Father, through the Son, and in the power of the Holy Spirit. We will have more to say about this in a moment.

Shared divine attributions

The New Testament writers also teach us that, beyond their distinctive redemptive activity, each redeeming person, Father, Son, and Holy Spirit, is God. How so? We note the following.

1. To each is applied the *divine names and titles* such as Lord and God. Nearly every epistle begins with a reference to 'God our Father' (e.g. Rom. 1:7; 1 Cor. 1:3; 2 Cor. 1:2; Eph. 1:2; etc.). Yet the apostle Paul refers to 'Christ who is God over all, blessed for ever' (Rom. 9:5), and the apostle John writes of Christ, 'the Word was God' (John 1:1, 14). We read of 'God our Saviour' (1 Tim. 1:1) and 'Christ Jesus our Saviour' (Titus 1:4; cf. John 20:28; Titus 2:13; 1 John 5:20). The believer, says the apostle Paul, is, as the temple of the Holy Spirit, the temple of God (1 Cor. 3:16; cf. Acts 5:3-4; 2 Pet. 1:21).

2. To each is applied the *divine attributes* such as eternality, omniscience, omnipotence, and immutability. The Word was 'in the beginning', says the apostle John, and the writer to the Hebrews speaks of the Spirit as 'eternal' (John 1:1-2; Heb. 9:14). Jesus 'searches mind and heart'; the Spirit 'searches everything, even the depths of God' (Rev. 2:23; 1 Cor. 2:10-11; Isa. 40:13-14). Jesus promises to be 'with [us] always', and the psalmist asks, 'Where shall I go from your Spirit? Or where shall I flee from your presence?' (Matt. 28:20; Psa. 139:7-16). Jesus is the 'Almighty', the 'Mighty God', and the apostle Paul speaks of the power of the Holy Spirit (Rev. 1:8; Isa. 9:6; Rom. 15:19; cf. Phil. 3:21). So it goes on. The apostle Paul writes of the Son, 'For in him the whole fullness of deity dwells bodily' (Col. 2:9). This means, says Warfield, that 'everything that enters into Godhead and constitutes it Godhead dwells in him'.[21]

3. To each is attributed the *divine works* of creation, providence, redemption, and judgment. God (the Father) created the heavens and

[20] Isaac Watts, 'Come, Holy Spirit, Heav'nly Dove'.
[21] Warfield, 'Biblical Doctrine of the Trinity', p. 46.

the earth (Gen. 1:1; cf. Psa. 102:25). Yet it was the Spirit of God who moved on the face of the deep (Gen. 1:2; Psa. 33:6), and John's prologue tells us that 'all things were made through him [i.e. Jesus], and without him was not any thing made that was made' (John 1:3), a truth which is repeated by the apostle Paul (Col. 1:16-17) and the writer to the Hebrews (Heb. 1:1-3).

God the Father providentially controls all things, 'declaring the end from the beginning' (Isa. 46:10), and works 'all things according to the counsel of his will' (Eph. 1:11) and for good (Rom. 8:28; cf. Acts 14:17). Yet the apostle Paul says of Jesus Christ that all things are in subjection under his feet, that 'in him all things hold together', and the writer to the Hebrews teaches that God 'upholds the universe by the word of his power' (Eph. 1:22; Col. 1:17; Heb. 1:3).

Judgment. The Father is the judge before whom the books will be opened. Yet Jesus says the Father has committed judgment to the Son (John 5:22-27; cf. Acts 17:31).

Redemption (which we have already seen), *creation*, *providence*, and *judgment*, the works of God, are attributed to each. Who else but God creates and governs all things? Who else but God judges? Who else but God can save? Yet each person, the Father, the Son, and the Holy Spirit, is said to create, govern, judge, and redeem.

4. To each is given *divine honour*. God declares through the prophet Isaiah, 'My glory I give to no other' (Isa. 42:8; cf. Jer. 9:23-24). Yet Jesus insists we are to 'honour the Son, just as [we] honour the Father' (John 5:22-23). Jesus calls on the Father to glorify him 'with the glory that I had with you before the world existed' (John 17:5). Jesus insists that we believe in him even as we believe in God (John 14:1). We are said to hope in Christ, and angels are said to worship him (1 Cor. 15:19; Heb. 1:6). The apostle Paul swears by the Holy Spirit, and Jesus teaches that the unforgiveable sin is not blasphemy of God generally, but of the Holy Spirit specifically (Rom. 9:1; Matt. 12:31, 32). Divine honour is spread in the threefold benedictions and salutations throughout the New Testament, as in the baptismal formula of Matthew 28:19 and the 'Grace' ('The grace of the Lord Jesus Christ and the love of God and the fellowship of the Holy Spirit be with you all'; 2 Cor. 13:14; cf. 1 Pet. 1:2; Jude 20-21; Rev. 1:4-5). The Westminster Larger Catechism asks,

'How does it appear that the Son and the Holy Ghost are God equal with the Father?' (Q. 11). It answers: 'The Scriptures manifest that the Son and the Holy Ghost are God equal with the Father, ascribing unto them such names, attributes, works, and worship, as are proper to God only.'

Distinct persons

Finally, the Scriptures teach that though the Father, Son, and Holy Spirit are one God, yet each is a *distinct person*. At Jesus' baptism the Father says, 'This is my beloved Son, with whom I am well pleased,' and the Holy Spirit descends like a dove to rest upon Jesus (Matt. 3:16-17). Three distinct persons are present. Jesus says, 'No one knows the Son except the Father' (Matt. 11:27; Luke 10:22). They enjoy what Warfield calls 'perfect mutual knowledge'.[22] Yet 'I and the Father are one' (John 10:30; cf. 10:38; 14:9; 17:5, 10, 11, 21; see also 5:18; 8:42). They are distinct; yet they are one. 'I came from God' (John 8:43)—distinction; yet 'we are one' (17:11)—unity. Jesus prays that 'the love with which you [the Father] have loved me may be in them [the disciples]', the Father's love for the Son 'before the foundation of the world' (17:24, 26; cf. 15:9).

Respecting the Holy Spirit, Jesus speaks of 'another Helper' whom the Father will give at the Son's request! 'And I will ask the Father, and he will give you another Helper, to be with you for ever, even the Spirit of truth, whom the world cannot receive, because it neither sees him nor knows him. You know him, for he dwells with you and will be in you' (John 14:16-17). 'The Holy Ghost,' says the Scottish Puritan George Hutcheson (1626–74) in his exposition of these verses, 'is a person in the godhead distinct from and equal with the Father and the Son.'[23] Yet Jesus says, '*I* will come to you' in the coming of the Spirit (John 14:28). 'It would be impossible,' says Warfield of the passage, 'to speak more distinctly of the three who were yet one.'[24]

[22] Warfield, 'Biblical Doctrine of the Trinity', p. 37.
[23] George Hutcheson, *The Gospel of John* (1657, 1841; Edinburgh: Banner of Truth Trust, 1972), p. 303. He continues: 'for he is "another comforter", distinct from the Son, and equal with him in that he is a "Comforter" also, as he is; and he is given by the Father, and so distinct from him' (p. 303).
[24] Warfield, 'Biblical Doctrine of the Trinity', p. 40.

Listen again: 'But when the Helper comes, whom I will send to you from the Father, the Spirit of truth, who proceeds from the Father, he will bear witness about me' (John 15:26). Jesus sends from the Father the Helper, the Spirit of truth, who yet bears witness to Jesus. Three persons, yet they are one (see also 16:7, 14). When Jesus encounters Nicodemus he tells that 'teacher of Israel' both that he must be 'born of the Spirit' and that he must believe in the 'lifted up' Son of Man if he is to enter the kingdom of the God who so loved the world (3:1-16). This, says Packer, is 'profound teaching about the Trinity'.[25] When Jesus speaks of the Father's love of the Son and the Son's love of the Father, the Spirit is not excluded. 'In some sense,' as Ferguson explains (citing Augustine), 'the Spirit is the bond of that embrace.'[26] Again, Warfield provides an insightful summary:

> As we read we are kept in continual contact with three Persons who act, each as a distinct person, and yet who are in a deep, underlying sense, one. There is but one God—there is never any question of that—and yet this Son who has been sent into the world by God not only represents God but is God, and this Spirit whom the Son has in turn sent into the world is also himself God. Nothing could be clearer than that the Son and Spirit are distinct Persons, unless indeed it be that the Son of God is just God the Son and the Spirit of God just God the Spirit.[27]

Calvin cites with delight the teaching of the church father Gregory of Nazianzus (329–89), who said, 'I cannot think on the one without quickly being encircled by the splendour of the three; nor can I discern the three without being straightway carried back to the one.'[28] Likewise Packer urges us 'to give equal emphasis in [our] thinking and [our] witness to the sovereign initiative of the Father who *planned* salvation, the atoning sacrifice of the Son who *obtained* salvation, and the mighty power of the Spirit who *applies* salvation. Let it prompt you to lay equal

---

[25] J. I. Packer, 'The Trinity and the Gospel', in *Celebrating the Saving Work of God: Collected Shorter Writings of J. I. Packer on the Trinity, Christ, and the Holy Spirit* (Carlisle: Paternoster, 1998), I:6.

[26] Ferguson, *Trinitarian Devotion of John Owen*, p. 36.

[27] Warfield, 'Biblical Doctrine of the Trinity', p. 41.

[28] Calvin, *Institutes*, I.xiii.17, p. 141.

stress on the love of each in the work of grace.'[29] Some Christians speak only of the Father's sovereignty in salvation. Others speak only of the cross and faith in Christ. Still others speak only of the Spirit's work in regenerating and sanctifying human hearts. 'Take care!' Packer warns. 'False proportions in our doctrine are the beginning of false doctrine itself .... So let the truth of the Trinity keep you balanced.'[30]

Historical

The doctrine of the Trinity, though revealed in Scripture, had to be hammered out on the anvil of church history. It took the church nearly 400 years to formulate precisely its nuances, usually in response to heresies. Over time the church, responding to what others were teaching, rebutted their errors and identified where the truth lay.

First heretical challenge: *Is the Son merely the highest creature?* Is he created, more than man but less than God? Likewise the Spirit: is he less than God, though, with the Son, one of 'God's two top creatures doing top jobs', in Packer's terms?[31] This was the Arian view, named for Arius (d. 336), a priest who served primarily in Alexandria, Egypt. The Council of Nicea (325) was called by the Roman Emperor Constantine in order to resolve the issue. Athanasius (296–373), the champion of orthodoxy, though often standing alone, *contra mundum* (against the world), guided the council into the truth. It condemned Arius and Arianism, and said that the Son is 'God of God, Light of Light, very God of very God, begotten, not made, being of one substance [or essence] with the Father'. That is, the Father and the Son consist of the same eternal, unchanging, and infinite substance (Gk *ousia*). So says the Nicene Creed.

Second: *Are the three (Father, Son, and Holy Spirit) merely three roles or perhaps three modes of existence of the one God?* That is, is there no distinct, permanent personhood of the Son and the Spirit? This was the challenge of Sabellianism, named for Sabellius, an early third-century figure about whom little is known. The Council of Constantinople (381) condemned Sabellianism, affirming the distinctive personhood

[29] Packer, 'Trinity and the Gospel', I:7 (emphasis added).
[30] *Ibid.*
[31] Packer, 'Trinity and the Gospel', I:2.

and deity of the Son and the Spirit. The Athanasian Creed was issued by the church at about this time (*c.* 381–428). It declared,

> The Father is God, the Son is God, and the Holy Ghost is God. And yet there are not three Gods, but one God. The Godhead of the Father, and of the Son, and of the Holy Ghost is all one, the glory equal, the majesty co-eternal. And in this Trinity none is afore or after other; none is greater or less than another, but the whole three Persons are co-eternal together and co-equal.

Third: *In what sense is the Son subordinate to the Father and the Spirit subordinate to both?* It was particularly important to answer this question because the Scripture does speak of subordination within the Trinitarian relationship. The Son does the will of the Father (John 6:38). The Spirit is sent by the Father and Son (15:26; 17:7ff.). Jesus even says, 'The Father is greater than I' (14:28), and the apostle Paul says, 'The head of Christ is God' (1 Cor. 11:3; cf. 3:23). How is this subordination to be understood?

The answer the church gave is that the subordination within the Godhead is *economic* or a matter of *order*, not *essential* or *ontological*. It is a matter of *function*, not of *being* or essence. It is a chosen subordination for the sake of accomplishing redemption. 'They cooperate according to a hierarchical pattern', says Packer.[32] As we have seen, the Father initiates redemption by *planning*, the Son acts as his agent by *going* and redeeming, and the Spirit executes the will of both by *applying* redemption. This hierarchy of labour says nothing of the essential, substantial unity and equality of the divine persons. Consequently the Son is 'begotten' but 'not made'. We are to speak of an *eternal generation* of the Son. So also the Holy Spirit 'proceeds from the Father and the Son' (*ex Patre Filioque*). We speak of an *eternal procession* of the Spirit.

The Larger Catechism summarizes the church's historic view:

> Question 9: How many persons are there in the Godhead?
> Answer: There be three persons in the Godhead, the Father, the Son, and the Holy Ghost; and these three are one true, eternal God, the same in substance, equal in power and glory; although distinguished by their personal properties.

[32] Packer, class notes.

Question 10: What are the personal properties of the three persons in the Godhead?

Answer: It is proper to the Father to beget the Son, and to the Son to be begotten of the Father, and to the Holy Ghost to proceed from the Father and the Son from all eternity.

Experiential

'Absolutely nothing worthwhile for the practical life can be made out of the doctrine of the Trinity', claimed the German philosopher (and sceptic) Immanuel Kant (1724–1804).[33] Many dismiss the doctrine, says Packer, 'as so much useless lumber for the mind'.[34] Having established the biblical basis and seen the historical confirmation of the doctrine of the Trinity, we are now in a position to prove Kant and others wrong.

For the Puritans, and, more generally, the whole Reformed tradition, communion with God is the purpose of man's existence. Our chief end, says the Shorter Catechism's first question, 'is to glorify God *and to enjoy him for ever*'. *Koinonia*, 'fellowship' or 'communion', flows from union with Christ which is ours by faith and consists in a mutual giving and receiving with each person of the Trinity. The full title of Owen's classic work is *Of Communion with God the Father, Son, and Holy Ghost, Each Person Distinctively, in Love, Grace, and Consolation, or, the Saints' Fellowship with the Father, Son, and Holy Ghost Unfolded*.[35] His meaning as summarized by Sinclair Ferguson: 'The Christian life is nothing less than fellowship with God the Trinity, leading to the full assurance of faith.'[36]

Under Owen's influence the following phrase was added to the section on the Trinity in the Westminster Confession of Faith when the

[33] Cited in Kapic, *Communion with God*, p. 147. Kapic also quotes Roman Catholic theologian Karl Rahner (1904–84), who said of the doctrine of the Trinity: 'as a reality it has nothing to do with us at all'; and Colin E. Gunton, who claims Trinitarian theology failed 'to be the living heart of worship and life' (p. 148).

[34] Packer, 'Trinity and the Gospel,' I:7.

[35] John Owen, *Works*, II, title page.

[36] Sinclair B. Ferguson, *John Owen on the Christian Life* (Edinburgh: Banner of Truth Trust, 1987), p. 74.

Puritan 'Independents' (Congregationalists) met at the Savoy Palace in 1658 in order to slightly revise it: 'which doctrine of the Trinity is the foundation of all our communion with God, and comfortable dependence upon him'.[37] As Scripture speaks of the Father, the Son, and the Holy Spirit distinctively, so believers are to have communion with each distinctively and yet in a united way as well. Of this the apostle John writes, 'That which we have seen and heard we proclaim also to you, so that you too may have fellowship with us; and indeed our fellowship is with the Father and with his Son Jesus Christ' (1 John 1:3).

John, we should remember, enjoyed personal fellowship with Jesus in his earthly ministry. He was one of the three who enjoyed the closest intimacy with the Redeemer. He had laid his head on Jesus' breast. He experienced the nearest and dearest fellowship in the flesh. This gives us insight into the word 'fellowship'. Now that Jesus was gone, John knew Jesus 'after a nobler sort', says Spurgeon. His fellowship with Christ was not 'less real, less close, less sweet, or less divine, than it had been when he had walked and talked with him, and had been privileged to eat and drink with him at that last sacred feast'.[38] The apostle Paul uses the same word, *koinonia*, in his 'grace': 'The grace of the Lord Jesus Christ and the love of God and the *fellowship* of the Holy Spirit be with you all' (2 Cor. 13:14).

Poole finds here 'eminent proof of the Trinity',[39] Hodge, 'a clear recognition of the doctrine of the Trinity, which is the fundamental doctrine of Christianity'.[40] Not only has each member of the Trinity made us and saved us, but we may experience a distinctive fellowship with each, the apostle Paul explicitly extending the mention of 'fellowship' to the Holy Spirit. 'This is surely why the Lord Jesus, in the darkest hours of his disciples' lives,' says Sinclair Ferguson, referring to John 14–17, the Upper Room Discourse and High Priestly Prayer, 'spent time teaching them the knowledge of God, and especially the

---

[37] Kapic, *Communion with God*, p. 156.

[38] C. H. Spurgeon, 'Fellowship with God', *The Treasury of the New Testament* (London: Marshall, Morgan & Scott, 1934), IV:474.

[39] Poole, *Commentary*, III:639.

[40] Charles Hodge, *A Commentary on 1 and 2 Corinthians* (1857, 1859; Edinburgh: Banner of Truth Trust, 1974), p. 690.

interrelations of the Father, the Son, and the Holy Spirit, and the significance of these relationships for believers.'[41]

Communion with the Father in love

The apostle Paul prays, 'The grace of the Lord Jesus Christ and the *love* of God [the Father] ... be with you all' (2 Cor. 13:14). 'The Father's love,' says Owen, 'is the fountain from whence all other sweetnesses flow.'[42] 'Our fellowship,' says the apostle John, 'is with the Father ...' (1 John 1:3). How do we enjoy fellowship with the Father? By contemplating the love of the Father in *planning* redemption. 'God [the Father] so loved the world ...' (John 3:16). Love is often singled out in the New Testament as the special characteristic of the Father in relation to us (see also John 14:21; Rom. 5:5; Titus 3:4). We are saved not because we loved God, but because 'he loved us and sent his Son to be the propitiation for our sins' (1 John 4:10). 'The Father himself loves you,' Jesus assures his disciples (John 16:27). Never should we think of the Son coercing love from a reluctant Father. Owen warns us against thinking of the Father only in terms of his 'terrible majesty, severity, and greatness', as though 'there is no sweetness at all in him towards us' except that purchased by the blood of Christ. While it is true that it is through Christ alone that the Father's love is received, yet 'the free fountain and spring of all is in the bosom of the Father' (see John 1:2). He urges: 'Let, then, this be the saints' first notion of the Father—as one full of eternal, free love towards them.'[43] Let the saints understand that he is 'the eternal fountain of all that rich grace which flows out to sinners in the blood of Jesus'.[44] Jesus Christ does not purchase the Father's love, rather he is the expression of it. 'The death of Christ is not the cause of the Father's love, but is its effect', explains Ferguson.[45] He continues, 'The Christian should therefore meditate on the eternal quality of God's love, the freeness and unchangeableness of its nature, and marvel at its characteristic distinguishing among men.'[46]

---

[41] Ferguson, *Trinitarian Devotion of John Owen*, p. 31.
[42] Owen, *Communion with God, Works*, II:22.
[43] *Ibid.*, II:32.
[44] *Ibid.*, II:35.
[45] Ferguson, *Trinitarian Devotion of John Owen*, p. 77.
[46] *Ibid.*

The redemption purchased by Christ is none other than that which was planned by a loving Father. Knowing this should endear the Father to us, and cause us to delight in him and rejoice in him. Knowing this should lead us to seek him, to find refuge and comfort in him. 'Exercise your thoughts upon this very thing,' says Owen, 'the eternal, free, and fruitful love of the Father, and see if your hearts be not wrought upon to delight in him …. Sit down a little at the fountain, and you will quickly have a farther discovery of the sweetness of the streams.'[47] Let us contemplate and respond to the Father's love by loving him in return: resting in him, delighting in him, reverencing him, and obeying him.[48]

Communion with the Son in grace

'Our fellowship is with the Father,' says the apostle John, 'and with his Son Jesus Christ' (1 John 1:3). While communion with the Father is primarily in love, communion with the Son is primarily in grace, says Owen. The apostle Paul prays, 'The *grace* of the Lord Jesus Christ … be with you all' (2 Cor. 13:14). Jesus is 'full of *grace* and truth', and we have received from him '*grace* upon *grace*' (John 1:14-17). This communion with the Son in grace is characterized, says Owen, by sweetness, delight, safety, support, and consolation. We enjoy communion with Christ as we contemplate incarnational love, instructional love, and sacrificial love: that he came, that he lived and taught, that he died an atoning death, and was raised again (Phil. 2:5ff.).

We enjoy communion with Christ when we contemplate what Owen calls his 'personal grace', that is, all that makes him suitable for the work of redemption: his virtues of mercy, holiness, moral perfection, love, patience, kindness, grace, tenderness, and so on, all that constitutes 'the desirableness of his person'.[49]

We also enjoy fellowship with Christ as we contemplate his 'purchased grace', all that is ours through his saving work as our substitute: bearing the wrath of God, satisfying the requirements of

[47] Owen, *Communion with God*, *Works*, II:36.

[48] See J. I. Packer, 'The Spirituality of John Owen', in *A Quest for Godliness* (Wheaton, IL: Crossway, 1998), p. 205; Owen, *Communion with God*, *Works*, II:28.

[49] Owen, *Communion with God*, *Works*, II:263.

justice, forgiving our sin, reconciling us to God, adopting us into the family of God, interceding on our behalf, and sanctifying and preserving us. Jesus is 'altogether lovely', says Owen, quoting the bride in Song of Solomon (5:16). Owen elaborates:

> Lovely in his *person*,—in the glorious self-sufficiency of his Deity, gracious purity and holiness of his humanity, authority and majesty, love and power.
>
> Lovely in his *birth* and incarnation; when he was rich, for our sakes becoming poor,—taking part of flesh and blood, because we partook of the same; being made of a woman, that for us he might be made under the law, even for our sakes.
>
> Lovely in the whole *course* of his life, and the more than angelical holiness and obedience which, in the depth of poverty and persecution, he exercised therein;—doing good, receiving evil; blessing, and being cursed, reviled, reproached, all his days.
>
> Lovely in his *death*; yea, therein most lovely to sinners;—never more glorious and desirable than when he came broken, dead, from the cross. Then had he carried all our sins into a land of forgetfulness; then had he made peace and reconciliation for us; then had he procured life and immortality for us.
>
> Lovely in his whole *employment*, in his great undertaking,—in his *life, death, resurrection, ascension*; being a mediator between God and us, to recover the glory of God's justice, and to save our souls—to bring us to an enjoyment of God, who were set at such an infinite distance from him by sin.
>
> Lovely in the glory and majesty wherewith he is *crowned*. Now he is set down at the right hand of the Majesty on high; where, though he be terrible to his enemies, yet he is full of mercy, love, and compassion, towards his beloved ones.
>
> Lovely in all those *supplies of grace and consolations*, in all the dispensations of his Holy Spirit, whereof his saints are made partakers.
>
> Lovely in all the *tender care, power, and wisdom*, which he exercises in the protection, safe-guarding, and delivery of his church and people, in the midst of all the oppositions and persecutions whereunto they are exposed.

Lovely in all his *ordinances*, and the whole of that spiritually glorious worship which he hath appointed to his people, whereby they draw nigh and have communion with him and his Father.

Lovely and glorious in the *vengeance* he taketh, and will finally execute, upon the stubborn enemies of himself and his people.

Lovely in the *pardon* he hath purchased and doth dispense,—in the reconciliation he hath established,—in the grace he communicates,—in the consolations he doth administer,—in the peace and joy he gives his saints,—in his assured preservation of them unto glory.

What shall I say? There is no end of his excellencies and desirableness;—'He is altogether lovely. This is our beloved, and this is our friend, O daughters of Jerusalem.'[50]

Jesus, says Owen, is an 'endless, bottomless, boundless' source of grace and compassion.[51] As we meditate upon these things, and give thanks for them, we enjoy fellowship with Christ.

Communion with the Holy Spirit in comfort

Owen maintains that the 'fellowship of the Holy Spirit' is mentioned in 2 Corinthians 13:14 along with the grace of Christ and the love of the Father 'because it is by the Spirit alone that we have fellowship with Christ in grace, and with the Father in love', plus 'we have also peculiar fellowship with him'.[52] How so?

We enjoy communion or fellowship with the Holy Spirit through his work of *applying* redemption. What the Father's love *planned*, and the Son graciously *accomplished*, the Holy Spirit *applies*. Thus there is an immediacy of communion with the Holy Spirit as he applies Christ and his benefits. The apostle Paul prays, 'and the fellowship of the Holy Spirit be with you all' (2 Cor. 13:14). Believers are regenerated by the Holy Spirit (John 3:5, 8), indwelt by the Holy Spirit (John 14:17; Rom. 8:9; 1 John 3:24), comforted and assured by the Holy Spirit (John 14:16-18; 16:7), and anointed by the Holy Spirit (1 John 2:20). He is our teacher (John 14:26), the Spirit of adoption (Rom. 8:16), and the

---

[50] Owen, *Communion with God, Works.*, II:77-78.
[51] *Ibid.*, pp. 61, 48.
[52] *Ibid.*, p. 20.

Spirit of supplication (Rom. 8:26). As we contemplate these gifts of the Spirit, as we meditate upon them and give thanks for them in our prayers and worship, we enjoy fellowship with the Holy Spirit.

The whole Christian life is a life lived in the Spirit. Our fellowship with him is constant. We are urged to walk in the Spirit (Gal. 5:16-17), be led by the Spirit (Rom. 8:26-27; Gal. 5:18), be filled with the Spirit (Eph. 5:18), and to avoid resisting the Spirit (Acts 7:51) along with all that might 'grieve' or 'quench' the Spirit or hinder his work (Eph. 4:3; 1 Thess. 5:19) He is our constant companion and the down payment or pledge of our heavenly inheritance (Eph. 1:13-14; 2 Cor. 5:5; Rom. 8:23).

* * *

When we worship, we worship the Holy Trinity. All our prayers are offered to the Father, through the Son, by the power of the Holy Spirit. 'Through him [Jesus],' says the apostle Paul, 'we both [Jews and Gentiles] have access in one Spirit to the Father' (Eph. 2:18). We rejoice in, give thanks for, offer praise to the Trinity as a whole, and to each person individually for his distinctive role and contribution. Packer cites another English Puritan, Thomas Goodwin (1600–80), who comments on 1 John 1:3 and John 14:17-23 in his *The Object and Acts of Justifying Faith*:

> sometimes a man's communion and converse is with the one, sometimes with the other, sometimes with the Father, then with the Son, and then with the help of the Holy Ghost; sometimes his heart is drawn out to consider the Father's love in choosing, and then the love of Christ in redeeming, and so the love of the Holy Ghost, that searcheth the deep things of God, and revealeth them to us, and taketh all the pains with us; and so a man goes from one witness to another distinctly, which I say, is the communion that John would have us to have.[53]

Goodwin urges that when we worship God we should not only offer him praise, or seek things from him, but should also

> take occasion to come into his presence on purpose to have communion with him …. When thou comest into his presence,

---

[53] Cited in Packer, *Quest for Godliness*, p. 208; quoting from Goodwin, *Works*, VIII:376.

be telling him still how well thou lovest him; labour to abound in expressions of that kind, than which … there is nothing more taking with the heart of any friend.[54]

Our God is one God in three persons who are the same in substance, equal in power and glory. Let us then pursue fellowship with our Triune God, united as one, and also with each person distinctively. Even as we have enjoyed their unique contribution to our salvation, let us also celebrate a distinctive communion with each.

---

[54] Packer, *Quest for Godliness*, p. 208.

THREE

'The Badges of Divinity':
The Incommunicable Attributes of God (1)

O LORD, you have searched me and known me!
You know when I sit down and when I rise up;
  you discern my thoughts from afar.
You search out my path and my lying down
  and are acquainted with all my ways.
Even before a word is on my tongue,
  behold, O LORD, you know it altogether.
You hem me in, behind and before,
  and lay your hand upon me.
Such knowledge is too wonderful for me;
  it is high; I cannot attain it.
Where shall I go from your Spirit?
  Or where shall I flee from your presence?
If I ascend to heaven, you are there!
  If I make my bed in Sheol, you are there!
If I take the wings of the morning
  and dwell in the uttermost parts of the sea,
even there your hand shall lead me,
  and your right hand shall hold me.

—Psalm 139:1-10

THE 139th Psalm is an extended meditation on the omniscience, immensity, and infinity of God. That the Bible devotes devotional space to such seemingly abstract doctrines may surprise some of us. What do these themes have to do with us? Yet

David ponders God's comprehensive understanding:

> O LORD, you have searched me and known me!
> You know when I sit down and when I rise up;
>   you discern my thoughts from afar.
> You search out my path and my lying down
>   and are acquainted with all my ways (Psa. 139:1-3; cf. 4-6).

David not only celebrates God's unlimited knowledge of his circumstances, he also contemplates his immensity or omnipresence, or perhaps his omnipresence as the basis of his omniscience:

> Where shall I go from your Spirit?
>   Or where shall I flee from your presence?
> If I ascend to heaven, you are there!
>   If I make my bed in Sheol, you are there!
> If I take the wings of the morning
>   and dwell in the uttermost parts of the sea,
> even there your hand shall lead me,
>   and your right hand shall hold me (Psa. 139:7-10).[1]

He delights in God's inescapable and unending presence. This knowledge of such a God, he affirms, is 'too wonderful for me' (139:6). 'How precious to me are your thoughts, O God! How vast is the sum of them!' (139:17). 'No escape and no regrets', is how J. A. Motyer (1924–2016) summarized David's meditation upon the omniscience and omnipresence of God.[2]

Would it occur to us to write 'a very pious devout meditation', as Matthew Henry calls it, on these themes as did David?[3] Would we know how to derive comfort from what Charnock, describing Psalm 139, calls 'that large meditation on the omniscience and omnipresence of God'?[4] Probably not. We suggested in our opening chapter that because we do not know God as we ought, we lack the rich resources such knowledge gives for living life in a fallen world. We struggle to make sense of things.

---

[1] The psalmist 'proves that such knowledge could not be in God, unless he were present in his essence in all places' (Charnock, *Existence and Attributes*, I:428).

[2] J. A. Motyer, Class notes, Trinity College, 1977–79.

[3] Henry, *Commentary*, introduction to Psalm 139.

[4] Charnock, *Existence and Attributes*, I:529.

Many of us today succumb to despair and become cynical, or bitter, hurt, and ineffective as Christians. Why? Perhaps it is because we are burdened with false expectations of the Christian life built directly on a false understanding of who God is. We are crippled by a shallow knowledge of a limitless God. We are confused because most issues return to the question of what we understand about God and his ways. Too often our understanding is superficial and defective. 'The fundamental problem' today, says David Wells, is that 'God rests too inconsequentially upon the church'.[5]

In this chapter we will focus our minds on the *difference* between God and all his creatures. James Henley Thornwell (1812–62), the outstanding Southern Presbyterian theologian of the nineteenth century, spoke of 'the immeasurable disparity' which exists 'between the most exalted creature in the universe and its infinite creator'.[6] Of what does this disparity consist? In what ways is God distinguished from us? He is beyond us in every way. The older theologians spoke in terms of the 'incommunicable' and the 'communicable' attributes of God. The incommunicable are those which are characteristic of God alone. Humanity does not and cannot share any of them. These characteristics (e.g. eternity, infinity, and immutability) cannot be transmitted to creatures. They highlight how different God is from us.

The communicable are those which God can impart to us, and in which we share to some finite, limited degree. God is good, gracious, and holy. There can be a corresponding goodness, graciousness, and holiness in us. There is 'some show or shadow' of the communicable attributes in us, says Swinnock, though even then, man 'is exceedingly unlike him, and falls infinitely short of him'.[7] Still, we are created in

---

[5] Wells, *God in the Wasteland*, p. 30. Here is Wells' full statement: 'The fundamental problem in the evangelical world today is not inadequate technique, insufficient organization, or antiquated music, and those who want to squander the church's resources bandaging these scratches will do nothing to stanch the flow of blood that is spilling from its true wounds. The fundamental problem in the evangelical world today is that God rests too inconsequentially upon the church. His truth is too distant, his grace is too ordinary, his judgment is too benign, his gospel is too easy, and his Christ is too common.'

[6] James Henley Thornwell, *The Collected Writings of James Henley Thornwell* (1875; Edinburgh: Banner of Truth Trust, 1974), I:198.

[7] Swinnock, 'Incomparableness of God', *Works*, IV:403.

God's image and likeness, and we share, though imperfectly, some of his communicable attributes.[8]

Our immediate concern, here, is with the incommunicable attributes of God, those which mark God as God and distinguish the Creator from his creation. According to Thornwell, the incommunicable attributes are those 'which separate God by an impassable chasm from every work of his hands. These,' he says, 'are the badges of Divinity—that glory which he will not and cannot give to another.'[9] Charnock and the older divines show the interrelatedness and interdependence of the incommunicable attributes. For example, if God were not immutable, he would not be *perfect*, for he would change for either the better or the worse; nor *simple*, because some part of him would remain and some part would be altered; nor *eternal*, because in all change something begins to exist or ceases to be: something non-eternal is added, or something non-eternal is subtracted; nor *infinite*, because if something is added to the infinite it, by definition, is not infinite.[10]

We will group these attributes under four headings: God's independence, immutability, infinity, and simplicity.[11]

God's independence

God is independent. He is *self-existent* and *self-sustaining*. Swinnock explains of God's independence that nothing in heaven or earth has ever contributed in the least towards the 'maintenance or continuance' of his being; 'neither the creatures' goodness nor their goods do him the least good'.[12] All created beings, in contrast, depend upon God and a host of secondary causes for their initial and continued existence. God has depended on no one. We are the product of a string of causation reaching back to the beginning. All creatures have their

---

[8] Even regarding the communicable attributes, there is but 'a reflection and faint resemblance in men', says à Brakel (*Christian's Reasonable Service*, I:90).

[9] Thornwell, *Collected Writings*, I:189.

[10] Charnock, *Existence and Attributes*, I:392-95.

[11] Bavinck provides this helpful reminder: 'The incommunicable attributes tell us about the way in which all that is in God exists in him; but they leave us in the dark about the content of the Divine being' (*Our Reasonable Faith*, p. 137). We will seek to fill in some of that content as we go along, especially in each successive study.

[12] Swinnock, 'Incomparableness of God', *Works*, IV:391.

being in and from God; in him they live, move, and exist (Acts 17:27-28). God, however, is the uncaused cause. Nothing has caused him to exist or keeps him in existence. Jesus said, 'For as the Father has life *in himself*, so he has granted the Son also to have life *in himself*' (John 5:26). When God appointed Moses to lead the children of Israel out of the bondage of Egypt, he revealed himself as "I AM WHO I AM" (Exod. 3:14). J. A. Motyer calls this 'an open-ended assertion of divine sufficiency'.[13] God's name signifies 'I am the only being, the root of all beings', and 'at the greatest distance from not being, and that is eternal', says Charnock.[14] His eternity points as well to his immutability, perfection, infinity, and blessedness. 'I am' indicates, Charnock continues, that 'I am that in every moment which I was, and will be in all moments of time; nothing can be added to me, nothing can be detracted from me. There is nothing superior to him, which can detract from him, nothing desirable that can be added to him.'[15] He is the self-existent, the self-dependent, self-sufficient one. 'Being self-existent,' says Matthew Henry, 'he cannot but be self-sufficient, and therefore all-sufficient, and the inexhaustible fountain of being and bliss.'[16] God is what he is and what he always has been, depending on nothing, needing nothing, and answering to no one. 'During a past eternity, God was alone: self-contained, self-sufficient, self-satisfied, in need of nothing', said A. W. Pink (1886–1952).[17]

Because God is independent, God is unobligated, unaccountable, and responsible only to himself. He is free to do *as* he wants, *when* he wants, and *how* he wants. 'His actions,' says Charnock, 'are not regulated by any law without him, but by a law within him, the law of his own nature.'[18] Indeed, 'he is his own rule'.[19] 'Our God is in the heavens; he does all that he pleases', the psalmist affirms (Psa. 115:3). The apostle Paul cites Exodus 33:19 where God announces, 'I will have

[13] J. A. Motyer, *The Message of Exodus: The Days of Our Pilgrimage*, The Bible Speaks Today: Old Testament (Downers Grove, IL: InterVarsity Press, 2005), p. 70.

[14] Charnock, *Existence and Attributes*, I:355.

[15] *Ibid.*

[16] Henry, *Commentary*, on Exod. 3:14.

[17] Pink, *Attributes*, p. 9.

[18] Charnock, *Existence and Attributes*, II:415.

[19] *Ibid.*, II:418.

mercy on whom I have mercy, and I will have compassion on whom I have compassion' (Rom. 9:15). The apostle concludes regarding God hardening Pharaoh's heart, 'So then he has mercy on whomever he wills, and he hardens whomever he wills' (Rom. 9:17-18). Paul affirms the absolute freedom of God, the potter's rights over the clay, not vice versa (9:21-23). 'He does according to his will among the host of heaven and among the inhabitants of the earth; and none can stay his hand or say to him, "What have you done?"' (Dan. 4:35). God 'works all things according to the counsel of his will' (Eph. 1:11) He consults not someone else's will, but his own, because he is independent and free to do what he pleases. A. W. Tozer (1897–1963), in his wonderful book *Knowledge of the Holy*, points out how unsettling the doctrine of God's absolute independence can be:

> We tend to be disquieted by the thought of one who does not account to us for his being, who is responsible to no one, who is self-existent, self-dependent, and self sufficient .... To admit that there is one who lies beyond us, who exists outside of all our categories, who will not be dismissed with a name, who will not appear before the bar of our reason, nor submit to our curious inquiries: this requires a great deal of humility, more than most of us possess, so we save face by thinking God down to our level, or at least down to where we can manage him. Yet how he eludes us![20]

Note as well that God is *self-sufficient*. Swinnock insists that 'the self-sufficient God gains nothing by all the suits and services, prayers and praises of his creatures; neither [does he] lose anything by their neglect of their duties'.[21] As the apostle Paul asks in Romans 11:35, 'Who has given a gift to [God] that he might be repaid?' He does not need us or our gifts. He did not have to create. He does not depend on us or rely on us. 'God was under no constraint, no obligation, no necessity to create,' explains A. W. Pink. 'That he chose to do so was purely a sovereign act on his part, caused by nothing outside himself, determined by nothing but his own good pleasure.'[22] The persons of

---

[20] A. W. Tozer, *The Knowledge of the Holy* (New York: Harper & Row, 1961), p. 33.
[21] Swinnock, 'Incomparableness of God', *Works*, IV:391.
[22] Pink, *Attributes*, p. 10.

the eternal Godhead, Father, Son, and Holy Spirit, are totally sufficient, blessed, and content in themselves and need nothing outside
of themselves. Edwards concurs: God 'is infinitely happy in himself'.
'There is no such thing as any pain, grief, or trouble in God.' He is
perfectly and unchangeably happy, absolutely happy with all possible
happiness. There can be 'no proper addition to the happiness of God,
because it is that which he eternally and unalterably had'.[23] Moreover,
'He has no occasion to go beyond himself for absolute blessedness',
says Thornwell.[24] 'The universe has added nothing to his bliss and can
subtract nothing from his fullness.'[25] He created, not out of compulsion
or the need to be loved or praised, but because of his own inscrutable
will (Rev. 4:11). His love 'is the love of him who is in himself all-sufficient, infinitely satiated with himself and his own glorious excellences
and perfections', says Owen. Within himself, within the mutual love
of the Trinity, 'he might rest with delight and complacency to eternity.
He is sufficient unto his own love'.[26] Again, A. W. Tozer demonstrates the
importance of understanding God's independence while condemning
common misconceptions of God's alleged neediness:

> Almighty God, just because he is almighty, needs no support.
> The picture of a nervous, ingratiating God fawning over men
> to win their favour is not a pleasant one; yet if we look at the
> popular conception of God that is precisely what we see.
> Twentieth-century Christianity has put God on charity. So lofty
> is our opinion of ourselves that we find it quite easy, not to say
> enjoyable, to believe that we are necessary to God. But the truth
> is that God is not greater for our being, nor would he be less
> if we did not exist .... Probably the hardest thought of all for
> our natural egotism to entertain is that God does not need our
> help. We commonly represent him as a busy, eager, somewhat
> frustrated Father hurrying about seeking help to carry out his
> benevolent plan to bring peace and salvation to the world ....

[23] Edwards, *Great and Glorious God*, pp. 15-17.
[24] Thornwell, *Collected Writings*, I:205.
[25] *Ibid.*, I:203. Again, Thornwell: 'God contains within himself the fullness of
perfection and blessedness—that nothing can be taken from him and nothing
added to him.' *Ibid.*, I:198.
[26] Owen, *Communion with God*, *Works*, II:32.

> Too many missionary appeals are based upon this fancied frustration of Almighty God. An effective speaker can easily excite pity in his hearers, not only for the heathen but for the God who has tried so hard and so long to save them and has failed for want of support. I fear that thousands of young persons enter Christian service from no higher motive than to help deliver God from the embarrassing situation his love has gotten him into and his limited abilities seem unable to get him out of. Add to this a certain degree of commendable idealism, and a fair amount of compassion for the underprivileged, and you have the true drive behind much Christian activity today.[27]

The God of the Bible has no needs. He is self-existent, self-sufficient, and self-dependent. He is independent and free.

God's immutability

'God is unchangeable in his essence, nature, and perfections,' Charnock explains.[28] He is what he always was and always will be. Because he is eternal he is eternally the same, that is, immutable. God does not and will not change, and therefore he is eternally consistent. God's character, ways, purposes, promises, plans, happiness, and glory are free from any change, free from both growth and decay. 'He wants nothing, he loses nothing, but doth uniformly exist by himself, without any new nature, new thought, new will, new purpose, or new place.'[29] God is 'incapable of the least alteration', insists Swinnock.[30] He does not change his mind or revise his decrees. There is no improvement or deterioration with God. 'In God there is nothing that looks like change, for better or worse,' says Thomas Watson; 'not better, because then he were not perfect; not worse, for then he would cease to be perfect.'[31] The psalmist, when speaking of the heavens and earth in

---

[27] Tozer, *Knowledge of the Holy*, pp. 40-41.

[28] Charnock, *Existence and Attributes*, I:380.

[29] *Ibid*.

[30] Swinnock, 'Incomparableness of God', *Works*, IV:393.

[31] Watson, *Body of Divinity*, p. 67. A. W. Pink says, 'He cannot change for the better, for he is already perfect; and being perfect, he cannot change for the worse' (*Attributes*, p. 37). See also Thornwell: 'Change is either from better to worse or from worse to better, and is grossly incompatible with the notion of the infinite' (*Collected Writings*, I:200); also Charnock, *Existence and Attributes*, I:383).

comparison with God, says, 'They will perish, but you will remain; they will all wear out like a garment. You will change them like a robe, and they will pass away, but you are the same, and your years have no end' (Psa. 102:26-27). The biblical writers regularly contrast the changing, deteriorating, temporary qualities of the created order with the unchanging nature of God (Psa. 90:1-2; Prov. 8:25-26; John 17:24; Eph. 1:4). James speaks of God as one in whom 'there is no variation or shadow due to change' (James 1:17). 'Here he sets forth God as essentially and immutably good', says Poole.[32] God declares through the prophet Malachi, 'For I the LORD do not change' (Mal. 3:6). 'God here disclaims all inconsistency', says Calvin. Rather, he 'continues in his purpose, and is not timid here and there like men'.[33] We may follow Packer in unfolding God's immutability under the following headings.[34]

First, God's *character* does not change. He is every bit as holy, gracious, righteous, and loving as he always was. The God of the New Testament is no less angry with sin than the God of the Old. The God of the Old Testament is no less love than the God of the New.[35] Our character can change over time. 'Man, after his revolt, can ascribe nothing constant to himself but his own inconsistency', says Charnock.[36] Once-honest people can become liars—not just tell a lie, but through repeated behaviour become liars. Once-faithful spouses can become adulterers—not just fall into adultery, but through habitual practice become adulterers. On the other hand, once-degraded sinners can become sanctified disciples of Christ. We change; God does not because he need not. Thomas Manton (1620–77), also commenting on James 1:17, says of God's immutability, 'This is an attribute that, like a silken string, through a chain of pearl, runneth through all the rest.'[37] It means that his mercy is an unchanging mercy, his love is

[32] Poole, *Commentary*, III:882.

[33] Calvin, *Commentaries on the Twelve Minor Prophets*, Vol. 5, *Zechariah and Malachi*, p. 579.

[34] Packer, *Knowing God*, pp. 68-72.

[35] See Leon Morris, *Testaments of Love: A Study of Love in the Bible* (Grand Rapids, MI: Eerdmans, 1981). He maintains, 'The love of God underlies the whole of our Old Testament' (p. 34).

[36] Charnock, *Existence and Attributes*, I:413.

[37] Thomas Manton, *A Commentary on James* (1693; Edinburgh: Banner of Truth

an unchanging love, his justice is an unchanging justice. Charnock concurs: 'Immutability is a glory belonging to all the attributes of God ... the centre wherein they all unite.'[38] 'There is no wrinkle upon the brow of eternity,' Manton maintains, 'and truly this is the church's comfort in the saddest condition ... the best cordial to refresh a fainting soul.'[39]

Truth does not change. God's mind does not change, his views do not change, his word and promises do not change, and his knowledge does not change. We humans change all of the above. We are fickle, indecisive. We change our minds and then have to go back on our word. We say things we do not mean. We are 'resolved to be as holy as angels in the morning', says Charnock, 'when the evening beholds us as impure as devils'.[40] Think of what two sweethearts may promise or claim in the tenderness of the moment and which they fail to fulfil. 'I thought I meant it', one may later lament; 'I thought I felt that way,' or 'I thought it was right.' How many times are we disappointed by broken promises—when someone promised to help, visit, or call, but did not follow through? However, Jesus teaches that 'Scripture cannot be broken' (John 10:35). 'For truly, I say to you, until heaven and earth pass away, not an iota, not a dot, will pass from the Law until all is accomplished' (Matt. 5:18). 'The grass withers, the flower fades, but the word of our God will stand for ever' (Isa. 40:6-8). God's truth did not fail then, nor will it fail now. The Dutch Puritan Wilhelmus à Brakel urges that believers should 'be comforted by the immutability of the Lord, for all the promises of which they are heirs will most certainly be fulfilled'.[41] God's word is a rock on which we can stand.

Third, God's *ways* do not change. His ways with us are consistent with his ways with Bible people. He treats us the same way he treated them. He saved them, pardoning their sin and reconciling them to

---

Trust, 1962), p. 113. So also Charnock: 'unchangeableness is a thread that runs through the whole web' (*Existence and Attributes*, I:381).

[38] Charnock, *Existence and Attributes*, I:381.

[39] Manton, *Commentary on James*, p. 114. 'He is unchangeably good, and can be no other,' says Trapp (*Commentary*, V:693).

[40] Charnock, *Existence and Attributes*, I:409.

[41] Cited in Richard A. Muller, *Post-Reformation Reformed Dogmatics: The Rise and Development of Reformed Orthodoxy, ca. 1520 to ca. 1725* (Grand Rapids, MI: Baker Academic, 2003), III:319.

himself through the blood of the Redeemer, the Lord Jesus Christ, whose benefits they received by faith. He blessed his people then with spiritual and material good, as he does now. He disciplined them when they were wayward, taught them through afflictions, led them by his word and Spirit, and sought their fellowship, just as he does now. The differences between the Testaments that we observe are matters of administration. They are external and relatively superficial. The fundamentals are identical (see Westminster Confession of Faith VII.5; XI.6; XIX.3). His unchanging ways are our link with the distant biblical past. As he did then, so he does now. Their experiences then were recorded for our instruction now (Rom. 15:4; 1 Cor. 10:6ff.).

Fourth, God's *purposes* do not change. 'God is not man, that he should lie, or a son of man, that he should change his mind. Has he said, and will he not do it? Or has he spoken, and will he not fulfil it?' (Num. 23:19). 'He wills or nills nothing to be in time, but what he willed and nilled from eternity.'[42] To change one's mind ('repent' KJV) means to revise one's plans and one's judgments. It implies a number of unforeseen developments, new and unexpected factors, unanticipated events for which one must accommodate by altering one's course of action. We change our minds because we had not realized what new circumstances would emerge. This is impossible with an all-knowing, all-powerful God. 'Such is the imperfection of man, and such the perfection of God', says Matthew Henry.[43] 'My counsel shall stand,' says God through the prophet Isaiah (Isa. 46:10). Watson explains:

> If he changed his decree, it must be from some defect of wisdom or foresight, for that is the reason why men change their purposes; they see something after, which they did not see before; but this cannot be the cause why God should alter his decree, because his knowledge is perfect, he sees all things in one entire prospect before him.[44]

[42] Charnock, *Existence and Attributes*, I:388.
[43] Henry, *Commentary*, on Num. 23:19.
[44] Watson, *Body of Divinity*, p. 69. 'God never does this,' says Packer of God changing his mind. 'He never needs to, for his plans are made on the basis of complete knowledge and control which extend to all things past, present, and future, so that there can be no sudden emergencies or unlooked-for developments to take him by surprise' (*Knowing God*, p. 71; see also Poole, *Commentary*, I:313). 'God is immutable in regard of knowledge,' says Charnock. 'God knows all things

There are a number of texts which refer to God 'changing his mind' (or 'repenting'): Genesis 6:6—for having made man; 1 Samuel 15:11—for having made Saul king; Jonah 3:4, 10—of his decision to destroy Nineveh; Isaiah 38:1, 5 (cf. 2 Kings 20:15; 2 Chron. 32:24)— of his decision to take the life of Hezekiah (and instead grant him fifteen more years of life); plus Jeremiah 18:8. However, in each case it is the human agent who changes; God then responds according to his unchanging nature to the altered circumstances. 'God always acts according to the immutable nature of his holiness', says Charnock.[45] Nineveh repents, and God shows mercy. Mercy is God's unchanging disposition towards the repentant. Hezekiah prays, and God grants the request. This is God's unchanging inclination towards those who humbly petition him. 'The change is always in the disposition of the creature,' Charnock explains, 'not in the nature of God or his will.'[46] When Scripture speaks of God 'changing his mind' it is accommodating itself to the limitation of human comprehension. It does not imply that God was taken by surprise, or that the human reaction was unforeseen. 'Immutability,' says Packer, 'is not the changelessness of an eternally frozen pose, but the moral consistency that holds him to his own principles of action and leads him to deal differently with those who change their own behaviour towards him (cf. Psa. 18:24-27).'[47] No change in his eternal plan is implied when God begins to curse the ungodly whom he has previously blessed, or bless the repentant whom he formerly cursed. Since God lacked 'not wisdom to frame his decrees, nor holiness to regulate them, nor power to effect them, what should make him change them?' asks Charnock. Why would he need to, 'since there can be no reason superior to his, no event unforeseen by him, no holiness comparable to his, no unrighteousness found in him, no power equal to his, to put a rub in his way'.[48]

---

by one intuitive act … there is no succession in his knowledge … God knows all things from eternity, and therefore perpetually … and therefore comprehends all knowable truths at once' (Charnock, *Existence and Attributes*, I:384-86).

[45] Charnock, *Existence and Attributes*, I:404.

[46] *Ibid*., I:406.

[47] J. I. Packer, 'God', in Sinclair B. Ferguson and David F. Wright (eds.), *New Dictionary of Theology* (Downers Grover, IL: InterVarsity Press, 1988), p. 276.

[48] Charnock, *Existence and Attributes*, I:389.

Fifth, *his Son* does not change. When God became man there was no change in the divine nature of the Son. 'There was an union of the two natures,' Charnock explains, 'but no change of the Deity into the humanity, or of the humanity into the Deity.'[49] He took the 'form of a servant' but he lost not the 'form of God' (Phil. 2:6-7). He 'emptied himself', not by taking away but by adding to. 'He assumed our nature without laying aside his own.'[50]

The God-Man 'Jesus Christ is the same yesterday and today and for ever' (Heb. 13:8). 'Jesus Christ is the same,' says Poole, in his comments on this verse, 'as in his person, so in his doctrine, faith, and conversation.' He is 'immutable in his care and love to his mystical body, and all the members of it'.[51] 'He is able to save to the uttermost those who draw near to God through him.' This is so 'since he *always* lives to make intercession for them' (Heb. 7:25).

The immutability of God is an anchor for us in a changing world. It is, says Charnock, our 'strongest prop for faith'. As such, 'it is not a single perfection, but the glory of all those that belong to his nature'.[52] Thornwell calls it 'the foundation of all our hopes' and 'the pledge of his faithfulness'.[53] Did Jesus choose men to be his disciples? He still does so today. Did Jesus call those who wished to be his disciples to leave their families and homes and follow him? He still does so today (Matt. 10:34ff.; Luke 14:26). Did he insist they calculate the cost (Luke 14:28), sell all their possessions (Luke 12:33), take up their cross, and follow him (Matt. 16:24)? Was Jesus moved with compassion when he saw the multitudes as sheep without a shepherd (Matt. 9:36)? Did he weep over Jerusalem (Luke 19:41)? Did he weep at the grave of Lazarus (John 11:35)? Did he welcome the weary and heavy-laden to himself (Matt. 11:28)? Did he welcome the tax collectors and sinners (Matt. 9:10)? Did he forgive the woman caught in adultery (John 8:3-4)? Did he forgive even his own murderers (Luke 23:34)? Did he promise to reward faithfulness and obedience (Matt. 5:13; 1 Cor. 15:58)? 'A steadfast obedience is encouraged by an unchangeable God to reward it.' Again,

[49] Charnock, *Existence and Attributes*, I:399.
[50] *Ibid.*, I:400.
[51] Poole, *Commentary*, III:876.
[52] Charnock, *Existence and Attributes*, I:412.
[53] Thornwell, *Collected Writings*, I:202.

'If God be unchangeable in doing us good, it is reason we should be unchangeable in doing him service.'[54] 'The pure, full, and entire religion of Christ is unchangeable, being simply, indivisibly, and constantly the same throughout all measure of time', Poole concludes.[55]

The great unchanging reality in our world, a world of frenetic change, a world in which few things last, and in which few people are consistent, is that our God and his Christ do not change. As he was in Bible times, so he is today and will be tomorrow (Heb. 13:8). Richard A. Muller, the great historian of Reformed Protestant orthodoxy, cites Benedict Pictet, the seventeenth-century Swiss Reformed Protestant, who said, 'This immutability of God is the fulcrum of our faith and the foundation of our hope.'[56] The renowned English Puritan Richard Baxter applies the doctrine of God's immutability with characteristic comprehensiveness:

> Our houses may be burned; our goods may be consumed or stolen; our clothes will be worn out; our treasure here may be corrupted; but our God is unchangeable, the same for ever. Our laws and customs may be changed; our governors and privileges changed; our company, and employments, and habitation changed; but our God is never changed. Our estates may change from riches to poverty; and our names that were honoured, may incur disgrace. Our health may quickly turn to sickness, and our ease to pain; but still our God is unchangeable for ever. Our friends are unconstant and may turn our enemies; our peace may be changed into war, and our liberty into slavery; but our God doth never change. Time will change customs, families, and all things here; but it changeth not our God. The creatures are all but earthen metal, and quickly dashed in pieces. Our comforts are changeable; ourselves are changeable and mortal; but so is not our God.[57]

---

[54] Charnock, *Existence and Attributes*, I:417.
[55] Poole, *Commentary*, III:876.
[56] Muller, *Post-Reformation Reformed Dogmatics*, 3:313.
[57] Richard Baxter, *The Divine Life*, *Works*, III:779.

FOUR

'The Badges of Divinity':
The Incommunicable Attributes of God (2)

O LORD, you have searched me and known me!
You know when I sit down and when I rise up;
*   you discern my thoughts from afar.*
You search out my path and my lying down
*   and are acquainted with all my ways.*
Even before a word is on my tongue,
*   behold, O LORD, you know it altogether.*
You hem me in, behind and before,
*   and lay your hand upon me.*
Such knowledge is too wonderful for me;
*   it is high; I cannot attain it.*
Where shall I go from your Spirit?
*   Or where shall I flee from your presence?*
If I ascend to heaven, you are there!
*   If I make my bed in Sheol, you are there!*
If I take the wings of the morning
*   and dwell in the uttermost parts of the sea,*
even there your hand shall lead me,
*   and your right hand shall hold me.*

—Psalm 139:1-10

HAVING looked at the first two of the 'badges of Divinity', God's independence and immutability, we move on to his infinity (his perfection, omnipotence, omniscience, eternality, omnipresence) and his simplicity. We are growing in our

61

awareness of the 'otherness' of God, an awareness that will only increase as we proceed.

The infinity of God

God is infinite—that is, God is free from all limits of character, power, knowledge, time, and space. Louis Berkhof (1873–1957), whose *Systematic Theology* is a twentieth-century classic, defines infinity as that 'perfection of God by which he is free from all limitations'.[1] 'God is infinite,' says nineteenth-century American Presbyterian W. G. T. Shedd (1820–94), 'and incapable of addition, of subtraction, or of division.'[2] David provides another poetic description of the infinity of God, to which Matthew Henry adds his comments: 'Your steadfast love, O LORD, extends to the heavens, your faithfulness to the clouds. Your righteousness is like the mountains of God; your judgments are like the great deep; man and beast you save, O LORD' (Psa. 36:5-6). His 'steadfast love' (Heb. *hesed*) 'extends to the heavens', extending 'in perfection and to eternity'; his 'faithfulness to the clouds', 'so that it does not change with the weather'. His 'righteousness is like the mountains of God', 'immovable and inflexible'; and his 'judgments are like the great deep', 'not to be fathomed [by] finite judgment' (Psa. 36:5-6).[3] Each is vast, beyond measure, exceeding the limits of our comprehension. David considers these, not as an end in itself, but that he might be confident of his deliverance from evildoers (Psa. 36:1-4, 10-12).

Character

The infinity of God can be seen first in that God is without limits in *character*. He is *perfect*. 'Be perfect, as your heavenly Father is perfect', Jesus told his disciples (Matt. 5:48). This is not a comparative perfection, says Poole, but an 'absolute perfection'.[4] God is 'unboundedly perfect in the highest manner', says Charnock, his perfection being even 'an infinite sublimity … without any shadow or taint of imperfection'.[5]

---

[1] Berkhof, *Systematic Theology*, p. 59.
[2] William G. T. Shedd, *Dogmatic Theology* (1888; Grand Rapids, MI: Zondervan, n.d.), I:473.
[3] Henry, *Commentary*, on Psa. 36:5-6.
[4] Poole, *Commentary*, III:26.
[5] Charnock, *Existence and Attributes*, I:268.

He is 'an ocean of all perfection'.[6] God is perfect holiness, perfect justice, perfect goodness. Consequently, when we speak of God's love, we speak of both a perfect or pure love, as to its character, and a limitless or boundless love, as to its extent. In contrast, human love suffers from defects in both areas: it is morally imperfect, and it is limited. In the first case, it suffers from a mixture of motives. It is tainted by selfishness, by self-interest, by sin. Human love is fickle. We easily cross the line from love to hate, from infatuation to jealousy, hatred, and a passion for revenge. In the second case, it is limited in scope, bound by the constraints of finite energy. Consequently, our love often does unlovely things, as when we withhold it in order to get our own way or when it fails simply because of exhaustion. Human love manipulates, disappoints, and breaks hearts. Sweet though it is, its imperfections carry with it much grief, sorrow, and pain.

However, God's love is perfect. He never plays games with us. He is never manipulative. He is never indecisive. Divine love 'never fails' (1 Cor. 13:8 NASB). What is true of God's love is true of all of his characteristics. He is perfect in his wrath, patience, anger, grace, righteousness, mercy, and justice. He is of flawless character.

Power

Second, God is without limits, not only in character, but also in *power*. He is *omnipotent*, of unlimited power. 'Power in God,' says Swinnock, 'is that attribute by which he effecteth whatsoever he pleaseth.'[7] He creates with a word. He governs all creatures and all their actions. As just mentioned, aside from moral imperfections, human love has physical limitations. We grow tired of caring for and loving others. We need rest; we need breaks. We are physically unable to love others as much as we would like or as much as we ought. We fall short because of physical frailties and the limitations of our bodies. The absolute perfection of God guarantees that God knows no such limits. 'As there is nothing too hard for God,' says Swinnock, 'so there is nothing hard to God.'[8] For God, 'it is as easy to create a world as to move a feather',

---

[6] Charnock, *Existence and Attributes*, I:416.

[7] Swinnock, *Incomparableness of God, Works*, IV:407.

[8] *Ibid.*, IV:439.

says Thornwell, 'to uphold all things as to speak a word'.[9] He is the Almighty (Psa. 91:1). Gurnall calls the 'all' in 'Almighty' the 'flower of his crown'.[10] He refers to God's almighty power as his 'incomparably sweet attribute'.[11] God is able to work according to the laws of nature and contrary to the laws of nature. He is able to work through ordinary means, 'yet is free to work without, above, and against them at his pleasure'.[12] He is able to make the sun stand still, nullify the power of fire, close the mouths of lions, make waters stand like a wall, heal diseases and raise the dead, multiply loaves, and walk on water. When he works above the laws of nature, we call it a miracle. Miracles are not a problem for Almighty God.

God's power can be seen not only in creation and providence, but also, even especially, in redemption. The apostle speaks of 'the immeasurable greatness of his power' towards believers, and of 'the working of his great might that he worked in Christ when he raised him from the dead and seated him at his right hand in the heavenly places' (Eph. 1:19-20). His redemptive power is characterized by 'immeasurable greatness'. His redemptive might is a 'great might'. For him, 'nothing [is] impossible' (Luke 1:37), and conversely, 'all things are possible' (Matt. 19:26). The prophet Jeremiah, startled by the command to buy land in a freshly conquered and exiled Israel, affirms as he prays, 'Nothing is too hard for you' (Jer. 32:17). When called upon in a crisis, God will not be asleep, nor will he be weary (Psa. 121:2-4). The troubles of the world will not have exhausted his supply of power, goodness, or justice. God is eternally with us with infinite resources. Those with eyes of faith are able to see that God always has their back, accompanying them through all of life's challenges with his great might. The enemies of our souls are meddling with one who is 'far above their match'.[13] God is limitless, boundless, eternally dealing with our world, and perfectly dealing with us according to his perfect goodness, justice, and wisdom.

---

[9] Thornwell, *Collected Writings*, I:204.
[10] Gurnall, *Christian in Complete Armour*, I:27.
[11] *Ibid.*, I:32.
[12] Westminster Confession of Faith V.3.
[13] Gurnall, *Christian in Complete Armour*, I:377.

Knowledge

Third, God is without limits in *knowledge*. A God who is omnipresent is aware of all that transpires. 'If God be present everywhere, he must needs know what is done everywhere', says Charnock.[14] 'The Creator has infinite knowledge at every instant,' says Shedd, 'and neither learns nor forgets.'[15] He is *omniscient*. He enjoys perfect knowledge of the world and of all possible worlds. He knows all things that can be known: all things that were, that are, that shall be, and that possibly could be, were God to will them to be, even 'though they shall never in the least peep up into being', as Charnock puts it.[16] He has a perfect knowledge of himself and of all that he has made, past, present, and future. He knows what happens by design and what happens by what we call 'chance'. He knows and foreknows the free and voluntary acts of man. God is never surprised. To think otherwise 'is to measure God by our short line', says Charnock, and 'an unworthy conceit of God'.[17] 'His understanding is infinite' (Psa. 147:5 NASB). 'God knows whatever is knowable', says Watson.[18] His knowledge is eternal; consequently, says Charnock, 'God sees all things in one instant.'[19] Indeed, says Swinnock, 'He doth by one pure, simple, undivided, eternal act of his understanding, know all things perfectly, immediately, distinctly, every moment.'[20]

His knowledge is complete. According to Swinnock, 'To his knowledge nothing can be given or added, from his knowledge nothing can be taken. His knowledge is so perfect that it admits not of an increase or decrease.'[21] More simply, 'God knoweth all things fully and perfectly.'[22]

Because God knows all things, he is able to prescribe laws that are perfectly suited to our nature. Because God knows all things, he is able

---

[14] Charnock, *Existence and Attributes*, I:447.
[15] Shedd, *Dogmatic Theology*, I:347.
[16] Charnock, *Existence and Attributes*, I:462.
[17] *Ibid.*, I:486.
[18] Watson, *Body of Divinity*, p. 55.
[19] Charnock, *Existence and Attributes of God*, I:484.
[20] Swinnock, *The Incomparableness of God*, *Works*, IV:415.
[21] *Ibid.*, IV:413.
[22] *Ibid.*, IV:414.

to judge justly. He is able to judge both our actions and our motives. He tests 'the minds and hearts' (Psa. 7:9). He 'weighs the spirit' (Prov. 16:2). He discerns 'the thoughts and intentions of the heart (Heb. 4:12). 'The hearts of the children of man' are 'open before the LORD' (Prov. 15:11). As we have seen, David expressed with poetic skill his wonder at God's comprehensive and exhaustive knowledge of him (Psa. 139:1-5). 'Such knowledge is too wonderful for me; it is high; I cannot attain it' (139:6). Indeed, 'no creature is hidden from his sight, but all are naked and exposed to the eyes of him to whom we must give account' (Heb. 4:13; cf. 2 Chron. 16:9; Prov. 15:3).

God is 'all eye … all understanding', says Charnock, and an 'unsleepy eye' at that.[23] Among our limitations is our inability to fix our attention on more than one thing at a time. We flatter ourselves about our capacity to 'multitask', when in reality what our eyes, ears, and attention are doing is moving rapidly from one thing to the next and back again. God, by way of contrast, is able to know all things comprehensively at once. His attention is fixed on everything at the same time, and not on one thing more than another. 'God is all eye', meaning he knows all things distinctly, infallibly, immutably, and perpetually. He knows the whole story, the good and the bad, the public and the private, the outward and the inward. 'He knows our frame; he remembers that we are dust' (Psa. 103:14). When others misjudge us, misreading our intentions or motives, our words or our actions, God knows our hearts. He discerns our thoughts 'from afar' (Psa. 139:2). He knows our intentions, even when our performance falters. 'God knows that we do that in the simplicity of our hearts, which may be judged by men to be done for unworthy and sordid ends.'[24] Conversely, he knows when we play the hypocrite and when our piety is self-serving; when we have cleaned the outside of the cup and left the inside full of corruption (Luke 11:39). *Cave! Deus videt*: Take heed! God sees. He knows our guilt. He also knows our innocence. 'If God were not omniscient, how could he reward the good, and punish the evil?' Charnock asks.[25] 'The exact discerning of these, without a possibility to be deceived, is necessary to pass a right and infallible

---

[23] Charnock, *Existence and Attributes*, I:464, 505.
[24] *Ibid*., I:526-27.
[25] *Ibid*., I:508.

judgment upon them.'[26] We can pray with the psalmist, 'Search me, O God, and know my heart! Try me and know my thoughts! And see if there be any grievous way in me' (Psa. 139:23-24).

Moreover, 'knowledge is the basis of providence', Charnock points out, citing Matthew 6:32 and Luke 11:13.[27] 'He understands our wants, appreciates our weakness and can accommodate his grace precisely to our case', Thornwell explains.[28]

Because his knowledge is infinite and his character is perfect, God always chooses the best means for the highest ends. That is, he is infinite in wisdom. 'Wisdom is the flower of knowledge,' says Charnock, 'and knowledge is the root of wisdom.'[29] Often it may seem otherwise to us; his 'judgments' to us are 'unsearchable' and his 'ways' are 'inscrutable' (Rom. 11:33). No one can know the mind of the Lord so as to reach perfect understanding. This is to be expected. 'It is not for a finite nature to understand an infinite wisdom', says Charnock.[30] The importance of God's omniscience in our understanding of his attributes is beautifully summarized by Charnock: 'His compassions to pity us, his readiness to relieve us, his power to protect and assist us, would be insignificant, without his omniscience to inform his goodness and direct the arm of this power ... without this knowledge of his, no comfort could be drawn from any other perfection.'[31]

Time

Fourth, God is not limited by *time*. He is eternal. God has no beginning or end. He created time and stands outside of it. 'God hath no succession in his duration,' says Swinnock; 'he dwelleth in one indivisible point of eternity.'[32] Indeed, 'he enjoyeth his whole eternity every moment'.[33] 'He possesses,' says Berkhof, 'the whole of his existence in one indivisible present.'[34] 'With him,' said Shedd, 'there is no

---

[26] Charnock, *Existence and Attributes*, I:508.

[27] *Ibid.*.

[28] Thornwell, *Collected Writings*, I:197.

[29] Charnock, *Existence and Attributes*, I:461.

[30] *Ibid.*, II:419.

[31] *Ibid.*, I:525.

[32] Swinnock, *The Incomparableness of God, Works*, IV:395.

[33] *Ibid.*

[34] Berkhof, *Systematic Theology*, p. 60.

distinction between the present, past, and future; but all things are equally and always present to him.'[35] All things are present to him though, in themselves, temporal things have temporal succession. Eternity also implies the omniscience we have just reviewed. Charnock cites Acts 15:17 in which James, before the Council of Jerusalem, affirms from Amos 9:11-12 that the things God knows are 'known from of old' (Gk *aiōnos*, eternity). 'God's knowledge is co-eternal with him,' says Charnock. 'He knows all things as present.'[36]

Eternity implies the immutability of God. According to Charnock, eternity is 'the essence of God'. Likewise, 'it is the essence of God to be immutable'.[37] The writer to the Hebrews joins the two in proving the deity of Christ from Psalm 102: 'But you are the *same*, and your years will have *no end*' (Heb. 1:12; cf. 13:8). 'It is contrary to the nature of immutability to be without eternity', Charnock claims.[38] Eternity is

> a denying of God any measures of time, as immensity is a denying of him any bounds of place; as immensity is the diffusion of his essence, so eternity is the duration of his essence …. As the essence of God cannot be bounded by any place, so it is not to be limited by any time; as it is his immensity to be everywhere, so it is his eternity to be always.[39]

His knowledge cannot be added to because all knowledge is equally present before him.

God never says, 'I wish I had done things differently.' Unlike us, he is not frustrated by an unrepeatable past or an unknown future, because he is beyond time. Time is a source of frustration to us. It races past us too quickly. We try to grab hold of it, but it eludes our grasp. We blink, and our children have grown and life is half over. 'Where has the time gone?' we ask. C. S. Lewis once wrote to Sheldon Vanauken, 'Notice how we are perpetually surprised at Time. ("How time flies! Fancy John being grown-up and married! I can hardly believe it!") In heaven's name, why? Unless, indeed, there is something in us which

[35] Shedd, *Dogmatic Theology*, I:385.

[36] Charnock, *Existence and Attributes*, I:361.

[37] *Ibid.*, I:359.

[38] *Ibid.*, I:357. Again, he says, 'Immutability and eternity go hand in hand together' (I:363).

[39] *Ibid.*, I:349.

is not temporal.'[40] We are made for eternity but trapped in time. The eternal God knows nothing of this unease.

Yet God does also stand in some relation to time and temporal things. He has *duration*, meaning continuance or endurance through time, without *succession*. God is the great 'I AM'—the ever-present, unchanging one (Exod. 3:14). Abraham called him 'the Everlasting God' (Gen. 21:33; cf. Isa. 40:28). 'Before the mountains were brought forth, or ever you had formed the earth and the world,' writes Moses in his contribution to the Psalter, 'from everlasting to everlasting you are God' (Psa. 90:2). The psalmist exclaims, 'But you, O LORD, are enthroned for ever … your years have no end' (Psa. 102:12, 27). That he is an 'everliving God' is our 'everlasting consolation', says Henry.[41] God declares through the prophet Isaiah, 'I am the first and I am the last; besides me there is no god' (Isa. 44:6). Again in the New Testament, '"I am the Alpha and the Omega," says the Lord God, "who is and who was and who is to come, the Almighty"' (Rev. 1:8). The apostle Paul speaks of the God 'who alone has immortality, who dwells in unapproachable light, whom no one has ever seen or can see. To him be honour and *eternal* dominion' (1 Tim. 6:16). 'To him be glory in the church and in Christ Jesus throughout all generations, *for ever and ever*' (Eph. 3:21).

God's characteristics and ways are as eternal as they are immutable. 'Without eternity,' says Charnock, 'what were all his other perfections but as glorious yet withering flowers, a great, but a decaying beauty!'[42] So it is that God's *mercy* endures forever (Psa. 136; 103:17); his *counsel* is eternal (Psa. 33:11), as are his *purpose* (Eph. 3:11), *kingdom* (Exod. 15:18), *power* (Dan. 6:27), and *glory* (1 Pet. 5:10); his *dominion* is everlasting (Dan. 7:14), as also are his *righteousness* and *truth* (Psa. 119:142). As quoted above from Charnock, 'It is contrary to the nature of immutability to be without eternity.'[43] The same may be said of God's infinity and perfection: 'If his being could fail, he were not perfect …. To be finite and limited, is the greatest imperfection, for it consists in a

---

[40] C. S. Lewis, cited in Sheldon Vanauken, *A Severe Mercy* (1977; London: Hodder & Stoughton; 1979), p. 93.

[41] Henry, Commentary, on Psa. 102:27.

[42] Charnock, *Existence and Attributes*, I:372.

[43] *Ibid.*, I:357.

denial of being. He could not be the most blessed being if he were not always so, and should not forever remain so.'[44]

Neither could he be omnipotent or almighty: 'Where there is no being, there is no power.'[45] If he could not preserve himself from non-being, that which was the cause of his non-being would be greater than he. His eternity and might are joined in Revelation 1:8: '"I am the Alpha and the Omega," says the Lord God, "who is and who was and who is to come, the Almighty."' 'He could not properly be *almighty*, that were not *always mighty*, Charnock explains.'[46] Consequently, he calls eternity 'the choice perfection of God', even 'the gloss and lustre of all others'. This is because 'every perfection would be imperfect if it were not always a perfection'.[47] He is the King eternal (1 Tim. 1:17) who inhabits eternity (Isa. 57:15), the Ancient of Days (Dan. 7:9, 27). According to Jonathan Edwards, 'The eternity of God's existence … is nothing else but his immediate perfect, and invariable possession of the whole of his unlimited life, together and at once …. It is equally improper to talk of months and years of the divine existence, and mile-squares of deity.'[48]

The eternality of God has practical implications. 'As the eternity of God is the ground of all religion, so the eternity of Christ is the ground of the Christian religion', says Charnock.[49] He explains: 'As God is infinite, he hath right to a boundless service; as he is eternal, he hath right to a perpetual service.'[50] Baxter applies the doctrine of God's eternality brilliantly. Because God is eternal, he says, our minds should be drawn away from the transitory and temporal to the enduring and eternal. Unlike the beasts, we were not made merely for the present, physical, material world. Our souls were made for the eternal God, and our happiness is to be found nowhere else but in him. Charnock

---

[44] Charnock, *Existence and Attributes*, I:357.

[45] *Ibid*.

[46] *Ibid*.

[47] *Ibid*., I:353.

[48] Jonathan Edwards, *A Careful and Strict Inquiry into the Prevailing Notion of the Freedom of the Will*, in *Works of Jonathan Edwards* (1834; Edinburgh: Banner of Truth Trust, 1974), I:72.

[49] Charnock, *Existence and Attributes*, I:361.

[50] *Ibid*., I:373.

concurs: 'Man is made for an eternal state.'[51] Consequently, man can never find happiness in that which is temporary. How can we live for this world when for all its pomp and pleasure it is 'passing away' (1 Cor. 7:31); when its greatest empires are dispersed by God like 'smoke out of the chimney' (Hos. 13:3 KJV)? The best of the world is but 'broken cisterns that can hold no water', incomparably inferior to God who is the 'fountain of living waters' (Jer. 2:13). Wealth 'suddenly … sprouts wings' and flies away (Prov. 23:4-5). 'The world is passing away along with its desires' (1 John 2:17). 'Truly if man had no other life to live but this,' Baxter writes, 'I should esteem him a very contemptible creature.'[52] Indeed, 'I think I should dig my grave, and lay me down in it and die, and perish, to escape the sorrows of a longer life', if there be no eternity.[53]

However, since there is an eternal God who inhabits an eternal realm, we should set our minds on things above, not on things below (Col. 3:2). We should seek the things above, where Christ is (Col. 3:1). The fact of eternity is what makes sense of the Christian life. Eternity is what gives *weight* to sin (it would otherwise be inconsequential), gives *value* to salvation and the means of attaining it, gives *necessity* to faith and the diligent pursuit of holiness, makes *folly* of ungodliness, makes *vanity* of worldly pursuits, and gives *worth* to God's favour. It is eternity that makes us 'so fearful of sinning, so diligent in holy duties, so cheerful and resolved in suffering', says Baxter. 'O play not, loiter not, do nothing by halves in the way of eternity.'[54] Listen as Baxter exhorts us to ponder eternity. First, the unbeliever:

> O methinks the very name of eternity should frighten the drunkard out of the ale-house, and the sleepy sinner out of his security, and the lustful, sportful, voluptuous sinner out of his sensual delights! Methinks the very name of eternity should call off the worldling to seek betimes a more enduring treasure, and should take down the gallant's pride, and bring men to look after other matters than the most do look after! Methinks to hear the name of eternity should, with men of any faith and reason, even

[51] Charnock, *Existence and Attributes*, I:371.
[52] Baxter, *The Divine Life, Works*, III:772.
[53] *Ibid.*, III:774.
[54] *Ibid.*, III:775.

blast all the beauty, and blur the glory, and sadden the delights, and weaken the temptations of the world, and make all its pleasure, pomp, and splendour, to be to our apprehensions as a smoke, a shadow, as the dirt that we tread upon! Methinks to hear the name of eternity should lay so odious a reproach on sin, and so nakedly open the folly, and shame, and misery of the ungodly, and so lively show the need and worth of faith and holiness, that men should be soon resolved in their choice, and soon be at the end of an ungodly course, and need no more words to make them the resolved servants of the Lord, before to-morrow![55]

Then the believer:

O methinks, that a thought of eternity should, with a believer, answer all temptations, and put life into all his prayers and endeavours! If we were never so cold, or dull, or sleepy, one would think a serious thought of eternity should warm us, quicken us, and awake us! O Christians, shall we hear carelessly or speak carelessly of eternity? Shall we pray coldly, or labour negligently, for eternity? Oh what an ocean of joy will eternity be unto the sanctified! It hath neither banks nor bottom.[56]

The unbeliever again:

Oh what a gulf of misery and woe will eternity be to the ungodly! Wonderful! that on their dying beds they quake not with the horror, and that they cry not out with greatest lamentation, to think what a bottomless gulf of misery their departing souls must be cast into! To be for ever, ever, ever under the most heavy wrath of God! This is the appointed wages of ungodliness; this is the end of wicked ways; this is it that sinners chose, because they would not live to God! This they preferred, or ventured on, before a holy, heavenly life![57]

Finally, the believer again:

And this is it that believers are labouring to escape in all their holy care and diligence! It is an infinite value that is put upon the

[55] Baxter, *The Divine Life, Works*, III:776.
[56] *Ibid.*
[57] *Ibid.*

blood of Christ, the promises of God, the ordinances and means of grace, and grace itself, and the poorest duties of the poorest saints, because they are for an infinite, eternal glory. No mercy is small that tastes of heaven (as all doth or should do to the believer). No action is low that aims at heaven. And oh how lively should the resolutions and courage of those men be, that are travelling, fighting, and watching for eternity! How full should be their comforts, that are fetched from the foresight of infinite, eternal comforts! As all things will presently be swallowed up in eternity, so methinks the present apprehension of eternity should now swallow up all things else in the soul.[58]

Space

Fifth, just as God cannot be measured or limited by time, neither can he be measured or limited by space. Charnock explains the relationship between eternity, immutability, and what the theologians call his *immensity*: 'As eternity is the perfection whereby he hath neither beginning nor end, immutability is the perfection whereby he hath neither increase nor diminution, so immensity or omnipresence is that whereby he hath neither bounds nor limitation.'[59]

'He transcends every change in time, for he is eternal, in space, for he is *omnipresent* ...', says Bavinck.[60] 'He is diffused through the whole world', says Charnock. He is '"higher than heaven, deeper than hell, longer than the earth, broader than the sea"'.[61] God is 'present in every point of space with his whole being', adds Berkhof.[62] Swinnock explains: 'He is neither shut up in any place nor shut out of any place. He is above place, without place, yet in all places .... God is in heaven, earth, sea, hell, and infinitely where there is neither heaven, nor earth, nor sea, nor hell.'[63]

[58] Baxter, *The Divine Life, Works*, III:776.
[59] Charnock, *Existence and Attributes*, I:423. He says again, 'As he is infinite, he is everywhere; as he is simple, his whole essence is everywhere; for in regard of his infiniteness, he hath no bounds; in regard of his simplicity, he hath no parts' (I:433).
[60] Herman Bavinck, *The Doctrine of God* (1951; Edinburgh: Banner of Truth Trust, 1977), 149 (emphasis added).
[61] Charnock, *Existence and Attributes*, I:268, citing Job 11:8.
[62] Berkhof, *Systematic Theology*, 60.
[63] Swinnock, *The Incomparableness of God, Works*, IV:398.

The limitations of space are another source of enormous frustration for mere mortals. I am needed *there*. However, because I am *here* I cannot be *there*. God experiences nothing of this. 'God in the fullness of his essence is present to every point of space in every point of time', Thornwell explains.[64] It should be carefully noted that while God inhabits space he is not part of space. Neither our meeting rooms nor our chairs are a part of God. 'God is not everywhere by any conjunction, composition, or mixture with anything on earth',' says Charnock.[65] His presence may be likened to light or air, which fills a space but retains its own nature. The confusion of the Creator with the creation is the error of pantheism, or pan-everything-ism (as Francis Schaeffer called it), where God is everything and everything is God.[66] God, Thornwell explains again, 'is as perfectly distinct from the universe and from every object in it as if he dwelt in distant and inaccessible regions'. Moreover, 'He is separated from the finite by a chasm as boundless as his immensity.'[67] Instead, he is mysteriously above space, while being present in every part of the universe. This is what is meant by the omnipresence of God. He is always everywhere. This also implies what Jesus told the woman at the well: 'God is spirit.' He is immaterial and cannot be localized. True worship, Jesus teaches her, is not a matter of geographic location, whether Samaria or Jerusalem, because God is spirit and therefore he is worshipped in spirit and truth (John 4:24).

Returning to Psalm 139 we read, 'Where shall I flee from your presence? If I ascend to heaven, you are there! If I make my bed in Sheol, you are there! (139:7-8).

'Whither shall I flee from thy presence?' the psalmist asks. 'Surely no whither', answers Trapp.[68] The Hebrew language uses contrasts to indicate *comprehensiveness*. For example, Moses refers to 'when you lie down, and when you rise', which means, 'in everything you do' (Deut. 6:7; 11:19). When the psalmist says, 'If I ascend to heaven, you are there! If I make my bed in Sheol, you are there' (Psa. 139:8), he

---

[64] Thornwell, *Collected Writings*, I:194; Charnock, *Existence and Attributes*, I:430.
[65] Charnock, *Existence and Attributes*, I:442.
[66] See Chapter VI, 'Our Governor and Preserver.'
[67] Thornwell, *Collected Writings*, I:195.
[68] Trapp, *Commentary*, II:680.

is saying that there is nowhere, from highest heaven to deepest hell, where one can escape from the presence of God. 'He not only knows both and governs both, but he fills both', says Henry.[69] In heaven, 'He there communicates to saints and angels the richest tokens of his love', says Thornwell. In hell, 'The impenitent and devils are made to feel the weight of his displeasure against sin.'[70] People can be avoided; God cannot. God, says Charnock, 'hath a presence of glory in heaven, whereby he comforts the saints; a presence of wrath in hell, whereby he torments the damned'.[71]

'God's centre is everywhere,' says Watson, 'and his circumference is no where.'[72] Solomon asked at the dedication of the temple, 'But will God indeed dwell on the earth? Behold, heaven and the highest heaven cannot contain you; how much less this house that I have built!' (1 Kings 8:27). 'Cannot contain you' because 'such is thine immensity', explains Trapp; 'thou fillest all places, and art comprehended of no place'.[73] 'Much less,' says Poole of Solomon's next phrase, 'for thy essence reacheth far beyond them, being omnipresent.'[74] In denouncing false prophets, God asked the rhetorical question through Jeremiah, 'Can a man hide himself in secret places so that I cannot see him? ... Do I not fill heaven and earth?' (Jer. 23:24). 'His presence,' says Charnock, 'is rendered as an argument to prove his knowledge.'[75] The apostle Paul said at the Areopagus in Athens, 'He is actually not far from each one of us, for "In him we live and move and have our being"' (Acts 17:27-28). If God were to make ten thousand worlds, says Swinnock, 'he would fill all, and his whole essence [would] be in every part of each world, and yet without the least extension, or multiplication, or motion'.[76]

---

[69] Henry, *Commentary*, on Psa. 139:7, 8.

[70] Thornwell, *Collected Writings*, I:196.

[71] Charnock, *Existence and Attributes*, I:426.

[72] Watson, *Body of Divinity*, 46. So also Swinnock, *Incomparableness of God*, *Works*, IV:397-98; Charnock, *Existence and Attributes*, I:423.

[73] Trapp, *Commentary*, I:557; Charnock, *Existence and Attributes*, I:431.

[74] Poole, *Commentary*, I:671.

[75] Charnock, *Existence and Attributes*, I:422; 'He that fills all, must needs see and know all.'

[76] Swinnock, *The Incomparableness of God*, *Works*, IV:398.

What are we to make of those passages which speak of God being in a specific place, such as sitting in heaven (Psa. 2:4); or when he is said to dwell in the ark and temple (Psa. 26:8), or in Jerusalem (Psa. 48:1ff.; Zech. 8:3)? What are we to understand when he is said to come to us and to depart from us? When he is said to be far from Gentiles (Eph. 2:17; Prov. 15:29), to dwell in believers (1 John 4:15), to depart from Saul (1 Sam. 16:14), and to come down to see a city (Gen. 11:5)? None of these depictions should be understood as speaking of God's essence; rather they speak of manifestations of his presence. His essence is present everywhere, but he manifests that presence differently according to his purposes. God's heavenly throne 'is the court of his majestical presence, but not the prison of his essence', says Charnock.[77] He is in heaven, says Owen, 'only by way of eminency, in respect of manifestations of himself and operations from his gracious presence'.[78] None of what we are affirming of God's universal presence denies his special presence, or peculiar presence, says Pictet, 'in certain places and persons, where he gives signs and effects either of his majesty, or his glory, or his grace'.[79] He is generally present to all, yet, explains Muller, 'he is present graciously and specially only to some'.[80] When God promises, 'I will never leave you nor forsake you' (Heb. 13:5), he is promising his *gracious* presence. When Jesus promises, 'I am with you always, to the end of the age' (Matt. 28:20), he is promising his *powerful* presence. Charnock summarizes what is meant when Scripture speaks of a localized presence of God:

> God is in heaven in regard of the manifestation of his glory; in hell by the expression of his justice; in earth, by the discoveries of his wisdom, power, patience, and compassion; in his people, by the monuments of his grace; and in all, in regard of his substance. … He fills hell with his severity, heaven with his glory, his people with his grace.[81]

---

[77] Charnock, *Existence and Attributes*, I:439.
[78] Owen, *Vindiciae Evangelicae, Works*, XII:90.
[79] Cited in Muller, *Post-Reformation Reformed Dogmatics*, III:345.
[80] Muller, *Post-Reformation Reformed Dogmatics,* III:345.
[81] Charnock, *Existence and Attributes*, I:440, 451.

Again, God is never limited to a place as we are—that is, so as to be there and nowhere else, in that place and so not in another. God is 'equally present everywhere', Owen explains.[82] 'God is *immense*,' says Owen, '*and indistant* to all things and places, absent from nothing, no place, contained in none, present to all by and in his infinite essence and being.' Yet he does manifest his power and glory in *all* places, *some* places or in *no* places 'as it seemeth good to him'.[83]

This doctrine of the divine omnipresence is both a comfort and unsettling: 'as much a comfort to a good man as it is a terror to a wicked one', says Charnock.[84] It is a comfort that God is always present. The great ones of the world are unavailable to most of us. Yet Almighty God is as close to us at all times as we are to ourselves. Furthermore, it is God in the fullness of his attributes who is present with us for our good. 'It is not a piece of God is here and another parcel there, but God in his whole essence and perfections,' says Charnock; 'in his wisdom to guide us, his power to protect and support us, his mercy to pity us, his fullness to refresh us, and his goodness to relieve us.' This is true whatever our circumstances or condition. 'If we are miserable, we have the presence of his goodness; if we want direction, we have the presence of his wisdom; if we are weak, we have the presence of his power.'[85] The believer, says Thornwell, 'can never be removed beyond the reach of his Redeemer and his Friend'.[86] Consequently, 'it is this that makes all other excellences of the divine nature sweet', says Charnock. 'What would grace, wisdom, power signify at a distance from us?'[87] However, it can also be somewhat unnerving to know that in everything I do and everywhere I go, God is there and knows. Thornwell reflects beautifully on the omnipresence of God:

> Go to the eternal snows of the north, the burning deserts of the tropics; climb from world to world and from sun to sun; or sink even to the deep vault of hell—everywhere you shall meet God. It is his hand that sustains the mountains, his breath that

---

[82] Owen, *Vindiciae Evangelicae*, in *Works*, XII:95.

[83] *Ibid.*, XII:92.

[84] Charnock, *Existence and Attributes*, I:450.

[85] *Ibid.*, I:453-54.

[86] Thornwell, *Collected Writings*, I:197.

[87] Charnock, *Existence and Attributes*, I:454.

scorches the desert, his arm that upholds the worlds. Surely we may ask with the psalmist, What is man that thou art mindful of him, or the son of man that thou visitest him? We are indeed as vanity and less than nothing in his sight.[88]

Consideration of his immensity leads us to conclude with Charnock, 'What little, little, little things we are to God.'[89] How can we not humble ourselves before him? Contemplation of the infinity of God, says Baxter, 'must raise admiring, reverent thoughts in the soul of the believer'.[90] The God with whom we have to do is infinite, without limits, without defects, perfect in character, boundless in knowledge and power, unlimited by time, unlimited by space. Another way of speaking of God's infinity is to speak of his *greatness*. William Perkins (1558–1602), regarded by many as the 'father of English Puritanism', wrote in his book *A Golden Chain*, 'His name is great, Jer. 10:6; Josh. 7:9; his power is great, Psa. 147:5; his acts are great, Psa. 111:2; his judgments are great, Exod. 7:4; he is great in counsel, Jer. 32:19, and mighty works, Jer. 32:19; Deut. 32:4.'[91] 'Great is the LORD and greatly to be praised' (Psa. 48:1; 96:4; 145:3). 'How we should never think of God without a holy admiration of his greatness, and a deep sense of our own littleness!' concludes Charnock.[92]

The unity or simplicity of God

We have looked at three of the incommunicable attributes of God and now we turn to the fourth, which is God's unity and his solidarity or simplicity. This attribute includes two ideas: first, God is numerically one, and, as such, unique. Thus Solomon, at the dedication of the temple, said, 'The LORD is God; there is no other' (1 Kings 8:60). Paul told the Corinthians, 'There is *one* God, the Father, from whom are all things and for whom we exist' (1 Cor. 8:6). He told Timothy, 'There is *one* God, and there is one mediator between God and men, the man Christ Jesus' (1 Tim. 2:5). As we saw in an earlier study, his uniqueness is indicated in Deuteronomy 6:4, the foundational creed

---

[88] Thornwell, *Collected Writings*, I:204, 205.
[89] Charnock, *Existence and Attributes,* I:448.
[90] Baxter, *The Divine Life, Works*, III:770.
[91] Cited in Muller, *Post-Reformation Reformed Dogmatics*, III:332.
[92] Charnock, *Existence and Attributes*, I:448.

of Israel. Moses calls out, 'Hear, O Israel: The LORD our God, the LORD is one': in other words, the 'LORD', Jehovah (Yahweh), is the only one entitled to be called God. Scripture emphasizes God's uniqueness by asking, 'Who is like you, O LORD, among the gods?' (Exod. 15:11). There are not many gods, nor even three gods, but one God, in three persons. Christianity is monotheistic. Father, Son, and Holy Spirit are the names of one God. He is the only God, unique, unparalleled, and unequalled. The oneness of God simplifies life for believers. There is but one God to whom we are accountable and whom we must acknowledge, praise, serve, and love.

Second, God is unified in being and character. The theologians speak of his *simplicity*. The simplicity of God is a natural corollary of the spirituality and unity of God. God is spirit (John 4:24). He is invisible (Heb. 11:1; Rom. 1:23; Col. 1:15; John 1:18; 1 Tim. 1:17; 6:16). He cannot be divided into parts. He is 'free from all composition and division', says Francis Turretin (1623–87), the outstanding Swiss Protestant Scholastic theologian of the seventeenth century.[93] 'The divine essence is indivisible and is entirely present everywhere', says Muller, explaining the orthodox Protestant view.[94] When we study his attributes, they are not parts of God. 'God is a most pure, simple, unmixed essence,' says Swinnock; 'he is incapable of the least composition, and therefore of the least division. He is one most pure, one without all parts, members, accounts, and qualities.'[95] The various attributes by which we describe him are 'one indivisible essence'.[96] His justice is his mercy and his wisdom and his patience; his knowledge is his faithfulness; his mercy is his justice, and so on.[97]

We comprehend the attributes differently, but they are all one in him. 'To speak properly,' says Lewis Bayly, 'there are not in God many attributes, but one only, which is nothing else but the Divine Essence itself, but what attribute soever you call it.'[98]

---

[93] Cited in Beeke and Jones. *A Puritan Theology*, 61 from Francis Turretin, *Institutes of Elenctic Theology*, ed. James T. Dennison, Jr., tr. George Musgrave Giger (Phillipsburg, NJ: P&R, 1992), Vol III, 7.1.

[94] Muller, *Post-Reformation Reformed Dogmatics*, III:343.

[95] Swinnock, *The Incomparableness of God*, *Works*, IV:397.

[96] *Ibid*.

[97] *Ibid*., IV:423.

[98] Bayly, *The Practice of Piety*, 23.

The Thirty-Nine Articles of the Church of England affirm, 'There is but one living and true God, everlasting, without body, parts, or passions' (Art. I; so also the Westminster Confession of Faith II.1). God is *impassible*: he is not characterized by changing human emotions. When he is described as having such passions, we are to understand them in the same way as we understand descriptions of God's body parts. The language is anthropomorphic. Unlike ours, his 'emotions' are chosen responses. He is never the victim, as are humans. Packer explains: 'No created beings can inflict pain, suffering and distress on him at their own will. In so far as God enters into suffering and grief (which Scripture's many anthropopathisms, plus the fact of the cross, show that he does), it is by his own deliberate decision; he is never his creatures' hapless victim.'[99]

We also may say that affections are attributed to God metaphorically. They describe the human emotions that would accompany the human actions that parallel those of God. For example, God's justice is described as anger or wrath resulting in retribution, pain, sorrow, and death. However, the anger and wrath themselves are metaphorical. 'If he be properly and literally angry, and furious, and wrathful,' Owen reasons, 'he is moved, troubled, perplexed, desires revenge and is neither blessed nor perfect.'[100] Love, mercy, and grace, he says, 'denote God's essential goodness and kindness, which is eminent amongst his infinite perfections'.[101] His jealousy and hatred (e.g. Psa. 5:4-5; Exod. 20:5; Deut. 32:21) describe not God as he is in himself, but the effects that will greet those who provoke God by their blasphemies and abominations. Again Owen: 'That which is inconsistent with absolute blessedness and all-sufficiency is not to be ascribed to God; to do so casts him down from his excellency.' Owen asks, 'Can he be blessed, is he all-sufficient, who is tossed up and down with hope, joy, fear, sorrow, repentance, anger, and the like?'[102] Our emotions are often involuntary; his are not. Moreover, God's happiness, his blessedness and contentedness, cannot be affected by finite creatures. 'God is a *perfectly happy* Being, in the most absolute and highest sense possible,'

---

[99] Packer, 'God', in the *New Dictionary of Theology*, 277.
[100] Owen, *Vindicae Evangelicae*, *Works*, XII:112.
[101] *Ibid*., XII:114.
[102] *Ibid*., XII:115.

says Edwards; 'in strict propriety of speech, there is no such thing as any pain, grief or trouble in God.'[103]

God is a simple, consistent, undivided unity. There are no elements in him which conflict. The various attributes are consistent with one another. God is 'totally integrated', says Packer.[104] Unlike man, as Packer points out, 'He cannot be torn different ways by divergent thoughts and desires.'[105] There is no gap between what he intends and what he accomplishes. Frail humans sometimes want to do something but for one reason or another cannot. As Jesus said, 'The spirit indeed is willing, but the flesh is weak' (Matt. 26:41; Mark 14:38). We may want to read but have a headache; or want to swim but have a pulled muscle; or want to pray but are tempted away by entertainment; or want to witness but fear what people might think; or want to be in full-time ministry but have financial obligations to meet; or want to continue our education and yet also want to start to work. In our experience we are torn back and forth by conflicting desires, by conflicting obligations and duties, and by conflicting thoughts and reasons. However, our experience is not God's. There is complete harmony in the being of God: Father, Son, and Holy Spirit. They agree in purposes, ends, and means. They are undivided regarding what they wish to do, how they wish to do it, and who is going to do what.

There is complete harmony in the eternal relations of the persons and in the character of God. His love does not conflict with his wrath; his justice does not conflict with his mercy. The being and virtues of God are a harmonious whole, united in all things, spiritual, simple. The simplicity of God means that there is nothing in God but infinite goodness: simple, pure, unmixed, uncompounded good; 'nothing but pure and perfect goodness', says Baxter; 'and therefore there is nothing in him to discourage the soul'.[106] His simplicity calls for a response of holy simplicity from us. 'We that serve a pure, simple God, must do it with simple, pure affections, and not with hypocrisy, or a double heart.' 'God will not accept of a half-heart,' Baxter warns: 'a double-minded, double-hearted, double-faced, or double-tongued person, is

---

[103] Cited in Gerstner, *Theology of Edwards*, II:59.
[104] Packer, 'God', *New Dictionary of Theology*, 271.
[105] Packer, *Knowing God*, 89.
[106] Baxter, *The Divine Life*, *Works*, III:777.

contrary to the holy simplicity of a saint.'[107] Our aim should be the testimony of a good conscience, that we might say with the apostle Paul 'we behaved in the world with simplicity and godly sincerity, not by earthly wisdom but by the grace of God' (2 Cor. 1:12).

How ought we to respond to the spirituality of God, to his invisibility? 'This must teach us to think most highly of the things that are invisible, and meanlier of these visible things,' Baxter urges.[108] Since God is the greatest, the best, the most blessed, the most delightful, and the most desirable of all beings, we must join the apostle and 'look not to the things that are seen but to the things that are unseen. For the things that are seen are transient, but the things that are unseen are eternal' (2 Cor. 4:18).

'Value not sight and sense too much,' Baxter cautions.[109] 'Set your minds on things that are above, not on things that are on earth' (Col. 3:2).

> Fix not your minds on sensible things. Remember that your God, your home, your portion, are unseen: and therefore live in hearty affections to them, and serious prosecution of them, as if you saw them … . Love him, and fear him, and trust him, and serve him, as you would do if you beheld him. 'Faith is the evidence of things not seen' (Heb. 11:1).[110]

* * *

What have we said? We have said much that is true about God, yet most of it goes far beyond our powers of understanding. Attributes are called attributes 'because they are attributed to him for our sakes', says Swinnock, 'so that we might better understand him, though they are not in him as they are in men or angels'.[111] Like a child who loves his brilliant father, and who knows things that are true about him, we know only in part. 'It is a thousand thousand fold more that we know not of him than that we know', says Baxter.[112] We 'see through a glass,

---

[107] Baxter, *The Divine Life*, *Works*, III:777.
[108] *Ibid.*, III:779.
[109] *Ibid.*
[110] *Ibid.*
[111] Swinnock, *The Incomparableness of God*, *Works*, IV:402.
[112] Baxter, *The Divine Life*, *Works*, III:771. 'The reason of God is inscrutable

darkly' (1 Cor. 13:12 KJV). 'We better understand what God is not, than what he is', says Charnock.[113] The infinite God, he insists, 'cannot be declared by human speech, perceived by human sense, or conceived by human understanding'.[114] As God is spirit and incapable of being seen, so he is 'incapable of being understood'. Furthermore, 'there is such a disproportion between an infinite object and a finite sense and understanding, that *it is utterly impossible either to behold or comprehend him*'.[115] Because we are finite, 'it is utterly impossible to have a notion of God commensurate to the immensity and spirituality of his being'.[116] 'This only can be known of God,' Swinnock insists, 'that he can never be known fully; and this only can be comprehended of him, that he cannot be comprehended.'[117] What we affirm is true as far as it goes, yet at all points there is more to be said. As Owen said, even in Christ we see but the 'back parts' of God (from the gospel revelation of Exod. 34:6-7). He makes this point with particular persuasiveness:

> all our notions of God are but childish in respect of his infinite perfections. We lisp and babble, and say we know not what, for the most part, in our most accurate, as we think, conceptions and notions of God. We may love, honour, believe and obey our Father; and therewith he accepts our childish thoughts, for they are but childish. We see but his back parts; we know but little of him.[118]

Because God is infinite, we will not know him as he is. We must rid our minds of any carnal or finite conceptions of God. 'Conceive of him,' says Charnock, 'as excellent, without any imperfections; Spirit without parts; great without quantity; perfect without quality; everywhere without place; powerful without members; understanding without ignorance; wise without reasoning; light without darkness.'

---

for us, unless we could understand God as well as he understands himself. … The rays of his infinite wisdom are too bright and dazzling for our weakness' (Charnock, *Existence and Attributes,* II:436-37).

[113] Charnock, *Existence and Attributes,* I:263.

[114] *Ibid.*

[115] *Ibid.*, I:266 (emphasis added).

[116] *Ibid.*, I:276.

[117] Swinnock, *The Incomparableness of God, Works,* IV:399-400.

[118] Owen, *Mortification, Works,* VI:65.

And then, 'when you have risen to the highest, conceive him yet infinitely above all you can conceive of spirit, and acknowledge the infirmity of your own minds'. In the end we must say, 'This is not God, God is more than this.'[119] 'Labour to get thine heart affected with thine ignorance', says Swinnock, commenting on 1 Corinthians 8:2.[120] In all that we know about God's infinity and immutability, we should realize there is infinitely more to be learned. Owen insists,

> we *cannot* know him. What else doth he intend where he calls himself invisible, incomprehensible, and the like?—that is, he whom we do not, cannot, know as he is. And our farther progress consists more in knowing what he is not, than what he is. Thus is he described to be immortal, and infinite,—that is, he is not, as we are, mortal, finite, and limited.[121]

'Our highest knowledge,' said Cyril of Jerusalem (*c.* 313–86), 'is to confess our ignorance.'[122] Yet we do and must affirm and even cling to all that God teaches us. 'Learn to admire where you cannot fathom', urges Thomas Watson.[123] 'Every attribute of God,' says Spurgeon, 'should become a fresh ray in the sunlight of our gladness.'[124]

God is independent, self-existent, self-sufficient, immutable, infinite, perfect, eternal, omnipresent, and simple. 'These are the attributes which distinguish God,' says Thornwell. 'It is these which render every other perfection divine.'[125] It is for these, as well, that we praise him.

> Immortal, invisible, God only wise,
>   In light inaccessible hid from our eyes,
> Most blessed, most glorious, the Ancient of Days,
>   Almighty, victorious, thy great Name we praise.
>
> Unresting, unhasting, and silent as light,
>   Nor wanting, nor wasting, thou rulest in might;

---

[119] Charnock, *Existence and Attributes*, I:279.
[120] Swinnock, *The Incomparableness of God*, *Works,* IV:489.
[121] Owen, *Mortification*, *Works,* VI:66.
[122] Cited in Thornwell, *Collected Writings,* I:158.
[123] Watson, *Body of Divinity*, 54.
[124] Spurgeon, *Morning and Evening* (1866; Grand Rapids, MI: Zondervan Publishing House, 1980), September 22.
[125] Thornwell, *Collected Writings*, I:203.

> Thy justice, like mountains, high soaring above
> Thy clouds, which are fountains of goodness and love.[126]

Each of the following chapters will demonstrate how the incommunicable attributes govern the communicable, so that the simple statement 'God loves me' begins to mean, 'God loves me because he freely chose to love me with a love that is unchanging, infinite, perfect, pure, boundless, eternal, and omnipresent.' Our God is one, says Watson, and he can 'supply all our wants, scatter all our fears, resolve all our doubts, conquer all our temptations'.[127] Indeed, says Swinnock,

> His incomparable power is thine to protect thee, Gen. 15:1-2; Exod. 15:9-12; his incomparable wisdom is thine to direct thee, Psa. 73:24; his incomparable mercy is thine to pity and relieve thee in thy miseries, Judg. 10:16; his incomparable grace is thine to pardon all thine iniquities, Mic. 7:18; Exod. 34:6-7; his incomparable love is thine to refresh and delight thy soul, Psa. 21:5-6; his incomparable justice is thine to accept thee as righteous for the sake of his Son, Rom. 3:24; his incomparable faithfulness is thine to fulfil all the gracious promises which he hath made to thee, Psa. 89:33-34; his incomparable majesty and beauty and glory are thine, to make thee great, and render thee comely and glorious for ever, Ezek. 16:14; Isa. 43:4; his incomparable joys and pleasures are thine to feed on, and be filled with, Psa. 36:8.[128]

'The LORD is my portion,' says Jeremiah (Lam. 3:24); 'my chosen portion,' says David (Psa. 16:5). Thomas Brooks (1608–80) would have us contemplate this carefully:

> He is a portion that is exactly suited to the condition of the soul in its desires, needs, wants, longings and prayers. All the soul needs is found in God. There is light to enlighten the soul, wisdom to counsel the soul, power to support the soul, goodness to supply the soul, mercy to pardon the soul, beauty to delight the soul, glory to ravish the soul, and fullness to fill the soul. Health is not more suitable to a sick man, wealth to a poor man, bread to

---

[126] Walter Chalmers Smith, 'Immortal, Invisible, God Only Wise'.
[127] Watson, *Body of Divinity*, 45.
[128] Swinnock, *The Incomparableness of God*, *Works,* IV:507-8.

a hungry man, drink to a thirsty man, clothes to a naked man, balm to a wounded man, ease to a tormented man, and pardon to a condemned man, than this portion is to all the needs of man.[129]

---

[129] Thomas Brooks, *An Ark for All God's Noahs*, *The Works of Thomas Brooks* (1861–67; Edinburgh: Banner of Truth Trust, 1980), II:27.

FIVE

'Our Creator God'

In the beginning, God created the heavens and the earth.

—Genesis 1:1

WE have entitled our studies *The Identity and Attributes of God.* Normally creation and providence are classified by the theologians under the 'works of God' rather than the 'attributes of God.' Yet acknowledging God as our Maker is fundamental to knowing God. We can hardly claim to know God at all if we do not know that he has made us. The theme of God the Creator provides the content of the first verse of the Bible, the first article of the Apostles' Creed ('Maker of heaven and earth'), and the first question in the Catechism for Young Children ('Who made you?'); and it is foundational to all subsequent divine awareness and self-awareness. 'Knowledge of the Creator,' says Berkhof, 'is the foundation of all ethical and religious life.'[1] The Creator's design for us as his creatures is the first principle of the life worth living and the first point of our evangelism. Moreover, because God's works manifest his attributes, it is sensible for us to pause to ponder his works, that they might illustrate for us what we have learned about those attributes. God's works are his attributes in action.

Creation, says à Brakel, 'is the proper work of God'.[2] It is what God does. To know God is to know not merely that he is independent,

[1] Berkhof, *Systematic Theology*, p. 126. 'The first verse of the Bible,' says Matthew Henry, 'gives us a surer and better, and a more satisfying and useful knowledge of the universe' as well as of 'the foundation of all religion … than all the volumes of the philosophers' (Henry, *Commentary*, introduction to Gen. 1).

[2] à Brakel, *Christian's Reasonable Service*, I:268.

immense, and immutable, but also that he has made us and all things. The awareness of the Creator–creature *relation*, not to mention its *distinction*, is fundamental to knowing God aright.

The God of Abraham, Isaac, and Jacob, the God and Father of our Lord Jesus Christ, the God of the Bible, is the Creator of all things. Before the moment of creation, God alone existed. Before the 'beginning' (Gen. 1:1), the universe and time did not exist. As we saw in our study of the Trinity,[3] the work of creation is a work of the Father, the Son, and the Holy Spirit (Gen. 1:1-2; John 1:2-3; Col. 1:16; Heb. 1:2). 'All things are at once out of the Father, through the Son, and in the Holy Spirit', says Berkhof.[4] Creation was a Trinitarian project.

We accept the divine creation of the universe as a given, as a fact for our consideration. 'By faith we understand that the universe was created by the word of God' (Heb. 11:3). There may be other occasions when we might debate creation versus evolution, or even young earth versus old earth, but this is not that occasion.[5] Given that we believe the Bible's testimony, what does God's work of creation teach us about God?

Nature reveals

The assumption of the Bible is that creation teaches us a great deal about the Creator. 'The heavens declare the glory of God,' says the psalmist (Psa. 19:1). God has set his glory 'above the heavens' (Psa. 8:1). God's 'invisible attributes, namely, his eternal power and divine nature, have been clearly perceived, ever since the creation of the world, in the things that have been made' (Rom. 1:20). Calvin called the creation a 'dazzling theatre' of God's glory.[6] 'Wherever you cast your eyes,' says Calvin, 'there is no spot in the universe wherein you cannot discern at least some sparks of his glory.'[7] The universe, he says, is 'a sort of mirror in which we can contemplate God, who is otherwise

---

[3] See Chapter 2 above, 'Our Triune God'.

[4] Berkhof, *Systematic Theology*, p. 129.

[5] We recommend Douglas F. Kelly, *Creation and Change: Genesis 1:1–2:4 in the Light of Changing Scientific Paradigms* (1997; Fearn, Ross-shire: Mentor, 2008).

[6] Calvin, *Institutes*, I.v.8, p. 61. Susan E. Schreiner has devoted an entire monograph to this single theme: *The Theater of His Glory: Nature and the Natural Order in the Thought of John Calvin* (Grand Rapids, MI: Baker Academic, 1991).

[7] Calvin, *Institutes*, I.v.1, p. 52.

invisible'.[8] Similarly, Lewis Bayly claims, 'Whatsoever excellency thou hast seen in any creature, it is nothing but a sparkle of that which is in infinite perfection in God.'[9]

What, then, is the purpose of creation? It is 'the glory of God and the manifestation of his perfections', says Charles Hodge.[10] Its purpose is to serve God's pleasure. This is always true of created things. Inventors, human creators, build or make what they do in order to serve specific purposes they have in mind. Creations serve their creators. Inventions serve their inventors. Buildings serve their builders. So it is with God. 'All things were created through him and *for* him' (Col. 1:16).

Why does God create? God creates to display his glory. 'It is God's good pleasure to bring the excellencies of his triune being into manifestation in his creatures, and so prepare glory and honour for himself in those creatures', Bavinck notes. The whole world, says Bavinck, is but 'a mirror in which he sees his excellencies at play'.[11]

God's rational creatures are meant to contemplate the glory of God in his creation. The visible is to direct us to the Invisible One. 'How clearly creation reveals the perfections of God!' says à Brakel.[12] All that is lovely, excellent, and desirable in creation is but a reflection of the same in God himself. Beauty in the world speaks to us of the greater beauty of its Maker. Power in creation points to the greater power of the Creator. 'Accustom yourself to behold creation in such a fashion that you may behold God in it', counsels à Brakel.[13] He directs us 'in a godly frame of mind' to 'go outdoors and lift up [our] eyes on high to observe the immeasurable dimensions of the universe … as well as its enormous space, and consider [ourselves] as grain[s] of sand surrounded by all this'.[14] Take in creation's beauty in the sky, among the trees, or along the seashore. Observe the diversity of colours, smells, tastes, sounds, and shapes. 'No education is required to discern what one may observe in, and learn from creation', à Brakel insists.[15]

[8] Calvin, *Institutes*, I.v.1, p. 52.
[9] Bayly, *Practice of Piety*, p. 27.
[10] Charles Hodge, *Systematic Theology* (1871; Grand Rapids, MI: Eerdmans, 1981), I:567.
[11] Bavinck, *Our Reasonable Faith*, p. 169.
[12] à Brakel, *Christian's Reasonable Service*, I:277.
[13] *Ibid.*, I:279.
[14] *Ibid.*, p. 281.
[15] *Ibid.*, p. 283.

Indeed, 'What dull scholars are we,' exclaims Stephen Charnock, if we fail to learn about God from the creation, 'when every creature is our teacher, every part of the creature a lively instruction.'[16] In all that is around us, à Brakel explains, 'we may observe the unsearchable *wisdom*, the infinite *power*, and the wondrous *goodness* of God, a view which will cause us to lose ourselves in amazement'.[17] If we look aright, we will see beyond created things to the glory of the Creator himself.[18] This is particularly the case with respect to the power, wisdom, and goodness of God.[19]

Power

Creation testifies to the *power* of God. That one being could create this vast universe is extraordinary. The Great Wall of China, the Pyramids of Egypt, the Interstate Highway system of the United States, and the Internet are remarkable testimonies to the creative power of humanity. Yet in comparison to this planet, indeed, in comparison with the whole universe, they are mere grains of sand, even molecules or atoms of a grain of sand.

After my two years of study in England, I sailed home on the ocean liner *Queen Elizabeth II*. One could gaze out from the stern of the ship and sense the tremendous energy of its engines as they seemed to churn up the ocean depths. Yet the ship was but a speck in an endless sea. The vast ocean, its length, breadth, and depth, provided a glimpse of the infinite power and immensity of God. As a boy in Southern California I would often sit on the beach in the late afternoon sun and stare at the expansive ocean as waves crashed upon the shore. It was so big, so powerful, so vast! I would think: How great must God be if he created all that!

Remarkably, God created all that there is *ex nihilo*, from nothing.[20] By 'nothing' we mean that God did not create with pre-existing

---

[16] Charnock, *Existence and Attributes*, II:27.

[17] à Brakel, *Christian's Reasonable Service*, I:283 (emphasis added).

[18] *Ibid.*, I:284.

[19] See *Westminster Confession of Faith,* IV.1 which states that God created in order to manifest "the glory of his eternal power, wisdom, and goodness."

[20] Theologians speak of 'original' and 'subsequent' creation. Strictly speaking, only Gen. 1:1 is *ex nihilo*; the subsequent creative acts are a fashioning of existing material.

materials. Neither did he place creation into a pre-existing place. *Ex nihilo* distinguishes God's creative activity from that of humanity. We do not actually create anything; we merely reorganize or reshape what is already there. God creates something out of nothing: 'By faith we understand that the universe was created by the word of God, so that what is seen *was not made out of things that are visible*' (Heb. 11:3). There was 'no pre-existent stuff', says Poole.[21] The apostle Paul describes God as one who 'calls into existence the things that do not exist' (Rom. 4:17). This is nearly impossible for us to understand. Can we even conceive of absolutely *nothing*? We may try to illustrate 'nothing' by several mind games. One is to draw a circle on the chalkboard and put a dot in the middle of it, erase the dot, then erase the circle. Another is to imagine a room full of furniture. Remove all the furniture, then remove the room. Yet neither of these attempts is adequate. Scripture emphasizes *ex nihilo* creation in order to deny, says Bavinck, 'that the world was made out of some stuff or matter or energy *which co-existed eternally alongside of God*'.[22] 'The thing that Holy Scripture is primarily on guard against,' Bavinck continues, 'is the confusion of God with his creation.'[23] God started with nothing, absolutely nothing. 'He merely spoke and things appeared, along with space and time for them to occupy', explains John Frame.[24] 'Some brag of their birth and ancestry; but how little cause they have to boast who came from nothing', says Watson.[25]

Consider as well the *ease* with which God created. He used no instruments or tools. He created with his bare hands (cf. Jer. 32:17). He had no helpers: 'I am the LORD, who made all things, who *alone* stretched out the heavens, who spread out the earth *by myself*' (Isa. 44:24). The vast oceans? He 'measured the waters in the hollow of his hand'. The vast starry host? He 'marked off the heavens with a span' ('so large handed is he', says Henry).[26] He numbered the stars 'calling them all by name'. The vast mountains? He 'weighed the mountains

[21] Poole, *Commentary*, III:860.
[22] Bavinck, *Our Reasonable Faith*, p. 166 (emphasis added).
[23] *Ibid.*
[24] John M. Frame, *The Doctrine of God* (Phillipsburg, NJ: P&R, 2002), p. 298.
[25] Watson, *Body of Divinity*, p. 114.
[26] Henry, *Commentary*, on Isa. 40:12.

in scales and the hills in a balance' (Isa. 40:12, 22, 26). These are all 'certain and evident proof of God's infinite power', says Poole.[27]

Let us attempt to grasp the scope of God's creative work. A light year is the distance that light, travelling at 186,000 miles per second, can travel in a year. The universe is believed by scientists to be 93 billion light years in diameter. This means that the distance from one end to the other is 8.80×10^{26} metres. If our solar system were represented on a twelve-inch ruler, our sun (which is more than 100 times the diameter of earth, scientists tell us) would be smaller than the period at the end of this sentence. On this same scale, our galaxy, the Milky Way, would be larger than the Pacific Ocean. Our galaxy alone is home to billions of stars. Yet there are countless galaxies. These unfathomable numbers give some indication of the immensity of God, who fills every corner of the universe with the whole of his essence. It also gives us some notion of the immensity of the power of the one who 'calls' it into existence. The universe is so vast that scientists play with the idea that the universe is infinite. Yet creating it and filling it is child's play for 'the everlasting God, the Creator of the ends of the earth' (Isa. 40:12, 28).

All God did to create our vast universe was speak and it was so. 'The disciples wondered that Christ could with a word calm the sea,' says Watson, 'but it was more with a word to make the sea.'[28] God created with a simple act of the will.

When I was in elementary school the State of California built the San Diego Freeway. Every day for weeks on end there was a seemingly endless line of diesel trucks bringing load after load of dirt for the elevated section near our house. Monumental effort was required. Enormous energy was expended to move a hill from one side of the state to another. Yet God creates 'with the greatest of ease'. Repeatedly in Genesis 1 God says, 'Let there be …' and we are told, 'And it was so' (verses 9, 15, 24). Creation required only a word. 'For he *spoke*, and it came to be; he commanded, and it stood firm', admires the psalmist (Psa. 33:9; cf. 148:5). God simply '*calls* into existence the things that do not exist' (Rom. 4:17). He 'calls'; they spring into existence. Scripture

---

[27] Poole, *Commentary*, II:414.
[28] Watson, *Body of Divinity*, p. 114.

teaches that this entire planet came out of nowhere, and took shape as it did, not by enormous exertions, but because God spoke. It was that simple, that easy. We repeat Thornwell's comment: for God 'it is as easy to create a world as to move a feather, to uphold all things as to speak a word'.[29]

Think of the seemingly effortless way in which the great athletes perform. Nadia Comăneci, the Romanian Olympian of a generation ago, hardly seemed to strain herself in her flawless gymnastic performances. Henry Aaron, baseball's greatest (chemically unenhanced) home-run hitter of all time, played the game with exceptional grace and ease. The same could be said of Michael Jordan's domination of professional basketball. That is the picture. God created effortlessly. He hangs the stars in the sky and moves whole planets into place without the slightest strain. Enormous energy is released by the splitting of the atom. But the creation displays the infinite, awesome power of God, who packs each atom with the power this division unleashes.

Wisdom

Creation also testifies to the *wisdom and knowledge* of God. The universe is unimaginably complex. Yet all the pieces fit together. Its complexity is complemented by its unity, or harmony. We find 'great exactness and accuracy', says Henry, and also 'great order; a mutual dependence of being, an exact harmony of motions, and an admirable chain and connection of causes'.[30]

We may use our microscopes and move from cells to molecules to atoms to electrons. Yet there is harmony; the parts of the machine work. The work of Henry F. ('Fritz') Schaefer, Director of the Graham Perdue Center for Computational Chemistry at the University of Georgia, demonstrates that atoms can be understood, mathematical formulas can predict their behaviour, and pharmaceutical companies can, on the basis of those predictions, design medicines that limit and even cure diseases.[31] Even in the post-Einstein world of relativity, most of the world is Newtonian: ordered, rational, predictable.

[29] Thornwell, *Collected Writings*, I:204.
[30] Henry, *Commentary*, on Gen. 1:1.
[31] See Henry F. Schaefer III, *Science and Christianity: Conflict or Coherence?* (Watkinsville, GA: Apollos Trust, 2003).

We may set aside our microscopes and gaze into our telescopes, and move from the moon to the planets to the sun to other solar systems, to other galaxies, and so on. Yet each element has its part to play. There is regularity, order, and harmony—the 'balance of nature', as it is called.

The universe shows ample evidence of extraordinary 'fine-tuning', as scientists, such as physicist Paul Davies (b. 1946), Professor and Director of BEYOND: Center for Fundamental Concepts in Science at Arizona State University, have called it. Astrophysicist Hugh Ross, in his book *The Creator and the Cosmos*, provides a list of twenty-five characteristics of the universe without which it could not support life.[32] For example, the precise relative strengths of gravitational and electromagnetic forces, fine-tuned to one part of 10^{40}, made possible the formation of stars like the sun; apart from them, these stars would not exist. The precision of the balance between the expansive energy of the universe and the counterbalancing gravitational force has been likened by Davies to taking aim at a postage stamp on the other end of the universe, 20 billion light years away, and hitting it.[33] This is remarkable precision. Similarly, the precise ratio of the size of the electron to the proton in the atom (1,836 times larger) makes the formation of molecules possible; without this, the elements of the universe could not have formed. Even the late physicist Stephen Hawking had to admit that 'the values of these numbers seem to have been very finely adjusted'.[34] Despite the claims of militant atheists

[32] Hugh Ross, *The Creator and the Cosmos: How the Greatest Scientific Discoveries of the Century Reveal God* (Colorado Springs, CO: NavPress, 1994).

[33] This analogy has been cited by John Polkinghorne, *One World: The Interaction of Science and Theology* (Philadelphia: Templeton Foundation Press, 2007), p. 69. Polkinghorne (b. 1930) was Professor of Mathematical Physics at the University of Cambridge, 1988–96, and winner of the Templeton Prize in 2002.

[34] Stephen Hawking, *A Brief History of Time* (New York: Bantam Books, 1998), p. 126. Here is more from Hawking: 'It would be very difficult to explain why the universe should have begun in just this way, except as the act of a God who intended to create beings like us. ... In fact, if one considers the possible constants and laws that could have emerged, the odds against a universe that has produced life like ours are immense. ... Why did the universe start out with so nearly the critical rate of expansion that separates models that recollapse from those that go on expanding forever, that even now, 10 thousand million years later, it is still expanding at nearly the critical rate? If the rate of expansion one second after the Big Bang had been smaller by even one part in 100 thousand million, million, the universe would have collapsed before it ever reached its present size.'

such as Richard Dawkins and Christopher Hitchens, 'settled science' does not disprove God; rather the opposite.[35] Physics in particular has forced atheism to posit 'multiverse' theories, according to which all possible universes exist simultaneously. We just happen, they say, to live in the one which is capable of supporting life. This is an 'atheism of the gaps' that parallels the much-scorned 'God of the gaps' (God as the explanation for whatever science does not yet understand). Atheists cannot explain either the 'fine-tuning' of the universe or its 'irreducible complexity', so they have sought refuge in a theory for which there is not a shred of evidence. 'The days of triumphalist scientism are over', claims one commentator.[36] As Charles Krauthammer has written of dogmatic atheism, 'There is nothing more anti-scientific than the idea that science is settled, static, impervious to challenge.'[37]

The 104th Psalm, which C. H. Spurgeon called 'a poet's version of Genesis',[38] praises God because he gives boundaries to mountains, valleys, and seas. He gives rivers to drink out of, grass on the ground for cattle, vegetation for man, trees for birds' nests, high mountains for wild goats, cliffs for rock badgers, even the sea for ships. The moon has its place, and the sun has its place. The lions come out at night and seek their food from God, and he feeds them; and then day comes, the lions retire to their dens, and man comes out and goes to work. The psalmist marvels at this wonderful harmony and says, 'O LORD, how manifold are your works! In wisdom have you made them all' (Psa. 104:24). Creation is an expression of God's wisdom (Prov. 3:19; 8:1, 22-36; Jer. 10:12; 51:15; Job 38–42). 'He has made everything beautiful in its time', wrote the preacher in Ecclesiastes 3:11. Indeed he has. Creation reveals the great mind of God.

We marvel at the complexity of the personal computer and the smartphone. We are awed by stealth combat planes and drones. Yet how much more complex and marvellous is God's creation! 'Plato,'

---

[35] See the mathematician Amir D. Aczel, *Why Science Does Not Disprove God* (New York: William Morrow, 2014).

[36] James Franklin, 'What's in the Details', in review article of Amir D. Aczel, *Why Science Does Not Disprove God*, *Wall Street Journal*, 30 April 2014, A13.

[37] Charles Krauthammer, 'The Myth of "Settled Science",' *Savannah Morning News*, 22 February 2014, 9A.

[38] C. H. Spurgeon, *Treasury of David* (1892; Grand Rapids, MI: Zondervan, 1950), V:1.

says Watson, 'was convinced of a Deity when he saw that all the world could not make a fly.'[39] The English poet William Blake (1757–1827) made the same deduction in his poem 'The Tyger':

> Tyger, tyger, burning bright,
> In the forests of the night;
> What immortal hand or eye,
> Could frame thy fearful symmetry?

When my first nephew was born, I was startled to hold that tiny fellow in my arms and to move his little fingers and let him grip my finger. Small as they were, all the parts worked: the bones, skin, veins, arteries, muscles, and nerves. How much more complex (not to mention beautiful) is an infant than a computer! Calvin, commenting on Psalm 8:2 ('Out of the mouth of babies and infants, you have established strength'), says, 'Infants, while they nurse at their mothers' breasts, have tongues so eloquent to preach his glory that there is no need at all of other orators.'[40] David confesses, 'I am fearfully and wonderfully made' (Psa. 139:14). Infants are a most impressive display of God's wisdom. Jeremiah summarizes for us: 'It is he who made the earth by his power, who established the world by his wisdom, and by his understanding stretched out the heavens' (Jer. 10:12). That God did so 'argues an unparalleled skill and understanding', says Poole.[41] Yet for all this, he consulted with no one. Isaiah asks:

> Who has measured the Spirit of the LORD,
> or what man shows him his counsel?
> Whom did he consult,
> and who made him understand?
> Who taught him the path of justice,
> and taught him knowledge,
> and showed him the way
>   of understanding?
>
> (Isa. 40:13-14)

---

[39] Watson, *Body of Divinity*, p. 116.
[40] Calvin, *Institutes*, I.v.3, p. 55.
[41] Poole, *Commentary*, II:531.

'*Who?*' 'None but his own essential wisdom', answers Trapp.[42] God required no instructors, no consultants, no advisers.

Goodness

Besides his power and wisdom, creation testifies to the *goodness* of God. The picture of the original creation in Genesis 1 and 2 is of divine beneficence. Everything God creates is good, and it is all created for the benefit of humanity. God fills the whole world with trees, shrubs, animals, fish, and all it contains. Then he says, 'Let us make man in our image, after our likeness. And let them have dominion over the fish of the sea and over the birds of the heavens and over the livestock and over all the earth and over every creeping thing that creeps on the earth' (Gen. 1:26).

All was designed for humanity's utilization. We were to rule over creation and subdue it for our use. It was made with our enjoyment in mind. In Genesis 2 God puts man in a garden. Notice, he does not put him in a desert. He did not put man in a wasteland with a hoe and a bag of fertilizer, and demand that he make something of it. He put him in a beautiful garden, whose trees were 'pleasant to the sight and good for food' (Gen. 2:9). The food was not just good food; it was lovely, too. 'God, as a tender father, considered not only Adam's profit, but his pleasure', says Henry.[43]

God could have created an ugly world, but he did not. All the world might have been created in shades of grey. There was even a river in the garden of Eden (Gen. 2:10). Adam had waterfront property, one might say. Finally, when something is not good, we see God faithfully moving to correct it (Gen. 2:18-22). Adam needs a wife, and God brings him one. 'An excellent wife who can find? She is far more precious than jewels' (Prov. 31:10).

God is concerned with beauty. He is concerned with our happiness. No doubt the garden was full of good melons and citrus fruits. Consider how wonderful a thing is a fresh strawberry, a fresh peach, or a watermelon. God made the world in such a way that the ground

---

[42] Trapp, *Commentary*, III:379.
[43] Henry, *Commentary*, on Gen. 2:8-15. We may suppose the garden 'to have been the most accomplished place for pleasure and delight that ever the sun saw'.

produces these gifts. The creation is beautiful and enjoyable to see, taste, touch, and smell. All that we must do to continue our existence in this world which the Creator has made pleasurable for us is breathe, eat, sleep, procreate, and work.

Since the fall, and sin, and all that accompanied it, the goodness of God can still be seen in creation when we have pleasant weather, luscious fruits, a productive land, beautiful landscapes, and picturesque coastlines. Still today God blesses us with 'fruitful seasons' and 'satisfies' our 'hearts with food and gladness' (Acts 14:17). Jesus himself invites us to learn of the goodness of God by observing the feeding of the ravens, who 'neither sow nor reap … and yet God feeds them' (Luke 12:24; Matt. 6:26). We should learn of the kindness of God by watching the birds. 'The *heirs* of heaven are much better than the *fowls* of heaven,' says Matthew Henry. 'Now he that feeds his birds surely will not starve his babies.'[44] He invites us to learn of his concern for beauty by observing the lilies of the field, which he clothes more beautifully than even 'Solomon in all his glory' (Luke 12:27; Matt. 6:29). 'Hang upon these fair flowers with the busy bee,' says Trapp, 'till you have sucked some sweet meditation out of them.'[45] The major point Jesus is making is that God supplies our needs. Yet God is no utilitarian provider: he lavishes his creation with beauty, even with regard to flowers which are here today and gone tomorrow.[46] Even in a fallen world we praise God for his goodness in 'richly provid[ing] us with everything to enjoy' (1 Tim. 6:17).

Power—wisdom—goodness: drawing on these three themes Isaac Watts (1674–1748) taught children to sing of the greatness of the Creator in his *Divine Songs* (1715), a children's hymnbook:

> I sing th' almighty *pow'r* of God,
>   That made the mountains rise,
> That spread the flowing seas abroad,
>   And built the lofty skies.

[44] Henry, *Commentary*, on Matt. 6:29.

[45] Trapp, *Commentary*, V:110.

[46] Jesus, says the modern commentator J. B. Green, can 'locate evidences of God's generosity and care in the world all around him' (J. B. Green, *The Gospel of Luke*, New International Commentary on the New Testament [Grand Rapids, MI: Eerdmans, 1997], p. 493).

I sing the *wisdom* that ordained
    The sun to rule the day;
The moon shines full at his command,
    And all the stars obey.

I sing the *goodness* of the Lord,
    Who filled the earth with food,
Who formed the creatures through the Word,
    And then pronounced them good.

Lord, how thy wonders are displayed,
    Where'er I turn my eye,
If I survey the ground I tread,
    Or gaze upon the sky.[47]

Response

'In the absence of any other proof,' said Sir Isaac Newton, 'the thumb alone would convince me of God's existence.'[48] Psalm 19 teaches us that God speaks to us through two books: what Matthew Henry called 'the book of the creatures' (verses 1-6), that is, creation, and 'the book of the Scriptures', that is, the Bible (verses 7-14).[49] The two are in

---

[47] Isaac Watts, 'I Sing Th' Almighty Power Of God' (emphasis added).

[48] Cited in Dr Paul Brand and Philip Yancey, *Fearfully and Wonderfully Made* (Grand Rapids, MI: Zondervan, 1980), p. 162. They cite a number of amazing facts about the human body. For example, the eye consists of 107,000,000 cells. It is easily capable of distinguishing a thousand shades of colour and a spectrum of light so broad that the brightest light it perceives is a billion times brighter than the dimmest. The ear can detect sound frequencies that flutter the eardrums as faintly as one-billionth of a centimetre. This vibration is transmitted by the three bones known as the hammer, anvil, and stirrup. When the middle C note is struck on a piano, the piston of bones vibrates at 256 times per second. One-fifth of our body weight comes from our bones. They are made of material that is extraordinarily light, yet strong enough to support the weight of the body and handle exceptional stress without breaking. The foot alone has twenty-six bones, about the same as the hand. Our sense of touch is so sensitive that it can distinguish between a smooth plane of glass and one etched with lines 1/2,500 of an inch deep. The top of the fingernail can distinguish between paper, fabric, wood, plastic, or steel. 'We can discern a thousandth of an ounce of pressure on the tip of a half-inch hair,' etc.

[49] Henry, *Commentary*, on Psa. 19.

harmony. Both teach us of the power, wisdom, and goodness of God our Creator. How, then, ought we to respond?

Worship and serve

First, the magnificence of creation ought to lead us to *worship and serve the Creator*. 'Worthy are you, our Lord and God, to receive glory and honour and power,' repeat the twenty-four elders in heaven. Why is he worthy? 'For you *created* all things, and by your will they existed and were created' (Rev. 4:11; cf. 14:7). The Creator is worthy of glory and honour because of his creation. 'God's power put forth in creation,' says Trapp, 'can never be sufficiently admired.'[50] 'Oh come, let us worship and bow down,' says the psalmist; 'let us kneel before the LORD, our *Maker*!' (Psa. 95:6). The 'Maker' is to be worshipped because he is *our* Maker. God's name is 'exalted above all blessing and praise', say the Levites in Nehemiah, for 'you made heaven, the heaven of heavens, with all their host, the earth and all that is on it, the seas and all that is in them; and you preserve all of them; and the host of heaven worships you' (Neh. 9:6; see also Psa. 8:3-9; 19:1-4; 33:6-9; 50:6; 89:5; 95:3-7; 98:7-9; 146:5-6; 148:1-14; Isa. 55:12). The essence of idolatry is to refuse to honour and thank God, to worship the *creature* rather than the *Creator* (Rom. 1:21-25). 'Worship is the most high and honourable of all our works', says Swinnock.[51]

More broadly, we should recognize that honour, glory, service, and obedience are *owed* to God. Why? Because he made us. If someone *saved* me from drowning, would I not be indebted to that person? What about the one who *made* me? We owe our existence to him. Consequently, we have an obligation to thank and honour him. This we are to do through the agent of creation, the eternal Word (John 1:3), God the Son (Col. 1:15-16; Heb. 1:2), the Lord Jesus Christ, through whom we are recreated or become new creations. Through Jesus Christ we are to trust, honour, serve and obey God (Eph. 2:10; 2 Cor. 5:17).

Like all creators, God has a particular design for us which we are to fulfil. God made us to know him, to love him, to serve him, to obey him, and to worship him. He made us for himself. We will never

---

[50] Trapp, *Commentary*, V:748.
[51] Swinnock, *Incomparableness of God*, *Works*, IV:503.

know peace, fulfilment, satisfaction, or joy until we begin to fulfil the design for which we were made; until we honour the divinely ordered purpose for our existence. Contemplation of God's power, wisdom, and goodness in creation is meant to lead us to Christ, through whom alone we may be reconciled to our Maker and begin to worship him in 'spirit and truth' (John 4:24).

Trust

Second, we ought to *submit, accept, and trust what God has created us to be.* God is *my* Creator, and he is *your* Creator. There is much about ourselves that we should *not* like: we have too much pride; we are too self-centred, stingy, hateful, and jealous. We cheat, lie, steal, and commit countless other evils. If we are unhappy about our character flaws, that is good. We should be upset about our failure to conform to the image of Christ. However, the problem for many of us is that we are unhappy with our created limitations, whether in the realm of beauty, intelligence, or athletic or artistic ability. We may even be angry with God because we are too short/too tall, or too skinny/too heavy. We may feel cheated by God because we lack coordination, intelligence, or looks, or because we are relatively unathletic, unattractive, or unacademic. What should we do?

Simply this: affirm before God that he has the right to make of us what he wishes. 'God is our Sovereign Lord Proprietor,' says Thomas Boston, 'and may do in us, on us, and by us, what he will.'[52] Does not the artist have the right to paint the picture as he wishes? Does not the carpenter have the right to build the house as he wishes? Why, then, would we deny this right to God when we grant it to our fellow dust? Yet God has done more than the artist or the builder. They work with existing materials, but God created us from nothing. 'Why should we enter a charge against him, because he hath not tempered us so strong in our bodies, drawn us with as fair colours, embellished our spirits with as rich gifts as others?' Charnock asks. 'Is he not the Sovereign of his own goods, to impart what, and in what measure, he pleaseth?'[53] Does

---

[52] Thomas Boston, *An Illustration of the Doctrines of Christian Religion*, in *The Complete Works of the Late Rev. Thomas Boston* (1853; Wheaton, IL: Richard Owen Roberts Publishers, 1980), I:176.

[53] Charnock, *Existence and Attributes*, II:497.

he not have the right to make of us what he wills? God himself warns us through Isaiah, 'Woe to him who strives with him who formed him! ... Does the clay say to him who forms it, "What are you making?"' (Isa. 45:9). 'This,' says Trapp, 'were an intolerable impetulancy.'[54]

Likewise, the apostle Paul asks, 'Who are you, O man, to answer back to God? Will what is moulded say to its moulder, "Why have you made me like this?" Has the potter no right over the clay?' (Rom. 9:20-21). Do not second-guess God. He knows in every case what he is doing. Trust his wisdom and goodness. God answered Job's presumptuous challenge of his purposes by asking, 'Where were you when I laid the foundation of the earth ... when the morning stars sang together and all the sons of God shouted for joy?' (Job 38:4, 7). Where? 'Then thou wast nowhere', answers Poole.[55] 'It is not so easy a matter as some think it,' says Henry, 'to contest with the Almighty.'[56] Instead, we should trust that 'God is great and God is good', as we learned in the childhood prayer. Everything has a purpose. This world is *not* the last word. When we are resurrected we will get new and perfect bodies (1 Cor. 15:35-58)! Until that time, God promises with Christ to freely give us all things (Rom. 8:32). All things work together for good for those who love God (8:28). When we are deprived of good it is always for a good reason. There are compelling reasons for what we lack—for why we are not more brainy, talented, athletic, or beautiful—though they are hidden and largely unknowable this side of eternity. Oliver Cromwell (1599–1658) famously asked that his portrait be painted 'warts and all'. He was reconciled to his flaws. Only God knows what evils we are being spared because of our warts. Consider the messed-up lives of our world's most beautiful people. Are they happy? Is Hollywood a happy place? Are the elite intellectuals and opinion-makers happy? Are the professional athletes happy? Is wealth making anyone happy? Is talent? Is beauty? God withholds no good thing from us (Psa. 84:11). Believe it! 'Our help is in the name of the LORD, who *made* heaven and earth' (Psa. 124:8).

---

[54] Trapp, *Commentary*, II:391.

[55] Poole, *Commentary*, I:1018; 'Thou wast ... not so much as a looker on', says Trapp (*Commentary*, II:400).

[56] Henry, *Commentary*, introduction to Job 38.

Enjoy

Our third response to our Creator, in addition to worship and trust, ought to be enjoyment. We ought to *enjoy the creation*. Matthew Henry, in *The Pleasantness of a Religious Life*, urges us 'to enjoy God in all our creature-comforts'. He directs us to 'look above second causes to the first, through the creature to the Creator'. Learn, he says, 'to say concerning everything that is agreeable and serviceable to us ... this I have from the hand of my heavenly Father'. He asks, 'Is it not pleasant to taste covenant-love in common mercies?'[57] We want to be cautious about saying this in a civilization addicted to entertainment. The pendulum swings so quickly from abuse to neglect that one cannot be sure which to address. On the one hand, there are Christians who know all about enjoying the creation—and little else. Off they go each weekend, neglecting their commitment to the church, spending exorbitant sums of money on extravagant pleasures, mindless of the poor, the lost, and the saints. To those who are rich (or aspire to be), the apostle Paul says, 'They are to do good, to be rich in good works, to be generous and ready to share' (1 Tim. 6:18). Calvin often cites the apostle Paul's admonition to the Corinthians, that because the time is short, those who buy are to be 'as though they had no goods, and those who deal with the world as though they had no dealings with it. For the present form of this world is passing away' (1 Cor. 7:30-31).[58]

On the other hand, we may also detect an undercurrent of guilt-inducing Neo-Platonism. The church never quite rids itself of monkish types who think the material world is evil and therefore to be avoided. They sharply divide life into the religious and the secular. In late antiquity there were thousands of monks who went into the desert, wrapped themselves in sheets, and lived their whole lives in caves, so as not to indulge the flesh. They avoided all sensual stimuli—sight, smell, taste, and touch—and devoted themselves to 'spiritual activity'. One monk, Simeon Stylites (*c.* 388–459), lived his last forty years on top of a stone column. Monks who followed his example were called 'Pillar Saints'. They eschewed all pleasure, suppressed the body's appetites, and avoided the material creation in order to devote themselves to

[57] Henry, *Pleasantness of a Religious Life*, pp. 54, 55.
[58] See Calvin, *Institutes*, III.x.1-3, pp. 720ff.

'spiritual things' such as prayer and fasting. While we admire monasticism's zeal, devotion to Christ, evangelistic fervour, and love of learning, we cannot endorse its asceticism.

These excesses may seem remote to us today. Yet some Christians have an uneasy conscience about recreation, play, vacations, and the like. Some of our more devoted brethren think 'time would be better spent' in 'religious activity' such as prayer, reading the Bible, reading Christian books, small-group study, and so on. They feel the need to justify pleasure and all so-called 'secular' activity in terms of it enabling us to rest and therefore devote more time to God in 'religious activity'. A measure of guilt accompanies every pursuit of leisure.

Over against this, we affirm that enjoyment of the creation is a proper activity for the Christian and need not be justified in terms of anything else. As we have said, this may be implied by the beauty of creation alone. Consequently, Calvin rightly argues, 'the use of God's gifts is not wrongly directed when it is referred to that end to which the Author himself created and destined them for us, since he created them for our good, not for our ruin'. He continues,

> Now if we ponder to what end God created food, we shall find that he meant not only to provide for necessity but also for delight and good cheer. Thus the purpose of clothing, apart from necessity, was comeliness and decency. In grasses, trees, and fruits, apart from their various uses, there is beauty of appearance and pleasantness of odour [cf. Gen. 2:9]. For if this were not true, the prophet would not have reckoned them among the benefits of God, 'that wine gladdens the heart of man, that oil makes his face shine' [Psa. 104:15]. ... Has the Lord clothed the flowers with the great beauty that greets our eyes, the sweetness of smell that is wafted upon our nostrils, and yet will it be unlawful for our eyes to be affected by that beauty, or our sense of smell by the sweetness of that odour? What? Did he not so distinguish colours as to make some more lovely than others? What? Did he not endow gold and silver, ivory and marble, with a loveliness that renders them more precious than other metals or stones? Did he not, in short, render many things attractive to us, apart from their necessary use?[59]

[59] Calvin, *Institutes*, III.x.2, pp. 720-21.

Again, God could have created an ugly world, but he did not. God made a beautiful and pleasurable world, and he is to be enjoyed through it all. Think of the parade of the animals in Genesis 2. Undoubtedly Adam roared with delight the first time he saw a giraffe; then again when he saw the hippopotamus. How could he not have been amused? Do the duck and the penguin not testify to the goodness of God, even the good humour, the affability, and the intention that the natural world should be enjoyed? Swimming, volleyball, horseback riding, eating, drinking, and even the most mundane of all activities can all glorify God (1 Cor. 10:31). He is honoured when we enjoy his gifts. Think of how parents are pleased when their children enjoy their birthday presents. The same is true of God. 'For everything created by God is good, and nothing is to be rejected ...,' the apostle Paul told Timothy (1 Tim. 4:4). The English Puritan Richard Sibbes (1577–1635) said, 'Worldly things are good in themselves, and given to sweeten our passage to heaven.'[60] God has created a beautiful world, and he wants us, his people, to enjoy it.

Consider the stars in heaven. Whatever could be more beautiful? Yet their primary function appears to be aesthetic. They beautify the heavens on our behalf and to the glory of God (Psa. 19:1). They are there for our enjoyment, and we ought to enjoy them, and enjoy and honour God through them. Of course we are capable of turning God's gifts into idols. When we give his gifts obsessive attention, or pursue the enjoyment of them in forbidden contexts, they become false gods and their design is thwarted. Yet in the proper proportions and proper contexts they are not to be refused. The apostle Paul told Timothy that it is God 'who richly provides us with *everything* to enjoy' (1 Tim. 6:17). The Westminster Shorter Catechism teaches, 'The chief end of man is to glorify God and to *enjoy* him for ever'—through his *word*, but through his *world* as well.

Learn

Fourth, we ought to *learn from the design of creation the will of the Creator.* Learn the mind of God through the works of God. If God

---

[60] Richard Sibbes, *The Danger of Backsliding,* in *Works of Richard Sibbes* (1862–64; Edinburgh: Banner of Truth Trust, 1982), VII:412-13; cf. Calvin, *Institutes,* III. ix.3-4, pp. 714-17.

is the author of nature, then nature has much to teach us about how life is to be lived. The wisdom of Proverbs is that of observation of the nature of things: human nature and the created order. We can 'go to the ant', observe its behaviour, and learn (Prov. 6:6). 'Does not nature itself teach you …?' the apostle Paul asks (1 Cor. 11:14). Nature teaches. The design of creation expresses the will of the Creator. When should I plant my crops? When should I harvest them? We plant in the spring and harvest in the autumn because of the nature of things. Scripture considers us foolish if we fail to observe nature and learn its lesson (Prov. 10:5; 20:4). There is only one reality: it is God's. It is not arbitrary; it is intentional. Learn to conform to the design of nature as God has made it, accepting its limitations and ordering life according to its principles.

Our moral conduct, among other things, is to be informed by the nature of things. I am a man and not a woman. How do I know? Because I have a male body. My wife is a woman. How does she know? Because she has a female body. Nature teaches us our identity. The human body is made up of one trillion cells, every one of which is either male or female, having either an XY or XX pair of chromosomes.[61] We do not have an inner identity that differs from that of our bodies. Those who exchange the 'natural function' of the male and female body for the 'unnatural' (the apostle Paul's terms) are failing to learn from the book of nature, not to mention the book of Scripture. They behave 'contrary to nature', and sadly ensure their own ruin (Rom. 1:26-27 NASB).

We may say the same for the whole list of sins in Romans 1:29-32. That which is 'dishonouring' of the body; those which are 'dishonourable passions'; those which are 'shameless acts'; those which are 'debased' are those things which are 'contrary to nature' and subsequently demeaning to us as human beings (Rom. 1:24, 26, 27, 28). There is a human nature, and there is that which is degrading to us as those made in the image of God. The apostle Paul highlights the

---

[61] Because we live in a fallen world there are some people, a tiny percentage, who are born with genuine gender confusion, having both male and female sex organs. Such are to be treated with compassion and understanding; see Nancy R. Pearcey (*Love Thy Body: Answering Hard Questions about Life and Sexuality*. Grand Rapids, MI: Baker Books, 2018).

sexual, particularly the homosexual, in Romans 1:24-28 because it is the most direct and blatant rejection of the natural for the unnatural. Likewise, sodomy, polygamy, prostitution, and other sexual deviancies are demeaning to us as human beings. So are adultery and fornication. The other sins of Romans 1:28-31 are included because finally *all sin is degrading because all sin is rebellion against the Creator's design for human beings*. Sin is a rejection of the Creator's plan for us, an attempt to create an alternative reality opposed to God's. That alternative reality is no reality at all, but an illusion, a phantom, a nightmare.

Our civilization defines freedom as the ability to do and be whatever we choose, without any constraints or limitations. Discovering the roots of this outlook is not simple. One highly influential source is mid-twentieth-century existentialism. Jean-Paul Sartre's philosophy of freedom, 'Existence precedes essence', means, according to Sarah Bakewell in *At the Existentialist Café*,

> As a human being, *I have no predefined nature at all*. I create that nature through what I choose to do. Of course I may be influenced by my biology, or by aspects of my culture and personal background, but none of this adds up to a complete blueprint for producing me. I am always one step ahead of myself, *making myself up as I go along*.[62]

This outlook now permeates the modern world. The US Supreme Court declared in its 1992 *Planned Parenthood vs Casey* decision preserving abortion 'rights' that 'At the heart of liberty is the right to define one's own concept of existence, of meaning, of the universe and of the mystery of life.' At the other end of the cultural spectrum, when a male celebrity told the world of his plans to live the remainder of his life as a woman, or to 'become a woman', as one tabloid put it, affirmations poured in. 'Kudos for feeling courageous enough to exist in *your truth*', said one fan. Another particularly head-on assault on reality asserted, 'People can bring up all of the chromosome mumbo jumbo that they want to, but *this is real*.' The biological reality, the *scientific* reality, of male and female chromosomes must fall before the

---

[62] Sarah Blackwell, *At the Existentialist Café* (New York: Other Press, 2016), quoted in Ruth Scurr, 'A Big, Busy Café of the Mind', *Wall Street Journal*, 29 February 2016.

right to create one's own reality. That biological reality becomes but 'mumbo jumbo'.

Reality, then, in current fashion, is not God-given. It is malleable. We can paint our own portrait of reality and inhabit it. Self-determination is thought to be fundamental to human dignity. The extent to which this is being taken can be seen in the cultural push to normalize the extreme step of transgender surgery. National news magazines and public radio have joined the crusade.[63] The federal government in the United States has ruled that Medicare can pay for sex 'reassignment surgery'.[64] Laws have been passed in California, New Jersey, and Massachusetts barring counsellors from attempting to restore normal gender consciousness to those minors with transgender feelings. The public schools in Massachusetts are being required to permit transgender youth to use the restrooms that correspond to their gender consciousness even if that is contrary to biological reality: transgender boys may use the girls' restroom and, we suppose, locker room. Reality is malleable. The transgendered become the transsexual.

The extent of cultural shift can be seen in the awarding of the ESPY's 2015 Arthur Ashe Courage Award to Bruce Jenner, also known as Caitlyn. It was not given to Lauren Hill, who played her final college basketball game with terminal brain cancer, nor to a deserving military war hero, but to a man who, with the aid of surgeons and cosmetics, is presenting himself as a woman. A *Wall Street Journal* sports writer who enthusiastically supported the ESPY's decision wrote of the rare privilege of hearing 'the wheels of the culture grind forward in real time'.[65] Rather than offering sympathy, counsel, or therapy, our culture now rewards this flight from reality and celebrates it as cultural progress. Sadly, Bruce Jenner's example will undoubtedly lead others, especially confused young people, to do the same. Many who otherwise might have passed through a youthful crisis of identity to live out normal adult lives will make catastrophic,

---

[63] Katy Steinmetz, 'The Transgender Tipping Point: America's Next Civil Rights Frontier', *Time Magazine* cover story, 9 June 2014.

[64] As of 30 May 2014.

[65] Jason Gay, 'Caitlyn Jenner and What Courage Means', *Wall Street Journal*, 20 July 2015, B9.

irreversible, life-altering decisions that will eventually leave them emotionally shattered. For the ESPY and cultural *avant-garde*, Jenner represents 'What Courage Means'. For Christians, Jenner represents secular society's massive delusions.[66]

Paul McHugh, former chief psychiatrist at the Johns Hopkins Hospital, deals with the transgender phenomenon with refreshing straightforwardness. It is, he says, 'a mental disorder that deserves understanding, treatment and prevention'. He calls the sense of being transgendered an 'intensely felt sense' which 'constitutes a mental disorder'. The idea of 'sex misalignment', he says, 'is simply mistaken— *it does not correspond with physical reality*'.[67]

He likens transgender consciousness to the disorder suffered by the anorexic and bulimic, whose self-perception 'departs from physical reality' in that they believe that they are overweight when, in fact, they are dangerously thin. 'The disordered assumption,' he says, 'is that the individual differs from what seems given in nature—namely one's maleness or femaleness.'[68] A more complete rejection of physical reality, of creation, and of the Creator can scarcely be imagined.

The emperor has no clothes. No surgical procedure coupled with a hormonal drug regimen can alter reality. The patient remains a man or a woman, though mutilated by the removal of certain organs. '"Sex change" is biologically impossible,' McHugh observes. 'Rather,' he continues, 'they become feminized men or masculinized women.'[69]

In *The Abolition of Man* C. S. Lewis points out that the aim of the wise men of previous ages was to 'conform the soul to reality'.[70] Reality was a given. The goal was to live in harmony with the universe as it was. Today the aim is 'to subdue reality to the wishes of men'.[71] The wise person will define freedom as the ability to become what I was made to be. The fish that refuses to be constrained by water, who finds

---

[66] Even more extreme is what is being called the 'body modification' movement: tongues split in half, horns placed under the scalp, tattoos on eyeballs, amputation of limbs, along with tattooing and scarring.

[67] Paul McHugh, 'Transgender Surgery Isn't the Solution', *Wall Street Journal*, 13 June 2014, A13 (my emphasis).

[68] *Ibid.*

[69] *Ibid.*

[70] C. S. Lewis, *The Abolition of Man* (1943; New York: Harper One, 2015), p. 78.

[71] *Ibid.*

it limiting and so flops out onto the land so that it can experience the open air, does not experience freedom but ruin. Its fins are not made for movement on land. Its gills are not made for breathing air. Freedom for the fish is found only in embracing its identity as a fish and thriving in the watery environment for which it was designed. Imagine an eagle for whom we perform species-altering surgery, clipping its wings and adding legs so that it might fulfil its wish to be a dog. Perhaps (we might speculate facetiously) it has always felt like a dog trapped in the body of a bird. Would surgery enable it to realize its 'inner dog' and experience true freedom from nature's restraints, or would such surgery be a mutilation, destroying the possibility of true freedom, true fulfilment, and true satisfaction for the eagle?

The man or woman who finds running or walking on the ground limiting and wants to fly does not find freedom by leaping off a building and flapping his or her arms. Freedom is found in honouring reality, the reality of gravity, and embracing the design of the human body. Design determines function. Design *limits* function. *Creation imposes limits*. Nature reveals the Creator's intentions for us.

Sin is lawlessness (1 John 3:4). It is a violation of the commands of God. The lawgiver is also our Maker. What he commands is suited to what he has designed. Consequently, sin is war against both God and nature. It is a rejection of both God's natural and his special revelation. It is an assault against reality. Freedom is found not in being and doing whatever I choose, but in developing and fully utilizing all that I was designed to be and do. Freedom is found in embracing the constraints, limitations, capacities, opportunities, and therefore the purpose of my design.

Learn, then, that we are all in rebellion, more or less, against God, his law, his design, and reality. Learn, then, that we are all in trouble, and that we all need a Deliverer, a Saviour—and turn to our Lord Jesus Christ, our Advocate and Redeemer. Learn from him that we were made for God; and let us find our true selves in conformity with his design for humanity generally, and for each of us individually.

Use

Finally, let us *use our God-given natural gifts*. Our abilities are not accidents of nature. They are what they are, not by 'the luck of the draw', but by divine purpose and intention. Identify, develop, and use them to the glory of our Creator. Assess what they are, and, whatever they be, whether skills, aptitudes, or brute strength, thank God for them and use them.

Let it be our ambition not to please ourselves but to please the God who made us (2 Cor. 5:9). We close with Thomas Boston's exhortation respecting the end for which we were made:

> Give away yourselves to God through Jesus Christ, making an hearty, a cheerful, and an entire dedication and surrender of your souls and bodies, and all that ye are and have, to him as your God and Father, resolving to obey him all the days of your life: that as he made you for his glory, *you may in some measure answer the end of your creation*, which is to shew forth his praise.[72]

---

[72] Boston, *Illustration of the Doctrines, Works*, I:176 (emphasis added).

SIX

'Our Governor and Preserver': The Providence of God

And he said to his disciples, 'Therefore I tell you, do not be anxious about your life, what you will eat, nor about your body, what you will put on. For life is more than food, and the body more than clothing. Consider the ravens: they neither sow nor reap, they have neither storehouse nor barn, and yet God feeds them. Of how much more value are you than the birds! And which of you by being anxious can add a single hour to his span of life? If then you are not able to do as small a thing as that, why are you anxious about the rest? Consider the lilies, how they grow: they neither toil nor spin, yet I tell you, even Solomon in all his glory was not arrayed like one of these. But if God so clothes the grass, which is alive in the field today, and tomorrow is thrown into the oven, how much more will he clothe you, O you of little faith!—Luke 12:22-28

THE next step for us in our study of God is to look at the Creator's relationship to his creation, a subject known as providence. Providence, says Louis Berkhof, is God's 'continued activity in the world for the realization of his plan'.[1] Like creation, providence is normally classified by theologians as a 'work' of God rather than an 'attribute'. Yet fundamental to our knowledge of God, and hence to our relationship with God, is understanding how God relates to the world he has created, and especially how he relates to those who alone are made in his image. When a car overruns a stop

[1] Berkhof, *Systematic Theology*, p. 167.

sign and slams into the side of my car; when I get the job that I always dreamed of having; when I get sick; when my lemon tree produces fruit; when the wind blows and a branch from a towering oak falls through my roof; when a wave crashes on the shore: in what relation does God stand to these and to all the other events of life?

Jesus invites us to 'consider the ravens', how, though they neither sow nor reap, 'God feeds them'. Similarly the lilies neither toil nor spin, yet 'God ... clothes the grass' (Luke 12:24, 27-28; cf. Matt. 6:26, 28-29). Jesus would have us understand that God is immediately active in his creation, feeding the animals and dressing the plants. 'Every pile of grass is a preacher of the lovingkindness of the Lord,' says Thomas Boston.[2] 'Each pile of grass speaks [of] a God, a wise, good, and powerful one.'[3] Jesus would even have us learn of the certainty of our Father's care for us, his children, from what we observe of his detailed care of the lesser creation. 'Will he not much more do so for you, O men of little faith?' (Matt. 6:30 NASB; Luke 12:28 NASB). God is no remote, detached, uninvolved deity, but a Father who can be counted on to feed and clothe his children. We learn about God not only by the *design* of creation (that he is powerful, wise, and good), but also by the *working* of creation. Jesus would have us understand the kind of God he is, not only by reading Scripture, but also by observing his management of the world. We may quickly dispense with three false views of providence.

False views

The first mistaken view is *deism*, a view of providence shared by historical figures such as Thomas Paine, Benjamin Franklin, and Thomas Jefferson. Deists view God as a clockmaker who long ago created the world, wound it up, and then set it aside. The universe unwinds according to the properties with which it was created and without any further divine activity. The God of deism is transcendent, but not immanent. He does not communicate with humanity. He does not answer prayer. He does not intervene in human affairs. He does not interact with the creation at all; he is distant, impersonal,

---

[2] Boston, *Illustration of the Doctrines*, *Works*, I:203.
[3] *Ibid.*, I:223.

unknown, and unknowable. A species of deism has reappeared on the contemporary scene in the form of what sociologist Christian Smith calls 'moralistic, therapeutic deism'.[4] He identifies this as the theology of America's youth culture: God is not relevant to life except that he wants us to be good and happy. Otherwise he may be ignored. Deism's failure: it does not relate the creation to the Creator.

The second mistaken view is *pantheism*. Pantheists believe that everything that exists is an extension of the essence or substance of God. A pantheist would say that the clockmaker is also the clock. The god of pantheism is immanent but not transcendent. Yet, like the god of deism, he is impersonal, unknown, and unknowable. Most Eastern religions are pantheistic. Their perspective is summed up by Maharishi Mahesh Yogi, the founder of Transcendental Meditation: 'I am *that*, thou art *that*, all this is *that*.'[5] Pantheists deny the distinct existence of the world and of a god who may be distinguished from the world. Their failure: they do not distinguish the creation from the Creator.

The third mistaken view is *dualism*. It posits two equally ultimate deities, one good and one evil. In this view God and Satan are co-equal adversaries battling it out, directing, influencing, and controlling events to good or evil ends, respectively. There is considerable practical dualism floating about even in Christian circles. Some think that God's purposes are frustrated by Satan, that things happen that are not his will and that he seems helpless to prevent. Their Satan is omniscient and omnipresent, and while not omnipotent, still a formidable opponent for God. Dualism's failure: it does not elevate the Creator over the creation.

Biblical view

What, then, is the right view of God's relation to the creation if deism, pantheism, and dualism are incorrect? The right and biblical view is that God is both *transcendent* and *immanent*. We have seen his tran-

---

[4] Christian Smith and Melinda Lundquist Denton, *Soul Searching: The Religious and Spiritual Lives of American Teenagers* (2005; New York: Oxford University Press, 2009).

[5] We note again the irony of the word 'Transcendental' in connection with Eastern thought. The 'Transcendent' one with whom one connects through meditation is the immanent god of pantheism.

scendence, God's otherness and apartness, in our study of his incommunicable attributes. 'Truly, you are a God who hides himself', says the prophet Isaiah (Isa. 45:15). God is far above us and beyond us, and so we 'are taught to trust God further than [we] can see him', says Henry.[6] Commenting on Isaiah 40, J. Gresham Machen (1881–1937), the brilliant New Testament scholar of Old Princeton and founder of Westminster Theological Seminary, wrote, 'The prophet celebrates especially the awful transcendence of God, the awful separateness between God and the world.'[7] As for God's immanence, the supreme example of this is found in the incarnation of Christ, the eternal Word who became flesh (John 1:1, 14). Jesus Christ, the God-Man in whom the divine and human are united but not confused, is Immanuel, 'God with us' (Matt. 1:23). The transcendent God demonstrates his immanence in Christ Jesus. He shows himself to be not a God who is remote, aloof, distant, and unknowable, but one who is actively engaged with his creation.

What is the nature of God's involvement in creation? 'God's works of providence,' says the Shorter Catechism, 'are his most holy, wise, and powerful preserving and governing all his creatures, and all their actions' (Q. 11). God *preserves* all things and God *governs* all things, and he does so according to his holiness, wisdom, and power. 'God keeps up what he sets up', says Swinnock.[8] To what purpose? He directs all things to their appointed end: to the consummation of the kingdom of God, the glory of Christ, and the good of his redeemed people.

God preserves

Almighty God *preserves* all things. Moment by moment, he keeps the universe in existence. God upholds all things. Theologians have sometimes referred to this as 'metaphysical preservation'.[9] Preservation, says Charles Hodge, is 'that omnipotent energy of God by which all created things, animate and inanimate, are upheld in existence, with all the

---

[6] Henry, *Commentary*, on Isa. 45:15.

[7] J. G. Machen, *God Transcendent* (1949; Edinburgh: Banner of Truth Trust, 1982), p. 17.

[8] Swinnock, *Incomparableness of God*, *Works*, IV:427.

[9] See Frame, *Doctrine of God*, p. 278.

properties and powers with which he has endowed them'.[10] Berkhof uses similar language to define preservation as 'that continuous work of God by which he maintains the things which he created, together with the properties and powers with which he endowed them'.[11] The Levites in Nehemiah not only praise God for having made the world:

> Stand up and bless the LORD your God from everlasting to everlasting. Blessed be your glorious name, which is exalted above all blessing and praise.
>
> You are the LORD, you alone. You have made heaven, the heaven of heavens, with all their host, the earth and all that is on it, the seas and all that is in them (Neh. 9:5-6).

They also praise him for preserving all things: 'and you preserve all of them; and the host of heaven worships you' (9:6). God preserves 'all of them', that is, all of heaven and its hosts, the earth and all that is upon it, and the sea and all that is in it. This is everything. He 'saves' or 'preserves' (NASB) man and beast (Psa. 36:6). 'He alone is the powerful Creator, the provident Disposer, the prudent Preserver of all things', says Trapp.[12] If God were to fail for a moment to maintain or preserve the existence of the universe, it would in that moment totally, absolutely, and completely vanish. The whole of the universe would completely disassemble the moment God withdrew his sustaining power. It would no longer adhere. It is only in Christ that 'all things hold together' (Col. 1:17). Christ 'upholds the universe by the word of his power' (Heb. 1:3). It is only *in him* that 'we live and move and have our being' (Acts 17:28). He gives us 'life and breath and everything' (Acts 17:25). Our infant children depend on us, their parents, for their being and continued existence. They are helpless. If we leave them to themselves, they will die. Infants are a compelling picture of dependence. Yet our dependence on God goes far beyond that of an infant. None of us is self-made, self-determining, or self-sustaining. The moment God withdraws his preserving power, we cease to exist.

There is a sense in which we can say that there are no natural laws on the basis of which the world functions. The 'laws of nature'

[10] Hodge, *Systematic Theology*, I:581.
[11] Berkhof, *Systematic Theology*, p. 170.
[12] Trapp, *Commentary*, III:472.

are merely human observations, human descriptions, of how God orders and regulates his universe. The dependability of those laws is a testimony to God's faithfulness. Thomas Chisholm's (1866–1960) beloved hymn based on Lamentations 3:22-23 ('his mercies … are new every morning') expresses this theme well:

> Summer and winter, and springtime and harvest;
> Sun, moon, and stars in their courses above
> Join with all nature in manifold witness
> To thy great faithfulness, mercy, and love.[13]

The natural order and regularity in nature are not inherent in any absolute sense. Rather, they testify to the faithfulness of God.[14] Natural laws describe how God normally works. When he stops, they stop. 'Man does not live by bread alone' because bread has no power to nourish apart from God's secret blessing (Deut. 8:3). Eating food would be like eating sand should God fail to bless. Bread nourishes because God at every point gives it the power to nourish. Rain does not cause crops to grow; God does. When he stops blessing the rain and soil, they will no longer enrich plants. We owe our continued existence and sustenance to the preserving power of God. Indeed, the continued existence of our fallen world and rebellious humanity is a testimony to the patience and mercy of God. 'The heavens and earth that now exist,' says the apostle Peter, are 'being kept [or 'preserved by God'] until the day of judgment and destruction of the ungodly' (2 Pet. 3:7). God preserves the world, withholding judgment, because he is patient. His preserving providence serves his purpose or plan, 'not wishing that any should perish, but that all should reach repentance' (2 Pet. 3:9).

[13] Thomas Chisholm, 'Great Is Thy Faithfulness'.
[14] It is of interest that the above-mentioned physicist Paul Davies has written in his book *The Mind of God: The Scientific Basis for a Rational World* that, 'Just because the sun has risen every day of your life, there is no guarantee that it will therefore rise tomorrow. The belief that it will—that there are indeed dependable regularities of nature—is an act of faith, but one which is indispensable to the progress of science' (quoted by Matt Emerson, 'At Its Heart, Science Is Faith-Based Too', *Wall Street Journal*, 3 March 2016). Hence the argument that the Christian faith was the necessary environment for the scientific revolution to occur.

God governs

Second, God *governs* all things. According to Hodge, this means that 'the external world, rational and irrational creatures, things great and small, ordinary and extraordinary, are equally and always under the control of God'.[15] How does he exercise this control? Sometimes he does so directly, by wielding his power. That is, sometimes God works above natural law or contrary to it, and we call this a miracle. Yet ordinarily God works indirectly, through created things in a manner consistent with their nature, that is, 'according to the nature of second causes'.[16] Normally God works through means. Theologians speak of 'divine concurrence': when the creature acts, God acts simultaneously. God's activity accompanies the creature's activity at every point, yet without depriving the creature of its natural freedom. God governs the physical universe according to the laws of nature, the animal world according to instinct, and the rational world according to the proper-ties of the mind and through 'circumstance, motives, instruction, per-suasion, and example', says Berkhof, as well as through the influence of the Holy Spirit on the mind, will, and emotions.[17]

The tension between divine sovereignty and human responsibility is present in the account of the crossing of the Red Sea. The children of Israel cry out to God and complain to Moses that they should never have left Egypt (Exod. 14:10-12). Yet Moses is confident. 'Fear not,' he says, 'and see *the salvation of the LORD*, which *he will work for you today*' (14:13). Again, 'The LORD will fight for you, and you have only to be silent' (14:14). The children of Israel have no faith, while Moses has unflinching faith. Yet God's response is instructive. Moses draws a rebuke in the form of a question: 'Why do you cry to me? Tell the people of Israel to go forward' (14:15).

This is a classic case of 'pray to God and row to shore'. Yes, God will save, and yes, the children of Israel are wrong to doubt. Yet if Moses' faith is passive; if his confidence in God absolves him of the responsibility to act, his faith is as defective as the people's. God will fight, but we must act if we are to be saved. 'Tell the people to go

---

[15] Hodge, *Systematic Theology*, I:582.
[16] Westminster Confession of Faith V.2.
[17] Berkhof, *Systematic Theology*, p. 176.

forward'; 'lift up your staff, and stretch out your hand over the sea and divide it, that the people of Israel may go through the sea on dry ground' (Exod. 14:16). God is sovereign, yet he typically exercises his sovereignty through means, and not apart from these means.

God's ordinary government of the world is 'suited to the nature of the creatures over which it is exercised', explains Hodge.[18] Whatever happens—though it happens through the activity of second causes, through means—happens ultimately by the hand of God, the first cause of all things. He does this not blindly or randomly, without a plan or purpose, but all for his own glory (Eph. 1:3-11).

Natural world

God's government incudes the most trivial of things, such as the roll of the dice (Prov. 16:33), a sparrow falling from a tree, and the number of hairs upon our heads at any given moment (Matt. 10:29; Luke 12:7). 'As nothing is too great to be above his power,' says Gurnall in his exhortation to prayer, 'so nothing is too little to be beneath his care.'[19] Jesus said that it is our Father who 'makes his sun rise on the evil and on the good, and sends rain on the just and on the unjust' (Matt. 5:45; cf. Acts 14:17; Psa. 104:19-20). The sun rises and rain falls, not of their own accord, but as God 'makes' them do so. He directs the wind and the lightning (Psa. 135:6-7), the snow, frost, and hail (147:16-17). When earthquakes hit, volcanoes erupt, and storms strike, they come by the hand of God. He feeds the ravens and he dresses the grass of the field (Matt. 6:30; Luke 12:24; Psa. 147:9). He turns the darkness to morning and the day to night (Amos 5:8-9). He fashions children in the womb (Psa. 139:13ff.). He leads the stars out each evening (Isa. 40:26). He feeds the animals, opening his hand and 'giv[ing] them their food in due season' (Psa. 104:27-28). 'God is a bountiful benefactor', says Henry.[20] He gives us fruitful harvests and fills our 'hearts with food and gladness' (Acts 14:17): 'Not only *food*, that we may live,' says Henry, 'but *gladness*, that we may live cheerfully.'[21] By God's 'appointment' the

---

[18] Hodge, *Systematic Theology*, I:585.
[19] Gurnall, *Christian in Complete Armour*, II:357.
[20] Henry, *Commentary*, on Psa. 104:28.
[21] *Ibid.*, on Acts 14:17.

heavens and the earth stand, and they are God's 'servants' (Psa. 119:91). It is right and proper that at Thanksgiving time we sing,

> We plough the fields and scatter
>   The good seed on the land,
> But it is fed and watered
>   By God's almighty hand;
> He sends the snow in winter,
>   The warmth to swell the grain,
> The breezes and the sunshine,
>   And soft, refreshing rain.
>
> He only is the Maker
>   Of all things near and far;
> He paints the wayside flower,
>   He lights the evening star;
> The winds and waves obey him,
>   By him the birds are fed;
> Much more to us, his children,
>   He gives our daily bread.

God 'sends the snow' and the 'warmth', the 'breezes and the sunshine', and the rain. He 'paints' the flowers, 'lights' the stars, and orders the winds and waves. He feeds the birds and gives us our 'daily bread'. Believers give thanks 'without ceasing' because we realize 'every good gift and every perfect gift is from above' (1 Thess. 5:17; James 1:17):

> All good gifts around us
>   Are sent from heav'n above;
> Then thank the Lord, O thank the Lord,
>   For all his love.[22]

'All good gifts ... are sent from heaven above.' According to the Westminster Confession of Faith, God 'doth uphold, direct, dispose, and govern all creatures, actions, and things from the greatest *even to the least*' (V.1).

---

[22] Matthias Claudius (1782), tr. Jane M. Campbell, 'We Plough The Fields And Scatter'.

Rational beings

God's control includes rational beings. When they act, he also acts. When they accomplish their purposes, he also, mysteriously, through them accomplishes his. When Cyrus, the pagan Prince of Persia, ordered the rebuilding of Israel's temple, Ezra says it was because 'the LORD stirred up the spirit of Cyrus king of Persia' (Ezra 1:1). Likewise, when Artaxerxes ordered the redecorating of the temple, Ezra says it was because God had put it into his heart to do so (Ezra 7:27). This is true in *everything*. When nations attack nations, we should know that God controls world politics (Psa. 22:28-29; 47:9). The apostle Paul tells us that God made every nation and has 'determined allotted periods and the boundaries of their dwelling place' (Acts 17:26). Nations rise and fall at his command and according to his purpose (Dan. 4:17, 25). 'All those changes in the face of the world, the revolutions of empires, the desolating and ravaging wars which are often immediately the birth of the vice, ambition, and fury of princes, are the royal acts of God as governor of the world', Charnock maintains.[23]

Evil empires get no further than God allows. The king in the ancient world had the last word on freedom and independence. The king could do as he pleased because he was sovereign; he was the lord of the realm. However, the Proverbs say, 'The king's heart [even the king's!] is a stream of water in the hand of the LORD; he turns it wherever he will' (Prov. 21:1). 'He speaks of the hearts of princes,' says Charnock, 'because in regard of their height, they seem to be more absolute and impetuous, as waters; yet God holds them in his hand, under his dominion.'[24] In all that kings do, as far as they go, in the last analysis they do only that which God has purposed them to do. 'Men are limited in their power,' says Watson, 'and cannot go one hair's breadth further than God's providence permits.'[25]

God's control extends beyond nations to individuals. 'The heart of man plans his way,' says Proverbs 16:9, 'but the LORD establishes his steps.' We make plans, we carry them out. Yet ultimately it is God who is in control, and his purposes stand. Man proposes but God disposes.

---

[23] Charnock, *Existence and Attributes*, II:451.
[24] *Ibid.*, II:425.
[25] Watson, *Body of Divinity*, p. 125.

'I know, O LORD, that the way of man is not in himself, that it is not in man who walks to direct his steps', says Jeremiah (Jer. 10:23). 'The prophet here acknowledges the sovereignty and dominion of the divine providence,' Henry explains, 'that by it, the affairs both of nations and particular persons are directed and determined.'[26] Ultimately, God is controlling the path we take. God raises up Pharaoh to prominence and orders him to let his people go, and then hardens his heart so that he will not do so until the appropriate time (Rom. 9:18). When Joshua goes into battle, God hardens the hearts of Israel's enemies to resist them, 'in order that they should be devoted to destruction and should receive no mercy but be destroyed' (Josh. 11:20). Eli's rebellious sons would not listen to him because 'it was the will of the LORD to put them to death' (1 Sam. 2:25). David's son Absalom failed to defeat his father completely because he followed poor advice rather than good. Why? 'For the LORD had ordained to defeat the good counsel of Ahithophel, so that the LORD might bring harm upon Absalom' (2 Sam. 17:14). Likewise, Solomon's son Rehoboam followed bad advice, oppressed the people, and thereby destroyed the kingdom. Yet we are told 'it was a turn of affairs brought about by the LORD' (1 Kings 12:15). The ten kings of Revelation give their kingdom to the beast because 'God has put it into their hearts to carry out his purpose by being of one mind and handing over their royal power to the beast, until the words of God are fulfilled' (Rev. 17:17).

Sinful acts

If God determines all these things, in what sense are we free? Does this mean that we are puppets on a string? Worse, does this make God the author of evil? We may begin to answer these questions by examining Isaiah 37 and Isaiah 10, which provide two of the most illuminating pictures of how God works in providence.

Through the prophet Isaiah God likens Assyria to a horse which he rides. God mounts the horse and swoops down on Israel in destructive judgment. When the mission is complete, God puts his hook in the horse's nose and the bit in its mouth, and turns it back to where it came from (Isa. 37:29). In this picture the *energy* belongs to the horse and the

[26] Henry, *Commentary*, on Jer. 10:23.

direction belongs to God. This led the late J. A. Motyer to conclude, 'The hard facts of human history are the plan of God … Divine Sovereignty … goes beyond the broad sweep of history to its small print.'[27]

The picture in Isaiah 10 is even more radical. Assyria is 'the rod of my anger' (verse 5). God compares the Assyrians to inanimate objects: a staff, an axe, a saw, a club, and a rod in his hands (verses 5, 15). 'Without forester and carpenter, axe and saw lie lifeless', observes Motyer.[28] All the energy, direction, and movement originate in God. God commissions Assyria to destroy Israel: 'take spoil and seize plunder, and … tread them down like the mire of the streets' (verse 6). Yet this inanimate object, Assyria, is condemned and its destruction promised (verses 16-19). Why? Because of its motives:

> But he does not so intend,
>   and his heart does not so think;
> but it is in his heart to destroy,
>   and to cut off nations not a few (verse 7).

Assyria did not 'so intend': it did not mean to carry out God's will, but to enlarge its empire. Ambition and covetousness motivated its brutalizing of nations.

The prophet also highlights its arrogance (verses 12-13):

> When the Lord has finished all his work on Mount Zion and on Jerusalem, he will punish the speech of the arrogant heart of the king of Assyria and the boastful look in his eyes. For he says:
>
> > 'By the strength of my hand I have done it,
> >   and by my wisdom, for I have understanding;
> > I remove the boundaries of peoples,
> >   and plunder their treasures;
> >   like a bull I bring down those who sit on thrones.'

'By the strength of my hand … wisdom … [and] understanding' is saying: 'I owe all my success to my own power, valour, and wise

---

[27] J. A. Motyer, *The Prophecy of Isaiah: An Introduction and Commentary* (Downers Grove, IL: InterVarsity Press, 1993), p. 283. 'All the energy, even violence, belongs to the horse—all the direction, wisdom, guiding touch belongs to the rider' (p. 283).

[28] *Ibid.*, p. 113.

conduct,' says Poole.[29] God destroyed Israel in a righteous judgment. Assyria destroyed Israel out of sinful arrogance and pride. 'For all Assyrian self-asserting,' says Motyer, 'it is nevertheless the Lord whose purpose controls all.'[30] God governs and directs evil, yet he is not its source. Assyria is responsible for its evil acts, as we are for our own. It is a mystery how it can be so. God's government includes evil actions, yet he is not the author of evil. The sinful acts of humanity, Hodge explains, 'are so under the control of God that they can occur only by his permission and in execution of his purposes'.[31] How can God determine that something should happen, and yet still hold the human agent responsible if it does? Because God's designs are righteous, and the agent's designs are evil. 'God has one end in wicked actions, and the sinner another. The sinner minds and intends evil, but God means and designs good by them all', says Boston.[32] Jesus said, 'The Son of Man goes as it is written of him, but woe to that man by whom the Son of Man is betrayed! It would have been better for that man if he had not been born' (Matt. 26:24). There was no excuse for Judas' sin of betrayal, even though it was part of God's plan that it should happen. 'He was not dragged into it', says Poole.[33]

The cross is the ultimate example of God's providential governance of evil actions. The crucifixion of Christ is without a doubt the worst crime the human race has ever committed. The only time the human race could get its hands on God, as we might put it, it defiantly and brutally murdered him. Yet the apostle Peter, in his Pentecost sermon, preaches, 'This Jesus, delivered up according to the definite plan and foreknowledge of God, you crucified and killed by the hands of lawless men' (Acts 2:23). There is the dilemma. Lawless men, in 'an act of prodigious sin and folly', were doing what God had predetermined according to his 'definite plan and foreknowledge, in infinite wisdom, and for holy ends', notes Henry.[34]

[29] Poole, *Commentary*, II:350.
[30] Motyer, *Isaiah*, p. 115.
[31] Hodge, *Systematic Theology*, I:589.
[32] Boston, *Illustration of the Doctrines, Works*, I:191.
[33] Poole, *Commentary*, III:126. He continues, 'God's decree as to the thing did neither take away the liberty of Judas' will in acting, nor yet excuse the fact he did.'
[34] Henry, *Commentary*, on Acts 2:23.

Again we read, 'For truly in this city there were gathered together against your holy servant Jesus, whom you anointed, both Herod and Pontius Pilate, along with the Gentiles and the peoples of Israel, to do whatever your hand and your plan had predestined to take place' (Acts 4:27-28). Herod, Pilate, and the rest intended evil, while God intended the salvation of the world.

A brilliant young student at California Institute of Technology, a devout Christian who was helping the US Center for World Missions set up its computers, was killed in the summer of 1978 in a hiking accident. It was a terrible tragedy, one impossible to understand. A leading theologian who attended his church said, 'I don't think this was God's will.' His comment raises a number of questions: Where does that leave us if it was not God's will? Does not God determine both the day of our birth and the day of our death? Did the theologian mean that God did not want this to happen, but it nevertheless did? Does that mean God could not *prevent* it? Or did he mean that God could have prevented it, but he chose not to? If he chose not to, did he not have reasons for choosing not to? If so, then what does it mean that 'it wasn't his will'? God had his purposes in the tragic death of that young man, even if it occurred as a result of carelessness, weakness, or simply what we would call 'an accident' (Eph. 1:11).

Satan

Even Satan does only what God allows him to do. He is allowed to do only what suits God's purposes. Satan is controlled. Evil is not equally ultimate with God. Satan must ask permission from God to afflict Job (Job 1–2), or Peter and the disciples (Luke 22:31-34). God restricts Satan's activity and allows him to go only so far and no further. 'He could not afflict Job without leave from God first asked and obtained, and then no further than he had leave', Henry maintains.[35] Satan does only what God gives him to do. The apostle Paul refers to Satan as the 'god of this world' who blinds 'the minds of the unbelievers' (2 Cor. 4:4). Yet elsewhere he attributes this blinding activity to God, saying, 'Therefore God sends them a strong delusion, so that they may believe what is false' (2 Thess. 2:11; see also Matt. 13:14-15). Satan, even

---

[35] Henry, *Commentary*, on Job 1:11.

at his worst, is doing God's bidding. He is serving God's purposes. Satan's motives, of course, are evil. He is in total rebellion. Yet the wisdom and power of God ensure that his rebellion serves only to further God's cause. God controls all spiritual forces. 'His empire reaches over the malignity of devils, as well as the nature of beasts', Charnock affirms.[36] Satan, we may say reverently, is God's Satan. He is a creature and is included among the 'all things' that are 'for him': 'For by him all things were created, in heaven and on earth, visible and invisible, whether thrones or dominions or rulers or authorities—all things were created through him and for him', the apostle tells us (Col. 1:16). The devil exists 'for God', and therefore he exists to suit God's purposes. He is among the 'rulers and authorities' that Christ has 'triumph[ed] over' (Col. 2:15). Satan is a vanquished enemy.

We have another striking example of God using or acting concurrently through Satan in 2 Samuel 24 and its parallel in 1 Chronicles 21. Note that 2 Samuel 24:1 says, 'The anger of the LORD was kindled against Israel, and he incited David against them, saying, "Go, number Israel and Judah."' It was wrong for David to number the people, yet this passage says 'the LORD … incited David against them'. However, 1 Chronicles 21:1 records the very same incident in this way, 'Satan stood against Israel and incited David to number Israel.' The chronicler tells us 'Satan … incited David'; 2 Samuel says 'the LORD … incited David'. Is this a contradiction? No. God did the inciting in that he ordained, permitted, and allowed (all three words are appropriate) Satan to 'incite'. God was the first cause of the incident; Satan was the second or immediate cause. God's reasons for his actions were righteous, holy, and good, while Satan's were vicious, wicked, and destructive. For wise and holy ends he permitted the devil to do it, Henry explains. Thus, in 1 Chronicles 'we trace this foul stream to its fountain,' as Henry puts it.[37] Satan tries to thwart God's purpose, yet ultimately he only serves to carry out God's plan. This is why the apostle Paul can speak of delivering an immoral brother over to Satan 'for the destruction of the flesh' (1 Cor. 5:5). Satan gladly does this sort of work. Yet the reason why God would have Satan do such a thing

---

[36] Charnock, *Existence and Attributes*, II:452.
[37] Henry, *Commentary*, on 1 Chron. 21:1.

is 'that his spirit may be *saved* in the day of the Lord'. The motives, the intent, are totally contrary, yet the act is the same. Satan aims to *destroy* a Christian's soul and so he destroys his flesh; God aims to *save* a Christian's soul and so he destroys his flesh through Satan. Satan's activity is 'approved' or 'allowed' by the Sovereign Lord. This does not mean it is good or praiseworthy, but that his activity accomplishes God's will and for that reason is permitted, allowed, and ordained. Satan and the human agents, Jew and Gentile, Herod and Pilate, race to do their absolute worst, and concurrently, God saves a multitude which no person can number (Rev. 7:9). While sin does its worst, God does his best, accomplishing his gracious purposes.

Whatever happens, though it happens through sinful people and Satan, ultimately happens by the hand of God. 'God is president in all the commotions of the world; his way is in every whirlwind', says Charnock.[38] Repeatedly the prophets emphasize this point so that the people of God might know that *they are always dealing with God.* Jeremiah asks, 'Is it not from the mouth of the Most High that good and bad come?' (Lam. 3:38). 'Whatever is done,' says Henry, 'God has the directing of it.'[39] Amos asks, 'Is a trumpet blown in a city, and the people are not afraid? Does disaster come to a city, unless the LORD has done it?' (Amos 3:6). God declares through Isaiah, 'I am the LORD, and there is no other. I form light and create darkness, I make well-being and create calamity, I am the LORD, who does all these things' (Isa. 45:6-7). Whether we encounter light or darkness, good or evil ('calamity' is the ordinary Hebrew word for 'evil'), it is the Lord 'who does all these things, either immediately by his own hand, or mediately by the hands of those he employs', explains Poole.[40] 'The Lord is executioner behind all the diversities of experience which life contains', says Motyer.[41] Bavinck says of all secondary causes that 'He governs and rules all things in such a way that they all cooperate and all converge upon the purpose he has established.' Bavinck continues: 'No accident and no necessity, no arbitrariness and no force, no mere caprice nor iron destiny controls the world and its history and the life

[38] Charnock, *Existence and Attributes*, II:503.
[39] Henry, *Commentary*, on Lam. 3:38.
[40] Poole, *Commentary*, p. 905.
[41] Motyer, *Isaiah*, p. 359.

and lot of mankind. Behind all secondary causes there lurks and works the almighty will of an almighty God and a faithful Father.'[42]

Whether life brings prosperity or poverty, well-being or disaster, health or disease, longevity or death, never am I facing random, meaningless events. I am always, always, always, dealing with God. He, in turn is always dealing with me. Whatever my circumstances may be, positive or negative, easy or difficult, I am always dealing with my Almighty Father, and he is always dealing with his beloved child. Packer provides a helpful summary:

> The doctrine of providence teaches Christians that they are never in the grip of blind fortune, chance, luck, or fate. All that happens to them is divinely planned, and each event comes as a new summons to trust, obey, and rejoice, knowing that all is for one's spiritual and eternal good (Rom. 8:28).[43]

God's purpose

Let us underscore what we have stated all along: the aim, purpose, or goal of God's preserving and governing providence is the fulfilment of his eternal purpose. God predestines 'according to [his] purpose'. He 'works all things', says the apostle—'powerfully and effectually', adds Poole[44]—'according to the counsel of his will' (Eph. 1:11). The apostle Paul summarizes this purpose as 'the praise of his glorious grace' (Eph. 1:6), as 'the summing up of all things in Christ, things in the heavens and things on the earth' (1:10 NASB), 'to the praise of his glory' (1:12, 14).

Similarly, the apostle Paul concludes his *Carmen Christi*, his hymn of Christ, saying, 'Therefore'—that is, given Christ's obedient death on the cross (Phil. 2:5-8)—'God has highly exalted him and bestowed on him the name that is above every name, so that at the name of Jesus every knee should bow, in heaven and on earth and under the earth, and every tongue confess that Jesus Christ is Lord, to the glory of God the Father' (2:9-11). The goal of God-directed history is the exaltation of Jesus Christ and the glory of God the Father.

[42] Bavinck, *Our Reasonable Faith*, p. 182.
[43] J. I. Packer, 'Providence', *The Reformation Study Bible* (Orlando: Ligonier Ministries, 2005), p. 900.
[44] Poole, *Commentary*, III:664.

Again, the apostle speaks of the reign of Christ, the defeat of all of God's enemies (including death itself), of their subjection under Christ's feet, and the consummation of the kingdom of God; he then concludes, 'When all things are subjected to him, then the Son himself will also be subjected to him who put all things in subjection under him, that God may be all in all' (1 Cor. 15:28). The goal of providence is 'that God may be all in all'. That goal, of course, includes the good of God's people, his glory being their blessing (Rom. 8:28ff.).

Application

We have gone to great lengths to demonstrate divine providence. The implications of this doctrine, especially when taken in conjunction with the doctrine of creation, are vast. Not only has God made me, but he has superintended every circumstance of my life. He has opened doors and closed doors, provided opportunities and denied opportunities. He has ordained all the events of life that have gone into making me what I am today. There is no good luck or bad luck. There is no fortune or misfortune. Nothing happens by chance or fate. Everything has a reason. Everything has a purpose. Everything is significant. 'Providence reacheth to all things,' says Boston, 'and in everything the finger of God is to be seen.'[45] There is, he continues, a 'web of providence wherein every moment we are wrapt up'.[46] God 'works all things according to the counsel of his will' (Eph. 1:11). *All things.* As his children we can take this a step further, as does the apostle Paul: 'And we know that for those who love God all things work together for good, for those who are called according to his purpose' (Rom. 8:28). I am *what* I am and *where* I am by the hand of God. 'Accustom yourself,' says à Brakel, 'by frequent meditations, attentive observations, and diligent exercises to believingly *observe God's hand in all things.*'[47]

Ordinary and other providences

The desire to see God act *supernaturally* has at times caused some to overlook this truth that God is continually at work *naturally*. God's

---

[45] Boston, *Illustration of the Doctrines, Works,* I:198.
[46] *Ibid.,* I:206.
[47] à Brakel, *Christian's Reasonable Service,* I:349 (emphasis added).

regular way of working is through natural means. Notice what we are saying: God is normally at work in and through the *ordinary*. The bias which can see the hand of God at work only in the miraculous is in direct conflict with our understanding of providence.

It is certainly wonderful when God suspends cause and effect and intervenes directly, miraculously. Yet equally wonderful is seeing the hand of God in all of life. How does God normally build his church? Sometimes he intervenes miraculously. Yet normally he works through the ordinary means of the word, sacraments, and prayer (see Shorter Catechism, Q. 88). How does God normally lead and shepherd his people (Psa. 5:8; 23:2; 25:5; 31:3; 43:3; 61:2; 80:1; 139:10; 143:10; Isa. 40:11; 42:16; 49:10; Jer. 31:9; Matt. 6:13; Rev. 7:17)? Ordinarily he leads through the circumstances of life: people, timing, events, prayer, Scripture. Our God is the God of the ordinary. Society wants the spectacular. The church wants the miraculous. But God normally works through ordinary circumstances and ordinary means.

Further, we can see God's hand in what we might call *amazing providences*. These are not miracles, though they sometimes are mislabelled as such. Rather, they are extraordinary coincidences. Natural law, cause and effect, are not disrupted. Yet circumstances converge in such a way as to unmistakably manifest the hand of God.

Perhaps the decisive month in my entire adult ministry took place during my one-month internship in Edinburgh, Scotland. Under the leadership of the Rev. C. Peter White I gained my first taste of ministerial practice, and was introduced to the Rev. William Still and the Crieff Fellowship. It was a life-changing, direction-setting, philosophy-determining time. On the train journey home we stopped at Newcastle to pick up passengers. At that moment my best friend from theological college, Christopher Bennett, walked across the platform, boarded my train carriage, and sat down next to me. There were a dozen other trains on which he might have returned to Bristol, and a dozen other carriages on my train that he might have boarded. The trip home was six to eight hours. But the time flew by. It seemed like but a few minutes as we intensely discussed all I was learning, solidifying and confirming those lessons. That was no mere coincidence, but what one might call a 'divine appointment'.

If we believe in providence—that God is sovereign in our circumstances—we will take seriously the people, events, and opportunities he puts in our path. Our circumstances do not arise by chance. God in his providential wisdom has placed us where we are and equipped us as he has for a good purpose. John Flavel (*c.* 1627–91), in his spiritual classic *The Mystery of Providence*, writes, 'Providence is wiser than you, and you may be confident it has suited all things better to your eternal good than you could do had you been left to your own option.'[48] Similarly, à Brakel urges, 'May you continually perceive God's hand working in and by secondary causes in such a manner as if these causes did not exist, but as if God worked these things immediately.'[49]

We understand that, at any given moment, interpreting the particulars of providence may be problematic. Is that barrier in my path a hurdle to overcome or a sign to alter my course? Seldom are events self-interpreting. If a manuscript has been turned down by a dozen publishers, does that mean that one should persevere or abandon the project? Because I have been turned down for a given job several times, does that mean that I should learn persistence or look in another direction? Does the young lady's refusal of my offer of dinner mean I should move on to another prospect or continue to pursue her and risk being seen as a 'creeper'? By saying that *everything is significant* we are not saying that *anything* in particular may be infallibly *interpreted*. Gurnall likens God's providences to bees that 'fly some this way, and some that, yea, one contrary to another, as, thou thinkest, impossible to trace them'. 'Yet,' he says, 'all [are] at work for thee; and thy soul is the hive wherein they will unlade the sweet fruit of all their labour.'[50] Often it is only in hindsight that it becomes clear what our Father in heaven was doing to us or for us. What was perceived at the time as a tragedy may later be understood as a bullet dodged, like the man for whom traffic caused him to miss his holiday flight home on a plane that subsequently crashed, killing everyone on board. As Flavel says, 'Sometimes providences, like Hebrew letters, must be read backwards.'[51]

[48] John Flavel, *The Mystery of Providence* (1678; Edinburgh: Banner of Truth Trust, 1963), p. 80.
[49] à Brakel, *Christian's Reasonable Service*, I:350.
[50] Gurnall, *Christian in Complete Armour*, I:504.
[51] John Flavel, *Navigation Spiritualized*, *The Works of John Flavel* (1820; Edinburgh: The Banner of Truth Trust, 1968), V:284.

Nevertheless, we can learn from the broad outlines of God's providential activity. Both adversity and prosperity are meant to persuade us to align ourselves with God's eternal purposes, so that whether we eat or drink or whatever we do, we do all to the glory of God (1 Cor. 10:31). 'The glory of God ought to eat up all other ends', says Trapp.[52] The prophet Amos tells us that food shortages, drought, water shortages, pestilence, plague, and war were all designed by God to bring Israel to repentance and avert more serious judgment (Amos 4:6-12). Adversity may be God's warning shot over our bow, designed to break us off from our idols and lusts and convince us to forsake them and turn to God. 'For where he causes changes to appear,' says Calvin, 'he warns that he is ready and, so to speak, armed for vengeance.'[53] Similarly, God's blessings may be designed to do the same. 'Or do you presume on the riches of his kindness and forbearance and patience,' the apostle Paul asks, 'not knowing that God's kindness is meant to lead you to repentance?' (Rom. 2:4). Let us not batter our heads against the wall of God's judgments and let us not presume upon his gifts. Rather, let us learn to interpret God's dealings with us, embracing his lessons and submitting to his will. 'They that are wise will be observers of providences', urges Thomas Boston.[54]

Calling

We can apply our understanding of providence to vocational decisions. What is my life's calling? What does God want me to do?

God has both created us and overseen our development, thereby making us who we are. A certain young man from childhood wanted to be a dentist. He did not know why; he just always loved the idea. As he matured, the desire persisted. When he became a serious Christian, he prayed fervently about his life's direction, and still he wanted to practise dentistry.

Given our understanding of providence, we might ask of this young man: why the affinity for dentistry? There were a number of factors, such as educated parents, a middle-class neighbourhood, and living in the twenty-first century and not in the sixth. Who determined all these factors? Who put him in that family, at that time, and

---

[52] Trapp, *Commentary*, V:539.
[53] Calvin, *Institutes*, IV.xii.17, p. 1243.
[54] Boston, *Illustration of the Doctrines, Works*, I:226.

in that neighbourhood? Who brought his friends to him? What about his teacher who sparked his interest in science? What about his natural aptitudes, desires, talents, and abilities? Had not God been provident in all these areas? Had not God made him what he is today? The man does not have to justify his love of dentistry; God made him that way. When he uses all those gifts, all those opportunities, all those talents and aptitudes, to their maximum potential, he honours the God who created and superintended all those factors.

We would include in the list of gifts and talents those that predate one's conversion. The apostle Paul, though converted on the Damascus Road (Acts 9), speaks of having been 'set apart' by God to be the apostle to the Gentiles 'before [he] was born' (Gal. 1:15). His whole life, then, was a preparation for this mission: his Roman citizenship, his classical education, his Jewish training under the greatest rabbi of that era, Gamaliel, and so on. If you, a believer, developed great writing skills as an unbeliever, thank God for them, and sanctify them. Keep writing for the local paper, but write for it as 'for the Lord' (Col. 3:23-24). God will be honoured, and he will be pleased that you are pleased. The wise preacher of Ecclesiastes says, 'So I saw that there is nothing better than that a man should rejoice in his work, for that is his lot' (Eccles. 3:22). 'Live a cheerful life', says Henry. You will be happier if you use and develop the gifts, interests, and abilities that God has given you, 'taking what is to be had', as Henry puts it, 'and making the best of it'.[55]

What should I do with my life? What is my calling? We answer this question by asking another: What has God equipped me to do? What are my *aptitudes*, my *abilities*, my *skills*? What do I love? What do I *desire* to do? Often our desires match our abilities. Rarely do we love that for which we have no aptitude. Further, we ask, how do my abilities and desires match my *opportunities*? Perhaps what I love above all else is building sand castles. Perhaps I am even especially skilled at building sand castles. Yet there is a problem in pursuing this as a life calling because it is virtually impossible to make a living building sand castles. We have to distinguish vocations from avocations. Given the whole mix of abilities, desires, and opportunities, and given that

---

[55] Henry, *Commentary*, on Eccles. 3:22.

God is sovereign over all these factors, what would God have me to do? How may I serve him? How may I know him? Understanding that God has both made me and overseen my development all along the way is vital if I am to answer that question.

Prosperity

This view of providence teaches us to give thanks for all that is right and good in life. 'Every good and perfect gift is from above, coming down from the Father of lights', James teaches us (James 1:17). Every moment of good health, every occasion of financial prosperity, every happy family gathering, every enjoyable meal, is a gift to us from God. There is not a wealthy, healthy, or famous person alive today for whom it could be said that with slightly altered circumstances they would be unknown and living in pain and poverty. 'The blessing of the Lord makes rich' (Prov. 10:22). Again the preacher in Ecclesiastes tells us, 'In the day of prosperity be joyful, and in the day of adversity consider: God has made the one as well as the other, so that man may not find out anything that will be after him' (Eccles. 7:14).

Our family was enduring one of those times of adversity when we decided to rendezvous at the beach for a weekend in order to get away from it all. Even there we were enveloped in sadness. The first evening we thumbed through the Yellow Pages at the last minute to find a place to eat outside, on the water, and surprisingly we were able to make reservations. We waited on the front porch of the restaurant until called, and then walked to our table. As we passed through the restaurant and to the back patio, a cool breeze swept over us as simultaneously we caught a glimpse of a beautiful sunset and a live band playing lovely music. I was immediately stunned with a sense of the goodness of God, of his tender care for us, as our sadness was overwhelmed by the beauty of that moment. That moment was a gift from God.

Our circumstances are not accidental. The apostle Paul asks the Corinthians, 'What do you have that you did not receive?' (1 Cor. 4:7). His rhetorical question expects 'Nothing' for an answer. Every good thing that we have we have received as a gift from God and it is an occasion for thanksgiving. For what may I thank God each day?

Adversity

Only with this view of providence will we learn to *trust God in adversity*. 'Does any affliction befall you?' asks Watson. 'Remember God sees it is that which is *fit for you, or it would not come*.'[56] With a lesser view of providence, the temptation in times of suffering is to remove God from the scene, to say (and we do so with the best of motives) that God is not responsible, that it was not God's fault, that God was not there. Yet by removing God from the picture we lose the opportunity to trust him.

The only reason why evil is a problem in this world, and the only reason why we need faith in tragic circumstances, is because God is both *sovereign* and *good*. Deny either side of the equation and we do not need faith. Deny his sovereignty and we can agree: God is good, and because he is good, he did not want the hurtful event to happen. This is the answer given by Rabbi Harold Kushner in his popular book *When Bad Things Happen to Good People*. God is nice, he says. However, God is incapable of preventing tragedy. He is not powerful enough, or he may not be present to stop bad things when they are happening to good people. Kushner denies the greatness of God.

Conversely, one may deny God's goodness, and affirm that he *is* powerful enough to prevent evil. However, he is not good. He does not want to relieve our pain. He likes suffering; he delights in evil. We thereby solve the problem of evil as sceptics and cynics have done from time immemorial.

Yet if God is great and good, sovereign and kind, there is a theological problem. As Christians we cannot deny one or the other and thereby escape the dilemma. Consequently, we must live with the antinomy and trust that God knows best. By faith we accept that there is more going on than we can see, and we receive our adversity from one who knows better than we. What are we to think when a child tragically dies? What are we to think when a loved one is crippled by a terrible accident, or when we contract a fatal disease? Flavel maintains, 'Providence has ordered that condition for you which is really *best for your eternal good*.'[57] Similarly, Boston reminds us how veiled God's purposes may be: 'The greatest cross may be wrapt up in what we take

---

[56] Watson, *Body of Divinity*, p. 125 (emphasis added).
[57] Flavel, *Mystery of Providence*, p. 78 (emphasis added).

to be our greatest comfort; and the greatest comfort may be inwrapt in what we call our greatest cross.'[58]

We speak not merely of physical but also of emotional and spiritual suffering. There may be times when God seems to withdraw our awareness of his presence, when the word no longer comforts, when God's people no longer encourage, when God seems to have abandoned us. There may be times when he leaves us with nothing but the naked promise that 'I will never leave nor forsake you', and says, 'Trust me' (Heb. 13:5). Many of us may face, at one time or another, the seeming disappearance of all tokens of God's love, both spiritual and material. Our spiritual ancestors spoke of 'the dark night of the soul' and of spiritual 'desertions'. We may cry with the psalmist, '*You* have put me in the depths of the pit, in the regions dark and deep ... O LORD, why do *you* cast my soul away? Why do *you* hide *your* face from me?' (Psa. 88:6, 14). With David we may want to cry, 'My God, my God, why have you forsaken me?' (Psa. 22:1). Jesus drank from that cup, and as the Puritan Joseph Symonds (d. 1652) said, 'It hath gone round ever since.'[59] Many of the great saints of old have gone through the same things. There may be times when everything around us and within us, subjective and objective, would tell us that God has no love for us. Yet, whatever our circumstances, we are to know, says Calvin, 'The Lord has willed it; therefore it must be borne, not only because one may not contend against it, but because he wills nothing but what is just and expedient.'[60]

Let us then receive suffering in faith, as from his hand, trusting it is for our good. Henry urges us 'to be fully reconciled to all the disposals of divine providence'.[61] Whatever our circumstances, be ready to say with David, 'Here I am, let him do to me what seems good to him' (2 Sam. 15:26). Watson reminds us from Romans 8:28, 'Our maladies shall be our medicine ... God makes our adversity our university.'[62]

---

[58] Boston, *Illustration of the Doctrines, Works*, I:223.

[59] Cited in Peter Lewis, *The Genius of Puritanism* (Haywards Heath: Carey Publications, 1977), p. 67.

[60] Calvin, *Institutes*, I.xvii.8, p. 220.

[61] Henry, *Pleasantness of a Religious Life*, p. 56.

[62] Thomas Watson, *The Art of Divine Contentment* (Morgan, PA: Soli Deo Gloria, 1984), pp. 134-35.

Our present circumstances, despite appearances, are best for us. 'God knows which is the fittest pasture to put his sheep in,' says Watson. 'Every cross-wind shall at last blow me to the right port.'[63] When God deals with us in the way of affliction, our response is to humbly receive it and learn. Watson urges us to 'Trust him where you cannot trace him. God is most in his way, when we think he is most out of the way.'[64] Nothing in life is accidental. God is always at work for our benefit. We cite Flavel again: 'He would rather hear me groan here than howl hereafter. His love is judicious, not fond. He consults my good rather than my ease.'[65] The English poet William Cowper (1731–1800) regularly endured deep depression. Yet out of his struggle came some of our richest hymns of praise, including 'There Is a Fountain Filled with Blood'. He wrote another hymn entitled 'God Moves in a Mysterious Way', in which he urges,

> Judge not the Lord by feeble sense,
> But trust him for his grace;
> Behind a frowning providence
> He hides a smiling face.[66]

All things for good

Finally, only with this high view of providence will we learn to see *good* in all things, and rejoice. All things are designed for the good of God's people and his own glory. 'Christians,' says Watson, 'believe that all God's providences shall conspire for your good at last.'[67] Again, the apostle Paul says in what Trapp calls 'that sweetest text',[68] 'God causes *all things* to work together for good to those who love God' (Rom. 8:28 NASB). Gladly we sing,

> Whate'er my God ordains is right:
> His holy will abideth;

---

[63] Watson, *Art of Divine Contentment*, p. 235.
[64] Watson, *Body of Divinity*, p. 76.
[65] Flavel, *Mystery of Providence*, p. 131.
[66] William Cowper, 'God Moves in a Mysterious Way'. The expression 'frowning providence' is also found in Gurnall, *Christian in Complete Armour*, II:98.
[67] Watson, *Body of Divinity*, p. 125.
[68] Trapp, *Commentary*, I:179.

I will be still whate'er he doth,
    And follow where he guideth.
He is my God; though dark my road,
He holds me that I shall not fall:
    Wherefore to him I leave it all.

Whate'er my God ordains is right:
    Here shall my stand be taken;
Though sorrow, need, or death be mine,
    Yet am I not forsaken.
My Father's care is round me there;
He holds me that I shall not fall:
    And so to him I leave it all.[69]

The God of providence controls all things and therefore is able to make even the worst evils work for our good. Consequently, we are able to 'rejoice in the Lord always', which would otherwise be an impossible command for us to obey (Phil. 4:4). The classic example we have already mentioned is the cross. God reversed the whole evil scheme of Satan. What Satan thought was God's greatest defeat was in fact his greatest victory. This is true of all evil. God overrules and reverses evil to bring about a greater good.

Aside from the cross, the greatest example of 'all things for good' may be found in the life of Joseph. Joseph was thrown into a pit by his brothers, who intended that he should die. Instead, he was sold into slavery. One can only imagine his heartbreak and sorrow at being separated from his family, a slave in a distant land. Yet Joseph prospered and became great in Egypt. He became Pharaoh's right-hand man, and through his wise management Egypt survived seven years of famine and was able to feed the world. When reunited with his brothers he says to them, 'You meant evil against me, but God meant it for good' (Gen. 50:20). God meant it! It was not an accident or a divine afterthought. 'God often brings good out of evil,' says Henry, 'and promotes the designs of his providence even by the sins of men.'[70] Joseph was not a victim of bad luck or misfortune. 'God meant it', and he caused it to work for good.

---

[69] Samuel Rodigast, 'Whate'er My God Ordains Is Right'.
[70] Henry, *Commentary*, on Gen. 50:20.

Luke tells us that 'there arose … a great persecution against the church in Jerusalem, and they were all scattered throughout the regions of Judea and Samaria' (Acts 8:1). Was this a great tragedy? In some respects, perhaps. Persecution meant displacement and suffering. Yet the effect was the spread, not the destruction, of the church: 'Now those who were scattered went about preaching the word' (Acts 8:4).

When the apostle Paul was imprisoned by the Romans the Philippians were very unsettled. Would they survive? Could the church get on without its great leader? What a blow for the infant church! Yet the apostle says that, on the contrary, his imprisonment had really served to 'advance the gospel' (Phil. 1:12). The whole Praetorian Guard had heard of the cause of Christ, and others had become far bolder because of Paul's example (1:13-14). We are to be assured, says Calvin, that 'there is no erratic power, or action, or motion in creatures, but that they are governed by God's secret plan in such a way that nothing happens except what is knowingly and willingly decreed by him'.[71] 'The dominion of God,' says Charnock, 'is manifest in appointing to every man his calling and station in the world.'[72]

Is this not the cure for our *anger* at what others have done, for how circumstances have conspired against us—to know that God is behind the occasion of dismay, working it for my good? What Watson calls 'distrustful' or 'distracting' worry 'is very dishonourable to God: it takes away his providence, as if he sat in heaven, and *minded not what became of things here below*'.[73] Since he does mind what becomes of things here on earth, will we not learn *contentment* if we are confident that his hand is in everything? Will we not learn *patience*, knowing that God governs all things, even those which frustrate and annoy, for my good? We are always to be 'looking beyond all creatures to God himself', says à Brakel.[74] Can we not in everything *give thanks* (1 Thess. 5:18) and rejoice always (Phil. 4:4), knowing that our Father has determined the outcome, whatever it be, for our good and his glory? Can we not find contentment, knowing that God has ordered our circumstances? Listen once more to Watson:

[71] Calvin, *Institutes*, I.xvi.3, p. 201.
[72] Charnock, *Existence and Attributes*, II:455.
[73] Watson, *Art of Divine Contentment*, p. 2 (emphasis added).
[74] à Brakel, *Christian's Reasonable Service*, I:351.

Whatever our condition be, God, the great umpire of the world, hath from eternity decreed that condition for us, and by his providence ordered all appurtenances thereunto. Let a Christian often think with himself, Who hath placed me here, whether I am in a higher sphere, or in a lower? not chance or fortune, as the purblind heathens imagined: no, it is the wise God who hath by his providence fixed me in this orb .... The wise God hath ordered our condition: if he sees it better for us to abound, we shall abound; if he sees it better for us to want, we shall want. Be content to be at God's disposal.[75]

That 'God causes all things to work together for good' is both a fact and a promise. Providence is on our side, and works for our good. Thomas Boston says of God's works of providence, 'In these his works no flaw is to be found, no mistake; nothing too much, nothing too little; nothing too soon done, nothing too late done; nothing misplaced, nothing in or over; nay nothing done that is not best done; nothing that man or angel could make better.'[76]

All things that happen happen for our good because they come to us not just from a sovereign God, but from a sovereign God who for us is also a loving, gracious, and tender Father who promises to freely give us all things. In the midst of troubling circumstances we know, says Packer, 'that the inscrutable God of providence is the wise and gracious God of creation and redemption'.[77] 'Oh how sweet it is,' says à Brakel, 'in contemplation of the fact that God is the moving cause of all things to bow before him and to worship him.'[78]

---

[75] Watson, *Art of Divine Contentment*, pp. 38, 40-41.
[76] Boston, *Illustration of the Doctrines, Works*, I:223.
[77] Packer, *Knowing God*, p. 96.
[78] à Brakel, *Christian's Reasonable Service*, I:351; we will revisit the issue of suffering in chapter twelve, looking there more broadly at the problem of evil in relation to the goodness of God.

SEVEN

'The Attribute of Attributes': The Holiness of God

In the year that King Uzziah died I saw the Lord sitting upon a throne, high and lifted up; and the train of his robe filled the temple. Above him stood the seraphim. Each had six wings: with two he covered his face, and with two he covered his feet, and with two he flew. And one called to another and said:

'Holy, holy, holy is the LORD of hosts;
the whole earth is full of his glory!'

And the foundations of the thresholds shook at the voice of him who called, and the house was filled with smoke. And I said: 'Woe is me! For I am lost; for I am a man of unclean lips, and I dwell in the midst of a people of unclean lips; for my eyes have seen the King, the LORD of hosts!'

Then one of the seraphim flew to me, having in his hand a burning coal that he had taken with tongs from the altar. And he touched my mouth and said: 'Behold, this has touched your lips; your guilt is taken away, and your sin atoned for.'

—Isaiah 6:1-7

WHEN Jesus taught us to pray, he instructed us to begin by recognizing God's paternity: 'Our Father'; by recognizing his supremacy and sovereignty over all things: 'who art in heaven'; and by recognizing his holiness: 'hallowed be thy name'. To 'hallow' is to treat or honour as holy. The 'name' represents the person. The first petition of the Lord's Prayer, and our first priority, as represented in our prayer-life, is that God would be acknowledged as holy.[1] Today's church has learned to call God 'Father', and perhaps learned (though less well) to recognize his supremacy in heaven, but it has sorely neglected to recognize and promote his holiness.

What the Bible teaches about God's holiness, his purity and perfection, his love of righteousness and truth, his abhorrence of sin, his rewarding of the good, his wrath and anger against evil, his demand for repentance, and his insistence upon the purified lives of his people, is a much confused, much maligned, and much neglected part of the Christian faith. Until the middle of the nineteenth century, nearly all *gospel* preaching was of the 'fire and brimstone' variety. Preachers proclaimed God's holiness, God's law, God's wrath and anger against sin, the necessity of the new birth, the need for faith *and* repentance, and the importance of holy living. Jonathan Edwards' 'Sinners in the Hands of an Angry God' is perhaps the supreme, if notorious, example of the older gospel message.[2] Whatever else might be said about it, such preaching did result in deep repentance, genuine faith, and a deep, deep appreciation of grace.

About the middle of the nineteenth century a shift occurred under the influence of post-Enlightenment romanticism and liberal theology. The emphasis in Christian preaching shifted from the holiness of God to the love of God. 'God is love' became the primary content of the gospel message, while 'God is light' (grammatically identical with the former) slipped into the background. The great American evangelist Dwight L. Moody experienced a moment of illumination in 1868 through the influence of Henry Moorhouse (1840–80). Moorhouses' sermon on John 3:16 at Moody's church in Chicago transformed Moody from a preacher of God's wrath to a preacher of God's love. Rather than driving sinners to Christ through fear of damnation he sought to draw them in by God's love. His preaching 'was to take on a different tenor to that of so much evangelistic preaching in the American tradition', says his biographer, Stanley N. Gundry.[3]

This shift suited the ethos of the times and was widely influential on subsequent evangelicalism. Modern people were becoming increasingly

---

[1] See Terry L. Johnson, *When Grace Comes Alive: Living through the Lord's Prayer* (Fearn, Ross-shire: Christian Focus, 2003), pp. 97-104.

[2] Jonathan Edwards, *Sinners in the Hands of an Angry God*, in *Works*, II:7-12.

[3] Stanley N. Gundry, *Love Them In: The Proclamation Theology of D. L. Moody* (Chicago: Moody, 1976), pp. 46, 116ff.

uncomfortable with the biblical picture of a God who in judgment would destroy whole nations, men, women, and children. They were uncomfortable attributing to God anger, jealousy, and violence, and such actions as destroying the world with a flood and raining fire and brimstone on Sodom and Gomorrah. They were uncomfortable describing God as 'a consuming fire' (Heb. 12:29). Modern people did not like the ideas of wrath, judgment, vengeance, eternal punishment, and hell. Such notions were considered unpleasant, discouraging, and even primitive. Some moderns even did not like the cross: it was far too violent, far too brutal and bloody, to attribute to God. They preferred a governmental or 'moral influence' view of the atonement.

God has been receiving a 'makeover' for some time now, as his 'harsher' attributes have been toned down or eliminated and his 'softer' attributes highlighted. Modern people have tamed and civilized the God of the Bible. The result is a God who is but a shadow of his former self. Although they would never have directly said, 'Let's make a new god', this essentially is what has happened. H. Richard Niebuhr (1894–1962) summarized the optimistic message of theological liberalism in this way: 'A God without wrath brought men without sin into a kingdom without judgment through the ministration of a Christ without a cross.'[4]

Decades later a host of 'conservative' Christians followed a similar path. 'The failure of modern evangelicalism,' says R. C. Sproul (1939–2017), 'is the failure to understand the holiness of God.'[5] 'The holiness of God,' says leading evangelical theologian David Wells, 'is given inhospitable treatment.' 'The modern church,' he points out, 'wants therapy not redemption, to be happy not holy; to feel good not be good; to avoid pain, not sin.'[6]

Jonathan Edwards convincingly argued in his great sermon 'Men Naturally Are God's Enemies' that people have always found the biblical God distasteful. It may not seem so. They may go to church, read their Bibles, pay tithes, keep the Sabbath, and even pray and worship. Yet in doing so they worship not the God of the Bible, but

[4] H. Richard Niebuhr, *The Kingdom of God in America* (1937; Middletown, CT: Wesleyan University Press, 1988), p. 193.

[5] R. C. Sproul, *The Holiness of God* (Wheaton, IL: Tyndale House, 1985), p. 232.

[6] David F. Wells, *God in the Whirlwind: How the Holy-Love of God Reorients Our World* (Wheaton, IL: Crossway, 2014), pp. 121, 126.

the god of their own imagination. If shown the biblical God, they will go nearly mad with rage. People hate that God and want nothing to do with him (Rom. 1:30). Edwards says of natural men, 'God is not such a being as they would have.' It is particularly God's holiness that is offensive. Specifically, when 'they hear God is an infinitely holy, pure, and righteous Being, they do not like him upon this account'. They have a 'distaste of the perfections', on account of which 'they dislike all his other attributes'.[7]

> They have greater aversion to him because he is omniscient and knows all things; and because his omniscience is a holy omniscience. They are not pleased that he is omnipotent, and can do whatever he pleases; because it is a holy omnipotence. They are enemies even to his mercy, because it is a holy mercy. They do not like his immutability, because by this he never will be otherwise than he is, an infinitely holy God.[8]

If we are honest, most of us would admit that at one time or another we have been tempted to refashion the biblical picture of God. We are ashamed to tell people about hell, and frankly we do not see how an eternity in flames could be fair. When someone says, 'What did I do to deserve that? I've never hurt anyone', we are dumbfounded and do not know what to say. We are ashamed to speak of repentance and a holy God's wrath against sin because we are afraid to 'turn people off'. We do not want to be negative and we do not want people to think poorly of us, so it is easier to talk about love and about gaining peace of mind, joy, and fulfilment. Yet in doing so, we attract them to a God different from the God of the Bible. When we do so, the apostle Paul is against us, for when he preaches the gospel, he begins by saying 'The *wrath* of God is revealed from heaven against all ungodliness and unrighteousness of men, who by their unrighteousness suppress the truth' (Rom. 1:18). Never do the biblical writers allow God's love, itself a vital theme, to cancel out his holiness.

Beware: when God is rejected, he is not rejected because of his power, wisdom, love, and grace. He is rejected because of his holiness. Humanity's 'unrighteousness' suppresses the truth (Rom. 1:18). It is

[7] Jonathan Edwards, *Men Naturally Are God's Enemies*, in *Works*, II:131.
[8] *Ibid.*

146

God's holiness with which we cannot live. 'They would own him in his power,' says Stephen Charnock, 'when they stood in need of deliverance; they would own him in his mercy, when they were plunged in distress; but they would not imitate him in holiness.'[9] Humanity has not given up religion; the human race is very religious. Rather, it is the holy God of the Bible who is rejected and replaced. At the heart of false religion, 'Christian' and otherwise, is a denial of God's holiness. False religions may say much that is true, but God's holiness is lost. 'To own all the rest,' Charnock continues, 'and deny him this, is to frame him as an unbeautiful monster—a deformed power. Indeed all sin is against this attribute; all sin aims in general at the being of God, but in particular at the holiness of his being.'[10] The apostle Paul describes the process in Romans 1 when he says of the human race in general: 'Claiming to be wise, they became fools, and exchanged the glory of the immortal [or 'incorruptible' KJV, NASB] God for images resembling mortal man and birds and animals and creeping things … they exchanged the truth about God for a lie and worshipped and served the creature rather than the Creator, who is blessed for ever! Amen' (Rom. 1:22-23, 25).

Pre-eminence

Packer suggests that Isaiah 6 could be used 'as a motto-text to sum up the theme of the whole Old Testament'.[11]

> In the year that King Uzziah died I saw the Lord sitting upon a throne, high and lifted up; and the train of his robe filled the temple. Above him stood the seraphim. Each had six wings: with two he covered his face, and with two he covered his feet, and with two he flew. And one called to another and said:
>
> > 'Holy, holy, holy is the LORD of hosts;
> > the whole earth is full of his glory!' (Isa. 6:1-3)

J. A. Motyer explains that 'Hebrew uses repetition to express superlatives or indicate totality.' The meaning of the threefold repetition of 'Holy, holy, holy', Motyer continues, is that 'holiness is supremely the

---

[9] Charnock, *Existence and Attributes*, II:243.
[10] *Ibid.*
[11] Packer, *Knowing God*, p. 83.

truth about God'. Indeed, a 'super superlative' had to be invented to express it. The threefold repetition indicates God's 'total and unique moral majesty'. 'Holiness is God's hidden glory; glory is God's all-present holiness.'[12] Holiness alone is given the threefold repetition because it uniquely comprehends the essence of God's nature. He is, says Poole, 'most eminently and unquestionably holy'.[13] The seraphim repeat not 'Grace, grace, grace', 'Love, love, love', or even 'Wrath, wrath, wrath', but 'Holy, holy, holy'. Why? Because 'holy' is the sum of all of God's attributes. What characterizes God, above all, is his holiness. It is his defining and distinguishing characteristic. What God is, first and foremost, is holy. While the New Testament mentions God's holiness less, 'the Old Testament revelation of the holiness of God and its demand for humility in man is presupposed throughout', says Packer.[14] The threefold repetition is found again in Psalm 99 (verses 3, 5, 9), and yet again in the concluding book of the New Testament:

> And the four living creatures, each of them with six wings, are full of eyes all round and within, and day and night they never cease to say,
>
> > 'Holy, holy, holy, is the Lord God Almighty,
> > who was and is and is to come!' (Rev. 4:8)

What is God? The heavenly worship focuses on the one essential attribute, that which summarizes what God is. Some have called holiness God's 'central and supreme perfection'. 'You alone are holy', the heavenly host chant (Rev. 15:4). God is 'righteous in all his ways' (Psa. 145:17; cf. 1 Sam. 2:2). God is 'majestic in holiness' (Exod. 15:11). Packer calls holiness *the attribute of attributes*. He says that 'all other attributes are comments on his holiness'.[15]

---

[12] Motyer, *Isaiah*, pp. 76, 77. Motyer adds, 'God's 'name' is qualified by the adjective 'holy' in the Old Testament more often than by all other qualifiers put together' (p. 77, n. 1).

[13] Poole, *Commentary*, II:337.

[14] Packer, *Knowing God*, p. 83.

[15] Packer, class notes. Packer says elsewhere, 'Holiness is the attribute displayed in all God's attributes; and thus the love of God is holy love, and must be viewed so, in explicit relation to the other aspects of God's being' (Packer, 'The Love of God: Universal and Particular', in *Collected Shorter Writings*, I:148).

Once this was widely understood, as can be seen in the classic authors. Edward Leigh (1602–71), a little-known but extraordinary leader among the Puritans, a Member of Parliament, a colonel in the Parliamentary army, and, though a lay theologian, a member of the Westminster Assembly, wrote in his *Treatise of Divinity* of God's original holiness as 'the incommunicable eminence of the divine Majesty' which is 'exalted above all, and divided from all other eminences whatsoever'. Zacharias Ursinus (1534–83) refers to the 'essential and uncreated holiness' of God, and Poole to God's holiness as the 'first cause' of all derivative holiness.[16] 'Holiness is the beauty of all God's attributes', according to Leigh. Remove holiness, and 'his wisdom would be but subtlety, his justice cruelty, his sovereignty tyranny, his mercy foolish pity'.[17] It is, says Thomas Ridgley (1667–1734) in his *Body of Divinity*, 'not so much one perfection as the harmony of all [God's] perfections, as they are opposed to sin'.[18] Holiness, according to Gurnall, is 'the glory of all God's attributes and works'. Without holiness, 'God himself would cease to be glorious; his sovereignty would degenerate into tyranny, his wisdom into craft, his justice into cruelty, etc'.[19]

Notice the commonalities in the foregoing assessments: holiness is the beauty, the harmony, the brightness, the splendour, the lustre, and varnish of the attributes, the essence of God's nature. Richard Muller summarizes the classic view of Reformed Protestantism:

[16] All cited in Muller, *Post-Reformation Reformed Dogmatics*, III:498-99.
[17] *Ibid.*, III:499.
[18] *Ibid.*, p. 500. Wilhelmus à Brakel describes holiness as 'the pure essence of the character of God' and 'the brightness of all his perfections' (*Christian's Reasonable Service*, I:121). 'The Lord is not merely called holy,' he insists, 'but is holiness itself' (*ibid.*, I:122. According to Charnock, 'If any, this attribute hath an excellency above his other perfections' (*Existence and Attributes*, II:191). It is, he says, 'the splendour of every attribute in the Godhead' (*ibid.*, II:269). 'Holiness,' agrees Thomas Boston, 'is the essential glory of the divine nature', even 'his very essence', as well as 'the lustre and varnish of all his other perfections', even 'the glory and beauty of God'. It 'hath a self-evidencing excellency in it' (*Illustration of the Doctrines*, *Works*, I:97, 103). Richard Baxter points out that 'holiness in us is called "the divine nature" (2 Pet. 1:4)' (*The Divine Life*, *Works*, III:805). John Flavel even says God's 'being and his holiness are one thing' (*An Exposition of the Assembly's Shorter Catechism*, *Works*, VI:153.
[19] Gurnall, *Christian in Complete Armour*, I:414.

God's holiness is in a sense the foundation of all his other virtues or 'excellencies' insofar as God must be characterized by this sacred self-regard or reflexive purity if he is to be perfect in wisdom, power, justice, and mercy and if he is to be properly regarded by his creation.[20]

Holiness, Muller continues, 'pervades all of his actions and interprets all of his other attributes'.[21] When God swears by it (Psa. 89:35; Amos 4:2), 'He singles it out', says Charnock, 'as if he were more concerned in the honour of it than all the rest.'[22] Indeed, it is the glory of all the rest. According to Scripture, God is 'the Holy One' (Job 6:10), 'the Holy One of Israel' (Isa. 41:20; 43:14), and the 'Holy One of Jacob' (Isa. 29:23), and it declares, 'Holy is his name' (Luke 1:49). Charnock summarizes the biblical witness:

His justice is a holy justice, his wisdom is a holy wisdom, his arm of power is a holy arm (Psa. 98:1); his truth or promise a holy promise (Psa. 105:42). Holy and true go hand in hand (Rev. 6:10). His name, which signifies all his attributes in conjunction, is holy (Psa. 103:1); yea, he is 'righteous in all his ways, and holy in all his works' (Psa. 145:17). It is the rule of all his acts, the source of all his punishments. If every attribute of the Deity were a distinct member, purity would be the form, the soul, the spirit to animate them. Without it, his patience would be an indulgence to sin, his mercy a fondness, his wrath a madness, his power a tyranny, his wisdom an unworthy subtlety. It is this [which] gives a decorum to all.[23]

John Howe, often regarded as the last of the great English Puritan divines, says that holiness 'may be styled a transcendental attribute, that as it were runs through the rest, and casts a glory upon every one'. Along with Packer, he calls holiness 'an attribute of attributes'. It is, he says, 'the very lustre and glory of his other perfections'.[24] To lose sight

---

[20] Muller, *Post-Reformation Reformed Dogmatics*, III:500.

[21] *Ibid*., III:501.

[22] Charnock, *Existence and Attributes*, II:192.

[23] *Ibid*., II:193.

[24] Howe, *Blessedness of the Righteous*, *Works*, II:59. Geerhardus Vos (1868–1949) said that holiness 'is not really an attribute to be coordinated with the other attributes distinguished in the divine nature. It is something co-extensive with and applicable to everything that characterizes him and reveals him, holy in his

of the holiness of God is to lose sight of God himself. Well might we all join with the heavenly chorus in praise of the holiness of God:

> Holy, holy, holy! Lord God Almighty!
>   Early in the morning our song shall rise to thee.
> Holy, holy, holy! Merciful and mighty,
>   God in three persons, blessed Trinity!
>
> Holy, holy, holy! All the saints adore thee,
>   Casting down their golden crowns around the glassy sea;
> Cherubim and seraphim falling down before thee,
>   Which wert, and art, and evermore shalt be.
>
> Holy, holy, holy! Though the darkness hide thee,
>   Though the eye of sinful man thy glory may not see,
> Only thou art holy; there is none beside thee,
>   Perfect in power, in love and purity.[25]

Holiness defined

Having established the *pre-eminence* of holiness among the attributes, what are the *characteristics* of holiness? The basic idea in 'holiness' is that of separation. According to Packer, the word 'holy' as applied to God not only 'signifies everything about God that sets him apart from us and makes him an object of awe, adoration, and dread to us'; but also points to the '"Godness" of God at every point', which 'covers all aspects of his transcendent greatness and moral perfection, and is characteristic of all his attributes'.[26] Classic definitions highlight God's moral purity, on the one hand, and his hatred of evil, on the other. 'God is light, and in him is no darkness at all' (1 John 1:5). He is 'of purer eyes than to see evil and cannot look at wrong' (Hab. 1:13).

---

goodness and grace, no less than in his righteousness and wrath' (Geerhardus Vos, *Biblical Theology: Old and New Testaments* [Grand Rapids, MI: Eerdmans, 1948], p. 266). R. C. Sproul adds, 'When the word holy is applied to God, it does not signify one single attribute ... the word holy calls attention to all that God is' (*Holiness of God*, p. 57).

[25] Reginald Heber, 'Holy, Holy, Holy'.

[26] Packer, 'God Is Light: Divine Holiness and Justice', in *Reformation Study Bible*, p. 168.

For example, Thomas Watson defines holiness as 'the intrinsic purity of his essence'.[27] For Edwards, it is the 'excellency and beauty of God's nature whereby his heart is disposed and delights in everything that is morally good and excellent'.[28] God, he says, is 'the infinite Fountain of purity and holiness in an infinitely pure flame' that shines with 'pure brightness', such 'that the heavens appear impure when compared with [him]'.[29] He is 'infinitely holy and opposite to sin'. It is 'his glory to be infinitely displeased with sin'.[30] Charles Hodge, writing in the nineteenth century, defined holiness as 'a general term for the moral excellence of God'.[31] God alone, he says, is 'absolutely pure and free from all limitation in his moral perfection'.[32] Holiness, Hodge continues, 'implies entire freedom from moral evil', as well as 'absolute moral perfection'.[33] Berkhof, writing in the twentieth century, demonstrated continuity in Reformed Protestantism as he defined holiness as 'that perfection of God, in virtue of which he eternally wills and maintains his own moral excellence, abhors sin, and demands purity in his moral creatures'.[34] David Wells, writing in the twenty-first century, considers the holiness of God 'a fundamental statement of who God is and what he is like. Holiness in God is everything that sets him apart from the sinful creation, and it is everything that elevates him above it in moral splendour.'[35]

[27] Thomas Watson, *The Lord's Prayer* (1692; Edinburgh: Banner of Truth Trust, 1960), p. 10. Flavel regards divine holiness as 'the infinite purity of his nature, whereby he delights in his own holiness, and the resemblance of it in his creatures, and hates all impurity' (*Exposition*, *Works*, VI:152). Charnock understands it as God's 'perfect and unpolluted freedom from all evil' (*Existence and Attributes*, II:194). Boston speaks of 'the absolute purity of his nature', as 'the perfect rectitude and integrity of the divine essence' (*Illustration of the Doctrines*, *Works*, I:97).

[28] Edwards, quoted in Gerstner, *Biblical Theology of Jonathan Edwards*, II:37.

[29] Edwards, *Great and Glorious God*, p. 171.

[30] *Ibid.*

[31] Hodge, *Systematic Theology*, I:413.

[32] *Ibid.*

[33] *Ibid.* So also, according to Shedd, 'Holiness is a general term denoting that quality in God whereby he is right (rectus) in himself, and in all his actions.' Moreover, he says, 'Holiness occupies a place second to none among the communicable attributes' (Shedd, *Dogmatic Theology*, I:363, 364).

[34] Berkhof, *Systematic Theology*, p. 74.

[35] Wells, *God in the Whirlwind*, p. 103.

Holiness revealed

How, then, does God manifest his holiness? We may examine four basic ways in which God makes his holiness known: his law, his Son, his people, and his love of righteousness coupled with his abhorrence of evil.

In God's law

First, God reveals his holiness *through his holy law*. The law of God, says the apostle Paul, is 'holy', and the commandment 'holy and right-eous and good' (Rom. 7:12). The Scriptures, he says, are 'holy Scriptures' (Rom. 1:2), and their promises are holy promises (Psa. 105:42). The law of God, says Baxter, is 'the rule of holiness'.[36] 'The moral law,' Shedd maintains, 'is the most important and clearest of the expressions of the Divine holiness.'[37]

The law of God is the life of a holy God as lived by man (cf. Eph. 4:18). Man is the image of God in the form of flesh; law is the image of God in the form of precept. Charnock terms the law 'the image of God's holiness, a transcript of his righteousness, and the efflux of his goodness'.[38] The two joined together animate the image of God in the life of man. The law is a detailing of what corresponds to the holiness of God in human behaviour and in human affairs. The law, says Bavinck, is 'the express image of God's will, as our Savior was of his person, and bearing a resemblance to the purity of his nature'.[39] Further, Bavinck continues, God 'formed the rational creature to manifest his holiness in that law whereby he was to be governed'.[40] The law of God (Heb. *torah*) is both a father's (Prov. 3:1; 4:2) and a mother's 'teaching' (Prov. 1:8; 6:20). Because God loves righteousness and hates wickedness, he publishes his law (Psa. 45:7). God's law is the rule of faith and practice

---

[36] Baxter, *The Divine Life, Works*, III:805.

[37] Shedd, *Dogmatic Theology*, I:363. Baxter defines God's law as 'the mere significa-tion of the wise and holy will of God concerning man's duty, with rewards and penalties, for the holy governing of the world' (Baxter, *The Divine Life, Works*, III:804).

[38] Charnock, *Existence and Attributes*, I:199.

[39] Bavinck, *Our Reasonable Faith*, p. 128.

[40] *Ibid.*, p. 190.

as given by a loving Father for his people's good. 'It is holy in what it enjoins us to do; just as in what it forbids us to do; and good in both', says Swinnock.[41]

We must be careful when reading our Bibles not to allow the New Testament polemic against legalism to blind us to the essential goodness and rightness of God's law. Jesus contended with the self-righteousness and legalism of the Pharisees, who 'preach, but do not practise' (Matt. 23:3ff.). Similarly, the apostle Paul contended with the legalism of the Judaizers, who were described by the Council of Jerusalem as teaching 'Unless you are circumcised according to the custom of Moses, you cannot be saved' (Acts 15:1). The Judaizers insisted that it was necessary for salvation that one be circumcised and keep the dietary laws, cleansing ordinances, and holy days of Judaism. They preached a 'different', a distorted, and 'contrary', gospel (Gal. 1:6-9; 2:11-14; etc.).

While we cannot be saved by law-keeping (because we are incapable of keeping it perfectly), the law of God does teach us what the holiness of God requires of us in every area of life. What corresponds to God's holiness in my role as a father or mother, as a son or daughter, as an employer or employee, as a citizen or ruler? What corresponds to God's holiness in my relationship with my parents, my regard for human life, my handling of sexual matters, my respect for the property of others, truth-telling, and my attitude towards the place and possessions of others (the Decalogue's last six commandments)? Do these 'good old friends', as Bishop J. C. Ryle (1816–1900) described the Ten Commandments in his nineteenth-century classic *Holiness*, still guide us?[42]

Even more fundamentally, the law reveals what corresponds to God's holiness in establishing the *who*, *how*, *what* (attitude), and *when* of worship (the Decalogue's first four commandments). Of this, God says on the occasion of the deaths of Aaron's sons Nadab and Abihu, who offered 'unauthorized' or 'strange' (KJV) fire—and by so doing, betrayed what Henry called, 'a carelessness, an irreverence, a want of

---

[41] Swinnock, *The Incomparableness of God*, *Works*, IV:449.
[42] J. C. Ryle, *Holiness: Its Nature, Hindrances, Difficulties, and Roots* (1877, 1879; Edinburgh: Banner of Truth Trust, 2014), p. 405.

faith, most surprising and lamentable'[43]—'By those who come near me I will be treated as holy, and before all the people I will be honoured' (Lev. 10:3 NASB).

God will be 'sanctified' (KJV) 'either in the *sincerity* of men's conversation, or in the *severity* of their condemnation', concludes Trapp.[44] Those who approach a holy God must do so as a holy people, holy as defined by God's holy law. If we wish to be God's holy people, God's law will be 'a lamp to [our] feet and a light to [our] path' (Psa. 119:105), leading, guiding, and directing us. We will long for God's law (119:40), be comforted by God's law (119:52), be thankful for God's law (119:62), and delight in God's law (119:77). His law for us will be sweet as honey (119:103), of more value than gold (19:10), and a joy to our hearts (119:111).

Following his exposition of the law of God in the Sermon on the Mount, Jesus said, 'You therefore must be perfect, as your heavenly Father is perfect' (Matt. 5:48). The law of God, rightly understood, guides us to that perfection. As regards the commandments, Jesus said, 'Whoever *does* them and *teaches* them [the commandments] will be called great in the kingdom of heaven' (Matt. 5:19). The apostle Paul teaches that 'the righteous requirement of the law [is to be] fulfilled in us, who walk not according to the flesh but according to the Spirit' (Rom. 8:4), meaning, said David Brown, the nineteenth-century Scottish commentator (1803–97), that 'the practical obedience which the law calls for' might be 'realized in us'.[45] The law of God is a revelation of the holiness of God in the form of commands. It is 'perfect', 'right', 'pure', 'true', and 'righteous' (Psa. 19:7-9). 'The law of God,' John Murray (1898–1975) summarizes, 'is the transcript of God's perfection; it is God's perfection coming to expression for the regulation of thought and conduct consonant with his holiness.'[46]

---

[43] Henry, *Commentary*, on Lev 3:10.

[44] Trapp, *Commentary*, I:235.

[45] Robert Jamieson, A. R. Fausset, and David Brown, *Commentary: Practical and Explanatory on the Whole Bible* (1864; Grand Rapids, MI: Zondervan, 1961), p. 1160.

[46] Murray, *Collected Writings*, II:307.

In God's attitude to good and evil

Second, the holiness of God is revealed *in his attitude towards good and evil*. On the one hand, we are repeatedly told that God is righteous and that he 'loves righteous deeds' (Psa. 11:7). 'He loves righteousness and justice' (33:5); 'the LORD loves justice' (37:28); 'Holy is he' (99:3, 5; cf. 99:9). He surrounds himself with holy angels (Rev. 14:10) and creates for himself a holy people (Isa. 62:12). No evil may dwell with him (Psa. 5:4).

On the other hand, because God is holy, he hates sin. Jonathan Edwards said, 'God's hatred of sin is infinite, by reason of the infinite contrariety of his holy nature to sin.'[47] The strongest language in the Bible is used of God's abhorrence of sin. We are told that God hates all who do iniquity and abhors the bloodthirsty and deceitful (Psa. 5:5); that God is indignant towards sin (Psa. 7:11); that he hates evil and perjury (Zech. 8:17); that he hated Judah's idolatry (Jer. 44:4); that he hated Israel's unrighteous festivals and feasts (Isa. 1:14). 'I hate, I despise your feasts, and I take no delight in your solemn assemblies', he says through Amos (Amos 5:21). He hates pride, the lying tongue, murder, false witnesses, troublemakers, and those who hurry towards evil (Prov. 6:16-19). 'I *hate* divorce' (Mal. 2:16 NASB). Various sins are declared by God to be 'abominations' (Lev. 18:22-30; Deut. 7:25; 29:17; Prov. 3:32; 8:7; Ezek. 33:29; Rev. 17:5), and others he is said to detest (Jer. 4:1; Amos 6:8; Luke 16:15).

Not only is the strongest language used, but also the strongest imagery. Sin is compared to the most nauseating, most revolting, most offensive things in human experience. It is compared to the smell of an open grave (Psa. 5:9); to a snake's poison (Psa. 140:3); to the vomit of a dog, and to the mire in which a sow wallows (2 Pet. 2:22). Ezekiel compares sin to the menstrual impurity of a woman (Ezek. 36:17). Many of the prophets compare it to harlotry, but none so graphically as Ezekiel. He likens the idolatry of Israel to the rudest sort of harlotry, as Israel 'spreads [her] legs to any passer-by' and even pays (rather than charges) her paramours (Ezek. 16:25, 33 NASB). So shocking is the imagery that the nineteenth-century Scot Patrick Fairbairn refused to

---

[47] Edwards, quoted in Gerstner, *Biblical Theology of Jonathan Edwards*, II:37.

closely comment on the passage lest he fall 'into some indelicacy'.[48] Charnock says God 'cannot look on sin without loathing it; he cannot look on sin but his heart riseth against it; it must needs be most odious to him, as that which is against the glory of his nature'.[49] God hates evil. He finds it as repulsive as we would a rat's dropping in a glass of water. Edwards vividly describes God's hatred of evil: 'The God that holds you over the pit of hell, much as one holds a spider, or some loathsome insect, over the fire, abhors you, and is dreadfully provoked … you are ten thousand times more abominable in his eyes, than the most hateful venomous serpent is in ours.'[50] God hates evil, abhors it, detests it, and will not be touched by it.

As we saw in our first study, God condemns Israel in the 50th Psalm for sinning without care. He says, 'You thought I was one like yourself. You thought I was as tolerant, as indifferent, as indulgent of sin as you are.' Commenting on this verse, Charnock asks us, 'Have we also created an idol?' He continues, 'May there not be many among us whose love to their lusts and desires of sinning without control, move them to slander God in their thoughts, rather than reform their lives, and are ready to frame, by the power of their imaginative faculty, a God not only winking, but smiling at their impurities?'[51] He adds,

> It is too common for men to fancy God not as he is, but as they would have him; strip him of his excellency for their own security. … Such notions of God render him a swinish being, and worse than the vilest idols adored by the Egyptians, when men fancy a God indulgent to their appetites and most sordid lusts.[52]

Rather, God is 'majestic in holiness' (Exod. 15:11). 'He cannot have more holiness, because he is perfectly holy; so he cannot have less holiness, because he is unchangeably holy', Thomas Watson explains.[53]

---

[48] Patrick Fairbairn, *Exposition of Ezekiel* (1851; Minneapolis: Klock & Klock, 1979), p. 169.

[49] Charnock, *Existence and Attributes*, II:251.

[50] Edwards, *Sinners in the Hands of an Angry God*, *Works*, II:10.

[51] Charnock, *Existence and Attributes*, II:243.

[52] *Ibid.*, II:244.

[53] Watson, *Body of Divinity*, p. 83.

In God's Son

Third, God reveals his holiness *through his Son*. Jesus is 'the image of the invisible God' (Col. 1:15). He is 'the radiance of the glory of God and the exact imprint of his nature' (Heb. 1:3). He is the Word that was in the beginning with God and was God and who became flesh (John 1:1, 14). To see Jesus is to see the Father (John 5:19). He makes manifest the perfections of God. He was 'that holy thing' (Luke 1:35 KJV). He lived a flawless, morally pure life. Jesus fulfilled all righteousness (Matt. 3:15). He is the perfectly obedient second Adam (Rom. 5:19). He is the 'lamb without blemish or spot' (1 Pet. 1:19). He 'offered himself without blemish to God' (Heb. 9:14). Our High Priest is 'holy, innocent, unstained' (Heb. 7:26). Jesus is holiness incarnate.

Jesus' spotless life is the one we are to imitate. He is our 'example', our pattern for holiness. We are to 'follow in his steps' (1 Pet. 2:21). We are to 'have [the] attitude … which was also in Christ Jesus', regarding others as more important than ourselves (Phil. 2:5 NASB). His resisting of the temptations of desire and power model for us the resisting of sin (Matt. 4:1-11). His sacrificial love is a model for our love (Eph. 5:21ff.; 1 John 4:10-11). The apostle Paul identifies our goal as reaching 'the stature of the fullness of Christ' (Eph. 4:13), which according to Murray 'is that of being filled with the grace, virtue, truth and wisdom, righteousness and holiness of which Christ is the embodiment'.[54]

Jesus' teaching also maps the way of moral purity. 'Blessed are the pure in heart', he teaches us (Matt. 5:8). 'Blessed are those who hunger and thirst for righteousness' (5:6). The Sermon on the Mount, the parables, his encounters with various people, his High Priestly Prayer, the Olivet Discourse: all of Jesus' teaching is designed to show us how we may live a life that is pleasing to a holy God. Jesus is the perfect revelation of the meaning of divine holiness in the life of a human being.

Nowhere is the holiness of God more clearly seen than in the cross of Christ. The price that God was willing to pay to have a holy people, that is, the suffering endured by Christ, provides the clearest of all demonstrations of our holy God's attitude towards both holiness and sin. Thomas Boston explains:

---

[54] Murray, *Collected Writings*, II:303.

Here his love to holiness and his hatred of sin is most conspicuous. All the demonstrations that ever God gave of his hatred of sin were nothing in comparison of this. Neither all the vials of wrath and judgment which God hath poured out since the world began, nor the flaming furnace of a sinner's conscience, nor the groans and roarings of the damned in hell, nor that irreversible sentence pronounced against the fallen angels, do afford such a demonstration of the divine holiness, and hatred of sin, as the death and sufferings of the blessed Redeemer.[55]

That he might drive home the point Boston asks us to consider the 'great dignity and excellency' of the one who suffered:

He was the eternal and only begotten Son of God, the brightness of his Father's glory, and the express image of his person. Yet he must descend from the throne of his majesty, divest himself of his robes of insupportable light, take upon him the form of a servant, become a curse, and bleed to death for sin. Did ever sin appear so hateful to God as here? To demonstrate God's infinite holiness, and hatred of sin, he would have the most glorious and most excellent person in heaven and earth to suffer for it. He would have his own Son to die on a disgraceful cross, and be exposed to the terrible flames of divine wrath, rather than sin should live, and his holiness remain for ever disparaged by the violations of his law.[56]

In the incarnation of Jesus Christ, John Murray summarizes, 'the holiness of God comes to perfect expression and illustration'.[57]

In God's people

Fourth, God created a holy people who would demonstrate to the world his holiness *by obeying his holy law and imitating his holy character*. Moses told Israel that God had set them apart from other nations: 'For you are a people holy to the LORD your God. The LORD your God has chosen you to be a people for his treasured possession, out of all the peoples who are on the face of the earth' (Deut. 7:6; cf. Lev. 20:26).

---

[55] Boston, *Illustration of the Doctrines, Works*, I:101.
[56] *Ibid.*
[57] Murray, *Collected Writings*, II:308.

The way of holiness for Israel was the way of *obedience*. The people of God are urged to 'remember and do all my commandments, and be holy to your God' (Num. 15:40). Moses warns them that they will be God's holy people only if they keep his commandments and walk in his ways (Deut. 28:8-9).

The way of holiness is also to be found in the way of *imitation*: 'For I am the LORD who brought you up out of the land of Egypt to be your God. You shall therefore be holy, for I am holy' (Lev. 11:45). This means that the people of God are to be 'separate from sin, and dedicated to God, in conformity to whom stands our happiness', says Trapp.[58] Israel failed to do this, and instead of God being glorified through Israel's obedience, his name was 'blasphemed among the Gentiles' because of their disobedience, and judgment fell upon them (Rom. 2:24). Jesus' warning was realized: 'Therefore I tell you, the kingdom of God will be taken away from you and given to a people producing its fruits' (Matt. 21:43). The kingdom was taken away from Israel as a political entity, and given to the church. Like Israel, the church is also called to holiness. It also must produce the fruit of holiness in holy living. The apostle Peter repeats the Old Testament requirement laid upon God's people: 'But as he who called you is holy, you also be holy in all your conduct, since it is written [quoting Lev. 11:45], "You shall be holy, for I am holy"' (1 Pet. 1:15-16). We (the church) are to be God's 'holy nation' so that we 'may proclaim the excellencies of him who called [us] out of darkness into his marvellous light' (1 Pet. 2:9).

Christians, then, like the ancient Hebrews, are to 'be imitators of God, as beloved children' (Eph. 5:1). Believers, says Herman Venema (1697–1787), are to 'imitate his actions and affections by conforming themselves to his holiness, so that they may reflect his image in themselves and in their lives'. God is 'a perfect pattern to us, the exemplar of all holiness, and therefore we should be perfect as he is perfect'.[59] Human holiness 'consists in conformity unto God', said Joseph Caryl (1602–73) in his twelve-volume *Exposition of Job*. We are to imitate God's attributes of patience, mercy, justice, faithfulness, truth, and love. We partake of his nature (as Peter describes

---

[58] Trapp, *Commentary*, V:706.
[59] Cited in Muller, *Post-Reformation Reformed Dogmatics*, III:501-2.

in 2 Pet. 1:4) 'when we love what God loves, when we hate what God hates, when, what pleases God, pleaseth us also'.[60] We purify ourselves, because he is pure (1 John 3:3). Murray, commenting on Ephesians 4:24 and Colossians 3:10, says, 'Likeness to God is the ultimate pattern of sanctification.'[61] Edwards put it this way: 'A true love to God must begin with a delight in his holiness, and not with a delight in any other attribute; for no other attribute is truly lovely without this, and no otherwise than as … it derives its loveliness from this.'[62]

The apostle Paul often summarizes our holiness as the goal of God's eternal plan. He says we were chosen in Christ 'before the foundation of the world, that we should be *holy* and blameless before him' (Eph. 1:4). The apostle identifies the work of the cross as having this single purpose: to create a holy people. We were 'predestined', says the apostle Paul, 'to be conformed to the image of his Son' (Rom. 8:29). We were reconciled to God by Christ that he might 'present [us] *holy* and blameless and above reproach before him' (Col. 1:22). The apostle says that Christ loved the church and gave himself up for her, 'that he might sanctify her, having cleansed her by the washing of water with the word, so that he might present the church to himself in splendour, without spot or wrinkle or any such thing, that she might be *holy* and without blemish' (Eph. 5:25-27). The apostle prays that God might 'sanctify [us] completely' and our 'whole spirit and soul and body be kept blameless' (1 Thess. 5:23). Gurnall argues that Christ would be but a 'minister of sins' if his design had been only to 'procure man a pardon, and not to restore his lost holiness'.[63] This would have 'set sin in the throne', and would have obtained 'a liberty for the creature to dishonour God without control'.[64] The point of redemption, the point of the whole *ordo salutis*—from election to justification, to sanctification, to perseverance, to glorification—is that we should be a holy people and, as such, should represent God in an unholy world. Thomas Watson asks,

> What are all the showers of ordinances for, but to rain down righteousness upon us, and make us holy? What are the promises

[60] Muller, *Post-Reformation Reformed Dogmatics*, III:502.
[61] Murray, *Collected Writings*, II:306.
[62] Edwards, quoted in Gerstner, *Biblical Theology of Jonathan Edwards*, II:36.
[63] Gurnall, *Christian in Complete Armour*, I:415.
[64] *Ibid.*

for, but to encourage holiness? What is the sending of the Spirit into the world for, but to anoint us with the holy unction? 1 John 2:20. What are all afflictions for, but to make us partakers of God's holiness? Heb. 12:10. What are mercies for, but loadstones to draw us to holiness? What is the end of Christ's dying, but that his blood might wash away our unholiness? 'Who gave himself for us, to purify unto himself a peculiar people.' Titus 2:14. So that if we are not holy, *we cross God's great design in the world*.[65]

Jesus Christ gave himself for us not only 'to redeem us from all lawlessness and to purify for himself a people for his possession', but that we should be a people 'who are zealous for good works', who have renounced 'ungodliness and worldly passions' and who 'live self-controlled, upright, and godly lives in the present age' (Titus 2:11-14; cf. 1:15; 3:8, 14). The Christian life may be summarized as it was by Jerry Bridges in the title of his classic work: *The Pursuit of Holiness*.[66] The writer to the Hebrews urges us to 'Pursue' (NASB) or 'Strive … for the holiness without which no one will see the Lord' (Heb. 12:14), leading Poole to remark, 'The result and quintessence of all the graces of the Spirit is holiness.'[67] Owen, commenting on this theme, refers to holiness as 'the means, the way to that eternal life, which … is [God's] gift by Jesus Christ'. He explains: 'Though it be neither the cause, matter, nor condition of our justification, yet it is the way appointed of God for us to walk in for the obtaining of salvation … and none shall ever come to that end who walketh not in that way; for without holiness it is impossible to see God.'[68]

Holiness may be pursued successfully because believers have been transformed by the power of the gospel (Rom. 1:16). We have become new creatures in Christ (2 Cor. 5:17). We have been sanctified, definitively, by the Holy Spirit (1 Cor. 1:30; Rom. 6:1ff.). Listen to the way that the apostle Paul exhorts the Corinthians. Citing Leviticus 26:12 ('I will be their God, and they shall be my people') and Isaiah 52:11 ('be separate from them … touch no unclean thing … and I will be a father to you'), he then urges, 'Since we have these promises, beloved, let us

---

[65] Watson, *Body of Divinity*, p. 85 (emphasis added).
[66] Jerry Bridges, *The Pursuit of Holiness* (Colorado Springs: NavPress, 1978).
[67] Poole, *Commentary*, III:871.
[68] Owen, *Communion with God*, *Works*, II:186.

cleanse ourselves from every defilement of body and spirit, bringing holiness to completion in the fear of God' (2 Cor. 7:1).

Holiness must be pursued to completion. The blood of Christ cleanses us from all sin (1 John 1:7), yet we are urged to 'cleanse ourselves from every defilement'. We are God's holy nation (1 Pet. 2:9), yet we must 'bring holiness to completion'. Murray says of this passage, 'We ourselves are to be actively engaged in cleansing ourselves from ... defilement.'[69]

The apostle Paul may exhort us in this fashion, urging actions for which we have no *natural* capacity, because we have been raised up with Christ to live a new life (Rom. 6:1ff.). That we might be a holy people, Christ has given us his *Holy* Spirit, who is himself a chief benefit of redemption, and whose task it is to apply the blood-bought benefits of Christ, regenerating, indwelling, sanctifying, and preserving us. He is our 'Helper' (John 14:16), the 'Spirit of truth' who 'dwells with [us] and will be in [us]' (John 14:17), who teaches us all things (1 Cor. 2:10-13) and leads us into 'all the truth' (John 16:13). We are born again by the Spirit (John 3:1ff.), walk by the Spirit (Gal. 5:16), and are led by the Spirit (Rom. 8:14), and his fruit means transformation of life (Gal. 5:22-23). Sin need no longer be master over us (Rom. 6:14). We become a holy people, not by our own exertions, but by the power of the Holy Spirit. Our 'new selves' that are to be 'put on' have been 'created after the likeness of God', says the apostle Paul, 'in true righteousness and holiness' (Eph. 4:24). This is practical holiness, life holiness, heart holiness. Let us then earnestly pursue holiness. 'Let the time past suffice us,' urges J. C. Ryle, 'to have been content with a half-and-half holiness.'[70]

Above all, our God is a holy God. His holiness is a thing of beauty, whether revealed in his law, in his attitude to good and evil, in his Son, or in his people. 'He that sees the beauty of holiness, or true moral good,' Edwards explains,

> sees the greatest and most important thing in the world, which
> is the fullness of all things, without which all the world is empty,
> no better than nothing, yea, worse than nothing. Unless this is

[69] Murray, *Collected Writings*, II:296.
[70] Ryle, *Holiness*, p. 406.

seen, nothing is seen that is worth seeing; for there is no other true excellency or beauty. Unless this be understood, nothing is understood that is worthy of the exercise of the noble faculty of understanding.

Holiness, Edwards continues, 'is the beauty of the Godhead, and the divinity of Divinity … the good of the infinite Fountain of good'.[71]

[71] Jonathan Edwards, *Select Works of Jonathan Edwards*, Vol. 3: *Treatise Concerning the Religious Affections* (London: Banner of Truth Trust, 1961), p. 200.

EIGHT

God's Holiness and Ours

But as he who called you is holy, you also be holy in all your conduct, since it is written, 'You shall be holy, for I am holy.'

—1 Peter 1:15-16

HOW are we to respond to the holiness of God? We finished the last chapter urging that holiness be pursued. The apostle Peter urges that we be holy because God is holy. Because 'he who called [us] is holy', we in turn must 'also be holy in all [our] conduct', which means, 'Separate from sin,' says Trapp, 'and be dedicated to God.'[1]

Let us ask ourselves several questions which will help us to determine if we have given due consideration to this 'attribute of attributes'. Augustine acknowledged in his *Confessions* that as a young man he would pray for deliverance from the bondage of his lust, yet the secret whispers of his heart were *non adhuc Domine*—not yet, Lord. Is the love of holiness and the abhorrence of evil characteristic of us?

Cost of atonement

First, *do I have a high regard for the cost of atoning for sin?* How may a polluted humanity approach a God who is the 'Father of lights', who dwells in 'unapproachable light' (James 1:17; 1 Tim. 6:16)? What did it take? What was required? Nothing less than the suffering of the infinitely holy, perfect God-Man Jesus Christ.[2] Or do I imagine that I can

---

[1] Trapp, *Commentary*, V:706.
[2] We will have much more to say on this as we look in Chapters 9 and 10 at the justice and righteousness of God.

approach the God who is 'a consuming fire' on the basis of my own virtue (Heb. 12:29)? Is moral living enough? Is sincere (though false) religion enough? Do I flatter myself by thinking that my (moral and religious) righteousness is sufficient? If so, I have not understood the holiness of God. Isaiah responds to his vision of God on his throne by saying, 'Woe is me! For I am lost; for I am a man of unclean lips, and I dwell in the midst of a people of unclean lips; for my eyes have seen the King, the LORD of hosts!' (Isa. 6:5)

When one understands the holiness of God, the result is an overwhelming sense of guilt and condemnation. 'The radiant beams of God's holiness had permeated every nook and cranny within Isaiah's being,' says David Wells, 'illuminating it all as if by a blinding flash of lightning.'[3] Woe is me, he says. Woe is all of us, we moan. 'We are never so low in our own eyes,' says Swinnock, 'as when we see the most high God.'[4]

'Then one of the seraphim flew to me, having in his hand a burning coal that he had taken with tongs from the altar' (Isa. 6:6). God sends a seraph with a burning coal, 'symbolic', says Motyer, 'of the wrath of God (Gen. 3:24; Num. 11:1-3), his unapproachable holiness (Exod. 3:2-6; 19:18-25), and the context of his holy law (Deut. 4:12, 33, 36)'.[5] The coal comes from the altar, the place 'where the holy God accepted, and was satisfied by, blood sacrifice (Lev. 17:11)', continues Motyer.[6]

'And he touched my mouth and said: "Behold, this has touched your lips; your guilt is taken away, and your sin atoned for"' (Isa. 6:7). The coal is applied to Isaiah's lips, showing, says Motyer, 'how God ministers to the sinner at the point of confessed need'. The result is forgiveness. Sin is atoned for (Heb. *kipper*), paying 'the price which justice required', and pointing ahead to the price that Jesus would pay for our sin (cf. John 12:41; Acts 28:25-27).[7]

Not the blood of bulls and goats but the blood of a lamb 'without blemish or spot' offered on the altar of Calvary was required (Heb. 10:4; 1 Pet. 1:19). The petitions denied in the garden of Gethsemane,

---

[3] Wells, *God in the Whirlwind*, p. 113.
[4] Swinnock, *The Incomparableness of God, Works*, IV:484.
[5] Motyer, *Isaiah*, pp. 77-78.
[6] *Ibid*., p. 78.
[7] *Ibid*.

the threefold plea that the cup would pass from Christ, and the cross be avoided, prove the necessity of the shed blood of the new covenant if sinners were to be saved (Matt. 26:36-46; Mark 10:45; Matt. 26:28). Nothing less would do.

Those who disputed the substitutionary view of the atonement were greeted by Anselm (1033–1109), in his classic *Cur Deus Homo*, with this retort: 'You have not considered what a heavy weight sin is.' Why did God become man? Anselm answers: because only man should pay the debt that man owes. Yet the debt is so great that only God could pay it. Consequently, it was necessary that the Saviour be both God and man.

Calvin elaborates beautifully on the same theme, arguing that it was imperative that our Redeemer be both true God and true man:

> It was his task to swallow up death. Who but the Life could do this? It was his task to conquer sin. Who but very Righteousness could do this? It was his task to rout the powers of world and air. Who but a power higher than world and air could do this? Now in short, since neither as God alone could he feel death, nor as man alone could he overcome it, he coupled human nature with divine that to atone for sin he might submit the weakness of the one to death; and that, wrestling with death by the power of the other nature, he might win victory for us.[8]

'You were bought with a price,' says the apostle Paul; 'so glorify God in your body' (1 Cor. 6:20). Those who seek peace with God through any lesser price than that of the blood of the God-Man Jesus Christ have not understood the holiness of God nor his abhorrence of sin.

Careful obedience

Second, *do I have a serious concern about sin and the need for careful obedience?* The apostle Paul teaches that 'the wages of sin is death' (Rom. 6:23). 'The soul who sins shall die', says the prophet Ezekiel (Ezek. 18:4). 'Sin is the great murderer,' said the Puritan William Greenhill (1591–1671); 'it let death into the world, and keeps death alive.'[9] One sin cast Adam and Eve out of the garden (Gen. 3). One

---

[8] Calvin, *Institutes*, II:xii.2, p. 466.
[9] William Greenhill, *An Exposition of Ezekiel* (1645–67, 1863; Edinburgh: Banner of Truth Trust, 1994), p. 440.

sin led to the destruction of Nadab and Abihu (Lev. 10:1-2). One sin led God to strike down Uzzah (2 Sam. 6:6-7). One sin resulted in the deaths of Ananias and Sapphira (Acts 5:5, 10). Violate one commandment and one is guilty of breaking all the commandments (James 2:10; Gal. 3:10). The Bible's serious outlook on sin, all sin, and even one sin, makes a casual attitude towards sin impossible.

Timothy is urged not to flirt with but to 'flee' from the 'love of money', which is 'a root of all kinds of evils', and to 'pursue righteousness, godliness, faith, love, steadfastness, gentleness'. He is to 'fight the good fight of the faith' (1 Tim. 6:10-12). 'Discipline' (NASB) or 'train yourself for godliness', the apostle urges (4:7).

The apostle employs vigorous, energetic language to describe how holiness is to be attained. That which must be pursued is that which cannot be attained apart from pursuit. It will not be passively acquired or easily attained. 'So flee youthful passions', he tells us. Yet do not do that alone. 'Flee' is the negative instruction. 'Flee youthful passions *and* pursue righteousness, faith, love, and peace, along with those who call on the Lord from a pure heart' (2 Tim. 2:22; cf. 1 Cor. 6:18). *Pursue* righteousness. *Pursue* faith. *Pursue* love. *Pursue* purity of heart. Actively, deliberately, energetically pursue righteousness. We are likened to soldiers, athletes, hard-working farmers, and industrious workers (2 Tim. 2:3-7, 15). 'Let everyone who names the name of the Lord *depart* from iniquity' (2:19). Do not play with it. Do not converse with it. Do not negotiate with it. Leave it. Run. 'Have nothing to do with' foolishness (2:23). 'Avoid such people', he says of the ungodly (3:5).

The apostle Paul likens the Christian life to a good fight and a race (2 Tim. 4:7). He reminds Titus of the graciousness of our salvation: the 'goodness' and 'loving kindness' of God that 'saved us, not because of works done by us in righteousness, but according to his own mercy' (Titus 3:4-5). We have been washed by 'regeneration' and by the 'renewal of the Holy Spirit'. This Spirit has been 'poured out on us richly through Jesus Christ our Saviour' (3:5-6). We have been 'justified by his grace' (3:7). Paul's application then is: 'I want you to insist on these things, so that those who have believed in God may be careful to devote themselves to good works' (3:8). 'Be careful,' he says, 'to devote'—using another energetic word. He sends greetings and then repeats himself: 'And let our people learn to devote themselves to good works, so as to help cases of urgent need, and not be unfruitful' (3:14).

The writer of the Hebrews tells us to 'strive to enter [our eternal] rest' (Heb. 4:11), and to 'strive ... for the holiness without which no one will see the Lord' (12:14). Those who understand the holiness of God will be eager to obey God comprehensively and precisely, knowing that this is what pleases him. 'Let not that man think he makes any progress in holiness,' warns John Owen, 'who walks not over the bellies of his lusts.'[10]

The Puritan Richard Rogers (*c.* 1551–1618), when criticized as too conscientious in his Christian walk, responded, 'Oh, sir, I serve a precise God.' Few today share his concern. The Puritans were scorned as 'precisionists'. Were we to attract that label we should wear it as a badge of honour. Our holy God seeks a people who are above reproach, who have no interest in accommodating his commands to their own convenience, who eschew compromise, who keep their promises even when it hurts (Psa. 15:4), and who walk with integrity in all things. May it be said of us as was said of those rebuilding the temple in the days of Jehoash: that no accounting was necessary, 'for they dealt honestly' (2 Kings 12:15). May be it said of us as was said of Daniel at a time when his enemies were attempting to entrap him: 'they could find no ground for complaint or any fault, because he was faithful, and no error or fault was found in him' (Dan. 6:4).

The United States Marine Corps' Officer Candidate School is a rigorous ten-week, humbling, ego-shattering, body-breaking course designed to turn young citizens into Marine officers. Among the tests that candidates must endure is a four-mile rapid-paced hike carrying fifty-pound packs. They walk fast, but they may not run. Among the rules are restrictions on their use of their canteens. They may drink from them. They may pour the contents over their heads. However, they may not pour out any of the water on the ground.

In a recent session, the highest-ranked candidate—the leading candidate in the classroom and in the field, a man recognized by the

---

[10] Owen, *Mortification, Works*, VI:14.

others as the outstanding participant—took a long drink, poured more water over his head, and then poured the small amount remaining onto the ground. When confronted, he said it was *just a little bit* of water. Confronted further, he became defensive and argued that it was *no big deal*. The Marines dropped him, the outstanding candidate, from the programme, with only two weeks of the ten-week programme remaining.

Thus cultural relativism confronts the reality of life and death on the battlefield, and loses. A few drops of water is no big deal. However, following commands is a big deal. Recognizing and admitting mistakes is a big deal. Later it was explained: We cannot test moral character. Candidates can give correct answers to any ethics test we might give. We know a candidate's character only by what he does. Those who lack integrity in the little things will lack integrity in the big things as well. Traditional military standards at times demonstrate more moral sense than much of the contemporary Christian community.

We are ethically sloppy today. Our obedience is not careful. Most of us will avoid committing notorious public sins, of the kind, for example, which make the newspapers. Most of us will never have a Watergate. However, the rubber of holy living hits the road of life in the little things, the average things. At seminary, a casual attitude towards sin was most apparent at the reserved shelf of the library. Books which were never supposed to leave that shelf had a way of disappearing around final exams time. No big deal? It may seem trivial, but at root the problem is the lack of honesty and integrity—that is, sin. 'Be killing sin,' Owen warns, 'or it will be killing you.'[11] It is only 'when sin lets us alone' that 'we may let sin alone'.[12]

Most of us are haters of sins which are not our own, but very tolerant, if not indulgent, of the sins with which we are tempted. We suffer from what Calvin describes as 'the almost inborn disease of being over strict and severe critics of others while approving of our own sins'.[13] Often we display the 'little white lie' syndrome: 'It was just a little sin', we say smugly; or 'I drank a little too much', we say with a twinkle in

[11] Owen, *Mortification, Works*, VI:9.

[12] *Ibid.*, p. 11.

[13] John Calvin, *A Harmony of the Gospels: Matthew, Mark, and Luke* (1555; Grand Rapids, MI: Eerdmans, 1972), II:94.

our eye. 'It was no big deal', or 'I didn't hurt anyone.' We are safe in hating murder and rape, because they may not be our problem or temptation. Yet how do we do in the areas in which we are vulnerable? What about the petty sins of whining and grumbling, griping and complaining (Phil. 2:14; 1 Cor. 10:10)? What about immodesty, gossip, materialism, and greed? 'We are apt to entertain slight thoughts of many sins', Boston warns.[14] How is our highway morality? How honest are we in filling out time-cards, or in giving an honest day's work? Do we cheat on tests? Or on homework? Do we lie to our parents about where we have been? Do we obey our parents? Do we obey the laws of the land? Is our 'yes', 'yes' and our 'no', 'no', as Jesus says they must be (Matt. 5:37)? Are we there at 8:00 p.m. when we say we will be there at 8:00 p.m.? Do we fulfil our obligations? Do we pay our bills on time? How about male and female relationships? Is there integrity in our relationships? Are we honest? Are we creating false hopes? Do we think that the God who sacrificed his own Son because of sin is as casual towards sin as we are?

Boston urges us to 'see the excellency of true gospel-holiness'.[15] If we are to draw near to God, we must 'cleanse [our] hands' and 'purify [our] hearts' (James 4:8). Carelessness about speech, viewing habits, drinking habits, work ethic, honesty, and integrity are epidemic and betray ignorance of the holiness of God, his love of righteousness, and his hatred of evil.

Grief over sin

Third, *do I grieve over sin or indulge it?* When Jesus said, 'Blessed are those who mourn', he was speaking primarily of our mourning over our sins (Matt. 5:4). Henry calls this 'penitential mourning', identifying it with the 'godly sorrow' of 2 Corinthians 7:11, 'a sorrow according to God; sorrow for sin, with an eye to Christ'.[16] Do I mourn over sin, or am I entertained by it? Do I abhor evil or laugh at it? Do I grieve over sin or play with it? Bible saints, when they confess their sin, do so with the utmost seriousness. Read the great prayers of confession in the

---

[14] Boston, *Illustration of the Doctrines, Works*, I:100.
[15] *Ibid.*, I:103.
[16] Henry, *Commentary*, on Matt. 5:4.

Bible, such as Psalm 51, Daniel 9, or Nehemiah 9. Daniel prays with 'fasting and sackcloth and ashes' (Dan. 9:3). Listen to just the beginning of his prayer:

> I prayed to the Lord my God and made confession, saying, 'O Lord, the great and awesome God, who keeps covenant and steadfast love with those who love him and keep his commandments, we have sinned and done wrong and acted wickedly and rebelled, turning aside from your commandments and rules' (Dan. 9:4-5).

This is no mere 'Forgive me for all my sins.' Five times in his first sentence he essentially says the same thing: the nation has 'sinned', 'done wrong', 'acted wickedly', 'rebelled', and turned 'aside'. He will go on to acknowledge 'open shame' and 'treachery' (verse 7), failure to obey, failure to walk in God's laws (verse 10), transgressions (verse 11), iniquities (verse 13), and wickedness (verse 15). 'Here observe the variety of words he makes use of to set forth the greatness of the provocations', Henry urges.[17] Daniel piles up the vocabulary so that his confession might be comprehensive and earnest. The Westminster Confession of Faith teaches us not to pray mere general prayers of confession, but to confess 'particular sins, particularly' (XV.5). Similarly, David confesses his transgressions, his sin, and his iniquity, and prays that he might be washed, cleansed, purified, delivered, have his sins blotted out, his heart cleansed, his spirit renewed, and his joy restored (Psa. 51). He does not trifle with sin, to say the least.

We should respond to sin in a manner similar to what the apostle Paul described of the Corinthian assembly: 'For see what earnestness this godly grief has produced in you, but also what eagerness to clear yourselves, what indignation, what fear, what longing, what zeal, what punishment!' (2 Cor. 7:11). Previously he had spoken to them of their failure to cleanse the church of immorality, and that they should have 'mourn[ed]' and must 'remove the wicked man from among [them]' (1 Cor. 5:2, 13 NASB). Yet now there was earnestness, godly grief, indignation, longing, and zeal, and the apostle commends them for it. James describes the proper response to sin: 'Be wretched and mourn and weep. Let your laughter be turned to mourning and your joy to

---

[17] Henry, *Commentary*, on Dan. 9:4ff.

gloom. Humble yourselves before the Lord, and he will exalt you' (James 4:9-10). Mourn 'savoury and soakingly', says Trapp, 'with a deep and downright sorrow'. And weep: 'Look not upon sin with dry eyes; paint every sin with a tear.'[18] This is the antithesis of flippancy.

When I was a young boy my pastor preached a sermon I will never forget. Entitling it 'The Unfunny Joke', he talked about how most humour in popular culture is based on immoral behaviour. 'My, my, isn't sex funny!' he said sarcastically. 'The comedians treat us to a constant barrage of winks and nods and double entendres. And then there's the drunk. Isn't drunkenness hilarious! He's slurring his speech. He's stumbling about. The happy drunk!' Then he leaned over the pulpit and said to us, 'If you think promiscuity is funny, why don't you come to my office when a fifteen-year-old girl in tears tells me she's pregnant. Sit with me then and have a good laugh. Or come with me down to our Skid Row mission and see the wasted lives. Come and laugh at the doctor who is lying in his own vomit in the gutter, his career destroyed, his family ruined, and then come back and tell me how funny sin is.'

Years ago, while on my way home from the UK, I watched my first James Bond movie. The Bond genre is considered fairly benign by today's standards. Yet his decadent lifestyle was glamourized throughout. Every half hour or so he was in bed with yet another woman. Yet this was supposed to be entertaining, even admirable and enviable. I determined not to watch another. Shortly thereafter a church deacon proudly showed me his complete collection of Bond films. Does he not see the discrepancy? I asked myself. Do we? Are we amused by Bond's sort of antics? Is this the kind of lifestyle we want to emulate? If not, why are we giving financial aid to this film industry so it can promote that which is destructive of Christian discipleship?

Let us ask ourselves: By what are we allowing ourselves to be entertained? Do we really think sin is desirable, humorous? Do we enjoy watching people destroy their souls? Do we enjoy watching devilish deeds, knowing the hellish consequences? Is my outlook fair to the *consequences* of sin? Is my attitude fair to the broken lives, the shattered families, and personal nightmares and suffering which are sure to

---

[18] Trapp, *Commentary*, V:701.

result? Does my attitude at all reflect the holy indignation of our Holy Father, who *hates*, utterly hates, sin? If we are not to 'touch' what is unclean, is it conceivable that we would be entertained by it (2 Cor. 6:17-18)? If we are to hate 'even the garment stained by the flesh'— which garment is, of course, an inanimate object and cannot be inherently evil—is it conceivable that we would be dancing about at the edge of sin (Jude 22-23)? Jude's point is, says William Jenkyn (1613–85) in his treasured commentary on Jude, 'that they should hate all incentives, occasions, inducements, or inlets to sin, and that both in respect of themselves and others'.[19]

How seriously are we to take sin? How careful is our obedience to be? Jesus said it would be better to pluck out the offending eye and cut off the offending hand and throw them away than—what?—than that 'your whole body be thrown into hell' (Matt. 5:29-30). Could it be put more strongly than that? Our ethical sloppiness, our foolishness, is inexcusable given the urgency with which our Lord Jesus instructs us. God requires that we mortify (Rom. 8:13)—also described as 'crucify'—the flesh and its passions and desires (Gal. 5:24). This means, Charnock insists, that a person ought to 'strike as full and deadly a blow at his lusts, as was struck at Christ upon the cross, and make them as certainly die as the Redeemer did'.[20] 'Sin must be loathsome to us,' says Baxter, 'because it is contrary to the holiness of God.'[21]

Grace and holiness

Fourth, *do I make grace a licence to sin or a motivation for holiness?* When the apostle Paul contemplates his past, as a persecutor of the church, and his present apostleship, he says, 'But by the grace of God I am what I am, and his grace towards me was not in vain. On the contrary, I worked harder than any of them, though it was not I, but the grace of God that is with me' (1 Cor. 15:10). Grace motivated him to labour 'all the more' (NASB). Grace understood and received enabled and motivated the apostle. It is by the 'mercies of God', understood

[19] William Jenkyn, *An Exposition upon the Epistle of Jude* (1653; Beaver Falls, PA: Soli Deo Gloria, n.d.), p. 355.
[20] Charnock, *Existence and Attributes*, II:214.
[21] Baxter, *The Divine Life*, *Works*, III:806.

and received, that we are prompted 'to present [our] bodies as a living sacrifice, holy and acceptable to God' (Rom. 12:1). The mercies of God motivate holiness. 'Let the consideration of them engage you to all manner of holiness and new obedience', says Poole.[22] Grace, not just law, trains us 'to renounce ungodliness and worldly passions, and to live self-controlled, upright, and godly lives' (Titus 2:11-12). 'Without the holiness of God,' warns David Wells, 'sin has no meaning and grace has no point.'[23] Does God's grace in Christ motivate me to new heights of holiness?

Or do I say, 'I'm not under law but under grace', even quoting the Bible as support (Gal. 5:18)? Do I hide behind 'All things are lawful' or 'eat and drink and be joyful' (1 Cor. 6:12; 10:23; Eccles. 8:15), and use such verses to justify sin? Am I guilty of saying, as the apostle Paul insists that we must not say, 'Why not do evil that good may come?' (Rom. 3:8; cf. 6:1). Gurnall warns us, 'The declarations of God's free grace, made on purpose to melt sinners' hearts, and draw them from their lusts to Christ, how oft are they abused to wedge and harden them in their sins, and keep them from him!'[24]

Jude warns of 'certain people', even 'ungodly people', who 'pervert the grace of our God into sensuality' (Jude 4). Because grace is free, it can be corrupted. 'The holiness of God is injured,' says Charnock, 'when men study arguments from the holy word of God to colour and shelter their crimes.' Do we in these ways presume on God's grace?

[22] Poole, *Commentary*, III:521.

[23] Wells, *God in the Wasteland*, p. 144. Wells goes on to say: 'for it is God's holiness that gives to the one its definition and to the other its greatness. Without the holiness of God, sin is merely human failure but not failure before God, in relation to God. It is failure without the standard by which we know it to have fallen short. It is failure without the presumption of guilt, failure without retribution, failure without any serious moral meaning. And without the holiness of God, grace is no longer grace because it does not arise from the dark clouds of judgment that obscured the cross and exacted the damnation of the Son in our place. Furthermore, without holiness, grace loses its meaning as grace, a free gift of the God who, despite his holiness and because of his holiness, has reconciled sinners to himself in the death of his Son. And without holiness, faith is but a confidence in the benevolence of life, or perhaps merely confidence in ourselves. Sin, grace, and faith are emptied of any but a passing meaning if they are severed from their roots in the holiness of God' (pp. 144-45).

[24] Gurnall, *Christian in Complete Armour*, II:234.

Do we make provision for the flesh and give in to sin, complacently reasoning, 'God understands' or 'God will forgive me' (Rom. 13:14)? By such thinking, 'Grace hath been turned into wantonness, and the abundance of grace been used as a blast to increase the flames of sin,' says Charnock. 'This is to feed the roots of hell with the dews of heaven', he insists.[25] Do we imagine that we can do as we please because God will forgive us? Will he do so? It is presumption to think so when the apostle Paul warns those who use their Christian freedom 'as an opportunity for the flesh' that they 'will not inherit the kingdom of God' (Gal. 5:13-21).

God's unconditional grace is not a *licence* to sin but an *inspiration* to holiness. We love God and love the brethren because he first loved us (1 John 4:10-11, 19). Jesus teaches that the one who is forgiven much loves much (Luke 7:47). God's redemptive love prompts and motivates our love. Because God loves us in Christ Jesus, we love him in return, and have no higher ambition than to please him (2 Cor. 5:9). Because God loves us, we love neighbours and even enemies, turning the other cheek, walking the extra mile, and giving the coat off our backs (Matt. 5:43-48). Grace, mercy and love ought to motivate us to pursue holiness.

Pursue trials and temptations

Fifth, *are trials and temptations a stimulus to holiness or the occasion of bitterness?* There are many obstacles to holiness. We face a trinity of evil: the world, the flesh, and the devil. We are surrounded by both trials and seductions. We are weak, and there is much that might entice us. Do I embrace my trials and temptations as for my good? Can I say with James, 'Count it all joy, my brothers, when you meet trials of various kinds, for you know that the testing of your faith produces steadfastness. And let steadfastness have its full effect, that you may be perfect and complete, lacking in nothing' (James 1:2-4)? Trials 'perfect' and 'complete' the saints. Can I consider these trials 'all joy', that is, 'full joy', says Trapp, 'complete and perfect'?[26] Can I 'rejoice', even 'exult in our tribulations', along with the apostle Paul (Rom. 5:3 NASB)? 'We rejoice in our sufferings, knowing that suffering produces

---

[25] Charnock, *Existence and Attributes of God*, II:246.
[26] Trapp, *Commentary*, V:693.

endurance, and endurance produces character, and character produces hope, and hope does not put us to shame, because God's love has been poured into our hearts through the Holy Spirit who has been given to us' (Rom. 5:3-5; cf. 1 Pet. 1:6-7).

No doubt these trials, temptations, and tribulations are difficult. Yet they are designed to encourage us in the path of holiness. Unpleasant circumstances are designed by our heavenly Father 'for our good, that we may share his holiness' (Heb. 12:10).

Perhaps you came from a broken home, or were neglected as a child, or were the victim of a crime, or were tempted by an overpowering image of illicit pleasure. Do you embrace your God-given circumstances, or are you embittered against God because he put you in a 'bad environment'? Do you blame him for your moral failures because he placed you in a bad family, a bad neighbourhood, a bad school, or among bad friends? Do you blame him for bringing a beautiful person by and thereby causing you to lust? Do you, like Adam in the garden, say, 'The woman whom you gave to be with me, she gave me fruit of the tree, and I ate' (Gen. 3:12)?

Life is not easy. The path to holiness is not easy. Little growth is possible apart from struggle and exertion. So it is that James must exhort those who have met 'trials of various kinds' (James 1:2) to 'draw near to God, and he will draw near to you. Cleanse your hands, you sinners, and purify your hearts, you double-minded' (James 4:8). We are to 'draw near to God'. We are to 'cleanse' our hands of sin. We are to 'purify' our hearts of our hidden pride, lusts, and self-righteousness. He places the initiative in our hands. We are to draw near to God that he might draw near to us. As we have seen, the apostle Paul urges the same: 'Since we have these promises, beloved, let us cleanse ourselves from every defilement of body and spirit, bringing holiness to completion in the fear of God' (2 Cor. 7:1).

We may have endured difficult circumstances. We may have faced terrible temptations, yet we have 'these promises' of the gospel. Indeed, 'There can be no more potent motive to persuade the perfection of holiness,' says Poole, 'than belief in the promises of God.'[27] They are to motivate us. We have the experience of reconciliation with God

[27] Poole, *Commentary*, III:628.

and fellowship with God (2 Cor. 5:17-21; 6:14-18). Consequently, we are to 'cleanse ourselves' of every 'defilement' (2 Cor. 7:1). We are to be 'bringing holiness to completion', or 'perfecting holiness in the fear of God' (NASB). We are to 'strive' for holiness (Heb. 12:14). All those who have the hope of seeing Christ when he 'appears' at his return, and of being 'like him', purify themselves 'as he is pure' (1 John 3:2-3). If I understand the holiness of God, I will pursue holiness and not be deterred by the circumstances in which I have had to struggle.

Holy people

Sixth, *do I cherish or ridicule holy people?* Are those who are especially zealous for God, who are especially faithful and especially obedient, objects of our admiration or targets for our ridicule? If I understand the holiness of God I will esteem holiness in God's people. 'He that honoureth the holy God,' says Baxter, 'will honour his image in his holy people.'[28] How easy is it to label someone who will not 'play along', who will not join with us in our sin, as a square, dead-head, or a legalist! 'Some are so desperately profane,' says Gurnall, 'that they dare flout and jeer at those who show any strictness in their lives, or zeal in the worship of God.'[29] The apostle Peter mentions those who are surprised when Christians do not run with them into all sorts of excesses (1 Pet. 4:4). Is that us? Whose side are we on? When we despise the holiness of the creature, we also despise the holiness of the Creator of which it is a reflection. That is why, for example, the apostle John says we cannot say we hate our brother and love God (1 John 4:20). The brother reflects the Father, and therefore to hate one is to hate both (cf. James 3:9-10). 'Despisers of holiness are despisers of God,' Boston warns. 'To despise holiness in the saints, and to make a mock of their holy lives and practices, is a high contempt of the holy God.'[30] Rather, our task is to 'consider how to stir up one another to love and good works' (Heb. 10:24).

[28] Baxter, *The Divine Life, Works*, III:806.
[29] Gurnall, *Christian in Complete Armour*, II:490.
[30] Boston, *Illustration of the Doctrines, Works*, I:104.

Preparation for worship

Seventh, *do we come to worship carefully prepared or without prior consideration?* If I understand the holiness of God, I will honour, fear, and reverence him. I will want not only to offer him the correct form of worship, but to do so in the proper spirit. I will want to worship him 'in spirit *and* truth' (John 4:24). I will prepare carefully because I understand that he is worthy of my best thoughts, my heartfelt devotion, and my undivided attention. My ambition will be that *'all that is within me'* should 'bless his holy name' (Psa. 103:1). My aim will be to worship him 'with reverence and awe' (Heb. 12:28).

'God is never to be approached or mentioned but with the greatest reverence', says Baxter, appealing to Isaiah 8:13 ('Let him be your fear, and … your dread') and Hebrews 12:28-29 ('let us offer to God acceptable worship, with reverence and awe').[31] Calvin, in his exposition of the first petition of the Lord's Prayer, insists that we 'should never speak or think of [God] without the highest reverence'.[32]

Or is public worship such a small matter to us that we slip in just under the wire or late? Do we casually survey those attending, whisper to our pew-mates a running commentary on the people and proceedings, and allow our thoughts to wander aimlessly, barely giving any effort or paying any attention to God? Then do we act like little gods and judge the sermon, the singing, and the prayers, and evaluate and criticize as though the service were a performance for our benefit? Do we act as though we were judges of the worship service when in fact God judges our worship? Do we not offend his holiness when we fail to prepare our hearts, to clean up our thoughts, and then to concentrate—truly concentrate—and to work at giving God our best efforts? 'Take heed,' says Baxter, 'lest irreverence, or deadness, or customary, heartless, worldly services should be brought before a holy God. Take heed of hypocritical, carnal worship. The holy God will not be mocked with compliments and shows.'[33]

Too often we burst into the presence of God unprepared. Charnock warns that we will offer God but 'slight service' if we do not believe in the

---

[31] Baxter, *The Divine Life, Works*, III:810.
[32] Calvin, *Institutes*, III.xx.41, p. 904.
[33] Baxter, *The Divine Life, Works*, III:807.

'excellency of his nature'. We must imagine him to be 'an easy, drowsy, unobservant God' if we fail to worship him in a manner befitting his perfections.[34] Carefully consider Charnock's further warning:

> The holiness of God is injured by our unprepared addresses to him, when, like swine, we come into the presence of God with all our mire reeking and steaming upon us. A holy God requires a holy worship; and if our best duties, having filth in every part, as performed by us, are unmeet for God, how much more unsuitable are dead and dirty duties to a living and immense holiness! … We condemn, then, his perfection, when we come before him without due preparation; as if God himself were of an impure nature, and did not deserve our purest thoughts in our applications to him; as if any blemished and polluted sacrifice were good enough for him, and his nature deserved no better. When we excite not those elevated frames of spirit which are due to such a being, when we think to put him off with a lame and imperfect service, we worship him not according to the excellency of his nature, but put a slight upon his majestic sanctity. When we nourish in our duties those foolish imaginations which creep upon us; when we bring into, and continue our worldly, carnal, debauched fancies in his presence, worse than the nasty servants, or bemired dogs, a man would blush to be attended with in his visits to a neat person. To be conversing with sordid sensualities, when we are at the feet of an infinite God, sitting upon the throne of his holiness, is as much a contempt of him, as it would be of a prince, to bring a vessel full of nasty dung with us, when we come to present a petition to him in his royal robes; or as it would have been to God, if the high priest should have swept all the blood and excrements of the sacrifices from the foot of the altar into the Holy of holies, and heaped it up before the mercy-seat, where the presence of God dwelt between the cherubims, and afterwards shovelled it up in to the ark, to be lodged with Aaron's rod and the pot of manna.[35]

---

[34] Charnock, *Existence and Attributes*, I:180.
[35] *Ibid.*, II:247.

Discipleship

Eighth, *do we love Christian discipleship, or do we think the demands of Christ are too difficult?* Jesus calls us to deny ourselves, take up our cross, and follow him. He insists we must lose ourselves if we are to save ourselves (Matt. 16:24-25). He demands that we love him more than we love our family members (Matt. 10:37-39). He says that if we love him, we will keep his commandments (John 14:15, 21, 23). Those who belong to Christ Jesus, says the apostle Paul, 'have crucified the flesh with its passions and desires' (Gal. 5:24).

What is our attitude to these requirements? Is it that of the psalmist? 'Oh, how I love your law!' he says (Psa. 119:97). The psalmist meditates on God's law day and night (1:2). He desires it more than gold and finds it sweeter than honey (19:10). The children of God find the yoke of Christ 'easy' and 'light' (Matt. 11:28-30). The children of God love the life they have in Christ, even its restrictions and requirements. 'His commandments,' says the apostle John, 'are not burdensome' (1 John 5:3).

Or do we find serious Christianity to be 'over the top'? 'Men naturally account God's laws too strict, his yoke too heavy, and his limits too strait', says Charnock.[36] Do we compartmentalize 'religion', giving it a few hours each month by periodic attendance at public services? Are we flippant about obedience as well as about our commitment to spiritual disciplines and to public services? Do we in this way accommodate God's absolute demands to our comfort, convenience, and desires, and thereby offend his holiness? Are we like those people that the apostle Paul warned of, who 'will not endure sound teaching, but having *itching ears … will accumulate for themselves teachers to suit their own passions*, and will turn away from listening to the truth and wander off into myths' (2 Tim. 4:3-4)?

Similarly, Isaiah condemned those 'who say to the seers, "Do not see", and to the prophets, "Do not prophesy to us what is right; speak to us smooth things, prophesy illusions, leave the way, turn aside from the path, let us hear no more about the Holy One of Israel"' (Isa. 30:10-11). The carnally minded did not wish to hear of the 'Holy One of Israel'—and the same is still true today. Charnock warns, 'To

---

[36] Charnock, *Existence and Attributes*, I:200.

charge the law with rigidness, whether in language or practice, is the highest contempt of God's holiness; for it is an implicit wish, that God were as defiled, polluted, disorderly, as our corrupted selves.'[37] Because the apostle Paul had experienced the Christ who 'loved me and gave himself for me', he thought nothing of his crucified life which he now lived by faith in the Son of God (Gal. 2:20). Let us, with him, think nothing of being crucified to the world, and the world to us (Gal. 6:14).

Influence

Finally, ninth, *is my life a stimulus to holiness for others or a stumbling block?* Does my life display the 'beauty' or the 'splendour of holiness' (Psa. 96:9)? Does it draw others to God? Does the light of my good works lead others to glorify our Father in heaven (Matt. 5:16)? Does my love for neighbours and enemies show me to be a child of the God who causes his sun to shine and rain to fall on the evil and on the good, on the righteous and on the unrighteous (Matt. 5:45)? Does my life 'adorn the doctrine of God our Saviour' (Titus 2:10)? Or am I a mass of contradictions, confusion, and compromise? Is the name of God blasphemed among unbelievers because of my hypocrisy (Rom. 2:24)? Am I a stumbling block for the weak, leading others into rebellion and ruin, wounding their consciences, and even destroying their faith (1 Cor. 8:9ff.; Rom. 14:12ff.)?

The apostle Paul urges, 'Be imitators of me, as I am of Christ' (1 Cor. 11:1). We are meant to be the same: imitators of Christ so that others might imitate us. Am I? Do I wish to be? Our usefulness, our effectiveness, our fruitfulness, as servants of Christ is directly related to our commitment to personal holiness. 'Useless and unprofitable' is how Gurnall characterizes those who do not maintain a holy life.[38] When commending his own ministry the apostle Paul reminded the Thessalonian church of 'how holy and righteous and blameless was our conduct towards you believers' (1 Thess. 2:10). The *credibility* of the apostle's ministry depended on the integrity of his life. The *fruitfulness* of his ministry depended upon the holiness of his life. And the

---

[37] Charnock, *Existence and Attributes*, II:179.
[38] *Ibid.*, I:425.

apostle urged the same for others. Look once more at Paul's instructions to Timothy: 'Therefore, if anyone cleanses himself from what is dishonourable, he will be a vessel for honourable use, set apart as holy, useful to the master of the house, ready for every good work' (2 Tim. 2:21). The blood of Jesus cleanses us from all sin (1 John 1:7). Yet we are to 'cleanse' ourselves, that we might be 'holy' vessels, 'useful to the master'. Usefulness is directly related to holiness.

The apostle continues, 'So flee youthful passions and pursue righteousness, faith, love, and peace, along with those who call on the Lord from a pure heart' (2 Tim. 2:22). We are to 'flee'—not flirt with youthful passions and evil desires. 'He that dares to dally with occasions of sin,' Owen warns, 'will dare to sin. He that will venture upon temptations to wickedness will venture upon wickedness.'[39] We are to 'pursue righteousness'. These are key ingredients in a fruitful and God-pleasing life. Earlier, after listing a number of destructive evils, Paul had urged Timothy, 'But as for you, O man of God, flee these things. Pursue righteousness, godliness, faith, love, steadfastness, gentleness' (1 Tim. 6:11). Once again, he tells him to 'flee' evil and 'pursue' righteousness, godliness, and so on. What Christian does not aspire to be 'useful to the master'? What Christian does not long to contribute? What Christian does not fear that his sin might somehow disqualify him—a fear, by the way, shared by the apostle Paul (1 Cor. 9:27)? Make no mistake: our personal holiness is a vital component in a life useful to Christ.

* * *

This concludes our study of the 'attribute of attributes', except to remind ourselves that the Father has given us in Christ all that we need for holy living. All the treasures of wisdom and knowledge are found in him (Col. 2:3). We have been blessed in Christ 'with every spiritual blessing in the heavenly places' (Eph. 1:3). All the fullness of deity is in him; he is full of grace and truth; and from his fullness we have received even 'grace upon grace' (Col. 1:19; John 1:14, 16).

To what end did Christ shed his blood, blood that not only atones but also cleanses, but that we should be holy (1 John 1:7, 9)? His blood

---

[39] Owen, *Mortification*, *Works*, VI:62.

is a 'fountain opened … to cleanse [us] from sin and uncleanness' (Zech. 13:1; cf. Heb. 1:3; 9:13-14).[40]

To what end does Christ himself intercede for us, praying for our sanctification, but that we should be holy (John 17:17)?

To what end has Christ given us his Spirit 'without measure' (John 3:34), and commissioned him to 'take what is mine and declare it to you' (John 16:15), but that we should be holy? The indwelling of the Holy Spirit, Owen insists, is 'the prime and principal gift of sanctification that we receive from Christ'.[41] Furthermore, 'His whole work upon us, in us, and for us, consists in preparing us for obedience; enabling of us thereunto, and bringing forth the fruits of it in us' (Gal. 5:17ff.).[42]

To what end, asks Owen from 2 Corinthians 5:17, 'hath God given us new hearts, and new natures? Is it that we should kill them? stifle the creature that is found in us in the womb? that we should give him to the old man to be devoured?'[43]

Rather, as our 'God is light, and in him is no darkness at all', let us 'walk in the light, as he is in the light'. As we do so, the apostle John promises, 'the blood of Jesus his Son cleanses us from all sin' (1 John 1:5-7). The apostle Peter agrees: 'As he who called you is holy, you also be holy in all your conduct' (1 Pet. 1:15). Likewise, the writer to the Hebrews urges, 'Strive for … the holiness without which no one will see the Lord' (Heb. 12:14). 'This is the will of God, your sanctification,' says the apostle Paul (1 Thess. 4:3). 'For God has not called us for impurity, but in holiness' (4:7; cf. 4:4).

---

[40] 'The two cardinal doctrines of justification and sanctification by the blood of Christ are therefore here brought out clearly' (T. V. Moore, *A Commentary on Zechariah* [1856; Edinburgh: Banner of Truth Trust, 1959], p. 205, on Zech. 13:1).

[41] Owen, *Communion with God, Works*, II:172.

[42] *Ibid.*, II:183.

[43] *Ibid.*, II:186.

NINE

'The Engines of Divine Dignity': The Justice and Righteousness of God

Truly God is good to Israel,
* to those who are pure in heart.*
But as for me, my feet had almost stumbled,
* my steps had nearly slipped.*
For I was envious of the arrogant
* when I saw the prosperity of the wicked. …*
All in vain have I kept my heart clean
* and washed my hands in innocence.*
—Psalm 73:1-3, 13

'MR Bain, you are a free man', the judge in a Florida courtroom told James Bain, aged fifty-four, after he had served thirty-five years for a crime he did not commit. When told that he had been exonerated, 'he got very quiet', recounted his attorney. 'I'm really happy', Bain soon said, as he began to weep. 'He was just a child when he went in there', his mother told the reporters. 'It was just like a death, because there was nothing we could do', his sister lamented. 'He was a family member and we couldn't bring him home. There was nothing we could do. It was like death. We had no control over it.'

Justice is elusive in this world. Hundreds of falsely accused inmates like James Bain have been released from prison in recent years, their innocence demonstrated by DNA testing. Each of us has had our own experiences of times when we were treated unfairly, when those with power and authority unjustly accused us or even condemned us for wrongs we did not commit. We know of occasions when rules have been applied inequitably, when people have been treated unfairly, when the unworthy were promoted and rewarded while the deserving were overlooked or punished.

So disturbing is human injustice for some that God's character or even his existence is called into question. Charnock calls challenges to God's justice in governing the world, such as can be seen in Job (e.g. Job 10:3, 7-8), or with the Israelites in the wilderness (e.g. Num. 16:41; 17:10), or with Jonah (Jon. 4:2), 'the epidemical disease of human nature'.[1] The 'prosperity of the wicked' is unsettling to those striving to live uprightly (Psa. 73:3). The arrogance, pride, violence, foolishness, oppression, malice, and scepticism of the wicked seem to go unpunished (73:6-15). They live and die fat and happy (verses 4-5). The faithful see this and are troubled. They are tempted to conclude that it is pointless living holy lives. 'I was almost ready to repent of my piety', says Poole, describing the psalmist's outlook.[2] 'All in vain have I kept my heart clean and washed my hands in innocence' (verse 13).

The psalmist confesses his vulnerability to cynicism and unbelief, brought on by the injustice of the world that God leaves uncorrected: 'But as for me, my feet had almost stumbled, my steps had nearly slipped' (verse 2). 'There are storms that will try the firmest anchors', Henry observes.[3]

Habakkuk raises the same issue when God fails to intervene to stop evil. He cries out for help against violence, iniquity, injustice, and the oppression of the righteous in contemporary Judah. Yet God fails to act (Hab. 1:1-4). Habakkuk complains bitterly. 'O LORD, how long shall I cry for help, and you will not hear? Or cry to you "Violence!" and you will not save? Why do you make me see iniquity, and why do you idly look at wrong? (1:2-3). When God reveals that he will raise up the Chaldeans to punish Judah and end the injustice (verses 5-11), Habakkuk's consternation is compounded. How does it make sense for a God who 'cannot look at wrong' to use the more wicked Chaldeans to punish the less wicked Judeans? He asks, 'You who are of purer eyes than to see evil and cannot look at wrong, why do you idly look

---

[1] Charnock, *Existence and Attributes*, I:219.
[2] Poole, *Commentary*, II:114.
[3] Henry, *Commentary*, on Psa. 73:2-3.

at traitors and remain silent when the wicked swallows up the man more righteous than he?' (verse 13). 'He debates with God about his providences', says Poole.[4] How can God 'idly look' and 'remain silent' in the face of unrighteousness? Will injustice, inequity, and oppression be perpetuated forever? 'Why is the juster oppressed by the unjuster?' Habakkuk wants to know.[5]

The same question is raised directly in the prophecy of Malachi: 'Where is the God of justice?' Appearances seem to indicate that God 'delights' in 'everyone who does evil' (Mal. 2:17; see 2:17–3:12; cf. Psa. 10). 'Either there is no God,' says Trapp of this meaning, 'or, at least, not a God of that exact, precise, impartial judgment.'[6] God's longsuffering is interpreted as indifference to sin.[7]

We also find the complaint expressed in Ecclesiastes. 'Because the sentence against an evil deed is not executed speedily, the heart of the children of man is fully set to do evil' (Eccles. 8:11). 'Thus doth man's venomous nature suck poison out of so sweet an attribute as God's patience', Manton comments on this verse.[8] If we are right to apply this principle to God's government of the world, we will conclude with Charnock that the ungodly 'could not think an infinite goodness and justice could be *so slow* to punish oppressors, and relieve the miserable, and leave the world in that disorder under the injustice of men'. Therefore they conclude that God does not govern the world, since his patience is 'beyond the line of [what is] fit and just'.[9]

Divine justice

God's answer to Malachi, and to us, is that a day of judgment is coming (Mal. 3:1-4). God has not yet settled his accounts, but he will. The day will come when God 'will draw near to you for judgement. I will

---

[4] Poole, *Commentary*, II:968.

[5] *Ibid.*

[6] Trapp, *Commentary*, IV:512.

[7] See T. V. Moore, *A Commentary on Haggai and Malachi* (1856; London: Banner of Truth Trust, 1960), pp. 142-43.

[8] Thomas Manton, *A Practical Commentary or An Exposition with Notes of the Epistle of Jude*, in *The Complete Works of Thomas Manton* (1870; Worthington, PA: Maranatha Publications, n.d.), V:149.

[9] Charnock, *Existence and Attributes*, II:511 (emphasis added).

be a swift witness against the sorcerers, against the adulterers, against those who swear falsely, against those who oppress the hired worker in his wages, the widow and the fatherless, against those who thrust aside the sojourner, and do not fear me, says the LORD of hosts' (Mal. 3:5)

Where is the God of justice? 'You shall know where he is,' says Henry, 'and shall know it to your terror and confusion.'[10] God will see to it that the wicked are punished and the helpless, the weak, the hired worker, the widow, the fatherless, and the sojourner are rescued. He will come as 'a swift witness against their crimes', says Moore.[11] Injustice will not be perpetual because the God who rules sovereignly over all creation is a God of justice. The God of the Bible is one who 'executes judgement' (Psa. 75:7). He is 'the judge of *all*' (Heb. 12:23).

God is both righteous and just (Heb. *saddiq*; Gk *dikaios*). He ensures that righteousness (Heb. *sedeq*; Gk *dikaiosunē*) and justice (Heb. *mishpat* and *sedeq*) are done. The vocabulary overlaps, as do the translations. According to Motyer, when 'righteousness' and 'justice' occur together, the former 'refers to righteous principles', and the latter 'righteous application and practice'.[12] 'Righteousness and justice are the foundation of his throne' (Psa. 97:2; cf. 89:14). Commenting on Psalm 97:1-2, Charnock says, 'These are the *engines of Divine dignity* which render him glorious and majestic.'[13] 'He loves righteousness and justice' (Psa. 33:5). He is 'exalted in justice, and the Holy God shows himself holy in righteousness' (Isa. 5:16). He is 'righteous in all his ways' (Psa. 145:17). He is 'the Judge of all the earth' who will 'do what is just' and see to it that right is done (Gen. 18:25; cf. Psa. 50:6). He is a 'righteous judge' (Psa. 7:11; 2 Tim. 4:8). His ways are just, his 'righteous acts have been revealed', and his judgments are 'true and just' (Rev. 15:3, 4; 16:7).

The Son of David—the Messiah, the Christ, our Lord Jesus— 'seeks justice and is swift to do righteousness' (Isa. 16:5). He '[loves] righteousness and [hates] wickedness', and 'a sceptre of uprightness' is 'the sceptre of [his] kingdom' (Psa. 45:6-7). His right hand is 'filled

---

[10] Henry, *Commentary*, on Mal. 3:5.

[11] Moore, *Haggai and Malachi*, p. 153.

[12] Alec Motyer, *Psalms by the Day: A New Devotional Translation* (Ross-shire, Scotland: Christian Focus, 2016), p. 82.

[13] Charnock, *Existence and Attributes*, II:432-33 (emphasis added).

with righteousness' (Psa. 48:10). The Prince of peace establishes and upholds the throne of David 'with justice and with righteousness from this time forth and for evermore' (Isa. 9:7).

David can confidently plead to a just God in his conflict with Saul, 'May the LORD judge between me and you, may the LORD avenge me against you' (1 Sam. 24:12), and further, 'May the LORD therefore be judge and give sentence between me and you, and see to it and plead my cause and deliver me from your hand' (1 Sam. 24:15).

God has pledged to 'judge the world in righteousness' (Psa. 96:13). Indeed, 'he will judge the world in righteousness', the apostle Paul repeats, adding that that judgment will be exercised through the man (Jesus Christ) whom God has appointed (Acts 17:31).

Justice defined

'The justice of God,' says Wilhelmus à Brakel, 'consists in giving each his worthy due, either by punishment or reward.'[14] For Edwards, it is the 'disposition of the divine nature to render to every one their own'.[15] That God is just means that we will all be treated *fairly*. We will all get that which we are *due*; we will all receive what we *deserve*.

God loves righteousness and hates wickedness. He demonstrates righteousness/justice in his law by what he prohibits and what he permits, by what he punishes and what he rewards.[16] He is just, righteous, and fair in ruling and governing all things. He is also just as Judge (Psa. 50:6). According to Edward Leigh, 'Justice … is the attribute whereby God is just in and of himself, and exercises justice towards all creatures, and giveth every one his due.'[17] His justice, then, is twofold: God is just *in himself* and just *in all his works*. God is just in his *word*, in that all that he declares is true, right, and equitable.

---

[14] à Brakel, *Christian's Reasonable Service*, I:127. It is, according to John Flavel, 'the perfect rectitude and equity of his nature; whereby he is just in himself, and in all his ways towards the creatures' (Flavel, *Exposition, Works*, VI:153).

[15] Cited in Gerstner, *Biblical Theology of Jonathan Edwards*, p. 43. Swinnock defines justice as 'the giving everyone their due'. It is 'that attribute [of God] whereby he disposeth all things according to the rule of equity' (*Incomparableness of God, Works*, IV:410).

[16] See Chap. 7, 'The Holiness of God'.

[17] Cited in Muller, *Post-Reformation Reformed Dogmatics*, III:481.

God is also just in his *deeds*, in that he governs the world equitably and renders to each one according to his deeds, without respect of persons (Deut. 16:19; Psa. 62:12; Prov. 24:12; Jer. 32:19; Ezek. 7:27; Matt. 16:27; John 5:29; Acts 10:34; Gal. 2:6; Eph. 6:9). The *justitia Dei*, says Richard Muller, summarizing classic Reformed views, is the principle by which God accomplishes the ends of creation and governance.[18] Righteousness will be rewarded and the righteous vindicated. Evil will be exposed and punished. The tyrants, the oppressors, the murderers, and the rebels of history will get away with nothing. The meek will inherit the earth (Matt. 5:5). 'Justice in God,' says Baxter, 'is the perfection of his nature, as it giveth every one his due, or governeth the world in the most perfect orders for the ends of government.'[19]

Justice revealed

The classic writers were quick to establish the connection between God's holiness and his justice. God must punish sin, says Edward Leigh, 'in order to give a manifestation of his holiness'.[20] Edwards describes the holiness of God as 'the infinite opposition of his nature to sin' which 'naturally and necessarily disposes him to punish sin', that is, to execute justice. Indeed, he says, 'His justice is part of his holiness.'[21] Shedd, citing both John Owen and Jonathan Edwards, views justice 'as a mode of holiness'.[22] It is, he says, 'that phase of God's holiness which is seen in his treatment of the obedient and the disobedient subjects of his government'.[23]

Reformed theologians have argued that vindicatory or punitive justice, punishing justice, is 'essential to God and must be exercised'.

[18] Cited in Muller, *Post-Reformation Reformed Dogmatics*, III:477.
[19] Baxter, *The Divine Life, Works*, III:805. 'Justice manifests itself especially in giving every man his due, in treating him according to his deserts' (Berkhof, *Systematic Theology*, p. 75).
[20] Cited in Muller, *Post-Reformation Reformed Dogmatics*, III:501. According to Joseph Caryl, 'God is so just, so pure in himself, that he neither doth nor can do wrong to any creature' (*ibid.*, III:482). 'His holy nature,' says Boston, 'prompts him to love righteousness, and consequently to hate and punish all unrighteousness' (*Illustration of the Doctrines, Works*, I:117).
[21] Edwards, *Great and Glorious God*, p. 170.
[22] Shedd, *Dogmatic Theology*, I:364.
[23] *Ibid.*, I:365.

'Indeed,' Muller continues, 'removal of this aspect of justice would render God *less than perfectly holy*.'[24] Vindicatory or punishing justice, says Leigh, 'is so essential to God, immutably, and inexorably, that he cannot remit the creatures' sin, nor free them from punishment, unless his justice be satisfied'.[25] Muller summarizes the view of punitive justice among the Reformed:

> Indeed, the case for an essential vindicatory justice in God is proven by the death of Christ, for God would not have subjected his beloved Son to death had there not been an inward necessity that his righteousness be satisfied by the infliction of punishment … in Christ we learn that God does not set aside sin without punishment, for the punishment of sin falls on Christ as Mediator.[26]

'Sin must be punished,' says C. H. Spurgeon, 'or God must cease to be.'[27] Let us then elaborate upon how God manifests his justice.

Governance of this world

First, God reveals his justice in *his governing of events in this world*. The ideals of divine government, even Messianic rule, are identified in Psalms 2, 45, 72, 82, and 101, among others. Broadly considered, righteousness is rewarded and evil is punished in the here and now. Even in this world, we reap what we sow (Gal. 6:7). The psalmist insists, 'Surely there is a reward for the righteous; surely there is a God who judges on earth' (Psa. 58:11).

It is not always the case that God's justice is realized in this life, as we have seen already. Justice may long delay. Yet 'Sometimes,' says Boston, commenting on Psalm 58:11, 'providence doth notably

---

[24] Muller, *Post-Reformation Reformed Dogmatics,* III:492 (emphasis added).

[25] From Leigh's *Treatise of Divinity* (1646), cited in Muller, *Post-Reformation Reformed Dogmatics*, III:492. Similarly, Benedict Pictet argued, 'If love of holiness, or hatred of sin is essential to God, then his avenging justice will be also' (*ibid.*, III:493). For Charnock, 'Divine holiness is the root of Divine justice, and Divine justice is the triumph of Divine holiness' (*Existence and Attributes*, II:209).

[26] Muller, *Post-Reformation Reformed Dogmatics*, III:492. We will return to this theme below.

[27] C. H. Spurgeon, 'Zealots', in *Metropolitan Tabernacle Pulpit* (1865; Cleveland: Pilgrim Press, 1973), XI:392.

interpose, and load obedience with blessings here in the world, to the conviction of all beholders, so that men are constrained to say, "Verily there is a reward for the righteous."'[28]

The 107th Psalm takes us through various occasions of distress: desert wasteland (verses 4-9), imprisonment (verses 10-16), afflictions (verses 17-22), and stormy seas (verses 23-32). Its point is that '[God's] providences are moral', as Motyer explains.[29] Verses 33-43 describe observable judgments and blessings from which both the wicked and the righteous learn: 'The upright see it and are glad, and all wickedness shuts its mouth' (107:42). God's moral governance can be seen. It is observable. When God turns 'a fruitful land into a salty waste because of the evil of its inhabitants' (verse 34), or when he 'turns a desert into pools of water, a parched land into springs of water' (verse 35), all may be exhorted: 'Whoever is wise, let him attend to these things; let them consider the steadfast love of the LORD' (verse 43). Learn, the psalmist is urging, from what can be observed from God's just rule, and adjust your conduct accordingly. 'Every morning he *shows forth* his justice,' says the prophet Zephaniah (Zeph. 3:5). The just wrath of God 'is *revealed* from heaven against all ungodliness and unrighteousness of men' (Rom. 1:18). It can be seen. Sodom and Gomorrah were reduced to ashes as 'an example' from which we all can learn, 'of what is going to happen to the ungodly' (2 Pet. 2:6).

We may consider the book of Proverbs as an extended meditation on the observable benefits of righteous and wise living. Live right and rewards follow:

> Honour the LORD with your wealth
>   and with the firstfruits of all your produce;
> then your barns will be filled with plenty,
>   and your vats will be bursting with wine (Prov. 3:9-10).
>
> A slack hand causes poverty,
>   but the hand of the diligent makes rich (10:4).

---

[28] Boston, *Illustration of the Doctrines, Works*, I:107.
[29] J. A. Motyer, 'Psalms', in *New Bible Commentary, 21st Century Edition*, eds. Gordon J. Wenham. J. A. Motyer, D. A. Carson, and R. T. France (Downers Grove, IL: InterVarsity Press, 1994), p. 558.

The righteous is delivered from trouble,
  and the wicked walks into it instead (11:8).

Poverty and disgrace come to him who ignores instruction,
  but whoever heeds reproof is honoured (13:18).

Disaster pursues sinners,
  but the righteous are rewarded with good (13:21).

In the house of the righteous there is much treasure,
  but trouble befalls the income of the wicked (15:6).

Whoever works his land will have plenty of bread,
  but he who follows worthless pursuits will have plenty
    of poverty.
A faithful man will abound with blessings,
  but whoever hastens to be rich will not go unpunished.
                                          (28:19-20)

A greedy man stirs up strife,
  but the one who trusts in the LORD will be enriched.
                                          (28:25)

'Every day's observation confirms the fact', says Charles Bridges (1794–1869) of Proverbs 10:4.[30] Tithe, work hard, live a morally upright life, stay humble, practise moderation, and well-being results. God blesses the righteous. There is 'great reward' in keeping God's commandments (Psa. 19:11). The obedient, says Henry, are 'unspeakable gainers'.[31]

The book of Job cautions us against imagining a one-to-one correlation. A substantial portion of the Psalter laments the suffering of the righteous at the hands of the wicked. Yet, broadly speaking, God governs the world in such a way that righteousness is rewarded and evil suffers. Sloth results in poverty (Prov. 6:9-11; 10:5; 18:9; 19:15; 20:4; 21:5-6). Gluttony results in bad health (21:17; 23:20-21). Promiscuity results in a host of maladies, from disease, to impotence, to ruin of the family, to poverty (5:8-14; 6:23-35; 9:13-18; 29:3; 31:3). Pride leads to recklessness and ruin (15:20; 16:18; 29:23). Drunkenness leads to loss of health, ruined relationships, and forfeiture of life itself (20:1; 23:29-35; 31:4-7). Generally

---

[30] Charles Bridges, *A Commentary on Proverbs* (1846; Edinburgh: Banner of Truth Trust, 1968), p. 92.

[31] Henry, *Commentary*, on Psa. 19:11.

speaking, live in God's world in God's way, and one will get along better than those who defy God's laws. David can even say (Psa. 18:20-24),

> The LORD dealt with me according to my righteousness;
>> according to the cleanness of my hands he rewarded me.
> For I have kept the ways of the LORD,
>> and have not wickedly departed from my God.
> For all his rules were before me,
>> and his statutes I did not put away from me.
> I was blameless before him,
>> and I kept myself from my guilt.
> So the LORD has rewarded me according to my righteousness,
>> according to the cleanness of my hands in his sight.

The personal 'righteousness' which he claims is a *relative* righteousness, a *comparative* righteousness (see also Psa. 7:8; 26:1ff.). He is clean, blameless, and guiltless relative to general human depravity as well as to the particular depravity of his enemies. He has not 'knowingly and wilfully forsaken God, and broken his laws, as wicked men do', Poole explains.[32] Accordingly, he is 'rewarded according to [his] righteousness'. Jesus promises reward for secret giving, praying, and fasting, without specifying if that reward will be in heaven or on earth (Matt. 6:2-8). However, following the encounter with the rich young ruler, Jesus responds to Peter's questioning by promising, 'There is no one who has left house or brothers or sisters or mother or father or children or lands, for my sake and for the gospel, who will not receive a hundredfold now in this time, houses and brothers and sisters and mothers and children and lands, with persecutions, and in the age to come eternal life' (Mark 10:29-30), which Henry interprets as 'the comforts of the Spirit sweetening their creature comforts'.[33]

Sometimes God rewards the righteous with *external* blessings. At other times, God rewards the righteous with *inward* blessings. Again, for the righteous, says Boston, 'There are fresh supplies and influences of grace, near and intimate communion with him, sweet manifestations of his favour and love, intimations of peace and pardon, and joy and peace in believing, etc.'[34]

[32] Poole, *Commentary*, II:26.
[33] Henry, *Commentary*, on Mark 10:30.
[34] Boston, *Illustration of Doctrines*, *Works*, I:107.

God's wrath is 'revealed' against ungodliness. To whom? To humanity. Where? 'From heaven', *in this world*. Wells calls this 'God's initial judgment'.[35] The apostle then delineates pagan humanity's turning to idols (Rom. 1:19-24) and to its lusts (1:25-28), and the resulting deterioration of society. As God gives them up to 'a debased mind', society unravels under his judgments:

> And since they did not see fit to acknowledge God, God gave them up to a debased mind to do what ought not to be done. They were filled with all manner of unrighteousness, evil, covetousness, malice. They are full of envy, murder, strife, deceit, maliciousness. They are gossips, slanderers, haters of God, insolent, haughty, boastful, inventors of evil, disobedient to parents, foolish, faithless, heartless, ruthless (1:28-31).

The apostle concludes: 'We know that the judgment of God rightly falls on those who practise such things' (Rom. 2:2).

Again, generally speaking, the wicked do not long prosper in this world. They sow the seeds of their own destruction through their evil deeds, which draw down the judgments of God. 'The wicked,' says the psalmist, 'are snared in the work of their own hands' (Psa. 9:16). 'All diseases and sicknesses, wars, pestilence, plagues, and famines, are designed to vindicate God's holiness and hatred of sin', says Boston.[36]

From Genesis to Revelation God reveals his judgments against sin even in this world. These are not eternal judgments, but temporal. Adam and Eve were banished from the garden because of their sin. The serpent was cursed, the ground was cursed, and the pain of childbirth was multiplied (Gen. 3:14-19). In the days of Noah, because of the evil of human hearts, God resolved to 'blot out man whom [he had] created from the face of the land' (6:7). God rained down fire and brimstone on Sodom and Gomorrah (Gen. 18-19) because, says Jude, they 'indulged in sexual immorality and pursued unnatural desire' (Jude 7). God sent plagues of blood, frogs, gnats, insects, pestilence, boils, hail and fire, locusts, darkness, and finally the death of the firstborn. He did so both in order to secure the release of his people and to judge Egypt (Exod. 7–12; Gen. 15:14). God ordered the worshippers of the golden

---

[35] Wells, *God in the Whirlwind*, p. 123.
[36] Boston, *Illustration of the Doctrines*, *Works*, I:99.

calf to be slaughtered, and three thousand were killed (Exod. 32:26-35). God consumed Nadab and Abihu with fire for ritual disobedience, for offering 'strange fire before the LORD, which he had not commanded' (Lev. 10:1 NASB). Korah led a rebellion challenging Moses' leadership, but God vindicated Moses by opening up the ground and causing it to swallow up Korah, his family, his followers, and all their possessions: 'So they and all that belonged to them went down alive into Sheol, and the earth closed over them, and they perished from the midst of the assembly' (Num. 16:33).

Joshua led the children of Israel in occupying the promised land. However, in doing so they wiped out whole cities, in some cases destroying every man, woman, child, and beast. Why did God require it? Because Israel was God's agent in judging the inhabitants of the land. In fact, Israel had to wait four hundred years until 'the iniquity of the Amorites' was 'complete' and they merited total destruction (Gen. 15:16). When Israel conquered Jericho, the people were forbidden to take anything from the city. But Achan stole some silver and gold, 'some of the devoted things', and therefore 'the anger of the LORD burned against the people of Israel' (Josh. 7:1). Achan's sin went undetected until the next battle, which they anticipated would be an easy victory. Instead, the Israelites were soundly defeated. Achan's guilt was uncovered by lot. Following his confession, they took him, his sons and daughters, his oxen, donkeys, and sheep, his tent, and all he possessed, and stoned them and burned them; thus 'the LORD turned from his burning anger' (Josh. 7:26).

Judges presents a cycle of sin, judgment, repentance, and restoration that repeated itself over and over again. During the period of the monarchy Saul's sin led to God's rejection of him as king (1 Sam. 15:1-23). David's sin (2 Sam. 11), followed by Solomon's (1 Kings 11) and Rehoboam's (2 Kings 12), divided and nearly destroyed the nation. The Northern Kingdom, Israel, was destroyed by God using Assyria because of its disobedience. Its people were carried off into captivity and have disappeared from history (2 Kings 17). Judah also was defeated, this time by the Babylonians, and carried into captivity as an act of God's wrath and anger (2 Kings 22:15-17). All the Old Testament prophets were covenant prosecutors warning of God's judgment upon Judah and Israel because of their covenant unfaithfulness.

In the New Testament we see Jesus warning that the kingdom would again be taken from Israel, that not one stone would be left upon another. Judgment was realized when in AD 70 the Romans destroyed Jerusalem (Matt. 21:43; 23:34–24:35). The apostle Paul said wrath had come upon the Jews 'to the utmost' (1 Thess. 2:14ff. NASB).

Ananias and Sapphira were struck dead on the spot for lying to the Holy Spirit (Acts 5:1-11). Herod was eaten by worms and struck dead because 'he did not give God the glory' (12:23). Elymas the magician was struck blind because he hindered the preaching of the gospel (13:11). Many were weak and sick and some had died in the Corinthian church because God had judged their disobedience with respect to the Lord's Supper (1 Cor. 11:29-32). The book of Revelation describes a series of fierce judgments, including warnings to the seven churches (Rev. 2–3), the seven bowls of God's wrath (15-16), and the judgment on Babylon (17:1–19:10).

This is just a selection of passages which speak of God's judgment in this world. Boston says, 'The end and design of all God's judgments is to witness to the world, that he is a just and righteous God. All the fearful plagues and terrible judgments which God has brought upon the world, proclaim and manifest his justice.'[37]

Justice in the next world

Second, God reveals his justice in his promise of rewards and punishments *in the world to come* in eternity, those rewards and punishments being completed on the day of judgment.

Regarding rewards, the Old Testament understanding is sketchy. The godly leaders of Israel are said to have been 'gathered to [their] people' (Deut. 32:50; cf. Num. 20:24, 26). David was confident that he (and all believers) would 'dwell in the house of the LORD for ever' (Psa. 23:6; so also throughout the Psalms, e.g. Psa. 21:4). Jesus brought much greater clarity. He promised his persecuted disciples, 'Your reward is great in heaven' (Matt. 5:12). Indeed, all the Beatitudes promise reward and vindication primarily in the next world: the kingdom of God, comfort, inheriting the earth, satisfaction, mercy, and seeing God (Matt. 5:3-12). Those who give, pray, and fast not to be seen by others

---

[37] Boston, *Illustration of the Doctrines, Works,* I:107.

but to please God are promised divine rewards (Matt. 6:1-18). Jesus promised those disciples who lost houses and families in this world full recompense and eternal life in the age to come (Mark 10:30). Believers are promised a heavenly inheritance (Acts 20:32; Eph. 1:11, 14; Col. 1:12; 2 Tim. 4:8). The righteous will hear the King say, 'Come, you who are blessed by my Father, inherit the kingdom prepared for you from the foundation of the world' (Matt. 25:34).

Regarding punishments, again, the Old Testament teaching is slender, yet the confidence of David was that the righteous, not the wicked, would 'stand in the judgment' (Psa. 1). The Bible promises punishments in the world to come. There will be a day of judgment when all things will be set right. The preacher affirms in Ecclesiastes, 'Moreover, I saw under the sun that in the place of justice, even there was wickedness, and in the place of righteousness, even there was wickedness. I said in my heart, God will judge the righteous and the wicked, for there is a time for every matter and for every work' (Eccles. 3:16-17). 'It is an unspeakable comfort to the oppressed,' says Henry, 'that their cause will be heard over again.'[38] 'All will soon be set right', Bridges concludes from verse 17.[39] The psalmist is heartened when he lifts his eyes from the prosperity of the wicked and perceives or discerns their end. They are in 'slippery places'; they will be 'destroyed in a moment' and 'swept away utterly by terrors' (Psa. 73:17-19).

Jesus teaches that the Father has given the Son of God 'authority to execute judgment' (John 5:27). He warns, 'Do not marvel at this, for an hour is coming when all who are in the tombs will hear his voice and come out, those who have done good to the resurrection of life, and those who have done evil to the resurrection of judgment' (5:28-29).

The books will be opened and all will be judged according to what they have done (Rev. 20:12). A great separation will take place:

> When the Son of Man comes in his glory, and all the angels with him, then he will sit on his glorious throne. Before him will be gathered all the nations, and he will separate people one from another as a shepherd separates the sheep from the goats.

---

[38] Henry, *Commentary*, on Eccles. 3:16-17.
[39] Charles Bridges, *A Commentary on Ecclesiastes* (1860; London: Banner of Truth Trust, 1961), p. 75.

> And he will place the sheep on his right, but the goats on the left. Then the King will say to those on his right, 'Come, you who are blessed by my Father, inherit the kingdom prepared for you from the foundation of the world.' ... Then he will say to those on his left, 'Depart from me, you cursed, into the eternal fire prepared for the devil and his angels.' ... And these will go away into eternal punishment, but the righteous into eternal life. (Matt. 25:31-34, 41, 46)

All wrongs will be made right. All injustices will be reversed. God's righteousness, says Wells, 'will one day become the broom that sweeps the universe clean'.[40]

According to Flavel, the second greatest demonstration of the justice of God (after the cross) 'is in the eternal punishment of sin in hell upon all that do not repent, and come to Christ by faith'; and the third 'is in making good all the mercies he promised to believers, exactly to a tithe'.[41] We will have more on these themes as we proceed to look at the characteristics of God's justice.

Justice described

Let us then look at the qualities which characterize God's justice.

Fair

First, God's justice is *fair*. We all get exactly what we deserve (Rom. 2:11; 3:22; James 2:1-13). God cannot be swayed by worldly criteria. There is no partiality with God (Rom. 2:11; Gal. 2:6; Eph. 6:9; Col. 3:25; 1 Pet. 1:17). He is not a 'respecter of persons', to use the language of the King James Version (Acts 10:34). He brings no bias to the bar of justice. He shows no favouritism. He cannot be bribed (Deut. 10:17). As Peter announced to Cornelius and the Gentiles, 'Truly I understand that God shows no partiality' (Acts 10:34). 'Outward things neither help nor hurt, please nor displease God, but as they are in a good or bad man', says Trapp.[42] Jonathan Edwards told the congregation in Enfield, Connecticut, in the sermon 'Sinners in the

---

[40] Wells, *God in the Whirlwind*, p. 125.
[41] Flavel, *Exposition*, *Works*, VI:154.
[42] Trapp, *Commentary*, V:443.

Hands of an Angry God', 'that you shall not suffer beyond what strict justice requires', which will mean infinite trouble for all who lack a redeemer.[43] Yet God will be fair. If we were ignorant, or did not know what God required, the Proverbs ask us rhetorically, 'Does not he who weighs the heart perceive it? Does not he who keeps watch over your soul know it, and will he not repay man according to his work?' (Prov. 24:12; cf. Luke 12:48). There will be no need to worry in eternity about bad judges, because there is only one Judge. Nor need we worry about bad juries, because God is judge and jury. Nor need we worry in eternity about bad laws, because God is the lawmaker. The whole judicial process is carried out by a holy and righteous God who cannot but be fair.

There is much that is frustrating, unfair, and unjust in human courts. The psalmist asks of mankind the questions that occur to us all: 'How long will you judge unjustly and show partiality to the wicked?' (Psa. 82:2).

The 1973 US Supreme Court *Roe vs Wade* decision, which redefined the unborn as outside the protection of the law, is one of the most arbitrary and unjust decisions ever made. It is arbitrary and unfair legally, medically, and morally, an exercise of what Chief Justice Rehnquist called 'raw judicial power'. Middle Eastern Muslim Islamic courts persecute Christian and other minorities in ways which are technically illegal even by their own laws. Southern courts in the Jim Crow era, rightly vilified by Harper Lee's *To Kill a Mockingbird*, were infamous for injustice. The courtroom of the notorious Nazi judge Roland Freisler, berating and badgering those accused of plotting against Hitler, was especially evil. The same was true of Cold War Soviet Bloc courts. All these courts were the opposite of what they should have been: they were (and are) oppressive, unjust, biased, and unfair.

In God's court, however, strict justice will prevail. 'He will judge the peoples with equity', says the psalmist (Psa. 96:10). The basis upon which God will judge is really very simple: deeds—what we have done and what we have failed to do. What could be fairer? Jesus tells of a coming day when those who have '*done good*' will be resurrected to

---

[43] Edwards, *Works*, II:10.

life, and those who have '*done evil*' will be resurrected to judgment (John 5:29). Jesus says, 'For the Son of Man is going to come with his angels in the glory of his Father, and then he will repay each person *according to what he has done*' (Matt. 16:27; cf. Rev. 20:12). We will be judged strictly according to our actions and culpable inactions.

We will all live or die according to our own sins, as Ezekiel explained centuries ago. Shall fathers eat sour grapes and their children's teeth be put on edge? No; 'The soul who sins shall die. The son shall not suffer for the iniquity of the father, nor the father suffer for the iniquity of the son. The righteousness of the righteous shall be upon himself, and the wickedness of the wicked shall be upon himself' (Ezek. 18:20). 'This is a most unquestionable truth', says Poole.[44] We are not accountable for what anyone else did, but only for what we have done. What could be fairer? The apostle Paul explains the same:

> He will render to each one according to his works: to those who by patience in well-doing seek for glory and honour and immortality, he will give eternal life; but for those who are self-seeking and do not obey the truth, but obey unrighteousness, there will be wrath and fury. There will be tribulation and distress for every human being who does evil, the Jew first and also the Greek (Rom. 2:6-9).

'He will judge men neither according to their professions nor their relations,' says Hodge, 'but according to their works.'[45] As a Junior High student I came within a hair's breadth of being punished for something I did not do. A couple of classmates lied and said they had seen me break into a locker. The vice-principal counted two against one and believed them rather than me. He said, 'I have been a cop for twenty years and I know when someone is guilty, and I think you're guilty.' I had no place to turn, no court of appeal, no jury of peers. Many of us will have been in similar or more serious situations, falsely accused and condemned with harmful consequences.

Abraham asked, 'Shall not the Judge of all the earth do what is just?' (Gen. 18:25). He will. Unlike my former vice-principal, God knows it all. He will not accuse us of something we did not do. Because he is

---

[44] Poole, *Commentary*, II:714.
[45] Hodge, *Romans*, p. 49.

holy, our reward or punishment will be just. The books will be opened and we will be judged according to our deeds (Rev. 20:12).

Comprehensive

Second, God's justice is *comprehensive*. All of our 'thoughts, words, and deeds' will be judged. Our Judge is an infinite God. He is infinitely holy; therefore sin will be relentlessly exposed and righteousness recognized. God is infinitely present, omnipresent; therefore he has always been there. No matter where I have been, he has been there and he knows. He is infinitely knowledgeable, omniscient; therefore he knows everything about all things. He knows not only *what* I did but also *why* I did it.

God's justice, then, includes the disclosure of *motives*. All those nice things I have done, things which everyone appreciated and admired, yet which I did because of a desire for prestige or because I wanted to be appreciated and admired, will be exposed and shown for what they were. When my motives were pure and yet I was accused of evil or self-serving motives, that injustice will be rectified. The apostle Paul told the Corinthian Christians that when the Lord comes he will 'disclose the motives of men's hearts' (1 Cor. 4:5 NASB), revealing all, says Hodge, that lies 'concealed in the recesses of the heart'.[46]

God's justice includes the disclosure of *closet* or *hidden behaviour*. All those awful things done in secret that no one knows about will be uncovered and exposed. Jesus said that what we have whispered in inner rooms will be shouted from housetops (Luke 12:2-3). Yet those who gave, prayed, and fasted in secret will be rewarded (Matt. 6:1-18). Nothing will be overlooked. 'For God is not unjust so as to overlook your work and the love that you have shown for his name in serving the saints, as you still do' (Heb. 6:10).

God's justice includes the disclosure of the *details*, from the greatest to the least. Jesus said we will render account on the day of judgment for 'every idle word' (Matt. 12:36 KJV). We will be condemned or rewarded not just for our acts, but also for our words; our profanity, our sarcasm, our destructive criticism, our gossip, and even our careless, unguarded jokes fall under judgment. Conversely, our virtuous, edifying, helpful,

---

[46] Hodge, *1 and 2 Corinthians*, p. 68.

grace-giving words will be rewarded (Eph. 4:29–5:4). The writer to the Hebrews describes a comprehensive judgment that includes the 'thoughts and intentions of the heart'! He writes of Christ, 'And no creature is hidden from his sight, but all are naked and exposed to the eyes of him to whom we must give account' (Heb. 4:13; cf. 4:12).

All things are 'laid open as by dissection', says Poole, by 'his most piercing eye'.[47] God's judgement is a *comprehensive* judgment. 'God hath an unerring eye to see,' says Charnock, 'as well as an unspotted holiness to hate, or an unbribable justice to punish'.[48]

Intense

Third, God's judgment will be *intense*. When studying the holiness of God we saw his attitude towards sin. Now we are examining God's active response to sin: anger and wrath. Classic definitions may help us. Leigh defines God's anger as 'an excellence of his own essence … *a settled and unchangeable resolution to punish sinners according to their sins*'.[49] Mueller explains that according to the Reformed understanding, 'the divine anger denotes, not a change of emotion in God, but his *constant purpose of punishing sin*'.[50] Packer describes God's wrath as 'the active manifestation of God's hatred of irreligion and moral evil'. John Murray calls it 'the holy revulsion of God's being against that which is the contradiction of his holiness'.[51]

There are more than twenty words in the Old Testament to describe the wrath of God. In total, there are 580 references to the anger or wrath of God in the Hebrew Scriptures. 'To the men of the Old Testament,' says Leon Morris (1914–2006) in his acclaimed work

[47] Poole, *Commentary*, III:825.

[48] Charnock, *Existence and Attributes*, I:472.

[49] Cited in Muller, *Post-Reformation Reformed Dogmatics*, III:585 (emphasis added).

[50] *Ibid*. (emphasis added).

[51] Cited in Packer, *Knowing God*, p. 166. Elsewhere Packer defines it as God's 'active judicial hostility to sin' (Packer, 'God Is Light', *Reformation Study Bible*, p. 168). God's wrath is exercised, says Wells, in order to restore 'to an unchallenged position all that is good, pure, true, beautiful, and right'. His wrath 'is the way in which God's holiness finally engages all that is wrong' (Wells, *God in the Whirlwind*, p. 121). 'It is the pure reaction of God to all that is impure' (*ibid.*, p. 122).

The Apostolic Preaching of the Cross, 'the wrath of God is both very real and very serious.' God's wrath, he says, 'is no capricious passion, but the stern reaction of the divine nature towards evil'.[52] Two words are used in the New Testament to describe God's wrath: *thumos* (anger) and *orgē* (wrath). God's *wrath* is specified in John 3:36; Romans 1:18; 9:22; Ephesians 5:6; Colossians 3:6; 1 Thessalonians 1:10; Revelation 11:18; 14:10; 16:19; 19:15; as well as Revelation 6:16, which speaks of the 'wrath of the Lamb'. *Anger* is attributed to God in Revelation 14:10, 19; 15:1, 7; 16:1; 19:15; as well as in parallel passages (without the vocabulary) in 2 Thessalonians 1:7-9; Romans 2:5-9; and Hebrews 12:29. The wrath of God, Morris continues, 'is not some irrational passion bursting forth uncontrollably, but a burning zeal for right coupled with a perfect hatred for everything that is evil'.[53] Wrath is a proper response of a holy God to sin. Packer further describes wrath as 'a right and necessary reaction to objective moral evil. God is only angry where anger is called for.'[54]

God's anger and wrath demonstrate his holy character and just government. The apostle Paul speaks of the day of wrath as a day which will reveal God's righteous judgment. He warns unrepentant sinners that 'because of your hard and impenitent heart you are storing up wrath for yourself on the day of wrath *when God's righteous judgment will be revealed*' (Rom. 2:5). As with God's *attitude* towards sin (his abhorrence of it), the Scriptures use the strongest language and imagery possible in describing God's *action* against sin. Deuteronomy 28:1-14 lists the blessings promised to Israel if they will obey; Deuteronomy 28:15-68 lists the curses pronounced should they fail to obey. Moses describes the wrath of God against sin manifesting itself in the most ghastly things: disease, war, famine, and brutal atrocities at the hands of a savage enemy. The wrath of God against sin is a fearsome thing indeed.

'He shall show his *indignation* against his enemies,' says the prophet Isaiah. 'For behold, the LORD will come in *fire*, and his chariots like the *whirlwind*, to render his *anger* in *fury*, and his rebuke with *flames*

---

[52] Leon Morris, *The Apostolic Preaching of the Cross* (1955; Grand Rapids, MI: Eerdmans, 1965), pp. 149, 150.

[53] *Ibid.*, p. 209.

[54] Packer, *Knowing God*, p. 136.

of fire' (Isa. 66:14, 15). God said that he would destroy Judah 'with an outstretched hand and a mighty arm, even in *anger* and *wrath* and great *indignation*' (Jer. 21:5 NASB). Jeremiah speaks of the 'storm of the LORD' which goes forth in wrath, 'a whirling tempest' which 'will burst upon the head of the wicked' (Jer. 23:19). Let us continue the story from our previous study in Ezekiel 16 (see Chapter 7) in which Israel plays the harlot and God reacts in wrath:

> And I will judge you as women who commit adultery and shed blood are judged, and bring upon you the blood of wrath and jealousy. And I will give you into their hands, and they shall throw down your vaulted chamber and break down your lofty places. They shall strip you of your clothes and take your beautiful jewels and leave you naked and bare. They shall bring up a crowd against you, and they shall stone you and cut you to pieces with their swords. And they shall burn your houses and execute judgments upon you in the sight of many women. I will make you stop playing the whore, and you shall also give payment no more. So will I satisfy my wrath on you, and my jealousy shall depart from you. I will be calm and will no more be angry. Because you have not remembered the days of your youth, but have enraged me with all these things, therefore, behold, I have returned your deeds upon your head, declares the Lord GOD. Have you not committed lewdness in addition to all your abominations? (Ezek. 16:38-43)

Israel's evil brings the 'wrath', 'jealousy', and 'anger' of an 'enraged' God. 'The words show how severely the Lord will deal with her,' says Greenhill of Israel, 'even like a husband whose rage and jealousy is up.'[55] God speaks further through Ezekiel of his 'jealousy' and 'blazing wrath' (Ezek. 38:19). Similarly, Nahum says, 'The LORD is a jealous and avenging God; the LORD is avenging and wrathful; the LORD takes vengeance on his adversaries and keeps wrath for his enemies' (Nahum 1:1-3). The psalmist says God 'will bathe his feet in the blood of the wicked' (Psa. 58:10-11).

The New Testament imagery of judgment becomes, if anything, even more vivid. The unmerciful servant in the parable is handed

---

[55] Greenhill, *Ezekiel*, p. 380.

over to torturers until he repays all he owes, and Jesus says, 'So also my heavenly Father will do to every one of you, if you do not forgive your brother from your heart' (Matt. 18:35). When Jesus compares the kingdom of heaven to a wedding feast, the man not dressed in wedding clothes is '[bound] hand and foot' and 'cast … into the outer darkness', into a place where there will be 'weeping and gnashing of teeth' (Matt. 22:13; cf. 25:30, 46). The evil servant who is not ready for his master's return shall be 'cut … in pieces' and assigned a place with the hypocrites: a place of 'weeping and gnashing of teeth' (Matt. 24:51). Jesus speaks of 'eternal punishment' (Matt. 25:46). He warns that it would be better to have a heavy millstone around our necks and be cast into the sea than to cause one of his little ones to stumble (Mark 9:42-50). It would have been better for Judas, Jesus said, never to have been born (Matt. 26:24; Mark 14:21). It would be better to have no hand, eye, or foot than to be led by them into what Jesus calls 'unquenchable fire, where the worm never dies and the fire is not quenched' (Mark 9:43-48). Jesus describes the rich man in the parable 'being in torment' and, lifting his eyes, wishing that Lazarus might 'dip the end of his finger in water and cool my tongue, for I am in anguish in this flame' (Luke 16:23-24). He pleads that someone might warn his brothers, 'lest they also come into this place of torment' (verse 28).

The apostle Paul speaks of a time when 'the Lord Jesus [will be] revealed from heaven with his mighty angels in flaming fire, inflicting vengeance on those who do not know God and on those who do not obey the gospel of our Lord Jesus. They will suffer the punishment of eternal destruction, away from the presence of the Lord and from the glory of his might' (2 Thess. 1:7-9).

James, sounding like an Old Testament prophet, warns of coming judgment:

> Come now, you rich, weep and howl for the miseries that are coming upon you. Your riches have rotted and your garments are moth-eaten. Your gold and silver have corroded, and their corrosion will be evidence against you and will eat your flesh like fire. You have laid up treasure in the last days. Behold, the wages of the labourers who mowed your fields, which you kept back by

> fraud, are crying out against you, and the cries of the harvesters have reached the ears of the Lord of hosts. You have lived on the earth in luxury and in self-indulgence. You have fattened your hearts in a day of slaughter. (James 5:1-5)

'Weep and howl', he says, warning of 'miseries' soon to be experienced. The luxury and wealth they enjoyed was but a fattening 'in a day of slaughter'. The apostle John portrays people pleading with the rocks and mountains to fall on them and hide them 'from the face of him who is seated on the throne, and from the wrath of the Lamb, for the great day of their wrath has come, and who can stand?' (Rev. 6:16-17).

Finally, John speaks of 'the wine press of the fury of the wrath [or 'fierce wrath'] of God the Almighty' (Rev. 19:15): not just wrath, and not just fierce wrath, but the fierce wrath of God the Almighty. He portrays hell as a 'lake of fire' (20:15). 'The great miseries of this life,' says Gurnall, 'are incomparably less than the least torment of hell.'[56] Hell is a place where he who can do the worst to you does the worst to you.

Yet the blessings of the righteous as described in Scripture are also intense, if that is the right word, also stretching human language to its capacity. The reward will be 'great' (Matt. 5:12). Repayment will be many times the loss (Mark 10:30). The righteous will experience 'fullness of joy' and 'pleasures for evermore' (Psa. 16:11). The apostle Paul cites Isaiah 64:4 as he promises the Corinthians and us, 'No eye has seen, nor ear heard, nor the heart of man imagined, what God has prepared for those who love him' (1 Cor. 2:9). Such things, says Poole, are 'not obvious to sense, nor to be comprehended by reason'.[57] Christian labourers will be rewarded (1 Cor. 3:8). Those who build on the foundation of Christ with 'gold, silver, [and] precious stones' 'will receive a reward', while others will 'suffer loss', their works being consumed; and while they themselves will be saved, it will be 'but only as through fire' (3:10-15). The saints across the ages have always had their eyes fixed on the heavenly reward (Heb. 11:26). The apostle John can speak of a 'full reward', and he hears Jesus promising, 'Behold, I

---

[56] Gurnall, *Christian in Complete Armour*, II:442.
[57] Poole, *Commentary*, III:544.

am coming soon, bringing my recompense with me, to repay everyone for what he has done' (2 John 8; Rev. 22:12).

As the apostle John describes our heavenly inheritance, he stretches the limits of earthly imagery: a city of pure gold; precious foundation stones of jasper, sapphire, chalcedony, emerald, sardonyx, sardius, and so on; gates of pearl; and streets of pure gold, like transparent glass (Rev. 21:18-21). He continues,

> And I saw no temple in the city, for its temple is the Lord God the Almighty and the Lamb. And the city has no need of sun or moon to shine on it, for the glory of God gives it light, and its lamp is the Lamb. By its light will the nations walk, and the kings of the earth will bring their glory into it (21:22-24).

'The scope of the whole,' says Poole, is 'to let us know that the mansions of heaven will be most glorious places, giving the souls of those to whom God shall give to enter into them, an infinite satisfaction, beyond what the most rich and glorious things in the world can give our outward senses.'[58]

Final

Fourth, God's judgment is not only fair, comprehensive, and intense, it is also *final*. His preliminary judgments will be followed by a final and irreversible judgment. God's judgment is eternal, everlasting. There is no court of appeal and no second chance. We will all stand before him. The sentence will be pronounced and that will be the end of it. There will be nowhere to hide, nowhere to run. There will be no one to help, no one to comfort, no one to listen. 'God's vindictive justice will appear strict, exact, awful and terrible, and therefore glorious', says Edwards.[59] God's final words will ring in our ears for all eternity. Our plight will be forever and unalterably fixed.

God's final verdict on the day of judgment will stand forever. The righteous will be blessed forever and the wicked cursed. Jesus uses the same word, 'eternal', in relation to both 'punishment' and 'life' (Matt. 25:46; cf. verse 41). The righteous will be eternally happy and the wicked eternally miserable. 'Eternity is the sting of the doctrine

---

[58] Poole, *Commentary*, III:1006.
[59] Quoted in Gestner, *Biblical Theology of Jonathan Edwards*, III:46.

of hell,' says Edwards, who admits 'this doctrine is indeed awful and dreadful'. He goes on to say, 'It is dreadful to think of it, but yet tis what God the eternal God who made us and who has us soul and body in his hands has abundantly declared unto us, so that so sure as God is true there will absolutely be no end to the misery of hell.'[60]

It is doubtful that anyone in the Christian tradition has thought more thoroughly about hell than did Edwards. Few have preached more on the subject than he did. Reviewing Edwards' sermons on Matthew 5:26 ('you will never get out until you have paid the last penny') and Mark 9:44 ('where their worm does not die and the fire is not quenched'), Gerstner reckons that Edwards 'annihilates annihilation'.[61] On the basis of Revelation 6:15-16 (the wicked crying for the mountains and rocks to fall on them), Edwards argues that 'Wicked men will hereafter earnestly wish to be turned to nothing and forever cease to be that they may escape the wrath of God.'[62] Annihilation is what they will want. 'See the insufferableness of wrath', says James Durham (1622–58) in his exposition of the book of Revelation.[63] 'Annihilation is the relief which the wicked, begging for, will never receive', says Gerstner.[64] What would be the point of Christ's suffering and dying if there were to be no suffering and death for the wicked?

Sinners must know that they face an eternity of torment. This is what God has promised, and he will keep his word. The climax of 'Sinners in the Hands of an Angry God' urges sober contemplation of this certainty:

> When you look forward, you shall see a long forever, a boundless duration before you, which will swallow up your thoughts, and amaze your soul: and you will absolutely despair of ever having any deliverance, any end, any mitigation, any rest at all; you will know certainly that you must wear out long ages, millions and

---

[60] Cited in Gestner, *Biblical Theology of Jonathan Edwards*, III:522, 523; see also Edwards, *Concerning the Endless Punishment of Those Who Die Impenitent, Works*, II:515-25.

[61] Gerstner, *Biblical Theology of Jonathan Edwards*, III:523.

[62] *Ibid.*, III:524.

[63] James Durham, *A Commentary on Revelation* (1658; Willow Street, PA: Old Paths Publications, 2000), p. 482.

[64] Gerstner, *Biblical Theology of Jonathan Edwards*, III:524.

millions of ages, in wrestling and conflicting with this almighty merciless vengeance, and then when you have so done, when so many ages have actually been spent by you in this manner, you will know that all is but a point to what remains. So that your punishment will indeed be infinite. Oh who can express what the state of a soul in such circumstances is! All that we can possibly say about it, gives but a very feeble, faint representation of it; tis inexpressible and inconceivable. For, *who knows the power of God's anger?*[65]

Many have struggled with reconciling God's goodness, mercy, grace, and even his justice with the idea of perpetual punishment. How is the endless torment of sinners consistent with the nature of God? The answer is that the punishment is proportionate to the offence. What is sin? We will let Edwards remind us: 'All sin may be resolved into hatred of God and our neighbour.'[66] 'Sin is of such a nature that it wishes ill, and aims at ill to God and man, but to God especially. It strikes at God. It would, if it could, procure his misery and death.'[67] Again: 'Sin calls contempt on the infinite glory and excellency of God. The language of it is that God is not an excellent being, but an odious one.'[68] According to an old Latin saying, *peccatum est deicidium*, sin is deicide, God-murder.

An offence committed against the Infinite requires infinite punishment. Sin against an infinite and blessed God is a sin of infinite evil incurring infinite guilt requiring infinite torments. Jonathan Edwards, in his revival sermon 'The Justice of God in the Damnation of Sinners' preached at Northampton during the Awakenings of 1734–35, warned, 'Sin against God, being a violation of infinite obligations, must be a crime infinitely heinous, and so deserving infinite punishment.'[69] If we fail to see the justice of this, says Edwards, it is because we lack 'a sense of the horrible evil of sin'. This leads us to 'pity the damned wretch' and view God badly for bringing this misery

---

[65] Edwards, *Works*, II:11.
[66] Edwards, *Great and Glorious God*, p. 169.
[67] *Ibid.*
[68] *Ibid.*
[69] Jonathan Edwards, *On Knowing Christ: Select Works of Jonathan Edwards* (Edinburgh: Banner of Truth Trust, 1990), p. 118.

upon them. We do this, Edwards continues, because 'we haven't sense enough of the evil of sin to stir up indignation enough in us against it' to balance our feelings of pity for the damned.[70] We fail to understand what Gerstner calls 'the infinite sinfulness of sin; the infinity of heinousness in wickedness'.[71]

Heaven, in contrast, will be a place of unimaginable happiness extending eternally in duration. The apostle Paul, 'caught up into paradise', heard 'inexpressible words' (2 Cor. 12:1-4 NASB). Edwards, while still a teenager, preached on Isaiah 3:10, recognizing that 'to pretend to describe the excellence, the greatness or duration of the happiness of heaven by the most artful composition of words would be but to darken and cloud it'.[72]

All the pleasures and comforts of earth are but a distant foretaste of the perfected and unfluctuating joys of heaven. The happiness of the saints will be progressive, as God gradually unveils his glory and as our capacity to grasp or receive that glory expands. This, too, will go on forever and ever. So it is that, whether for blessing or curse, God's judgment will be final and irreversible. 'It is appointed for man to die once,' says the writer to the Hebrews, 'and after that comes judgment' (Heb. 9:27).

Let us not trifle with such a God. Let us fear his judgment and flee from the wrath to come (Luke 3:7). If his justice is precise, according to what we have done; if it is both temporal and eternal; if it is fair, exhaustive, intense, final, and irreversible, let us heed the warning of the apostle Paul to the ancient Athenians: God, he said, 'has fixed a day on which he will judge the world in righteousness by a man whom he has appointed; and of this he has given assurance to all by raising him from the dead.' 'Now,' the apostle says, 'he commands all people everywhere to repent' (Acts 17:30-31).

[70] Edwards, cited in Gerstner, *Biblical Theology of Jonathan Edwards*, III:536.
[71] Gerstner, *Biblical Theology of Jonathan Edwards*, III:537.
[72] Cited in *ibid.*, III:544.

TEN

'Just and Justifier':
Righteousness Satisfied and Conferred

But now the righteousness of God has been manifested apart from the law, although the Law and the Prophets bear witness to it—the righteousness of God through faith in Jesus Christ for all who believe. For there is no distinction: for all have sinned and fall short of the glory of God, and are justified by his grace as a gift, through the redemption that is in Christ Jesus, whom God put forward as a propitiation by his blood, to be received by faith. This was to show God's righteousness, because in his divine forbearance he had passed over former sins. It was to show his righteousness at the present time, so that he might be just and the justifier of the one who has faith in Jesus.—Romans 3:21-26

W E have established that God is just. We have *defined* the justice of God as that virtue in God that guarantees that everyone gets what they deserve. We have examined how God *reveals* his justice, in his rewards and punishments in time and in eternity. We have explained the character of his justice: he ensures a fair, comprehensive, intense, and final judgment. However, we must know *by what standard moral creatures are to be judged*. If we are to be judged, what will be the criteria for judgment?

Standard of justice

The answer is that we will be judged by the criteria of God's law. God's law provides the terms of justice. It defines what is righteous and unrighteous, what is right and wrong, what is innocent and

213

blameworthy. 'The precepts of the LORD are right … the rules of the LORD are true, and righteous altogether' (Psa. 19:8-9; cf. 119:142, 151, 160). We are judged according to whether we have obeyed or violated God's righteous laws as summarized by the two great commandments and/or the Ten Commandments. Have I loved God and loved my neighbour (Luke 10:27; Deut. 6:5)? Have I honoured my parents (fifth commandment)? Have I guarded my neighbour's life (sixth commandment)? his marriage (seventh commandment)? his property (eighth commandment)? his reputation (particularly in a legal proceeding; ninth commandment)? Has my heart-attitude towards my neighbour been right (tenth commandment)?

Likewise, have I given God his due right to exclusive service, prescribed worship, with reverence, on the authorized day (first to fourth commandments)? God's law determines who is righteous. God's law determines what justice requires. By God's law we are and shall be judged. Sin is lawlessness (Gk *anomia*, 1 John 3:4). Sin is defined by God's law and is an offence against God. The standard of justice is the law of God in its integrity. What does God require of us? 'Perfect and perpetual obedience', to use the language of the Larger Catechism (Q. 20). Keep the whole law yet stumble at one point, says James, and one is guilty of breaking all (James 2:10). Fail to 'do' and 'abide by all things written in the Book of the Law', and one is cursed (Gal. 3:10). The soul that sins shall die (Ezek. 18:4). The wages of sin is death (Rom. 6:23). The justice of God requires that every act of unrighteousness be punished with eternal death.

What, then, is the principle by which we are punished and rewarded? The principle of equitable compensation is expressed in the *lex talionis*, the principle of an eye for an eye and a tooth for a tooth (Exod. 21:24). This principle was probably never taken literally, but rather expresses the principle of fair, proportionate, and suitable compensation (see also Lev. 24:17-21; Deut. 19:21).[1] If you take a life, you lose a life. If you kill your neighbour's animal, you must 'make it good', restoring it in kind (Lev. 24:21). 'Nor could any law be more just', says Henry.[2] Modern insurance policies embody this principle. If you damage your

---

[1] See Poole, *Commentary*, on Exod. 21:24.
[2] Henry, *Commentary*, on Deut. 19:21.

neighbour's house or car, the value lost must be compensated through either monetary means, replacement, or repairs. The punishment must fit the crime; penalties must be proportionate to the costs incurred. Jesus does not revoke this principle but rather disallows its application in cases of personal vengeance (Matt. 5:38-42), which would result in 'universal confusion', says Henry, 'and make men like the fishes of the sea'.[3] Again, we ask, what could be fairer than the *lex talionis*?

The principle of proportionality means that there will be degrees of punishment and reward in eternity. According to Edwards, 'The punishment and misery of the wicked man in another world will be in proportion to the sin that they are guilty of.'[4] Jesus spoke of it being 'more tolerable' on the day of judgment for Sodom and Gomorrah than for Capernaum and the cities of Galilee (Matt. 11:20-24). The criteria are 'not only how bad we were, but how much better we might have been', says Henry.[5] 'Men's offences are increased by their obligations', adds Trapp.[6] Some will receive worse punishment than others. The wicked are 'storing up wrath ... on the day of wrath' (Rom. 2:5). They 'accumulate a store of wrath for themselves', says Hodge;[7] that is, with each sin unrepentant sinners are compounding the wrath that will be poured out upon them. The 'damned in hell would be ready to give the world if they could to have the number of their sins to have been one less', Edwards insists.[8] One single sin was enough to cast Adam and Eve out of the garden and them and their descendants into hell. On the basis of Matthew 5:22 (where Jesus speaks of increasing guilt and punishments, from the court to the Supreme Court, to 'the hell of fire'), Edwards argues that by a second act of sin the sinner 'now deserves twice so hot a place in hell'.[9] The notion that one may as well 'live it up' now on earth since one is going to hell anyway is tragically mistaken. The wicked by their sins are gathering sticks for their own fire. Punishment in hell will be in exact proportion to the sins

---

[3] Henry, *Commentary*, on Exod. 21:24.
[4] Edwards, cited in Gerstner, *Biblical Theology of Jonathan Edwards*, III:511.
[5] Henry, *Commentary*, on Matt. 11:20-24.
[6] Trapp, *Commentary*, V:163.
[7] Hodge, *Romans*, p. 49.
[8] Edwards, cited in Gerstner, *Biblical Theology of Jonathan Edwards*, III:512.
[9] *Ibid.*, III:514.

committed. Even in hell itself, as the wicked rebel against their plight, cursing God and complaining of his injustice, they will be punished further, increasing their misery—a pattern that will continue forever, compounding their guilt and intensifying their suffering eternally.

Likewise, there will be degrees of reward in heaven. The imperfect works of Christians will be accepted as they are offered in Christ, and rewarded (2 Tim. 1:18; 4:8; Dan. 12:2, 3). Jesus speaks of the 'great' reward awaiting those persecuted for righteousness' sake (Matt. 5:12). These are rewards of grace, not merit. The Westminster Confession of Faith puts it this way:

> Notwithstanding [their flawed lives], the persons of believers being accepted through Christ, their good works also are accepted in him; not as though they were in this life wholly unblamable and unreprovable in God's sight; but that he, looking upon them in his Son, is pleased to accept and reward that which is sincere, although accompanied with many weaknesses and imperfections (XVI.6).

The Confession's Scripture proofs point us to passages already familiar to us in our study: Hebrews 6:10 and the promise that 'God is not unjust so as to overlook your work'; and Jesus' likening judgment day to the master saying to his wise servant, 'Well done, good and faithful servant' (Matt. 25:21, 23). The 'work' of Hebrews 6 and the 'good' of Matthew 25 are both relative, not absolute. They are counted as good because God looks upon them in his Son and because they were done in sincerity. Good works performed with good motives will be rewarded. The more good works, the greater the rewards.

There will be degrees of blessedness as well. All the saints will be filled with joy, but, as we have seen, they will vary in their capacities to be filled. There are vessels of varying sizes and crowns will be awarded with differing lustre. 'We ought to seek high degrees of glory in heaven', says Edwards.[10] Those who sow sparingly will reap sparingly. Those who sow bountifully will reap bountifully (2 Cor. 9:6). Consequently, we ought to 'abound in every good work', that God might 'increase the harvest of [our] righteousness' (2 Cor. 9:8-10; cf. Luke 6:38; Matt. 10:41).

---

[10] Edwards, cited in Gerstner, *Biblical Theology of Jonathan Edwards*, III:553.

Justice confirmed and satisfied

Are we doubtful at all about the certainty, necessity, and severity of divine justice as the Bible describes it? Yet it is confirmed in the design of the cross. The justice of God in relation to sinners may be satisfied in one of two ways. Sinners themselves may suffer in hell forever, or Christ may suffer on their behalf. We have argued that, because sin is against an infinite God, it is an offence of infinite evil requiring infinite punishment. If the sinner is to bear his guilt himself, his punishment could not be of infinite strength, because finite beings would be consumed immediately by wrath of infinite proportions. Consequently, the justice of God is satisfied through punishment that is of infinite length. Hell's torments are eternal. 'The punishment of the wicked cannot be infinite in *intensity*,' says Edwards, 'and therefore it is so in *duration*.'[11]

What is the alternative to our own personal eternal punishment? Might there be a substitute? 'God could not redeem us without ... the presence of that which is of infinite worth and value', says Edwards. This was 'absolutely necessary', he insists. 'There was no other way to satisfy God's justice.' He continues: 'It came to this: either we must die eternally or the Son of God must spill his blood; either we or God's own Son must suffer God's wrath, one of the two.'[12] That is to say, the infinite payment that God's justice requires his mercy provides. The mercy of God moved him to provide a means of pardon for sinners. 'The greatest evidence that ever was given of the justice of God,' says Flavel, 'was in his exacting full satisfaction for our sins upon Christ.'[13] Owen agrees: 'The death of Christ is a most solemn exemplar of the last judgment.'[14] God is not like the unjust judge who winks at sin. Forgiveness must be extended in a way that gives expression to God's grace while not compromising the requirements of his justice. His mercy must not undermine the moral foundation of the universe. 'O

[11] Edwards, cited in Gerstner, *Biblical Theology of Jonathan Edwards*, III:57 (emphasis added). Gurnall says much the same: 'their sufferings are infinite *extensive*—extensively, because everlasting; but his were infinite intensive—intensively (*Christian in Complete Armour*, I:497).
[12] Edwards, *Great and Glorious God*, p. 30.
[13] Flavel, *Exposition, Works*, VI:154.
[14] Owen, *Communion with God, Works*, II:106.

deceive not yourselves, poor souls,' Gurnall warns. 'God will not make war between his own attributes to make peace with you!'[15]

The solution—the only solution that would satisfy both the mercy and the justice of God—was the cross. 'God gave his beloved Son to the death for this end, that it might be known what a just and righteous God he is', says Boston.[16] The wages of sin is death (Rom. 6:23). Forgiveness of sin is possible only through the offering of a blood sacrifice (Heb. 9:22). 'God did not design that, in his manner of dealing with mankind, men should be pardoned and accepted without atonement', says Edwards.[17] God's insistence upon atonement, Edwards continues, 'is represented by all the prodigious expense and labour, the multitude of services and ceremonies, so great an apparatus, and so great pomp, which with so much exactness were prescribed' in the Old Testament.[18] Yet 'it is impossible for the blood of bulls and goats to take away sins' (Heb. 10:4). If there were to be a satisfaction for human guilt, a sacrifice was required that encompassed infinite value.

God's answer was nothing less than the incarnation of the eternal Son of God (John 1:1ff.; Phil. 2:5ff.), the Lamb of God who would take away the sin of the world (John 1:29). In him, justice and mercy 'kiss each other' (Psa. 85:10). Through his suffering Christ offered to God what was 'fully and completely equivalent to what we owed to divine justice for our sins'.[19]

This is the burden of the apostle Paul's presentation of the atonement in Romans 3:21-26. Jesus' death was a propitiatory sacrifice ('propitiation by his blood')—that is, one which satisfied or averted the just wrath of God against sin.[20] The fearful reality of God's wrath is where the apostle Paul began his presentation of the gospel in Romans 1. Wrath, as we have seen, is the response of a just God to the 'ungodliness and unrighteousness of men' (1:18). An adequate payment or sacrifice for human guilt was essential because for generations God 'in his divine forbearance … passed over former sins' (3:25).

---

[15] Gurnall, *Christian in Complete Armour*, I:512.
[16] Boston, *Illustration of the Doctrines, Works*, I:108.
[17] Edwards, *Great and Glorious God*, p. 187.
[18] *Ibid*.
[19] *Ibid*., p. 186.
[20] See Packer, *Knowing God*, pp. 163-69 for a succinct discussion of propitiation.

Abraham, Moses, David, Isaiah, and all the Old Testament saints received pardon without an adequate blood sacrifice, though in anticipation of a future sufficient sacrifice. There is a sense in which this forbearance was extended to pagan humanity as well. 'In past generations [God] allowed all the nations to walk in their own ways,' says the apostle (Acts 14:16). Again, he preached, 'The times of ignorance God overlooked'—meaning, says John Murray, 'God did not visit man with wrath commensurate with their sins' (Acts 17:30). God's forbearance, Murray continues, 'was liable to be interpreted as indifference to the claims of justice'.[21] Yet 'it was to show his righteousness at the present time, so that he might be just and the justifier of the one who has faith in Jesus' (Rom. 3:26). In the fullness of time Christ offered that essential propitiatory blood sacrifice, and God thereby vindicated his justice, 'show[ing] his righteousness at the present time'. The cross was a 'demonstrat[ion]' (NASB) not only of God's love (Rom. 5:8), but also of his righteousness. His passing over sin made it necessary for him to demonstrate what Murray calls his 'inherent justice' by showing 'that justification demands nothing less than the propitiation made in Jesus' blood'.[22] To what end? 'That he might be just and the justifier of the one who has faith in Jesus'; that he might be just in justifying sinners (3:26). At the cross the demands of the law were met. At the cross the demands of justice were met. 'In the propitiation,' says Robert Haldane, 'the justice of God in the salvation of sinners shines conspicuously.'[23]

God is both 'just' (one who executes perfect justice) and 'the justifier' (the one who justifies repentant and believing sinners, declaring their sins forgiven and crediting them with righteousness; Rom. 3:21–4:12). C. E. B. Cranfield (1915–2015), one of the great exegetes of the twentieth century, understood the apostle Paul's meaning to be 'that God might be righteous even in justifying'—that is, 'that he might justify righteously without compromising his own righteousness'.[24] This is why the

---

[21] John Murray, *The Epistle to the Romans* (Grand Rapids, MI: Eerdmans, 1968), p. 119.

[22] *Ibid.*, p. 120.

[23] Haldane, *Epistle to the Romans*, p. 153.

[24] C. E. B. Cranfield, *A Critical and Exegetical Commentary on the Epistle to the Romans* (Edinburgh: T&T Clark, 1975), p. 213.

death of Christ had to be a propitiation, a *hilastērion*: 'For God to have forgiven man's sins lightly—a cheap forgiveness which would have implied that moral evil does not matter very much—would have been altogether unrighteous, a violation of his truth and profoundly unmerciful and unloving toward man, since it would have annihilated their dignity as persons morally accountable.'[25] Cranfield continues: 'the purpose of Christ's being *hilastērion* was to achieve a divine forgiveness which is worthy of God, consonant with his righteousness, in that it does not insult God's creature man by any suggestion that it is after all of but small consequence'.[26]

The classic authors agree. According to Thomas Boston, 'Christ stepped in, and made a sufficient satisfaction by his death and sufferings, that so God might exercise his mercy without prejudice to his justice. Thus the blood of the Son of God must be shed for sin, to let the world see that he is a just and righteous God.'[27] Jesus, the apostle Paul teaches, became a curse for us and thereby 'redeemed us from the curse of the law', that we might be saved (Gal. 3:10-14). We are redeemed, said the Scottish Puritan James Ferguson (1621–67), commenting on these verses, only 'by payment of a sufficient price, and by giving a just satisfaction to a provoked God'. Redemption, he says, means 'a delivery obtained by a payment of a just price'.[28] Those who would understand the justice of God need only look at the cross and behold the suffering of the God-Man Jesus Christ. Hear his plea in the garden of Gethsemane for an alternative means of redemption. See him sweat drops of blood, and realize that there was no other way to honour both God's mercy and his justice. See the beatings, the

---

[25] Cranfield, *Romans.*, pp. 213-14.

[26] *Ibid.*, p. 214; Hodge explains in his comment on the phrase 'just and justifier': 'A judge is unjust when he allows a criminal to be pronounced righteous, and treated accordingly. On the other hand he acts justly when he pronounces the offender guilty, and secures the infliction of the penalty which the law announces. What the apostle means to say is, that there is no such disregard to the claims of justice in the justification of the sinner who believes in Christ' (Hodge, *Romans*, p. 98).

[27] Boston, *Illustration of the Doctrines, Works*, I:108.

[28] James Ferguson, *The Epistles of Paul to the Galatians, Ephesians, Philippians, Colossians and Thessalonians* (1659–74, 1841; Edinburgh: Banner of Truth Trust, 1978), p. 54.

mockery, the humiliation, the nails, and the cross, and understand what justice required. Indeed, says John Owen,

> To see him who is the wisdom of God, and the power of God, always beloved of the Father; to see him, I say, fear, and tremble, and bow, and sweat, and pray, and die; to see him lifted up upon the cross, the earth trembling under him, as if unable to bear his weight; and the heavens darkened over him, as if shut against his cry; and himself hanging between both, as if refused by both; and all this because our sins did not meet upon him;—this of all things doth most abundantly manifest the severity of God's vindictive justice.[29]

The cross shows us the seriousness with which God takes his justice. Again, Owen says, 'Never was sin seen to be more abominably sinful and full of provocation, than when the burden of it was upon the shoulders of the Son of God. ... Would you, then, see the true demerit of sin—take the measure of it from the mediation of Christ, especially his cross.'[30] Similarly, Stephen Charnock maintains,

> Not all the vials of judgments, that have, or shall be poured out upon the wicked world, not the flaming furnace of a sinner's conscience, nor the irreversible sentence pronounced against the rebellious evils, nor the groans of the damned creatures, give such a demonstration of God's hatred of sin, as the wrath of God let loose upon his Son.[31]

Judgment, then, is the certain, necessary, and severe work of God, satisfied at the cross or, for those who will not repent, on the day of judgment. If God ordained the cross at great cost to himself, we can know with certainty that a day of judgment will come. Boston insists, 'When we hear that God exposed his own Son to the utmost severity of wrath and vengeance, may we not justly cry out, O the infinite evil of sin! O the inflexible severity of divine justice! It is a fearful thing to fall into the hands of the living God.'[32]

[29] Owen, *Communion with God*, *Works*, II:85.
[30] *Ibid.*, II:96-97.
[31] Charnock, *Existence and Attributes*, I:211. He says again, 'Justice indeed gave the stroke, but holiness ordered it.' (*Ibid.*).
[32] Boston, *Illustration of the Doctrines*, *Works*, I:109.

Response

What does all this mean for us? How are we to respond?

Flee from sin

First, because God is judge, let us *flee from sin*. Swinnock reminds us not only of the heinousness of sin, but also of its foolishness. Sin is a kind of insanity. When we sin we war against Deity, we fight against a God 'who is stronger than millions of armies, who is almighty, and [we] provoke him to destroy [us] who can wink [us] into the other world, and look [us] into the eternal lake, and hiss [us] into hell-flames'.[33] Swinnock warns us,

> I tell thee thou provokest a God who is incomparable in holiness, and hath threatened thy destruction; who is incomparable in power, and can accomplish what he hath threatened; and who is incomparable in truth, and cannot but make good with his arm what he hath spoken with his mouth.[34]

'Here is sauciness indeed,' he says, 'for a pitiful nothing to challenge almightiness to battle.'[35]

Not only is sin foolhardy, but it is contrary to self-interest: 'What a madman is he who will stake a million against a mite, a crown against a crumb, substance against shadows, all things against nothing, the blessed boundless God against a moment's sensual delight!'[36] Ponder carefully what sin would have us forfeit:

> Friend, think of it seriously the next time thou art tempted to sin, will this oath, or this cup, or this theft, or this wantonness, or this neglect of duty, balance the everlasting loss of the incomparable God? Will this lust, this moment's pleasure, make amends for the loss of him who is eternal life, a river of unconceivable and unchangeable pleasures? Shall I be so besotted, bewitched, distracted, as to lose real mercies for lying vanities, the fountain of living waters for broken cisterns, the food of angels for the

---

[33] Swinnock, *Incomparableness of God*, *Works*, IV:461.
[34] *Ibid.*, IV:462.
[35] *Ibid.*
[36] *Ibid.*, IV:463.

world's scraps, a precious soul, an inestimable Saviour, an incomparable God, for a toy, a trifle, a poor empty gilded nothing?[37]

Swinnock continues at length. To lose God is to lose everything worth having:

> To depart from the incomparable God for ever, to lose the only paradise of pleasures, the only fountain of living waters, the only author of true felicity; to lose the unsearchable mine of riches, the inexhaustible well of salvation, the inestimable Sun of righteousness; to lose the dearest father, the wisest guide, the strongest shield, the sweetest love, the closest friend, the tenderest mercy, the richest grace, the highest honour, the only happiness; to lose the Lord of life, the Lord of glory, the Lord of lords; to lose the God of hope, the God of all grace, the God of all consolation, the God of peace, the God of gods, the God and Father of our Lord Jesus Christ, the incomparable God; and to lose him totally and for ever, is the loss of all losses, is such a loss as no tongue can declare, no mind can conceive, is such a loss as never was the like before it, nor shall, nor can be the like after it. He that hath lost God, hath nothing left that is good, he hath lost all that was worth having or saving.[38]

Consider the horror when in eternity the damned realize their folly:

> Ah, sinner, when thou shalt know and believe what a vast treasure, what a river of pleasure, what a perfect good, what fullness of joy, what solid comfort, what real satisfaction, what a weight of glory thou hast lost for ever, without the least hopes and possibility of regaining, and lost for base, vile, sordid lusts, for a little foolish brutish momentary pleasure; what thoughts, thinkest thou, will then seize thee? What anguish and remorse surprise thee? Ah, how wilt thou loathe and hate, and curse thyself for thy folly and madness! Thou wilt gnash thy teeth for envy at them that sit at heaven's table, feasting with the fruit of the tree of life, and drinking of the pure rivers of water which flow from the throne of God and the Lamb: and thou wilt weep and wail for thy own distraction, that thou shouldst refuse the offers of all

---

[37] Swinnock, *Incomparableness of God*, *Works*, IV:463.
[38] *Ibid.*, IV:463-64.

those dainties, and delicates, and delights, when they were made to thee in the day of thy life; that thou shouldst shut thy own mouth, and wilfully refuse all those rich and costly cordials, and shut the door of heaven and happiness against thee with thine own hands. Ah, sinner, little dost thou know at the present what it is to lose this God.[39]

For sin, one not only loses everything worth having in losing God, but one also gains an infinite foe: 'As there is no friend like God, and therefore their privative misery must be great, exceeding great, inconceivably great; so there is no enemy like God; and therefore the positive misery of sinners must be matchless and beyond all comparisons.'[40]

In the eternal world, God 'puts off all pity, all tenderness, all bowels towards' the unrepentant; and furthermore,

the other world is the place wherein his justice, that is now clouded and eclipsed, shall shine forth in its full force and strength, and appear in all its beauty and brightness. And therefore, it must of necessity be a fearful thing for a poor creature to fall into the hands of the living God; to have nothing but his naked flesh, his own weak soul, to bear the stroke of infinite power, set on and urged to strike home by infinite anger, and that forever.[41]

With good reason Swinnock asks of those who choose sin over God,

Ah, why then shouldst thou, for a little profit, a little pleasure, a little honour for a few days,—for thy life is but a vapour,—bring thyself under a necessity of frying in the flames, and boiling in the furnace of the Almighty God's anger for ever and ever? O friend, be wise on this side the other world.[42]

Flee to the cross

Second, because God is judge, let us *flee to the cross*. Jesus satisfies the requirements of God's justice for us, as we have just seen. A favourable

[39] Swinnock, *Incomparableness of God*, *Works*, IV:465-66.
[40] *Ibid.*, IV:466.
[41] *Ibid.*, IV:467.
[42] *Ibid.*

verdict on judgment day is impossible apart from Christ. Not only the apostle Paul, but also the apostle John teaches that if we sin we have an 'advocate with the Father, Jesus Christ the righteous'. He adds that 'he is the propitiation for our sin' (1 John 2:1-2). Christ alone satisfies for us all that the justice of God requires. He alone quenches God's wrath so that repentant sinners might be spared, forgiven, and cleansed (1 John 1:9). Again, John writes, 'In this is love, not that we have loved God but that he loved us and sent his Son to be the propitiation for our sins' (1 John 4:10). Jesus' death is the blood sacrifice that alone turns away the wrath of God 'so that we might live through him' (1 John 4:9). Which shall it be? Shall Jesus remove my infinite guilt? Shall he pay my debt on my behalf? Or shall I do so, through an eternity of hell's torments? Shall he die or shall I? Jesus alone 'delivers us from the wrath to come' (1 Thess. 1:10). Only those who believe in the Son of God will 'not perish' on the day of judgment (John 3:16). Those who refuse to believe are 'condemned already' (John 3:18), and 'the wrath of God remains on [them]' (John 3:36).

Gurnall refers to the justice of God as his 'fiery attribute', the 'naked consideration' of which, apart from mercy, or contemplated 'without gospel comment' ('through which alone it can be safely and comfortably viewed by a sin-smitten soul'), 'must needs appal and dispirit him, whoever he be, yea, *kindle a fire of horror in his bosom*'. Only by faith can the soul 'walk in this fiery attribute with his comforts unsinged'.[43] Do not allow the day of death to come and not be prepared. Do not imagine that we can stand before God empty-handed, pleading our own virtue, without a Saviour, without an advocate, with nothing between ourselves and a holy God. Do not imagine facing judgment day clothed, not in the righteousness of Christ, but only in 'filthy rags' of our own righteousness (Isa. 64:6 KJV). Augustus Toplady (1740–78) made powerful use of this theme in the last stanza of his well-loved hymn 'Rock of Ages':

> While I draw this fleeting breath,
> When mine eyelids close in death,
> When I soar to worlds unknown,
> See thee on thy judgment throne,

---

[43] Gurnall, *Christian in Complete Armour*, II:107 (emphasis added).

> Rock of Ages, cleft for me,
> Let me hide myself in thee.

When we draw our last 'fleeting breath' and 'see thee', the great God of heaven and earth, 'on [his] judgment throne', what is there to do but plead,

> Rock of Ages, cleft for me,
> Let me hide myself in thee?

Flee to Christ. Flee to the cross. He bore our sins in his body (1 Pet. 2:24). He died, once for all, the just for the unjust, that he might bring us to God (3:18).

Live holy lives

Third, because God is Judge, *we ought to live holy lives*. The apostle Paul says that we have been 'saved by him from the wrath of God' (Rom. 5:9). Yet we are not to grow complacent. Knowledge of the coming judgment ought to inspire us to lead a godly life. Hell's torments will be both 'intolerable and interminable', as Gurnall puts it, both 'endless and easeless'.[44] Fear of that judgment is not the highest motive for the Christian life, but it is a valid one. 'And if you call on him as Father who judges impartially according to each one's deeds,' says the apostle Peter, 'conduct yourselves *with fear* throughout the time of your exile' (1 Pet. 1:17). While we enjoy 'this sweet relation of a Father to us in Christ', Alexander Nisbet (*c*. 1623–69) explains from 1 Peter 1:17, 'we ought also to cherish other considerations of him and look upon him as standing in other relations to us, especially that of a Judge'. Peter urges this, 'that so our hearts may be kept in awe and fear of offending [God], and our homeliness [i.e. familiarity] may not mar our reverence'. Notice, Nisbet continues, 'the apostle holds forth both these relations between the Lord and his children to be jointly considered by them'.[45]

The apostle Paul warns the Corinthian Christians about doing works consisting of wood, hay, or straw as opposed to gold, silver, and

---

[44] Gurnall, *Christian in Complete Armour*, II:435, 509.
[45] Alexander Nisbet, *1 and 2 Peter* (1658; Edinburgh: Banner of Truth Trust, 1982), p. 42.

precious stones. He says 'the Day'—the judgment day—'will disclose' its quality: 'fire will test what sort of work each one has done'. Defective works will be consumed, while those built on Christ 'will receive a reward' (1 Cor. 3:13-14).

The works of Christians will be judged, and Christians are to be motivated by the promise of reward as well as by the warning of loss. Judgment, says the apostle Peter, begins at the household of God (1 Pet. 4:17). Nisbet describes this judgment as not only loving discipline to the godly (Heb. 12:6), but also 'acts of his holy justice, correcting and humbling them'.[46] Let each one take care how he builds upon the foundation (1 Cor. 3:10). Were we thinking that any service might be acceptable to God, whatever the motive, whatever the aim, whatever the attitude? 'Take care', the apostle urges. Rewards will be distributed accordingly.

The apostle Paul expresses the same expectation of judgment, reward, and loss in 1 Corinthians 4 as he does in 1 Corinthians 3. As he seeks to restrain the Corinthians' judgmentalism, he says, 'It is the Lord who judges me' (1 Cor. 4:4). He urges them to withhold judgments because when the Lord comes, he 'will bring to light the things now hidden in darkness and will disclose the purposes of the heart'. The judgment of which he speaks is of believers: 'Then each one will receive his commendation from God' (4:5). Only believers will receive commendation on judgment day, though the implication is that not all will receive the same commendation or be commended in the same way or to the same degree. 'Each one' receiving 'his' commendation underscores the distinctive distribution of God's rewards. Particularly in view are 'the things now hidden in darkness'—that is, what was true of us in private, what never became public, the person that we were when no one was around or when we were anonymous. 'The purposes of the heart', our true motives, our aims, our designs, are in view. Our behaviour, not just externally, but internally, will be judged and rewarded accordingly. Our contributions to God's kingdom will be assessed. They will not simply be rubber-stamped, evaluated, or blindly commended; their true nature will be revealed. Judgment day will disclose the motives of even believing hearts (4:7). The apostle's

---

[46] Nisbet, *1 and 2 Peter*, p. 183.

aim is to motivate us by reminding us of the thoroughness of the judgment to come.

Listen to the apostle Paul warning certain believers who are indulging in sexual immorality (1 Thess. 4:3-6). Their sanctification is the will of God. He urges them to abstain, to control their bodies in holiness and not in passion. He urges them not to 'transgress and wrong [their] brother in this matter'. Why? 'Because the Lord is an avenger in all these things.' Paul warns of judgment. This was not the first time the apostle taught this; he continues, 'as we told you beforehand and solemnly warned you'. The apostle Paul uses what James Ferguson calls 'this inferior motive' of judgment to 'dissuade even believers'. Ferguson would have us learn from the apostle: 'There must be not only love to the commander to constrain, but also the terror of God to persuade.' The apostle, he says, appeals not only to the will of God but also to 'God's vengeance and terror'.[47] He uses not just the good news of the gospel, not just the teaching of justification, but also the threat of divine vengeance ('the Lord is an avenger') to motivate obedience.

The writer to the Hebrews warns against defiant and wilful disobedience by referring to God's judgment:

> For if we go on sinning deliberately after receiving the knowledge of the truth, there no longer remains a sacrifice for sins, but a fearful expectation of judgment, and a fury of fire that will consume the adversaries .... For we know him who said, 'Vengeance is mine; I will repay.' And again, 'The Lord will judge his people.' It is a fearful thing to fall into the hands of the living God (Heb. 10:26-27, 30-31).

The certainty of 'judgment', of fiery judgment, of divine vengeance, of 'the Lord' who 'will judge his people' is meant to motivate his readers (then and now) not to 'shrink back' and be 'destroyed' but to 'have faith and preserve their souls' (Heb. 10:39). He again urges us to faithfulness in 12:29, motivating us by reminding us that 'our God is a consuming fire'. 'His gospel law, in the contempt of it,' says Poole, 'will be as the fiery law at Sinai, adjudging such sinners unto fire unquench-

---

[47] James Ferguson, *Epistles of Paul*, p. 420.

able.'[48] The author of Hebrews writes as he does not to undermine our assurance but to expose our presumption, if we are guilty of such.

The apostle Paul likewise warns Gentile believers of their haughty attitude towards Jews. He says,

> They were broken off because of their unbelief, but you stand fast through faith. So do not become proud, but fear. For if God did not spare the natural branches, neither will he spare you. Note then the kindness and the severity of God: severity towards those who have fallen, but God's kindness to you, provided you continue in his kindness. Otherwise you too will be cut off (Rom. 11:20-22).

The danger of being 'cut off' and becoming a subject of God's 'severity', like that then being experienced by unbelieving Jews, was meant to motivate believers then and now to 'continue in his kindness'.

Jesus himself warns of people who prophesy, cast out demons, and perform miracles *in his name* (emphatic in its repetition) to whom he will nevertheless say, 'I never knew you; depart from me, you workers of lawlessness' (Matt. 7:21-23). Clearly Jesus is concerned about unbelief of professing believers masked by self-deception. 'Men are wondrous apt to deceive themselves in point of salvation', warns Trapp.[49] The Lord's warning of rejection on judgment day is meant to motivate us to know our own hearts and not make that error.

None of these warnings undermines the fact of the eternal security of believers. Yet there can be no room for complacency among the children of God. In an age of cheap grace and carnality, this needs to be said. If we call ourselves Christians and yet lead unholy lives, we, like those in Matthew 7, will find ourselves on the wrong side of eternity. True believers cannot lose their salvation, yet some may *profess* Christ but not *possess* him. Some may not have trusted Christ but presumed on him. So multiple passages warn us: we must continue in obedience or be cut off. We must persevere to the end in order to be saved (Matt. 24:13). Scripture does not hesitate to motivate us through fear at this point. It may not be the purest form of motivation, but, if nothing else, the terror of who God is and of what he can do ought

---

[48] Poole, *Commentary*, III:874.
[49] Trapp, *Commentary*, V:133.

to inspire us to pursue holiness. The apostle Paul discloses that the 'judgment seat of Christ' motivates his Christian service, for he says, 'Knowing the fear of the Lord, we persuade others' (2 Cor. 5:10-11).

Warn unbelievers

Fourth, because God will judge the world, *our evangelism ought to warn of his judgment*. The apostle Peter explained to the Gentiles in Caesarea his task as a preacher in relation to the judgment seat of Christ. He said that God had 'commanded us to preach to the people and to testify that [Christ] is the one appointed by God to be judge of the living and the dead' (Acts 10:42). The apostle Paul likewise concludes his gospel presentation to the Athenians by saying that God 'commands all people everywhere to repent, because he has fixed a day on which he will judge the world in righteousness by a man whom he has appointed; and of this he has given assurance to all by raising him from the dead' (Acts 17:30-31).

Fear of being labelled a 'fire and brimstone' preacher has largely muffled this warning today. At times people have been exhorted by preachers to be saved, yet not known exactly from what they are to be saved. Today's evangelism is often insipid, failing to tell people of sin and judgment. Do we really believe God will judge the world? That there is a day of wrath? Do our friends and families get any impression from our words and actions that such a fate awaits them? Do we ever warn them—in fact, have we ever even once warned them—of the day of wrath which awaits them? We shy away from this because we are afraid of using 'fear tactics'. We do not want to scare them into the kingdom. Yet we should ask: Why does God use them? Why are there such vivid warnings of wrath if he does not intend to put his fear into us and lead us by that fear to repentance? Why does he appeal to our enlightened self-interest with rewards and punishments? If he uses such 'tactics', then why not we?

The apostle Paul calls unbelievers 'children of wrath' (Eph. 2:3), 'vessels of wrath' (Rom. 9:22), and those who are 'storing up wrath' for 'the day of wrath' (Rom. 2:5). It is doubtful that more than a handful of unbelievers today know their peril, given the church's unconscionable neglect of the solemn matters of eternity, the jokes about sin and lightning bolts, and the irreverent references to the 'big man upstairs'. Again, as noted above, the apostle Paul warns, 'For we must all appear before the judgment seat of Christ …. Therefore, knowing the fear of the Lord, we persuade others' (2 Cor. 5:10-11). This is urgent business because a day of wrath is coming. Jude describes salvation as 'snatching' people from the fire (Jude 23), indicating, says Jenkyn, that 'no persuasions should be so vehement, no pains so great, as those we take for souls'.[50] Spurgeon asks the pertinent question: 'How can I see souls damned, without emotion? How can I hear Christ's name blasphemed, without a shudder? How can I think of the multitude who prefer ruin to salvation, without a pang?'[51] For us a statement like Jude's above is almost a parody. Baxter, by way of contrast, urges,

> let the dreadfulness of God prevail with every believing soul to pity the ungodly that pity not themselves. O pray for them, O warn them, exhort them, entreat them, as men that know the terrors of the Lord, 2 Cor. 5:11. If they knew, as well as you do, what sin is, and what it is to be children of wrath, and what it is to be unpardoned, unjustified, and unsanctified, they would pity themselves, and cry for mercy, mercy, mercy, from day to day, till they were recovered into a state of life, and turned from the power of Satan unto God. Alas! they know not what it is to die, and to see the world to come, and to appear before a dreadful God: they know not what it is to be in hell-fire; nor what it is to be glorified in heaven.[52]

However, because we know what is coming:

> pity, and warn, and help the miserable. Tell them how much easier it is to escape hell, than to endure it; and how much easier a holy life on earth is, than the endless wrath of the most dreadful God. Tell them that unbelief, presumption, and security, are the certain means to bring their misery, but will do nothing to keep it off; though they may keep off the present knowledge and sense of it, which would have driven them to seek a cure. Tell them that death and judgment are at hand, and that when

[50] Jenkyn, *Jude*, p. 355.
[51] Spurgeon, 'Zealots', *Metropolitan Tabernacle Pulpit*, XI:392.
[52] Baxter, *The Divine Life*, *Works*, III:810.

they laugh, or sport, or scorn, and jest at the displeasure of the dreadful God, it is posting toward them, and will be upon them before they are aware; and when they slumber, their damnation slumbereth not; but while unbelieving sinners say, Peace, peace, sudden destruction will come upon them, as unexpected travail on a woman with child, and they shall not escape. O tell them how dreadful a thing it is, for a soul that is unregenerate and unsanctified, to go from that body which it pampered and sold its salvation to please, and to appear at the tribunal of God; and how dreadful it is for such a soul to fall into the hands of the living God. At least save your own souls, by the faithful discharge of so great a duty; and if they will take no warning, let them at last remember, when it is too late, that they were told in time, what they should see and feel at last, and what their latter end would prove; and that God and man did warn them in compassion, though they perish because they would have no compassion or mercy upon themselves. Thus let the terribleness of God provoke you to do your duty with speed and zeal, for the converting and saving of miserable souls.[53]

Rejoice

Fifth, because God is judge, *rejoice in the triumph of good over evil.* 'The justice of God,' says Baxter, 'is the consolation of the just.' It is 'the terror of the ungodly', but it is our consolation.[54] Hardly a psalm can be found in which the righteous do not complain of the unwarranted taunts, attacks, and persecutions of the wicked (Psa. 3; 4; 5; 6; 7; etc.). Other psalms complain that the wicked prosper in this world while the righteous suffer (e.g. Psa. 10; 37; 73). Particularly in the short-term, within the span of one's own lifetime, the ungodly seem to get away with their evil. They seem to suffer no ill consequences for their deeds.[55] We may return to the complaint of the 73rd Psalm:

---

[53] Baxter, *The Divine Life, Works,* III:810-11.

[54] *Ibid.*, p. 805.

[55] See what we observed about the blessings of God upon the righteous in the long run in Chapter 9, '"The Engines of Divine Dignity": The Justice and Righteousness of God'.

> For I was envious of the arrogant
>> when I saw the prosperity of the wicked.
> For they have no pangs until death;
>> their bodies are fat and sleek.
> They are not in trouble as others are;
>> they are not stricken like the rest of mankind ...
> Their eyes swell out through fatness;
>> their hearts overflow with follies ...
> Behold, these are the wicked;
>> always at ease, they increase in riches.
> All in vain have I kept my heart clean
>> and washed my hands in innocence.
>
> (Psa. 73:3-5, 7, 12, 13)

There were times as an undergraduate at the University of Southern California when I struggled with envy for the lifestyle of the wicked. I envied the racy, party-boy lifestyle and all its forbidden pleasures. When I endured my first month of rain and English food as a graduate theological student in the UK, I again had serious moments of doubt about what I was doing. I envied my friends who, like me, had graduated from college, but who now had money to spend and were enjoying the world's finer things. I questioned if it was really worth it. Yet, like the psalmist, I needed to return to the presence of God and view things from an eternal perspective:

> But when I thought how to understand this,
>> it seemed to me a wearisome task,
> until I went into the sanctuary of God;
>> then I discerned their end.
> Truly you set them in slippery places;
>> you make them fall to ruin.
> How they are destroyed in a moment,
>> swept away utterly by terrors!
> Like a dream when one awakes,
>> O LORD, when you rouse yourself,
>>> you despise them as phantoms (73:16-20).

The psalmist 'discerned their end' and was comforted. God's mill grinds slow, as the ancient saying goes, but it grinds exceeding fine.

The prosperity of the wicked is 'short and uncertain', says Henry,[56] their destruction is 'sure, and sudden, and very great'. This world is not the last word. There is a day coming when the score will be evened, when all the wrongs will be righted, when Christ will wipe away every tear (Rev. 21:1ff.). God's justice is an aspect of his goodness. 'Could you account him good, if he did always with pleasure behold evil, and perpetually suffer the oppression of the innocent under unpunished wickedness?' Charnock asks.[57] Of course not. Consequently, 'is not a hatred of what is bad and unworthy, as much a part of divine goodness, as a love to what is excellent?' Charnock asks again.[58] God is not indifferent to evil. He will arise and not allow the wicked to prevail (Psa. 9:19-20; 10:12, 14-18). He stands against the oppressors and tormenters of humanity. Remember, 'the destruction of the oppressor is the rescue of the innocent', as Charnock puts it. 'Not to punish evil would be a want of goodness to himself', he insists.[59] The salvation of Israel means the destruction of Egypt. God is the great defender of the weak, the defenceless, the poor, the crippled, the orphaned, and the widowed, and he guarantees that they will have their day. Packer says,

> God will see that each man sooner or later receives what he deserves—if not here, then hereafter … the character of God is the guarantee that all wrongs will be righted some day; when 'the day of wrath and revelation of the righteous judgment of God' (Rom. 2:5) arrives, retribution will be exact, and no problems of cosmic unfairness will remain to haunt us. God is the Judge, so justice will be done.[60]

'The righteous will rejoice when he sees the vengeance', says David, as God 'bathe[s] his feet in the blood of the wicked' (Psa. 58:10). The righteous rejoice because justice is thereby vindicated, the oppressions of the wicked are stopped, and God's people are rescued. 'The final proof that God is a perfect moral Being, not indifferent to questions

---

[56] Henry, *Commentary*, on Psa. 73:17-19.
[57] Charnock, *Existence and Attributes*, II:299.
[58] *Ibid.*
[59] *Ibid.*, II:301. Charnock continues, 'The goodness of God is an indulgent goodness, in a way of wisdom and reason; not a fond goodness, in a way of weakness and folly.' He asks, 'Would it not be a weakness, always to bear with the impenitent?'.
[60] Packer, *Knowing God*, p. 129.

of right and wrong,' says Packer, 'is the fact that he has committed himself to judge the world.'[61]

> But the LORD sits enthroned for ever;
>   he has established his throne for justice,
> and he judges the world with righteousness;
>   he judges the peoples with uprightness.
> The LORD is a stronghold for the oppressed,
>   a stronghold in times of trouble.
> And those who know your name put their trust in you,
>   for you, O LORD, have not forsaken those who seek you.
>   (Psa. 9:7-10)

---

[61] Packer, *Knowing God*, p. 130.

ELEVEN

'The Captain Attribute': The Goodness of God

And God saw everything that he had made, and behold, it was very good.—Genesis 1:31

THE first prayer many of us learned began, 'God is great and God is *good*.' First lesson: God is a big God and he is not mean, cruel, or bad. 'Give thanks to the LORD, for he is good [Heb. *tob*]', Scripture urges repeatedly (Psa. 106:1; 107:1; 135:3; 136:1; 2 Chron. 5:13; 7:3; Jer. 33:11; Nah. 1:7). Jesus said, 'No one is good [Gk *agathos*] except God alone' (Mark 10:18). God's goodness is of such a complete and perfect character that all other goodness is as no goodness at all.

Not only is God good in himself (Psa. 25:8; 100:5), but he expresses that goodness continuously. 'Everything created by God is good [Gk *kalos*]', said the apostle Paul (1 Tim. 4:4). All that he creates is 'very good' (Gen. 1:4, 10, etc.; 1:31). 'You *are* good and *do* good' (Psa. 119:68). 'The LORD is good to all' (145:9), and he is particularly good to the 'pure in heart' and to those who wait for him (73:1; Lam 3:25). His goodness, says the psalmist, is 'abundant' (Psa. 145:7). 'How great is his goodness!' exclaims the prophet Zechariah (Zech. 9:17). And his goodness is accessible: 'Oh, taste and see that the LORD is good!' David urges (Psa. 34:8).

God is compared to and identified with whatever is good in this world (Jas 1:17): a fountain (Psa. 36:9); light (John 1:9), bread (John 6:51), water (John 4:10), and rest (Psa. 116:7). He is likened to a dwelling place (Psa. 90:1), and associated with health (Psa. 42:11-17); peace (2 Cor. 13:11), protection, and defence (Gen. 15:1); a wall of fire (Zech.

2:5); a refuge (Psa. 57:1); a rock, a fortress, and a high tower (Psa. 18:2). He is compared to riches (Job 22:24; Eph. 3:8); to honour and glory (Isa. 33:21); and to joy and pleasure (Psa. 43:4). Using the analogy of human relations he is a father (2 Cor. 6:18) and a husband (Hos. 2:19). Depending on how one interprets the Song of Solomon, he is likened to beauty which delights the eyes (Song of Sol. 5:10-16); to sweet smells which delight the nostrils (1:3; 4:10); and to harmonious music which delights the ears (2:12-14).[1] After citing multiple psalms which commend to us the goodness of God (e.g. 31:19; 73:1; 34:8; 100:5; 145:9; 135:3), Baxter explains, 'If there be a thought that is truly sweet to the soul, it is the thought of the infinite goodness of the Lord.'[2]

Goodness described

As we delve into the goodness of God, we will borrow heavily from Discourse XII, 'On the Goodness of God', in Stephen Charnock's *The Existence and Attributes of God*, an unmatched meditation on multiple aspects of God's goodness. God is the original good, he says, good of himself and the source of all good. All creaturely good is derived from him and is a reflection of him. All that is morally good and all that is beneficial or pleasant may be traced to its source in God. All that I touch, taste, see, feel, and know that is pleasing and enjoyable is but a reflection, indeed a dim reflection, of the goodness of God from which it originates. 'Every good and perfect gift is from above', says James, and so is an occasion for thanksgiving (James 1:17). 'God,' says George Swinnock, 'hath all good eminently and virtually in himself.' Whatever excellencies are scattered throughout the universe, 'they are all united in, and centred after an infinite manner in the Creator'.[3] Moreover, 'God is not one good. Rather,' says Swinnock, 'all the good, all the excellences that are in men and angels, are not worthy to be a shadow, or foil to set off those excellences that are in God.'[4]

The *bonitas Dei*, the goodness of God, is both an 'essential attribute' as well as what theologians would call a 'primary affection of the

---

[1] See James Durham, *The Song of Solomon* (1688, 1840; Edinburgh: Banner of Truth Trust, 1982).

[2] Baxter, *The Divine Life*, *Works*, III:785.

[3] Swinnock, *The Incomparableness of God*, *Works*, IV:392.

[4] *Ibid*., IV:393.

divine will'.⁵ Wilhelmus à Brakel places goodness at 'the very essence of God's being'.⁶ God's goodness should be understood not as his way of behaving, nor even as a characteristic he possesses, but as essential. 'Goodness is not a quality in him,' says Charnock, 'but a nature; not a habit added to his essence, but his essence itself.'⁷ Further, his goodness is 'as inseparable from his nature as his holiness'.⁸ God is perfectly good and immutably good. 'Nothing can add to him, or make him better than he is; nothing can detract from him, to make him worse.'⁹ He is all good. 'There is no mixture of anything which can be called not good in him.'¹⁰ God is infinitely good. His goodness is as infinite as his essence. 'He cannot be weary of doing good, no more than a fountain or sea are of flowing.' Indeed, 'It is a part of his goodness not to be weary of showing it.'¹¹ His goodness is 'boundless and bottomless'.¹² He is 'not only good, but best', says Charnock; 'not only good, but goodness itself, the supreme inconceivable goodness'.¹³ He is the *summum bonum*, the greatest good. 'Goodness is a choice perfection of the divine nature', Charnock continues. God possesses 'whatsoever is comely, excellent, desirable' and is the 'highest good' and the 'first good'.¹⁴

Because God is the greatest good, he is to be sought above all else. 'He contains in himself,' says Charnock, 'the sweetness of all other goods, and holds in his bosom plentifully what creatures have in their nature sparingly.'¹⁵ The good things of earth are but morsels of the goodness that is in God himself. Charnock explains this in language similar to that of Swinnock above:

> If anything be desirable because of its goodness, God is much more desirable because of his, since all things are good by a

⁵ Muller, *Post-Reformation Reformed Dogmatics*, III:503.
⁶ à Brakel, *Christian's Reasonable Service*, I:122.
⁷ Charnock, *Existence and Attributes*, II:285.
⁸ *Ibid.*, II:288.
⁹ *Ibid.*, II:286. .
¹⁰ *Ibid.*, II:287. 'He is a good without mixture, good without weariness—none good but God, none good purely, none good inexhaustibly, but God' (II:387).
¹¹ *Ibid.*, II:388.
¹² *Ibid.*
¹³ *Ibid.*, II:277.
¹⁴ *Ibid.*, II:280.
¹⁵ *Ibid.*, II:392.

> participation, and nothing good but by his print upon it: as what being creatures have was derived to them by God, so what goodness they are possessed with they were furnished with it by God; all goodness flowed from him, and all created goodness is summed up in him.[16]

Again, he urges,

> If the sparkling glory of the visible heavens delight us, and the beauty and bounty of the earth please and refresh us, what should be the language of our souls upon those views and tastes but that of the Psalmist, 'Whom have I in heaven but thee? and there is none upon earth that I can desire beside thee' (Psa. 73:25). No greater good can possibly be desired, and no less good should be ardently desired.[17]

Goodness defined

God's goodness is that which sets him apart from all malice, cruelty, and harshness, and characterizes him as kind, generous, trustworthy, and gracious. Charnock defines the goodness of God as 'the bounty of God'.[18] Citing another author, he describes God's goodness as 'his inclination to deal well and bountifully with his creatures'. It is, he says, 'that perfection of God whereby he delights in his works, and is beneficial to them'.[19]

Additional classic definitions may help us. Edward Leigh defines God's goodness as 'an essential property whereby he is infinitely and of himself good, and the author and cause of all goodness in the creature'.[20]

---

[16] Charnock, *Existence and Attributes*, II:392.
[17] *Ibid.*
[18] *Ibid.*, II:283.
[19] *Ibid.*, II:283-84.
[20] Cited in Muller, *Post-Reformation Reformed Dogmatics*, III:507. Similarly, goodness, or benevolence, was defined by Herman Venema (1697–1787) as 'the love of God towards his creatures' by which he acts to 'promote their happiness and perfection' (*ibid.*, III:509). John Flavel, like the others, sees goodness as 'an essential property of [God's] nature'. It means that God 'is absolutely and perfectly good in himself, and the fountain of all communicated goodness to the creature' (Flavel, *Exposition, Works*, VI:155; see also Boston, *Illustration of the Doctrines, Works*, I:119).

God, according to Thomas Manton, 'is good of himself, good in himself; yea, good itself'.[21] Goodness is 'the chiefest name by which we conceive of God'.[22] 'Goodness is the very opposite of harshness, cruelty, gruffness, severity, [and] mercilessness', explains à Brakel. By God's goodness we mean 'the loveliness, benign character, sweetness, friendliness, kindness, and generosity of God'.[23] Packer defines God's goodness as 'his cosmic generosity'.[24] Louis Berkhof completes our survey of definitions of the goodness of God by describing it as 'that perfection of God which prompts him to deal bountifully and kindly with all his creatures'. 'God,' he agrees, 'is the *summum bonum*, the highest good, for all his creatures.'[25] Hence we are to seek him above all else as our greatest good. Our good is to be 'near God' (Psa. 73:28). We are to say with David, 'I have no good apart from you' (Psa. 16:2).

Goodness is a comprehensive attribute. What is true of the holiness of God is true of his goodness as well. 'All his attributes are summed up in this one', Charnock maintains.[26] When Moses pleads, 'Show me your glory' (Exod. 33:18), God answers, 'I will make all my *goodness* pass before you' (33:19). 'God's goodness is his glory,' says Henry, 'and he will have us know him by the glory of his mercy more than the glory of his majesty.'[27] Moses is allowed to gaze upon what Charnock describes as 'the train of all his lovely perfections springing from his goodness',[28] namely, his mercy, grace, patience, lovingkindness, truth, and justice (Exod. 34:6). Twice Amos urges, 'Seek the LORD and live.' The third time he alters it to 'Seek *good*, and not evil, that you may live' (Amos 5:4, 6, 14). To seek God is to seek good, goodness being the sum of his essence. According to Flavel, 'all his other attributes flow out of it as their fountain: the other acts of God are but effuxes of his goodness' (Exod. 33:19).[29] Goodness, says Charnock, is 'the lustre of all

[21] Thomas Manton, *Psalm 119* (1680; Edinburgh: Banner of Truth Trust, 1990), II:96.
[22] *Ibid.*, II:97.
[23] à Brakel, *Christian's Reasonable Service*, I:122.
[24] Packer, *Knowing God*, p. 111.
[25] Berkhof, *Systematic Theology*, p. 70.
[26] Charnock, *Existence and Attributes*, II:365; cf. II:284, 285.
[27] Henry, *Commentary*, on Exod. 33:19.
[28] Charnock, *Existence and Attributes*, II:284.
[29] Flavel, *Exposition*, *Works*, VI:155.

his attributes'.[30] Goodness 'puts a gloss upon all his other attributes'.[31] It is 'the splendour and loveliness of all divine attributes'.[32]

Typically, theologians have treated God's love, grace, mercy, and patience under the classification of 'goodness'. Goodness is the genus; the others are the species: *gratia, amor, misericordia, patientia*. All of these are expressions of God's goodness, 'streams from this fountain'.[33] Charnock explains:

> When [goodness] confers happiness without merit, it is grace; when it bestows happiness against merit, it is mercy; when he bears with provoking rebels, it is long-suffering; when he performs his promise, it is truth; when it meets with a person to whom it is not obliged, it is grace; when he meets with a person in the world, to which he hath obliged himself by promise, it is truth; when it commiserates a distressed person, it is pity; when it supplies an indigent person, it is bounty; when it succours an innocent person, it is righteousness; and when it pardons a penitent person, it is mercy: all summed up in this one name of goodness.[34]

'This is the captain attribute,' Charnock insists, 'that leads the rest to act.'[35] Goodness is the 'heart and spirit' of God's wisdom, knowledge, and power; it 'animates all'.[36] Only when we contemplate the other attributes as 'marching under the conduct and banners' of goodness do they refresh as well as amaze us.[37] Bavinck, writing two hundred years after Charnock, said much the same. Goodness

> is called longsuffering or forbearance when it is manifested to the guilty (Rom. 3:25), grace when it is manifested to those who receive the forgiveness of sins (Eph. 2:8), and love when God, out of grace towards his creatures, shares himself with them (John 3:16 and 1 John 4:8). It is called loving-kindness or mercy when this goodness of God is manifested to those who enjoy his favour

[30] Charnock, *Existence and Attributes*, II:377.
[31] *Ibid.*, II:380..
[32] *Ibid.*, II:398.
[33] *Ibid.*, II:276.
[34] *Ibid.* II:284-85.
[35] *Ibid.* II:285.
[36] *Ibid.*, II:376.
[37] *Ibid.*, II:385.

(Gen. 39:21; Num. 14:19; Isa. 54:10; and Eph. 2:7), and good will or good pleasure when the emphasis falls on the fact that the goodness and all its benefits are a free gift (Matt. 11:26; Luke 2:14; 12:32; and 2 Thess. 1:11).[38]

Goodness revealed

How does God reveal his goodness? Where might we turn to see it?

Creation

First, the revelation of God's goodness begins with the act of creating. 'By his goodness,' says Charnock, 'the whole creation was brought out of the dark womb of nothing.'[39] God was not obliged to create; the decision to do so was undertaken freely. He was eternally and blissfully happy in himself, having no need to create anything outside himself. Charnock explains: 'When [God] was alone from eternity, he contented himself with himself, abounding in his own blessedness, delighting in that abundance; he was incomprehensively rich in the possession of an unstained felicity.'[40] God created, not out of necessity, not out of need, not because of some lack in himself, but because he freely determined to do so. His creative acts, then, were voluntary acts that arose out of his goodness, expressed his goodness, and reflected his goodness. His creative acts were 'a voluntary goodness'.[41] God created that he might bring into existence those beings who might be the beneficiaries of his bounty. Indeed, 'the very act of giving to nothing a being, was an act of choice goodness'.[42]

Consequently, God's goodness is the most visible of his attributes. 'No perfection of the divine nature is more eminently, nor more speedily visible in the whole book of the creation than this.'[43] Why did God create? Because he is good. What did God create? Only that which was 'good' and 'very good'. While God's power enabled his

---

[38] Bavinck, *Our Reasonable Faith*, p. 140-41.
[39] Charnock, *Existence and Attributes*, II:306.
[40] *Ibid*. II:307.
[41] *Ibid*., II:290.
[42] *Ibid*. II:289.
[43] *Ibid*., II:280.

work of creation, and his wisdom designed it, 'nothing can be adored as the motive of his work, but the goodness of his nature'.[44] Indeed, 'his power in making, and his wisdom in ordering, are subservient to his goodness'.[45]

Wherever we cast our eyes, the goodness of God may be seen. At every turn we encounter God's goodness. The apostle Paul therefore upbraids humanity for its inexcusable ingratitude in not receiving God's self-revelation in creation. The goodness of God in nature is unmistakable (Rom 1:18-21). Yet humanity 'did not honour him as God or give thanks to him'. God's goodness is manifest at every hand, requiring a response of gratitude. Wherever we gaze, even in a fallen world, we see evidence of his goodness, not the least of which is being itself, rather than non-being.

God's goodness, then, is diffusive. It is active and expressive. His is 'not an idle, enclosed, pent up goodness'.[46] It is creative and expansive. We are able to 'mount by steps from the consideration of the goodness of created things to acknowledge one infinite ocean of sovereign goodness, whence the streams of created goodness are derived'.[47] Indeed, there is 'not a drop of creation, but is a drop of his goodness'.[48]

God's goodness is seen more particularly in the design of creation for humanity. All this created goodness was for our benefit. 'The world was made for the support and delight of man.'[49] God created man and placed him in a garden, surrounding him with beauty and natural delights (Gen. 2:8). He made man his vice-gerent, with 'dominion' over all other living creatures 'and over all the earth' (1:26). The whole earth was theirs to have, 'fill', 'subdue', and rule over (1:27-28). Notice how the words 'every' and 'all' underscore the sheer magnitude of the benefits our first parents received:

> And God said, 'Behold, I have given you *every* plant yielding seed that is on the face of *all* the earth, and *every* tree with seed in its fruit. You shall have them for food. And to *every* beast of

[44] Charnock, *Existence and Attributes.*
[45] *Ibid.*
[46] *Ibid.*, II:288.
[47] *Ibid.*, II:286.
[48] *Ibid.*, II:307.
[49] *Ibid.*, II:310; see Chapter 5 above, 'Our Creator God'.

the earth and to *every* bird of the heavens and to *everything* that creeps on the earth, *everything* that has the breath of life, I have given *every* green plant for food.' And it was so (1:29-30).

God gave not only that which was good for man, or useful, or interesting, but also that which was a delight to him: 'And out of the ground the LORD God made to spring up every tree that is *pleasant* to the sight and good for food. The tree of life was in the midst of the garden, and the tree of the knowledge of good and evil' (2:9).

When that which was 'not good' was identified, God made the woman, one 'fit' or 'suitable' for man, a 'helper', so that he should not be 'alone' (2:18-23). 'How God graciously pitied his solitude!' Henry exclaims.[50] God instituted marriage, wherein the man and the woman might enjoy the pleasures of becoming 'one flesh' with each other (2:24-25). Charnock elaborates:

> God provided for innocent man a delightful mansion-house, a place of more special beauty and curiosity, the garden of Eden, a delightful paradise, a model of the beauties and pleasures of another world, wherein he had placed whatsoever might contribute to the felicity of a rational and animal life, the life of a creature composed of mire and dust, of sense and reason (Gen. 2:9).[51]

Even in a fallen world, this goodness continues. God has given to man the 'bespangled heavens' above and the 'solid earth' beneath with its wonderful tapestry of terrain and vegetation.[52] 'The air is his aviary, the sea and rivers his fish-ponds, the valleys his granary, the mountains his magazine.'[53] Listen to Charnock at his best:

> There is not the most despicable [i.e. insignificant] thing in the whole creation but it is endued with a nature to contribute something for our welfare: either as food to nourish us when we are healthful; or as medicine to cure us when we are distempered; or as a garment to clothe us when we are naked, and arm us against the cold of the season; or as a refreshment when we are weary; or as a delight when we are sad: all serve for necessity

[50] Henry, *Commentary*, on Gen. 2:18.
[51] Charnock, *Existence and Attributes*, II:312.
[52] *Ibid.*, II:311.
[53] *Ibid.*

or ornament, either to spread our table, beautify our dwellings, furnish our closets, or store our wardrobes.

Further, God gave humanity the physical capacity to enjoy these outward benefits:

> He did not only give variety of senses to man, but provided variety of delightful objects in the world for every sense; the beauties of light and colours for our eye, the harmony of sounds for our ear, the fragrancy of odours for our nostrils, and a delicious sweetness for our palates.

Still further, God gave humanity the faculty of reason by which to understand what we perceive of the 'delightful objects' in creation:

> He hath set up a sun in the heavens, to expose their outward beauty and conveniences to our sight; and the candle of the Lord is in us, to expose their inward qualities and conveniences to our knowledge, that we might serve ourselves of, and rejoice in, all this furniture wherewith he hath garnished the world, and have wherewithal to employ the inquisitiveness of our reason, as well as gratify the pleasures of our sense.[54]

Brush the cheek of a newborn baby with your finger; feel a cool ocean breeze blow over your warm skin on a hot day; or enjoy a warm fire on a cold night—and give thanks for the sense of touch.

Drive along Big Sur in California and absorb the breathtaking beauty of the rugged cliffs and the blue waves crashing against the rocks; or head to New England in the fall and drink in the beauty of the changing colours of the leaves; or head to the Mid-West and look out over the vast fields of grain—and give thanks for the sense of sight.

Peel a fresh orange and bite into a wedge; or slice into a fresh peach or watermelon on a hot summer day; or enjoy bananas, apples, lemons, strawberries, blueberries, and countless other products of the earth that spring from the ground of their own accord, and realize these are the gifts of a good God to us—and thank him for the sense of taste.

Consider the sweet sounds of the chirping birds, the thunderous crashing of the waves, the rustling of the brook, the whistling of the wind through the trees, the melodies of the human voice, the

---

[54] Charnock, *Existence and Attributes*, II:312

symphonies of Beethoven—and give thanks that God has both created a world full of delights and given us senses with which to perceive and enjoy these delights. Every good thing is a reminder of the goodness of the 'God from whom all blessings flow'. More so than the other attributes of God, his goodness, says Boston, is 'eminently visible in the whole book of the creatures'.[55] Created things, with all their variety and beauty, 'are so many beams and apparitions of his goodness'.[56]

Finally, let us not forget that God's goodness is seen in imparting to humanity his own nature. God created man 'in his own image' (Gen. 1:27). He made us, sings David, 'a little lower than the heavenly beings and crowned [us] with glory and honour'. He gave to us 'dominion over the works of [his] hands' and 'put all things under [our] feet' (Psa. 8:5-6). He gave to us alone the capacity to know him and enjoy fellowship with him. 'He imparted to [man] a spark of his own comeliness,' says Charnock, 'in order to a communion with himself in happiness.'[57]

Providence

Second, God's goodness can also be seen in his providential care of all that he has created. God not only constructed the world, he also manages it.[58] The infinite, eternal, and almighty God cares for and provides for everything, from the grass to the beasts that feed upon it, from fallen humanity to redeemed humanity. There is nothing so small or insignificant as to be outside the range of God's goodness. What sort of God rules over the universe with such almighty power? Jesus told us to consider the birds of the air: they do not sow, reap, or gather into barns; yet our heavenly Father feeds them (Matt. 6:26). Jesus said that God clothes the grass of the field so lavishly that even Solomon's wardrobe cannot compare (6:30). Jesus speaks of the common, seemingly insignificant creatures to highlight God's goodness. God is so good that he faithfully and consistently feeds and clothes birds and grass.

---

[55] Boston, *Illustration of the Doctrines, Works*, I:119.

[56] *Ibid.*, I:120.

[57] Charnock, *Existence and Attributes*, II:308.

[58] *Ibid.*, II:348. 'Without his government everything in the world would jostle against one another: the beauty of it would be more defaced, it would be an unruly mass, a confused chaos, rather than a *kosmos*, a comely world' (*ibid.*).

Jesus says that not a single sparrow falls to the ground apart from his Father's will (Matt. 10:29). Not one of them, as apparently inconsequential and worthless as it might be, is ever forgotten (Luke 12:6). The young ravens cry and God opens his hand and feeds them (Psa. 147:9). The lions seek their meat from God (Psa. 104:21). God opens his hand and satisfies the desire of every living thing (Psa. 145:16).

Charnock explains from Psalm 104 that 'the goodness of God is the river that waters the whole earth'.[59] God preserves man and beast (Psa. 36:6). He gives to all 'fruitful seasons', and '[satisfies] our hearts with food and gladness' (Acts 14:17). He crowns the year with his bounty as rich harvests are gathered (Psa. 65:9-11; 107:35-36). 'Every day shines with new beams of his divine goodness.'[60] Never for a moment indulge the thought that God is a detached or indifferent deity, remote and unconcerned about anything below. Nothing escapes his loving care and generous provision.

God extends his care for the lower forms of creation by insisting that his people also be good to them. 'As the lawgiver to the Jews, he took care that the poor beast should not be abused by the cruelty of man.'[61] Livestock were to do no work on the Sabbath (Exod. 20:10). Oxen were not to be muzzled while threshing grain (Deut. 25:4). The mother hen and her young were not to be seized on a single occasion, with this incentive for those who were obedient: 'that you may live long' (Deut. 22:6-7; cf. Psa. 147:9; 104:21, 25-28). 'He would revenge the cruelty to dumb creatures with the shortness of the oppressor's life.'[62] A cow or a ewe and their young were not to be killed for sacrifice on the same day (Lev. 22:28). What was the point? God was teaching his people to be merciful to their animals. 'He is so good,' says Charnock, commenting on Leviticus 22:28, 'that he would have worship declined [delayed] for a time in favour of a distressed beast.'[63] An animal caught in a pit on the Sabbath was to be rescued (Matt. 12:11; Luke 14:5). 'He seems to remit for a time the rights of the Deity for the rescue of a mere

[59] Charnock, *Existence and Attributes*, II:349.
[60] *Ibid*. II:350.
[61] *Ibid*.
[62] *Ibid*., II:351.
[63] *Ibid*., II:351.

animal.'[64] God even commanded his people that if they besieged a city they were not to destroy its fruit trees (Deut. 20:19). That God insists that trees and animals be treated appropriately and kindly is a token of his goodness. He commits himself to caring for the lower forms of creation and commands his people to do likewise. God himself makes sure that all creatures have ample supplies, ample food, and ample protection. Charnock continues:

> He who possesses the praises of angels, leaves not off the care of the meanest creatures: and that majesty that dwells in a pure heaven, and an inconceivable light, stoops to provide for the ease of those creatures that lie and lodge in the dirt and dung of the earth. How should we be careful not to use those unmercifully, which God takes such care of in his law, and not to distrust that goodness, that opens his hand so liberally to creatures of another rank![65]

Further, the God who rules over the universe with his almighty power cares particularly for society's cast-offs, the weak, the helpless, and the despised. God insisted upon mercy towards slaves (Deut. 15:18; 21:14, 15), fugitives (23:15-16), criminals convicted of lesser crimes (25:3), the poor (Lev. 19:10; 23:22), and debtors (Exod. 22:25). He identifies himself as the God of the widow and orphan and of the fatherless and sojourner, and he demands that his people treat the same with love and impartiality (Psa. 146:9; 68:5; 82:2-4; Exod. 22:21; Lev. 19:33-34; Deut. 10:17-19). Even the wicked and unbelieving are the beneficiaries of God's goodness. 'The earth is full of the goodness of the LORD' (Psa. 33:5 KJV), and the just as well as the unjust partake of that goodness. Commenting on Matthew 5:45, Charnock says, 'The earth affords its riches, the heavens its showers, and the sun its light, to those that ignore and blaspheme him.'[66] Though the earth and its fullness is his, he shares it with all (Psa. 24:1). He is kind and merciful to ungrateful and evil men (Luke 6:35-36). His people, then, are to be the same. 'The wickedest breathe in his air, walk upon his earth, and drink of his

---

[64] Charnock, *Existence and Attributes,* II:351.
[65] *Ibid.,* II:351.
[66] *Ibid.,* II:352.

water, as well as the best.'[67] If God cares for all these, can we not then be sure of his care for us too? Indeed we can.

As for his people, every day he leads us to 'green pastures' and 'still waters'. He prepares a table for us and fills our cup (Psa. 23:5). He is our 'stronghold' (27:1), our refuge and strength (46:1), our shield and fortress (18:1-2). He protects us from the 'terror of the night' and 'the arrow that flies by day' (91:5). He watches over our goings out and our comings in (121:8). He assigns his angels to watch over us (91:11). God has 'a tenderness for all', says Charnock, but 'a peculiar affection' for his covenant people.[68]

God's providential goodness can be seen in his laws governing human relations. From the very beginning God gave commands to our first parents, and through them to us, that are for our good. God has given to humanity a nature. That which is fitting to human nature is permitted by his law, and that which is contrary to human nature is prohibited. Those things that are suited to our nature and conducive to our pleasure and happiness are permitted. Those things which are not suited to our nature and are destructive of our pleasure and happiness are forbidden. The Sabbath principle, that it was 'made for man', can be applied to all of God's laws (Matt. 12:8; Mark 2:27). They were all designed by a good God to promote our well-being. They are good for us physically. They are good for us spiritually. They are good for our health. They point the way to grow wealth. His law is *torah* (Heb.), fatherly instruction for his children (Prov. 4:1ff.). When properly received, God's commands kindle a 'delight' (Psa. 1:2). They are not grievous (1 John 5:3); they are just and good (Rom 7:12). They are righteous (Psa. 119:164). The keeping of them satisfies the soul (Psa. 119:165; 19:7). When kept, they impart 'peace … like a river' (Isa. 48:18). 'What a good master we serve,' says Henry, 'all whose institutions are for our own benefit.'[69]

Our first parents were commanded to 'be fruitful and multiply and fill the earth' (Gen. 1:28). They were suited for this task, made for it, and designed to find fulfilment in it. They were commanded to

---

[67] Charnock, *Existence and Attributes*, II:352.
[68] *Ibid.*, II:350.
[69] Henry, *Commentary*, on Mark 2:27.

'subdue [the earth] and have dominion over ... every living thing that moves on the earth' (1:28). They were commanded to 'work' and 'keep' the garden. They were forbidden to eat of the tree of the knowledge of good and evil (2:15-17). These commands were for the good of Adam and Eve. They were designed for them and given for their well-being.

After the fall, God's laws continue to promote human flourishing, continue to be suited to human nature, and are designed for our well-being. God forbids neglect of parents, murder, adultery, theft, dishonesty, and covetousness in the second table of the law. He ordains civil government for the purpose of restraining evil (Gen. 9:6). Thus does he 'still the roaring of the waves, the tumult of the peoples' (Psa. 65:7). Charnock says, 'God hath commanded nothing but what doth conduce to our happiness. All disobedience implies that his law is a snare to entrap us, and make us miserable, and not an act of kindness, to render us happy.'[70] Writing two hundred years later, Spurgeon said much the same: 'The law of the Ten Commandments is a gift of great kindness to the sons of men, for it tells us the wisest and happiest way of living. It forbids us nothing but what would be to our injury, and it withholds from us nothing which would be a real pleasure to us.'[71] 'Every violation of the divine law,' says Charnock, 'is a contempt of God's goodness as well as his sovereignty.'[72]

Even God's justice, his threats of punishment, and his promises of reward should be seen as aspects of his goodness. Charnock explains, 'He promises that he might be a rewarder, and threatens that he might be a punisher; the one to elevate our hope, and the other to excite our fear, the two passions whereby the nature of man is managed in the world.'[73] Owen would have us understand that 'the most bitter threats' are precious to believers, and even in them 'see him to be excellent, desirable, and beautiful'.[74] Indeed, his goodness 'shines in his justice', says Charnock, 'for without being just he could not be good'.[75] The point of God's law, his warnings, his discipline, his

---

[70] Charnock, *Existence and Attributes*, II:365.
[71] Spurgeon, 'God's Love to the Saints', *Treasury of the New Testament*, IV:540.
[72] Charnock, *Existence and Attributes*, II:365.
[73] *Ibid.*, II:315.
[74] Owen, *Communion with God*, *Works*, II:76.
[75] Charnock, *Existence and Attributes*, II:298.

temporal judgments, and his rewards is to encourage goodness and discourage wickedness.[76] Punishment is never the primary intention of God. His prohibitions and threatenings are meant to be a 'bar to evil' and so 'prevent evil', says Charnock, to prevent 'any occasions of severity against his creature'.[77] So it is that God speaks of his wrath as his 'strange work' (Isa. 28:21), strange, says Charnock, not because it is 'against his nature, as the governor of the world, but against his first intention, as creator, which was to manifest his goodness'.[78] He does not afflict willingly (Lam. 3:33). He does not delight in the death of the wicked (Ezek. 33:11), whereas he does delight in blessing and pleasing.

Using language familiar to us today, Charnock maintains, 'God only hates the sin, not the sinner. He desires only the destruction of the one, not the other.'[79] So it is that God does not send judgments unless he first warns, as with Jonah and all the prophets, so that those judgments might not have to be sent. Even his judgments, when executed, have goodness in them, in that, in Charnock's quaint phrasing, 'he strikes some, to reform others that are spectators'.[80] So Jesus would have us 'remember Lot's wife', that her fate might not be our own (Luke 17:32-33). The apostle Paul makes us 'spectators' of the judgments upon Israel in the wilderness, that we might not repeat their errors (1 Cor. 10:1-14). 'Now these things happened to them as an example,' he tells us, 'but they were written down for our instruction' (10:11; cf. Rom. 15:4). 'How could God be a friend to goodness, if he were not an enemy to evil?' Charnock asks.[81]

Even our afflictions are signs of his goodness, as through suffering he corrects that which would harm us, and strengthens us through our pain, that we might never succumb to evil again. He 'disciplines us for our good, that we may share his holiness'. Painful discipline 'yields the peaceful fruit of righteousness' (Heb. 12:10-11). 'Is it not a greater

---

[76] Charnock, *Existence and Attributes*, II:299-300. 'All of his attributes, which are parts of his goodness, engage him to punish sin; without it, his authority would be vilified, his purity stained, his power derided, his truth disgraced, his justice scorned, his wisdom slighted' (*ibid*,. II:302).

[77] *Ibid.*, II:302.

[78] *Ibid.*

[79] *Ibid.*

[80] *Ibid.*

[81] *Ibid.*, II:304.

goodness to separate us from the world to happiness by his scourge, than to leave us to the condemnation of the world for our sins? Is it not a greater goodness to make us smart here than to see us scorched hereafter?'[82] We shall look at this in greater detail as we proceed. For now, understand the goodness of God's law: of its instruction, its promises, and its warnings. It is 'a lamp to [our] feet and a light to [our] path' (Psa. 119:105).

Response

Let us pause to consider what we have seen so far of God's goodness in creation and providence. How ought we to respond?

Gratitude

First, we should respond with gratitude. Give thanks for the delights of creation. Give thanks for all that pleases our senses of taste, touch, sight, sound, and smell. Has he not richly provided us with everything to enjoy (1 Tim. 6:17)? What is true of food is true of all that God has made: these were 'created to be received with thanksgiving by those who believe and know the truth' (4:3).

Often a twisted sense of entitlement mars our perception of God's goodness. We focus on what we do not have rather than on what we do have. God 'gives to all mankind life and breath and everything' (Acts 17:25). *Everything.* All that is good comes to us by his hand (James 1:17). Yet the twist of sinful human nature is such that we will tend to fixate on the one thing we do not have rather than on the ninety-nine that we do have. We have food on our tables, clothes on our backs, roofs over our heads, family, friends, jobs, a church home, and all the blessings of redemption (which we have not yet begun to elaborate on—see the next chapter), and yet we obsess over the one thing that we are denied. That one thing robs us of our peace and joy. That one thing steals away our contentment. That one thing leads us to question the goodness of God. What pitiful ingrates we are! Does the Good Shepherd not daily lead us into the green pastures and by the still waters? Does he not daily, even in danger, spread a table for us and ensure that our cup overflows with his provisions (Psa. 23:1ff.)? Shall we not, then, 'Rejoice

---

[82] Charnock, *Existence and Attributes*, II:305.

always' and 'give thanks in all circumstances', knowing that 'this is the will of God in Christ Jesus for [us]' (1 Thess. 5:16, 18)? Recognize the goodness of God that surrounds you, and give thanks.

Trust

Second, we should respond to God's goodness with trust. This is the point of Jesus' appeals to God's care for the birds and the grass (Matt. 6:26-30). God unfailingly feeds the birds. He lavishly clothes the grass. What are we meant to learn? To trust God's goodness: 'Look at the birds of the air: they neither sow nor reap nor gather into barns, and yet your heavenly Father feeds them. Are you not of more value than they?' (6:26). Since we are of 'more value', can we not count on his provision? Since God is good to the birds, can we not count on him to be good to us? So also the grass: 'But if God so clothes the grass of the field, which today is alive and tomorrow is thrown into the oven, will he not much more clothe you, O you of little faith?' (6:30). Grass is virtually worthless and insignificant. It is 'alive' one day, and the next it is 'thrown into the oven'. Yet God clothes it more lavishly than 'Solomon in all his glory' (6:29). If he is so extravagantly good to the grass, can we not count on his being good to us? 'Shall the great housekeeper of the world water his flowers, prune his plants, fodder his cattle, and not feed and clothe his children?' Trapp asks.[83]

Can we not trust God to protect us and provide for us? Jesus asks, 'And which of you by being anxious can add a single hour to his span of life?' (Matt. 6:27). Our anxieties accomplish nothing. We should instead look to the birds and to the grass, and see how God cares for the inconsequential. If his goodness extends to them, will it not also extend to us? If we grasp this, does it not make sense for Jesus to urge, 'Do not be anxious about your life, what you will eat or what you will drink, nor about your body, what you will put on. Is not life more than food, and the body more than clothing?' (6:25). Again, 'Therefore do not be anxious, saying, "What shall we eat?" or "What shall we drink?" or "What shall we wear?"' (6:31). Can we not set aside our anxieties about food, clothing, and shelter, knowing that God's good hand will care for us too? Can we not follow Jesus' exhortation, 'But seek first

[83] Trapp, *Commentary*, V:110.

the kingdom of God and his righteousness, and all these things will be added to you' (Matt. 6:33)? This 'great duty', says Henry, is 'the sum and substance of our whole duty'.[84] Surely we can seek Christ's gospel kingdom first, given that we are immersed in his goodness, knowing that as we do so we lose nothing. We only gain. All these things will be added to us; the goodness of God ensures it. Let us allow Swinnock to help us:

> All the sheets in the explication of the doctrine speak somewhat of him, but not the thousand thousandth part of that excellency that is in him. Read, I may tell thee, when God is offered thee, the greatest good that ever was, that ever will be, that ever can be, is offered thee; there never was, or can be, the like offered thee; more than heaven and earth, than both worlds, than millions of worlds, is offered thee. This God who is offered thee is the King of kings, the Lord of lords, the God of gods, the blessed and glorious potentate, the first cause, the original being, self-sufficient, all-sufficient, absolutely perfect, incapable of any addition or diminution. This God who is offered thee is the high and lofty One that inhabiteth eternity every moment, to whom a thousand years, yea, millions of ages, are but as one day, as one moment, whose duration is incapable of the least accession, who is boundless in his being, omnipotent in his power, unsearchable in his wisdom, inconceivable in his grace, and infinite in all his perfections. He dwelleth in that light that is inaccessible; before him angels, the highest of creatures, veil their faces; to him the whole creation is less than nothing, and vanity. This God who is offered thee made all things, and infinitely more than all things, influenceth all things, and is all things, and infinitely more than all things.[85]

Again,

> The God who is offered thee is the well of salvation, the Lord of life, the God of all consolation, a hive of sweetness, a paradise of pleasure, a heaven of joy. He is the richest grace, the dearest love, the surest friend, the highest honour, the vastest treasure,

[84] Henry, *Commentary*, on Matt. 6:33.
[85] Swinnock, *Incomparableness of God*, *Works*, IV:493.

the exactest beauty, the chiefest good, and the fullest felicity. He is one that can enlarge and suit all thy faculties, relieve and answer all thy necessities, fill up and satisfy all the capacities of thy heaven-born soul. God is a good which Christ died to purchase for thee, Eph. 2:13; 1 Pet. 3:18. And surely if Christ thought him worth his blood, he is worthy thine acceptance. God is a comprehensive universal good, not one, but all good; riches, honours, pleasures, friends, relations, health, life, earth, heaven, this world, the other world, all the good of both worlds, and infinitely more; and art thou not covetous of such wealth, that is better worth than both worlds? [86]

---

[86] Swinnock, *Incomparableness of God*, *Works*, IV:493-94.

TWELVE

'God's Victorious Goodness'

Now the serpent was more crafty than any other beast of the field that the LORD God had made. He said to the woman, 'Did God actually say, "You shall not eat of any tree in the garden"?' And the woman said to the serpent, 'We may eat of the fruit of the trees in the garden, but God said, "You shall not eat of the fruit of the tree that is in the midst of the garden, neither shall you touch it, lest you die."' But the serpent said to the woman, 'You will not surely die. For God knows that when you eat of it your eyes will be opened, and you will be like God, knowing good and evil.' So when the woman saw that the tree was good for food, and that it was a delight to the eyes, and that the tree was to be desired to make one wise, she took of its fruit and ate, and she also gave some to her husband who was with her, and he ate. Then the eyes of both were opened, and they knew that they were naked. And they sewed fig leaves together and made themselves loincloths.—Genesis 3:1-7

WE have defined what we mean by the goodness of God, and we have investigated how God reveals his goodness in creation and providence. We have meditated on the ways in which God blesses us each day through all that he has made and all that he has ordained.

Goodness challenged

Yet God's goodness does not go unchallenged. In his play *J. B.*, Archibald MacLeish (1892–1982), American poet, writer, and Librarian of Congress, gave voice to the complaint of many when he said, 'If he is God, he cannot be good; if he is good, he cannot be God.'[1] Similarly, the nineteenth-century French poet and art critic Charles Baudelaire (1821–67) said, 'If there is a God, he is the devil.'[2] More recently, Gil Martins, the Scottish-born FBI agent who narrates Philip Kerr's novel *Prayer*, emerges from a crisis of faith brought on by his work on cases of domestic terrorism with renewed belief in God, but it is a God 'indifferent to good and evil'.[3]

Why these cynical conclusions about the nature of God? Because for some, the existence of misery and suffering cannot be reconciled with the existence of a good God. The child's prayer with which we began our study of this theme exposes the mystery of the problem of evil. There would be no mystery if God were not both great and good. If God were either not great and not able to prevent evil, or not good and consequently disinclined to prevent it, evil could be explained. However, because he is great and good, and not weak and evil, the persistent existence of evil is a mystery.

As we have seen, Genesis 1 and 2 present a clear picture of God's goodness prior to the fall. Everything he creates is *good*. He creates a good world, a good man, and a beautiful garden. Man is surrounded by beautiful things to see, taste, touch, smell, and hear. Then, when it is *not* good for man to be alone, God creates a good woman. Eden was paradise: perfect fellowship with God, perfect relationships between its inhabitants, in a perfect environment, and all coming from a loving and good God. This lavish display of God's goodness is the context in which we encounter the fall (Gen. 3). The event of the fall can be divided into three stages, all of which centred around a dispute with respect to God's goodness. The fall of man may be understood as a direct assault upon the goodness of God, one which succeeded despite the unmistakable goodness of the garden. It was an onslaught which has continued ever since.

[1] Cited in Francis A. Schaeffer, *Escape from Reason* (Downers Grove, IL: Inter-Varsity Press, 1968), p. 81.
[2] Cited in Francis A. Schaeffer, *The God Who Is There* (Downers Grove, IL: InterVarsity Press, 1968), p. 100.
[3] Phillip Kerr, *Prayer* (New York: Putnam, 2014); cited in Tom Nolan, 'Romantics But Not Rebels', *Wall Street Journal*, 17-18 March 2014, C6.

Doubting God's goodness

First, Satan cast *doubt* upon the goodness of God. The serpent asked, 'Did God actually say, "You shall not eat of any tree in the garden"?' (Gen. 3:1). The answer should have been 'No!' This is not at all what God said. 'He quotes fallaciously, as if it were a prohibition, not only of that tree, but of all', Henry observes.[4] God's instructions were, 'You may surely eat of every tree of the garden, but of the tree of the knowledge of good and evil you shall not eat, for in the day that you eat of it you shall surely die' (2:16-17).

God had said that they could eat from all the trees *except* just this one. Why this one? The one tree was forbidden to Adam for no other reason than God would have it so. He reserved it for himself, says Charnock, 'as a mark of his sovereignty'.[5] Charnock calls the tree 'a visible memorial of [God's] sovereignty' by which God let Adam know that he 'was not his own lord, nor was [he] to live after his own sentiments'.[6] Given the surrounding bounty, this was a minimal and extremely reasonable restriction. However, Satan suggested otherwise. 'It is the subtlety of Satan to blemish the reputation of the divine law as uncertain or unreasonable', Henry observes.[7] Satan suggested that God would not let them eat from *any* tree, maximizing the prohibition. 'He, by aggravating the exception, endeavours to invalidate the concession', says Henry.[8] Satan was challenging the goodness of God. He was raising doubts. 'Might it be that God is withholding things from you? Might it be that he is limiting your potential? Does it seem that God is restricting your freedom?' The implication here was that God did not seem to have the man and the woman's best interests in mind. He was not good. 'The divine law cannot be reproached unless it first be misrepresented.'[9]

[4] Henry, *Commentary*, on Gen. 3:1.
[5] Charnock, *Existence and Attributes*, II:429. Charnock continues, 'This was neither good nor evil in itself; it received its sole authority from the absolute will of God ... in [Adam's] obedience to it, nothing but the sole power and authority of God, which is the proper rule of obedience, could have been respected, not any reason from the thing itself' (*ibid.*).
[6] *Ibid.*, II:477.
[7] Henry, *Commentary*, on Gen. 3:1.
[8] *Ibid.*
[9] *Ibid.*

Notice how the woman answered: 'And the woman said to the serpent, "We may eat of the fruit of the trees in the garden, but God said, 'You shall not eat of the fruit of the tree that is in the midst of the garden, neither shall you touch it, lest you die'" (3:2-3). The woman denied *most* of what Satan said. She said, 'Oh, no, you've got it wrong. We *can* eat from the trees in the garden.' However, she accepted the principle behind Satan's question. She did not mention that God had said they could eat from 'every tree', underscoring his generous provision. Instead, she spoke merely of eating from 'the trees'. Then she too maximized and even expanded the prohibition, the one negative command. 'Neither shall you touch it', she misquoted God as saying. 'The tree in the middle—we can't eat of it, and *we can't even touch it*.' 'They had imposed on themselves the additional requirement of not touching the forbidden fruit', explains J. A. Motyer.[10] Satan planted the seed of doubt and it had taken root. The law of the garden did not mention *touch*. It said, 'Don't *eat*.' However, the woman was beginning to see God as an enemy. She was beginning to focus all of her attention on the prohibition. Motyer describes the woman's response as a 'mini-assent to the proposition that life in the garden is restrictive rather than free'.[11] It is a matter of perspective. Is life with God one of almost limitless possibilities or of unreasonable constraints? There are only ten commandments. Are these unbearable restrictions? Or, because they are *only* ten in number, does this open to us a vast array of opportunities? The woman and her successors, even in the light of all this goodness, see God primarily in light of that which is prohibited. '[Satan] leads our first parents into *hard thoughts of God*', says Owen.[12]

Denying God's goodness

Second, Satan *denied* the goodness of God: 'But the serpent said to the woman, "You will not surely die"' (3:4). 'Satan teaches men first to doubt and then to deny', Henry warns.[13] The devil denied God's word; he denied the truthfulness or trustworthiness of God. His word could

---

[10] J. A. Motyer, *Look to the Rock: An Old Testament Background to Our Understanding of Christ* (Leicester: Inter-Varsity Press, 1996), p. 114.

[11] *Ibid.*

[12] Owen, *Communion with God, Works*, II:35 (emphasis added).

[13] Henry, *Commentary*, on Gen. 3:4.

not be relied on. What God had threatened was false. Then Satan questioned God's motive: 'For God knows that when you eat of it your eyes will be opened, and you will be like God, knowing good and evil' (3:5). Satan says, in effect, 'God is lying in order to mask his self-interest.' 'He insinuates to them that God has no good design upon them', says Henry.[14] He just doesn't want you to be like him. He regards you as a rival. He hasn't made this law for your good; he's holding you down. He's denying you positive pleasures and experiences. God has deceived you. He doesn't care about you. He made his law only for reasons of self-promotion. 'Satan paints God with his own colours', says Charnock, and 'represents him as envious and malicious as himself'.[15] This 'slur on the character of God', adds Motyer, involves accepting both 'an assault on the veracity of what [God] had said' and 'a questioning of his benevolence', even a 'denigration of his character'.[16] It was, says Henry, 'a reproach to his goodness'.[17]

A friend of mine in college 'quit' being a Christian essentially because he came to doubt God's goodness. He said he only had four years in college and he was not going to deny himself the never-to-be-repeated experiences available to him there. Essentially, he was denying God's goodness, denying that what God permits and forbids has our best interests at heart. This is the outlook of all those who think that if they follow Christ 'life will end'. Life under God, they suppose, means unrelenting boredom and unreasonable deprivation. Like for the defiant kings and rulers of Psalm 2, life under God is 'bonds' and 'cords' (Psa. 2:1-3).

Defying God's goodness

Third, Adam and Eve *defied* the goodness of God. Their defiance entailed the total nature of man rebelling against the total revealed prohibitive will of God: 'So when the woman saw that the tree was good for food, and that it was a delight to the eyes, and that the tree was to be desired to make one wise, she took of its fruit and ate, and she also gave some to her husband who was with her, and he ate' (Gen. 3:6).

---

[14] Henry, *Commentary*, on Gen. 3:5.
[15] Charnock, *Existence and Attributes*, II:365.
[16] Motyer, *Look to the Rock*, pp. 115, 116.
[17] Henry, *Commentary*, on Gen. 3:5.

This was not a slight misstep. It was not a momentary lapse. Notice that the whole person, faculties fully engaged, rebelled against God.

(1) The *emotions* or *desires* were engaged: the woman *saw* that the tree was 'good'; it was a 'delight' to her eyes. 'Good' was no longer defined by the word of God; rather, it was now determined by what appealed to the senses or to the appetites. God should not want to deny me what I desire, what my senses crave. What could be wrong with experiencing something so delightful?

(2) The *mind* or *intellect* was engaged: she consented in her mind, thinking, 'It is good to be wise.' '[Satan] could not have persuaded them to run the hazard of ruining themselves,' says Henry, 'if he had not suggested to them a great probability of bettering themselves.'[18] The tree was called a tree of knowledge, and what could be more reasonable than to seek knowledge? 'There is a logic at work here,' says Motyer, 'and it has every appearance of soundness.'[19] Notice that the mind followed the emotions, an inversion of the natural order. Human beings are not meant to be driven by their instincts like beasts. Rather, the emotional response should be shaped by the understanding. Theology should shape behaviour. Because the fruit was forbidden, she should have hated it as one hates poison, though it be ever so colourful. However, like the cat which leaps into the pool while chasing a colourful butterfly, the woman allowed her desires to govern her understanding, to her own destruction. Morality drove her theology. Desire determined behaviour.

Finally, (3) the *will* or *volition* was activated: 'she took of its fruit and ate' (3:6). 'No sooner a sinner than a tempter', says Henry.[20] She gave it to her husband, and he ate.

For any act, these three must consent. Her *mind* consented to her *desires* and then her *will* followed. The result was that the total person revolted against the total known will of God. Man in his totality acted against God in his totality; man, with his emotions, mind, and will, rejected the word of God. The total known prohibitive will of God amounted to one negative precept. It was distorted, then it was rejected. What is sin? Sin is 'lawlessness' (1 John 3:4). 'His sin was, in

---

[18] Henry, *Commentary*, on Gen. 3:5.
[19] Motyer, *Look to the Rock*, p. 116.
[20] Henry, *Commentary*, on Gen. 3:6.

one word, *disobedience*,' says Henry.[21] Humanity overthrew the law of God. While the woman was deceived, the apostle Paul implies that it was not innocently but with clarity of mind that Adam flouted the will of God (1 Tim. 2:14).

The arguments of Satan were accepted. God's goodness was denied. Man, says Charnock, joined 'in league with hell against heaven'.[22] Think of the irony: the God who is only good and had showered man with his benevolence was regarded by man as a self-seeking tyrant. What was the fall, asks Charnock, 'but ingratitude to divine bounty, and rebellion against divine sovereignty'?[23] Consider, says Charnock again, that 'every offence was infinite, as being committed against a being of infinite dignity; it was a stroke at the very being of God, a resistance of all his attributes'.[24] So it was, said Calvin, that 'Adam… as far as he was able, extinguished *the whole glory of God*.'[25]

Let us be wise to the ways of Satan. The apostles would not have us be 'outwitted by Satan' or be 'ignorant of his designs' or 'schemes' (2 Cor. 2:11 NASB). At the top of his list of schemes is his plan to convince us that God is not good. He would have his victory in the garden often repeated in our lives. 'Satan, as he is the accuser of the brethren before God, so he accuses God before the brethren', Henry warns.[26] Am I thinking that God's commands and laws are burdensome? They are not (1 John 5:3). Yet if I begin to convince myself that they are too restrictive, that they are unreasonable, that what they require limits or denies me too much, the devil has achieved a preliminary victory in my life which he is seeking to complete with my total destruction. He is firing 'flaming darts' in my direction, stirring up doubts and fears (Eph. 6:16). Will God really provide for me? I am so needy. I must have that job. I must have that relationship. I must have that wealth or that recognition. The tempter is tempting me to compromise my integrity and faith (1 Thess. 3:5). He is a roaring lion seeking to devour me (1 Pet. 5:8). 'Has God said?' Satan asks. 'You will not die!' he assures me.

---

[21] Henry, *Commentary*, on Gen. 3:6.
[22] Charnock, *Existence and Attributes*, II:327.
[23] *Ibid.*
[24] *Ibid.*, II:328.
[25] Calvin, *Institutes*, II.i.4, p. 246 (emphasis added).
[26] Henry, *Commentary*, on Gen. 3:5.

Recognize his strategy; recognize his tactics. If he can get us to doubt God's goodness, it is but a short step to convincing us that we must take matters into our own hands, redefine the 'good' as that which we desire, defy his word like Eve, and make catastrophic decisions. Without the full armour of God, we fall prey to his schemes (Eph. 6:11). Without the shield of faith, the fiery darts of doubt hit the mark. We wrestle not with 'flesh and blood', but against 'spiritual forces of evil' (Eph. 6:12).

'Yes!' Even in the face of rebellion, while Adam and Eve were 'shifting the sin rather than suing for mercy', he clothed the rebels in animal skins, replacing 'Adam's fig-leaf armour', and promised them a Redeemer.[27] The *proto evangelion*, the first announcement of the gospel, came in Genesis 3:15: the seed of the woman would bruise the head of the serpent. In the fullness of time, this promise would be fulfilled in the coming of the Son of God, our Lord Jesus Christ (Gal. 4:4-7).

Redemption

Having seen God's goodness, first, in creation and, second, in providence (see Chapter 11), we will now, third, see that God's goodness is revealed supremely in *redemption*.

What was the impact of the fall? Human nature was corrupted and bent against God. Man now hid from God, 'as if the thickness of the trees could screen him from the eye of the Creator'.[28] The man and woman feared the presence of God (Gen. 3:8). 'Adam sinned and defiled our nature,' says Gurnall, 'and now our nature defiles us.'[29] We, the sons of Adam, are, like Adam himself, enemies of God, rebels in revolt against the living God (Rom. 5:10). It is not that, as one evangelist put it, 'We've sort of done a few things that God isn't pleased with.' Jonathan Edwards maintains that we would pull him down from heaven 'to dethrone him if [we] could'.[30] We are *mortal* enemies, totally *alienated* from and *hostile* towards God (Rom. 8:7; Col. 1:21). Gurnall speaks of our 'envenomed nature that teems with

---

[27] Gurnall, *Christian in Complete Armour*, I:46, p. 52.
[28] Charnock, *Existence and Attributes*, I:517
[29] Gurnall, *Christian in Complete Armour*, I:407.
[30] Edwards, *Men Naturally Are God's Enemies*, *Works*, II:132.

enmity towards God'.[31] God has cursed us with death, and we ourselves would destroy him if we could. In fact, the one time God came within our reach, within our grasp, we rejected him. Although Jesus was the most beautiful, the most innocent, and the loveliest man who ever lived, we brutally executed him. Edwards writes with profound insight of the nature of fallen humanity:

> when once God became man, and came down to dwell here, among such vipers as fallen men, they hated and persecuted him; and never desisted till they had imbrued their hands in his blood. There was a multitude of them that appeared combined in this design. Nothing would do, but he must be put to death. All cry out, *Crucify him, crucify him. Away with him.* They had rather Barabbas, who greatly deserved death, should live, than he should not die. Nothing would restrain them from it; even all his preaching, and all his miracles: but they would kill him. And it was not the ordinary kind of execution that would satisfy them; but it must be the most cruel, and most ignominious they possibly could invent. And they aggravated it as much as they could, by mocking him, and spitting on him, and scourging him. This shows what the nature and tendency of man's enmity against God is; here it appeared in its true colours.[32]

Every sin, says Charnock, aims at the destruction of the being of God. It is 'a virtual undeifying of him'.[33] The apostle Paul says we are even 'haters of God' (Rom. 1:30). Fallen humanity opposes God's honour, glory, interests, kingdom, and declared designs. We think lowly of him. He is distasteful to us. He is 'not such a being as [we] would have'.[34] We are enemies of God in our judgments, tastes, wills, affections, and practices. 'A natural man is as full of enmity against God', Edwards insists, 'as any viper or any venomous beast, is full of poison.'[35]

Moses says of humanity from Adam to Noah, 'every intention of the thoughts of his heart was only evil continually' (Gen. 6:5). The

---

[31] Gurnall, *Christian in Complete Armour*, II:114.
[32] Edwards, *Men Naturally Are God's Enemies, Works*, II:132.
[33] Charnock, *Existence and Attributes*, I:189..
[34] Edwards, *Men Naturally Are God's Enemies, Works*, II:131.
[35] *Ibid.*, II:132.

prophet Jeremiah warns that 'The heart is deceitful above all things, and desperately sick' (Jer. 17:9). The apostle Paul characterizes natural men as living 'in the passions of [their] flesh, carrying out the desires of the body and the mind, and [being] by nature children of wrath' (Eph. 2:3). Again, Edwards maintains, 'The heart of a natural man is as destitute of love to God, as a dead, stiff, cold corpse is of vital heat.'[36] There is not the least spark of love towards God in us. Our every faculty and motive for action is hostile towards God. Our hatred of God is so great that it cannot be overcome or conquered by any finite force. It takes supernatural, divine action to turn our hearts from their hatred of God.

What, then, is God's response to these 'children of wrath'? To his hating, blasphemous, poison-spitting image-bearers? God judges them. He cursed the serpent (Gen. 3:14), the woman (3:15-16), the man, and all creation (3:17-19). The curse of death was reaffirmed: 'to dust you shall return' (3:19). However, God did not stop being good even though humanity no longer deserved his goodness. As we have noted, he does good to those who hate him. Jesus says, 'He is kind to the ungrateful and the evil' (Luke 6:35). He redeems. He is good to those who not only do not deserve love but who actually deserve the opposite. God's goodness, expressed in his love, is 'contrary to desert', says Packer, because it is given to those 'who merit only condemnation and final banishment from his presence'.[37] It is for reasons such as these that Packer says, 'It is staggering that God should love sinners; yet it is true. God loves creatures who have become unlovely and (one would have thought) unlovable. There was nothing whatever in these objects of his love to call it forth; nothing in man could attract or prompt it.'[38]

We have seen God's goodness in creation and providence. Let us now examine more closely his goodness in redemption. 'The whole gospel,' says Charnock, 'is nothing but one entire mirror of divine goodness.' Charnock calls God's goodness in redemption 'pure goodness'.[39] Let us consider how this is so, letting Charnock guide us through the discussion.

[36] Edwards, *Men Naturally Are God's Enemies, Works*, I:132.
[37] Packer, *Knowing God*, p. 112.
[38] *Ibid*.
[39] Charnock, *Existence and Attributes*, II:317, 318.

Redemption's source

First, redemption's *origin or source is in God's goodness.* Remember, God was not required to redeem. He was not obliged to save. God did nothing to rescue fallen angels. Similarly, 'he might as well forever have let man lie in the chains wherein he had entangled them'.[40] God's freedom not to save must be maintained. 'He was under no obligation to pity our misery, and repair our ruins,' Charnock insists.[41] Nothing outside God demanded it of him. Nothing lacking inside him prompted it. Nothing in us required it. 'Certainly that God who had no need of creating us, had far less need of redeeming us,' Charnock maintains.[42] Yet God determined to redeem us. Why? Because he is good.

As he warns those who practise wickedness that will not escape the judgment of God, the apostle Paul asks, 'Or do you presume on the riches of his kindness and forbearance and patience, not knowing that God's kindness is meant to lead you to repentance?' (Rom. 2:4-5). 'Kindness', 'forbearance', 'patience': redemption is a work of God that arises out of his goodness. God's 'kindness', an expression of his goodness, 'is meant to lead [us] to repentance'. 'The shining of God's mercies on us should dishearten and extinguish lust in us', says Trapp.[43]

Redemption's benefits

Second, consider further redemption's *benefits.* Are not our sins forgiven? Are we not reconciled to God? Have we not been given the gift of eternal life? Have we not been regenerated, justified, sanctified, preserved, and glorified? By this goodness, says Charnock, 'we are delivered from the corruption of our nature, the ruin of our happiness, the deformity of our sins, and the punishment of our transgressions; he frees us from the ignorance wherewith we were darkened and from the slavery wherein we were fettered'.[44] Further, 'He hath sought us out when we were lost, ransomed us when we were captives; he hath pardoned us when we were condemned, and raised us when we were

[40] Charnock, *Existence and Attributes*, II:321.
[41] *Ibid.*, II:318.
[42] *Ibid.*
[43] Trapp, *Commentary*, V:492.
[44] Charnock, *Existence and Attributes*, II:319.

dead.'[45] Why do we enjoy all of these good effects? Because God is good.

Redemption's cost

Third, God's goodness can be seen in the *cost of redemption*. God's goodness in redemption exceeds his goodness even in creation. It is both a more difficult goodness and a 'more expensive' goodness, Charnock maintains. In order to redeem humanity,

> God must be made man, eternity must suffer death, the Lord of angels must weep in a cradle, and the Creator of the world must hang like a slave; he must be in a manger in Bethlehem, and die upon a cross on Calvary; unspotted righteousness must be made sin, and unblemished blessedness be made a curse. He was at no other expense than the breath of his mouth to form man; the fruits of the earth could have maintained innocent man without any other cost; but his broken nature cannot be healed without the invaluable medicine of the blood of God. View Christ in the womb and in the manger, and his weary steps and hungry bowels, in his prostrations in the garden, and in his clotted drops of bloody sweat; view his head pierced with a crown of thorns, and his face besmeared with the soldiers' slobber; view him in his march to Calvary, and his elevation on the painful cross, with his head hanged down, and his side streaming blood; view him pelted with the scoffs of the governors, and the derisions of the rabble; and see, in all this, what cost Goodness was at for man's redemption! In creation, his power made the sun to shine upon us, and, in redemption, his bowels sent a Son to die for us.[46]

Charnock's observations are profound. 'He was desirous to hear him groaning, and see him bleeding, that we might not groan under his frowns, and bleed under his wrath; he spared not him, that he might spare us.'[47] 'In God's giving Christ to be our Redeemer, he gave the highest gift that it was possible for divine goodness to bestow.'[48]

[45] Charnock, *Existence and Attributes*, II:319.
[46] *Ibid.*, II:320.
[47] *Ibid.*, II:322-23.
[48] *Ibid.*, II:324.

'He had but one Son in heaven and earth, one Son from an unviewable eternity, and that one Son he gave for a degenerate world.'[49] 'It was the triumph of divine goodness, to give so great, so dear a person, for so little a thing as man.'[50] With reference to Romans 5:10, Boston exclaims, 'O what an expansive goodness and love was this!'[51] Think often of the goodness of God in bearing the cost of our redemption.

Redemption's extent

Fourth, God's goodness can be seen in the *extent of redemption*. We are not merely forgiven of our sins. We are not merely justified before our Judge. We are not merely reconciled to our Creator. No, this was not enough. We must also be adopted into the family of God (Rom. 8:14-16; Gal. 4:4-7). As Christ was raised, so we are raised (Rom 6:1ff.). As he was exalted to the right hand, so we are seated with him in the heavenly places (Eph. 2:6). The benefits of Christ's exaltation are extended to us.

> This goodness gave him to be debased for us, and ordered him to be enthroned for us: as it gave him to us bleeding, so it would give him to us triumphing; that as we have a share by grace in the merits of his humiliation, we might partake also of the glories of his coronation; that, from first to last, we may behold nothing but the triumphs of divine goodness to fallen man.[52]

In giving us his Son, God with him freely gives us 'all things' (Rom 8:32). *All things.*

Redemption's terms

Fifth, the goodness of God can be seen in the *easy terms of redemption*. What does God require of us but that we believe? No lower condition can be imagined, nor one 'so small and reasonable', or 'so slight'.[53] He does not require perfect obedience to his laws. He does not require a great mass of good works. He does not demand elaborate rituals or

---

[49] Charnock, *Existence and Attributes*, II:325.
[50] *Ibid.*
[51] Boston, *Illustration of the Doctrines, Works*, I:120.
[52] Charnock, *Existence and Attributes*, II:326.
[53] *Ibid.*, II:337.

multiple ceremonies. He only requires that we believe in Jesus. 'Believe in the Lord Jesus, and you will be saved' (Acts 16:31). 'What prince could require less upon any promise he makes his subjects than to be believed as true and depended on as good?'[54] Can we imagine an easier requirement? One less demanding? One less difficult? Even then, the faith that he requires is also a gift that he gives (Eph. 2:8-9).

Beyond this, God's goodness can even be seen in his accepting the good works of the redeemed which confirm the authenticity of their faith, though they be flawed (James 2:14-28; 1 John 2:3-4). He requires of us, says Charnock, not 'the perfection of obedience, but the sincerity of obedience; an uprightness in our intention, not an unspottedness in our action; an integrity in our aims, and an industry in our compliance with divine precepts'.[55] Though our obedience is 'weak and defective', says Calvin, God accepts our good works out of his 'free kindness'.[56]

Redemption's methods

Sixth, God's goodness can be seen in the *methods he uses to bring us to himself.* His methods, says Charnock, are characterized by 'gentleness and sweetness'. Charnock speaks of God's 'wooing goodness' and 'bewailing goodness' in drawing sinners to himself. 'Come now, let us reason together', God pleads (Isa. 1:18). He urges us with 'alluring promises and pressing exhortations'.[57] God laments, 'All day long I have held out my hands to a disobedient and contrary people' (Rom. 10:21; Isa. 65:2). Charnock describes these as 'melting expressions of a tender God soliciting a rebellious people'.[58] The prophet Isaiah said of Jesus, 'a bruised reed he will not break, and a smouldering wick he will not quench' (Matt. 12:20; Isa. 42:3). He is gentle and tender in his handling of the fragile soul and barely smouldering spirit. Richard Sibbes, in his famous 'Bruised Reed' sermon, remarks, 'There is more mercy in Christ than sin in us.'[59]

---

[54] Charnock, *Existence and Attributes*, II:337.
[55] *Ibid.*; See also Westminster Confession of Faith XVI.6.
[56] Calvin, *Institutes*, IV.x.15, p. 1193.
[57] Charnock, *Existence and Attributes*, II:340.
[58] *Ibid.*
[59] Sibbes, *Bruised Reed, Works*, I:47.

Jesus implores, 'Come to me, all who labour and are heavy laden, and I will give you rest. Take my yoke upon you, and learn from me, for I am gentle and lowly in heart, and you will find rest for your souls. For my yoke is easy, and my burden is light' (Matt. 11:28-30). Jesus pleads. He urges. He is gentle and humble. His yoke is easy. His burden is light.

Through Isaiah God invites us, 'Come, everyone who thirsts, come to the waters; and he who has no money, come, buy and eat! Come, buy wine and milk without money and without price' (Isa. 55:1). 'The Lord even thirsteth to be thirsted after', says Trapp.[60] Through Isaiah God urges us, 'Seek the LORD while he may be found; call upon him while he is near' (Isa. 55:6).

Listen to God entreat us through his apostle: 'Therefore, we are ambassadors for Christ, God making his appeal through us. We implore you on behalf of Christ, be reconciled to God' (2 Cor. 5:20). Commenting on this verse, Charnock says, 'It is as if divine goodness did kneel down to a sinner with ringed hands and blubbered cheeks, entreating him not to force him to re-assume a tribunal of justice in the nature of a judge, since he would treat with man upon a throne of grace in the nature of a father.'[61]

Through Ezekiel God pleads, 'Why will you die, O house of Israel?' (Ezek. 33:11). 'A yearning tenderness here manifests itself,' says Fairbairn, 'still seeking, not withstanding all that has taken place.'[62] Through Hosea God speaks, says Henry, as a 'tender father reasons with himself':[63] 'How can I give you up, O Ephraim? How can I hand you over, O Israel? How can I make you like Admah? How can I treat you like Zeboiim? My heart recoils within me; my compassion grows warm and tender' (Hos. 11:8). 'He never used his justice to crush men,' says Charnock, 'till he had used his kindness to allure them.'[64]

---

[60] Trapp, *Commentary*, III:413.
[61] Charnock, *Existence and Attributes*, II:340.
[62] Fairbairn, *Ezekiel*, p. 360.
[63] Henry, *Commentary*, on Hos. 11:8.
[64] Charnock, *Existence and Attributes*, II:340-41.

Redemption's provisions

Seventh, God's goodness in redemption may be seen in his *various provisions for his redeemed people.* His goodness may be seen in his giving us his *Scripture* to guide us to Christ, in whom we have been given 'all things that pertain to life and godliness' (2 Pet. 1:3). Through God's word we are born again and come to faith (1 Pet. 1:23-25; Rom. 10:17). We grow by its 'pure … milk' (1 Pet. 2:2), and we are sanctified by its truth (John 17:17). The Scriptures make us wise for salvation (2 Tim. 3:15). The Scriptures profitably teach, reprove, correct, train, and equip us for every good work (2 Tim. 3:16-17). God's word, says Charnock, 'is a lamp to our feet, and a medicine for our diseases; a purifier of our filth, and a restorer of us in our faintings'.[65]

God's goodness is seen in his giving us *prayer* by which we can call upon him, and in promising to answer, giving 'good things' to those who ask (Matt. 7:11). He is eager to answer us, promising, 'Before they call I will answer; while they are yet speaking I will hear' (Isa. 65:24). 'It is a wonder that God should condescend so much, that he should hear prayers so weak, so cold, so wandering, and gather up our sincere petitions from the dung of our distractions and diffidence.'[66]

God's goodness may be seen in his *readiness to forgive.* We confess our sins and he forgives them (Psa. 32:5; 1 John 1:9). The father runs towards the prodigal and interrupts his confession (Luke 15:20-22). 'He delights in steadfast love' (Mic. 7:18). 'For you, O LORD, are good and forgiving, abounding in steadfast love to all who call upon you (Psa. 86:5; cf. 130:3-4). 'He acts not according to the rigour of the law,' Charnock would have us understand, 'but willingly grants his pardon to those that fly into the arms of the mediator.'[67]

God's goodness may be seen in the *sacraments*, wherein he 'complies with our senses, and condescends to our weakness; he instructs us by the eye, as well as by the ear; he lets us see, and taste, and feel him, as well as hear him; he veils his glory under earthly elements, and informs our understanding in the mysteries of salvation by signs familiar to

[65] Charnock, *Existence and Attributes*, II:357.
[66] *Ibid.*, II:360.
[67] *Ibid.*, II:388.

our senses'.[68] He 'seals [the covenant] to our sense in a sacrament, to give us strong consolation', to 'strengthen our weakness, and support our security ... to keep up our tottering faith and preserve us constant in our obedience'.[69] Moreover, not only is Christ represented to us, but he is also communicated to us, or conferred. 'If Christ himself be received by faith in the word (Col. 2:6),' says Charnock, 'he is no less received by faith in the sacrament.' Through baptism we are made one body with Christ (1 Cor. 12:13). Through the bread and cup believers enjoy 'fellowship' (Gk *koinonia*), with Christ (1 Cor. 10:16). Even as the *unworthy* partaker 'eats and drinks judgment on himself', so the *worthy* partaker 'eats and drinks' salvation (1 Cor. 11:29). 'The infinite wise, gracious, and true God would never give us empty figures without accomplishing that which is signified by them, and suitable to them.'[70]

Redemption's limits

Eighth, God's goodness is even seen in the *incompleteness of our redemption*, as when we encounter trials, temptations, and suffering. 'It is good for me that I was afflicted', says the psalmist (Psa. 119:71). God designs and limits our temptations. 'God is at the beginning and end of every temptation: he measures out both the quality and quantity.'[71] He shortens our afflictions so that we can endure them, and he provides a way of escape lest we be overwhelmed. 'No temptation has overtaken you that is not common to man. God is faithful, and he will not let you be tempted beyond your ability, but with the temptation he will also provide the way of escape, that you may be able to endure it' (1 Cor. 10:13; cf. Dan. 11:35).

All temptations are 'common', not exceptional. All temptations are within our 'ability'. 'He proportioneth the burden to the back, and the stroke to the strength of him that beareth it', says Trapp.[72] All temptations have a divinely provided escape route, a 'way of escape'. 'The strong blast Satan breathes cannot blow, nor the waves he raises

[68] Charnock, *Existence and Attributes*, II:342.
[69] *Ibid.*, II:343-44.
[70] *Ibid.*, II:344.
[71] *Ibid.*, II:362.
[72] Trapp, *Commentary*, V:538.

rage one minute beyond the time God allows them', Charnock assures us.[73] If there is to be no escape, he strengthens us to withstand. 'If he doth not restrain the arm of Satan from striking, he gives us a sword to manage the combat, or a shield to bear off the blow (Eph. 6:14, 17).'[74] 'When we have not a strength by nature, he gives it us by grace.'[75]

Sometimes God uses our afflictions and temptations to prevent sins to which we would have been vulnerable if left unafflicted. The apostle Paul's thorn in the flesh was a 'messenger of Satan' yet was used by God to prevent him from exalting himself (2 Cor. 12:7-10). Our suffering is 'for our good, that we may share his holiness'. It yields the 'peaceful fruit of righteousness' (Heb. 12:10, 11). 'The goodness of God makes the devil a polisher, while he intends to be a destroyer.'[76] God may take us into a wilderness 'to bring down our loftiness, to starve our carnal confidence, and to expel our rusting security' (Deut. 8:2).[77]

When afflicted, trust his goodness. 'When he bestows anything upon his people, he sees it best they should have it; and when he removes anything from them, he sees it best they should lose it.'[78]

Redemption's scope

Ninth, God's goodness in redemption may be seen in its *scope*. All creation is to be redeemed. The created order was 'subjected to futility' because of the fall, and it 'groans', says the apostle Paul, under the effects of sin (Rom. 8:20, 22). It longs to be 'set free from its bondage to corruption and obtain the freedom of the glory of the children of God' (8:21). 'The honour of [created things] was stained,' says Charnock, 'when they were debased to serve the lusts of a traitor, instead of supporting the duty of a subject.' The creation is alienated from its intended use. 'The drunkard's cup, and the glutton's table, the adulterer's bed, and the proud man's purple, would groan against the abuser of them'—that is, if they could.[79]

[73] Charnock, *Existence and Attributes*, II:362.
[74] *Ibid.*
[75] *Ibid.* II:363.
[76] *Ibid.*, II:364.
[77] *Ibid.*
[78] *Ibid.*, II:395.
[79] *Ibid.*, II:347.

Redemption not only restores humanity to its true end, but also restores the created order to its true use. Hereafter, created things shall only serve righteousness, as they were designed to do. 'The world,' says Charnock, 'shall be nothing but a universal smile.' One day humanity and creation will be in harmony. No longer will we work by the 'sweat of [our] face'. The curse on the ground will be lifted (Gen. 3:17-19). No longer will we be in danger of wild animals, violent storms, annoying insects, and natural disasters. 'There shall be no affrighting thunders, choking mists, venomous vapours, or poisonous plants.'[80] Charnock beautifully summarizes the vast scope of God's goodness in redemption:

> How great is that goodness, when by sin we were fallen to be worse than nothing, that he should raise us to be more than what we are; that restored us, not to the first step of our creation, but to many degrees of elevation beyond it! not only restores us, but prefers us; not only striking off our chains, to set us free, but clothing us with a robe of righteousness, to render us honourable; not only quenching our hell, but preparing a heaven; not re-garnishing an earthly, but providing a richer palace: his goodness was so great, that, after it had rescued us, it would not content itself with the old furniture, but makes all new for us in another world; a new wine to drink; a new heaven to dwell in; a more magnificent structure for our habitation; thus hath goodness prepared for us a straiter union, and a fuller glory; all more excellent than was within the compass of innocent Adam's possession.[81]

Response

We have already partially responded to God's goodness in redemption, urging that we do not fall prey to the devil's scheme to doubt the goodness of God. Let us now respond further.

---

[80] Charnock, *Existence and Attributes*, II:348.
[81] *Ibid.*, II:346.

Receive the greatest gift

First, *receive the greatest of God's gifts*, the gift of his Son, Jesus of Nazareth, Jesus the Christ. Baxter would have us see God's goodness in his nature, his works, his laws, but especially 'in the face of Christ, and behold his love in the design of our redemption, in the person of the Redeemer, and in the promises of grace, and in all the benefits of redemption'.[82] 'Gift' is the language the Bible uses to describe salvation (Rom. 6:23; Eph. 2:8-9). Is not the gift of God's Son—his only Son (Gen. 22:2, 16; John 3:16), his beloved Son, his Son with whom he is well pleased (Matt. 3:17)—proof of his goodness? Love, an aspect of his goodness, is demonstrated 'in that while we were still sinners', even 'enemies', 'Christ died for us' (Rom 5:8, 10). Now that God has demonstrated and proven his goodness at the cross, can we not count on that goodness in all things? Is not this the apostle Paul's argument in Romans 8? 'He who did not spare his own Son but gave him up for us all, how will he not also with him graciously give us all things?' (Rom. 8:32). Paul argues from the greater to the lesser. Having given us his Son—the greatest of all gifts—can God not be counted on to give us all lesser things? 'The gift of Christ,' says Hodge, 'includes all other gifts.'[83]

Conversely, is refusing the greatest of all gifts from the hand of the gracious God not the greatest of all evils? Charnock maintains, 'Since the sending of his Son was the greatest act of goodness that God could express, the refusal of him must be the highest reproach of that liberality God designed to commend to the world in so rare a gift.'[84] For us to turn our backs on this gift is to act 'as though the richest gift of heaven were not so valuable as a swinish pleasure on earth'.[85] Receive God's gift of salvation through Jesus Christ the Lord of all.

Enjoy the lesser gifts with thankfulness

Second, *enjoy God's lesser gifts as expressions of his goodness*. Every good thing enjoyed, every moment of pleasure experienced, should be

---

[82] Baxter, *The Divine Life*, *Works*, III:784.
[83] Hodge, *Romans*, p. 288.
[84] Charnock, *Existence and Attributes*, II:369.
[85] *Ibid.*

allowed to kindle love and gratitude for God, since he is its source. Primarily we are to love God for 'the excellence of His own nature', for who God is in himself.[86] Yet, secondarily, we are to love God for his benefits. Explaining how enjoying the goodness of created things ought to lead us to love God even more, Charnock explains, 'If we love a little spark of greatness in this or that creature, if a drop be so delicious to us, shall not the immense sun of goodness, the ever-flowing fountain of all, be much more delightful?'[87] He continues:

> We love creatures for what we think to be good in them, though it may be hurtful; and shall we not love God, who is real and unblemished goodness, and from whose hand are poured out all those blessings that are conveyed to us by second causes? The object that delights us, the capacity we have to delight in it, are both from him.[88] ... Shall we love a horse or dog, for the benefits we have by them? And shall not the spring of all those draw our souls after it, and make us aspire to the honour of loving and embracing him who hath stored every creature with that which may pleasure us?[89]

The problem with these lesser gifts is that fallen humanity tends to turn them into idols to be worshipped. The propensity of human nature is not gratefully to receive God's 'witness' to himself in the form of 'rains from heaven and fruitful seasons' that satisfy our hearts 'with food and gladness' (Acts 14:17), but to turn them into false gods and 'worship and serve the creature rather than the Creator' (Rom. 1:25). Our inclination is to lose all sense of proportion and become obsessed with the pleasure, activity, or thing, to bow down, worship, and serve it. There are two ways to sin. One is to violate God's commands: to kill, commit murder, steal, lie, and so on. The other, less obvious way is to indulge in lawful, permitted and approved things to idolatrous proportions. It is not enough to have money: we worship it (Matt. 6:24). It is not enough to enjoy food: our belly becomes our god (Phil. 3:19. It is not enough to have plenty: we consume our lives building bigger

---

[86] Charnock, *Existence and Attributes*, II:382.
[87] *Ibid.*
[88] *Ibid.*, II:366.
[89] *Ibid.* II:382.

barns (Luke 12:16-21). We abuse God's goodness, says Charnock, when 'we enjoy the mercies and forget the donor'.[90] This was the sin of Israel while still in the wilderness. 'They forgot God, their Saviour, who had done great things in Egypt' (Psa. 106:21). Once they prospered in the land of Canaan, they forgot the source of their well-being, as Moses had warned would happen (Deut. 6:12; 8:11, 14, 17) and as God through Hosea explains: 'And she did not know that it was I who gave her the grain, the wine, and the oil, and who lavished on her silver and gold, which they used for Baal' (Hos. 2:8). 'God took it ill, and well might he,' says Gurnall of this verse, 'that they should entertain Baal at his cost.'[91]

When we place our trust in God's gifts, or 'glue our choicest affections to them', we abuse God's goodness.[92] Bitter is the irony in that God 'receives no blows from men, but by these instruments he gave them to promote their happiness'.[93]

Likewise, we abuse God's goodness when we attribute our blessings to causes other than God, as Israel did with her lovers (Hos. 2:5, 12), Belshazzar his idols (Dan. 5:23), and Nebuchadnezzar his own power and wisdom (Dan. 4:29ff.; cf. Deut. 6:10-15; and especially 8:17-18). Of the last, Charnock says, 'We eclipse the glory of Divine goodness, by setting the crown that is due to it upon the head of our own industry.'[94] He warns us, 'We are descended as low as brutes, if we understand him not to be the perfect good; and we are descended as low as devils, if our affections are not attracted by it.'[95]

Let all of God's gifts lead us to God himself. Let all of the good things of this life direct us to the greater good, the greatest good—that is, God himself. 'We should look upon the world not as a god, but as a gift from God, and never think the present better than the donor.'[96] Instead of being led astray by God's gifts to serve them rather than the giver, let these gifts lead us to love and serve him. The greatness and

---

[90] Charnock, *Existence and Attributes*, II:366.
[91] Gurnall, *Christian in Complete Armour*, I:418.
[92] Charnock, *Existence and Attributes*, II:371.
[93] *Ibid*., II:373.
[94] *Ibid*. II:373-74.
[95] *Ibid*., II:380.
[96] *Ibid*., II:396.

number of God's benefits lay upon us an unequalled motivation and obligation to honour and serve him. 'He hath a claim to our choicest affections' and to our 'most exact obedience'.[97]

Learn contentment

Third, *learn contentment.* Whatever our circumstances may be, we know that they are ordained by a God who is good and who has our well-being in mind. David, writing Psalm 84 in a time of deprivation, cut off from the worship of God for which his soul longed (verse 2), nevertheless could sing. 'For the LORD God is a sun and shield; the LORD bestows favour and honour. No good thing does he withhold from those who walk uprightly' (Psa. 84:11). 'No good thing does he withhold'? David has learned to view his deprivations as engineered by God to serve the greater good of 'those who walk uprightly'. So yes, he is suffering. Yes, he is enduring deprivation. Sometimes 'the chariot wheels of divine goodness move slow', says Charnock. Sometimes our prayers 'hang too long for an answer'.[98] Yet David knows that 'Not an ill will, but a good will directs his scourge'; that God 'is not an idle spectator of our combats'.[99] In fact, the truth is that we receive more blessings than we are worthy of receiving, and fewer afflictions than we deserve. 'How doth he provide for us above our deserts, even while he doth punish us beneath our merits!'[100]

Yet often we are tempted to grumble, complaining that God has mistreated us. Job, under the initial pressure of his afflictions, 'did not sin or charge God with wrong' (Job 1:22). Yet this is rare. 'Scarce a man is to be found without unjust complaints of God, and charging him under their crosses with cruelty.'[101] Job himself, when tormented by his friends, succumbed to despair and said, 'God has wronged me' (Job 19:6 NASB). Jeremiah, under the pressure of Pashhur's persecutions, accused God of deception (Jer. 20:7). The psalmist wondered, 'Has God forgotten to be gracious?' (Psa. 77:9). He complained, 'All in vain have I kept my heart clean and washed my hands in innocence'

[97] Charnock, *Existence and Attributes*, II:386.
[98] *Ibid.*, I:529.
[99] *Ibid.*, II:389.
[100] *Ibid.*
[101] *Ibid.*, II:367.

(73:13). 'All murmuring,' says Charnock, 'either in our own cause or others', charges God with a want of goodness.'[102] The complaints in the wilderness that things were better in Egypt (e.g. Exod. 16:3; Num. 11:5, 18) were an assault upon God's goodness. It ought to 'set us a blushing before him', says Charnock, 'when we should consider the multitude of his benefits, and our unworthy behaviour'.[103] Even when we suffer the loss of a beloved object, 'there is more cause to be thankful that we have enjoyed it so long, than to murmur that we possess it no longer'.[104]

Why does God allow evil? If God is good, why does he allow suffering and pain? For the *greater good*. Twice in Jesus' ministry he declared that sickness and death were ordained and permitted for the greater good. Jesus said of Lazarus' illness, 'It is for the glory of God', that is, 'so that the Son of God may be glorified through it' (John 11:4). 'Let this reconcile us to the darkest dispensations of providence, they are all for the glory of God,' says Henry; 'and if God be *glorified*, we ought to be *satisfied*.'[105] Similarly, when asked concerning the man born blind, 'Who sinned, this man or his parents, that he was born blind?', Jesus answered that it was neither; rather, the man had been born blind 'that the works of God might be displayed in him' (John 9:2-3). Calvin cites Augustine: 'It pertained to [God's] most omnipotent goodness to bring good out of evil things *rather than not to permit evil things to be.*'[106] We can see this most clearly at the cross, where the greatest evil brought about the greatest good (Acts 4:27-29).

All trust in God assumes that he is good; all distrust assumes that he is evil. Israel complained that God had brought them into the wilderness only to kill them (Num. 14:3)! Listen instead to the apostle Paul as he writes from a Roman prison as an ambassador of Christ in chains (Eph. 6:20; cf. Col. 4:18; 2 Tim. 2:9), and, heightening his distress, betrayed by fellow Christian ministers (Phil. 1:15-18; cf. 2 Tim. 1:15; 4:10-11, 16): 'I have learned in whatever situation I am to be content. I know how to be brought low, and I know how to abound. In

---

[102] Charnock, *Existence and Attributes*, II:368.
[103] *Ibid.*, II:394.
[104] *Ibid.*, II:368.
[105] Henry, *Commentary*, on John 11:4 (my emphasis).
[106] Augustine, *On Rebuke and Grace*; cited in Calvin, *Institutes*, III.xxiii.7, p. 956 (emphasis added).

any and every circumstance, I have learned the secret of facing plenty and hunger, abundance and need' (Phil. 4:11-12).

Why was the apostle content? Because God is great and God is good. This good God 'will supply every need of yours according to his riches in glory in Christ Jesus' (Phil. 4:19). He is sovereign, and he ordains only that which is for the good of his people. All things work together for their *good* (Rom. 8:28). As noted above, our suffering is the Father's loving hand disciplining us that we might 'share his holiness' and yield 'the peaceful fruit of righteousness' (Heb. 12:10-11). We may 'count it all joy … when [we] meet trials of various kinds' because their aim is that we may be 'perfect and complete' (James 1:2-4). Simply put, 'suffering produces … character' (Rom. 5:3-5). Let us then 'draw near to God' whatever our circumstances may be, as Baxter urges, 'and have no low undervaluing thoughts of his infinite goodness'.[107]

Gratefully serve

Fourth, *gratefully serve*. As beneficiaries of the vast goodness of God, goodness expressed through creation, providence, and redemption, we ought to respond in grateful service. When pleading with God, Nehemiah condemned the people of Israel because they had enjoyed 'your great goodness that you gave them', yet 'they did not *serve* you or turn from their wicked works' (Neh. 9:35). It is in view of the 'mercies of God' that we 'present [our] bodies as a living sacrifice, holy and acceptable to God', which is our 'spiritual service' (NASB) or 'worship' (Rom. 12:1). It is by the 'mercies of God' that we are inspired to serve (see Rom. 12:2ff.). As Baxter says, 'The goodness of God obligates us to serve him, not to offend him.'[108]

Be good and do good

Fifth, and finally, *be good and do good*. Imitate God's goodness. 'Beloved, do not imitate evil but imitate good,' instructs the apostle John. 'Whoever does good is from God; whoever does evil has not seen God' (3 John 11). Jesus transforms his disciples so that they have the capacity to be good and do good. Because God is 'kind to the ungrateful and

---

[107] Baxter, *The Divine Life, Works*, III:785.
[108] *Ibid.*

the evil', Jesus exhorts us to 'love [our] enemies, and *do good*'. 'Do good to those who hate you … pray for those who abuse you' (Luke 6:35, 27-28). 'Goodness' is a fruit of the Holy Spirit (Gal. 5:22). 'Do not be overcome by evil,' the apostle insists, 'but overcome evil with *good*' (Rom. 12:21). 'Let us not grow weary of *doing good*', the apostle urges (Gal. 6:9). May our '*good* works' lead others to glorify our Father in heaven (Matt. 5:16; 1 Pet. 2:12). And may we all one day hear those words of divine commendation: 'Well done, *good* and faithful servant … Enter into the joy of your master' (Matt. 25:23).

THIRTEEN

'The Love of God'

*See what kind of love the Father has given to us, that we should be called children of God; and so we are. The reason why the world does not know us is that it did not know him. ... Beloved, let us love one another, for love is from God, and whoever loves has been born of God and knows God. Anyone who does not love does not know God, because God is love. In this the love of God was made manifest among us, that God sent his only Son into the world, so that we might live through him. In this is love, not that we have loved God but that he loved us and sent his Son to be the propitiation for our sins. Beloved, if God so loved us, we also ought to love one another. No one has ever seen God; if we love one another, God abides in us and his love is perfected in us.—*I John 3:1; 4:7-12

JOHN was an elderly man by the time he wrote his first epistle. Somewhere between thirty and sixty years had passed since the resurrection. As a younger man he had had the privilege of walking daily with Jesus during his three years of public ministry. He had heard the great sermons, seen the spectacular miracles, and witnessed first-hand his dealings with both friend and foe. He had even been a part of the inner circle along with Peter and James. He had seen his hopes crushed as he watched Jesus die. He had known the incomparable thrill of realizing that Jesus had risen from the dead. He had been there at Pentecost. He had watched the church grow and spread during its early decades. He had led and taught congregations for decades. He knew first-hand the power of the gospel. John had been through it all.

Yet, when John begins to write about the love of God, he can still hardly contain himself. The truth has not become stale for him. It is still alive; it is still a cause of wonder and amazement. 'The holy apostle is here in a transport,' says Matthew Poole, 'in the contemplation of the glorious ... privilege, to be called [God's] sons.'[1] 'See', he says, using the aorist imperative; 'Look'—or perhaps the Elizabethan English is still the best: 'Behold' (KJV). Then he uses a word (Gk *potapos*, 'what kind') which originally meant 'from what country?' and is used of something that is foreign, unusual, or inexplicable.[2] It has been translated 'How great' (NASB) or 'what manner' (KJV). It indicates that God's love (Gk *agapē*) is of a different order, or different kind—exceptional, outstanding, unique, superior—from all other loves. It is 'out of this world', says Ian Hamilton.[3] What is it about God's love, which he has 'given to us' that calls for this exuberance? John continues: 'that we should be called children of God; and so we are' (1 John 3:1).

The highest expression of God's love, as John sees it, is the love which results in our salvation. The fact that, in Christ, God is our Father and we are his adopted children thrills his soul. 'The wonder of it all grips John', Leon Morris observes.[4] Such a love is amazing, incredible. Not only are we 'called children of God', but 'so we are'. We have not just the name, but the reality.

'Behold', John says. Open your eyes! His urgency 'reproves men's squint-looking', as New England's John Cotton (1584–1652) put it so quaintly.[5] Be amazed and astonished at the love of God. 'The love of Christ ... surpasses knowledge', says the apostle Paul (Eph. 3:19). The love of Christ, says John Stott commenting on Ephesians 3:18, 'is

[1] Poole, *Commentary*, III:934.

[2] For example, after Jesus quieted the storm the people asked, 'What kind [or 'sort', *potapos*] of man is this?' (Matt. 8:27). The disciples, when they pointed to the massive stones used in building Herod's temple (40' by 10' by 12') and the massive buildings themselves, said, 'Behold [or 'Look'], ... what wonderful [*potapos*] stones and what wonderful buildings!' (Mark 13:1).

[3] Ian Hamilton, *Let's Study the Letters of John* (Edinburgh: Banner of Truth Trust, 2008), p. 33.

[4] Leon Morris, '1 John', in G. J. Wehnam, J. A. Motyer, D. A. Carson, R. T. France (eds.), *The New Bible Commentary: 21st Century Edition*, 1953 (Downers Grove, IL: InterVarsity Press, 1994), p. 140.

[5] John Cotton, *An Exposition of First John* (1656; Lafayette, IN: Sovereign Grace Publishers, 2001), p. 312.

"broad" enough to encompass all mankind ... "long" enough to last for eternity, "deep" enough to reach to the most degraded sinner, and "high" enough to exalt him to heaven'.[6] B. B. Warfield speaks of 'the immeasurable greatness' of the love of God and of its 'unfathomable profundities'.[7] Isaac Watts taught us to sing of God's 'amazing pity! grace unknown! and *love beyond degree*'.[8]

'Beloved, let us love one another, for love is from God, and whoever loves has been born of God and knows God. Anyone who does not love does not know God, because God is love' (1 John 4:7-8).

'God is love' (Gk *agapē*). With this we come to what Robert Law, writing in 1909, called 'the summit of all revelation',[9] and what Stott called 'the most comprehensive and sublime of all biblical affirmations about God's being'.[10] John does not say that 'God is loving'. It is not God's behaviour but his essential nature which is in view. God 'is love in his inmost being'.[11] 'God loves,' Morris adds, 'but not in an incidental or haphazard fashion. He loves because it is his nature to love, because it is his nature to give himself unceasingly in love.'[12] All love is 'from God' (1 John 4:7). He is the origin and source of love. 'Here is the principal shining forth of the hidden glory of the divine nature,' said J. W. Alexander (1804–59), son of the founding theologian of Princeton Theological Seminary, Archibald Alexander, and a renowned pastor and theologian in his own right. 'Here is the central truth of Christianity.'[13] God is the 'fountain of love', says John Calvin.[14] God's nature, his being, his character, his essence, is love.

[6] John R. W. Stott, *The Message of Ephesians: God's New Society*, *The Bible Speaks Today* (Leicester: Inter-Varsity Press, 1979), p. 137.

[7] B. B. Warfield, 'God's Immeasurable Love', in *The Savior of the World* (New York: Hodder & Stoughton, 1913), pp. 103, 112.

[8] Isaac Watts, 'Alas! And Did My Saviour Bleed' (emphasis added).

[9] Robert Law, *Tests of Life*; cited in John Stott, *The Epistles of John: An Introduction and Commentary*, Tyndale New Testament Commentaries (1964; Grand Rapids, MI: Eerdmans, 1975), p. 159.

[10] Stott, *Epistles of John*, p. 160.

[11] *Ibid.*; cf. Morris, *Testaments of Love*, p. 136.

[12] Morris, *Testaments of Love*, p. 136.

[13] J. W. Alexander, *God Is Love* (1860; Edinburgh: Banner of Truth Trust, 1985), pp. 20-21.

[14] John Calvin, *The First Epistle of John*, David W. Torrance and Thomas F. Torrance (eds.) (Grand Rapids, MI: Eerdmans, 1959), p. 290.

Classifications and definitions

Where do we place love among the attributes? 'From goodness flows love', says Francis Turretin.[15] Love is an aspect of the goodness of God, as also are his mercy, grace, and patience. *Mercy* is God's goodness expressed towards the suffering. *Grace* is God's goodness expressed towards the unworthy. *Patience* is God's goodness expressed towards those who have long provoked him. God's *love* is his goodness expressed towards the good, as he sees it in creation and foresees it in redemptive recreation. The classic theologians, agreeing with the modern exegetes cited above, defined the love of God as 'an essential attribute of God'.[16] Indeed, it is more than an attribute. 'The love of God by definition,' says Wilhelmus à Brakel, 'is the loving God himself.'[17]

Intra-Trinitarian

The love of God, then, begins with divine self-love, as God himself is the greatest good. The 'primary object of God's love is himself', says Edward Leigh, 'for he taketh great pleasure in himself, and is the author of greatest felicity toward himself'.[18] Jesus teaches that 'the Father loves the Son' (John 3:35) and the Son loves the Father (14:31). The persons of the Trinity love each other. 'God is a society,' says Packer, 'a community of mutual love.'[19] The love of God is triune love. The gospel, says Jonathan Edwards in his wonderful work *Charity and Its Fruits*,

> brings to light the love eternally existing between the Father and the Son, and declares how that same love has been manifested in many things; how that Christ is God's well-beloved Son, in whom he is ever well pleased; how he so loved him, that he has raised him to the throne of the mediatorial kingdom, and appointed him to be the judge of the world, and ordained that all mankind should stand before him in judgment.

---

[15] Turretin, *Elenctic Theology*, p. 241.

[16] à Brakel, *Christian's Reasonable Service*, I:123.

[17] *Ibid*.

[18] Cited in Muller, *Post-Reformation Reformed Dogmatics*, III:565. Muller comments: God 'loves the ultimate goodness of his own Being as the foremost and highest object of love' (*ibid.*).

[19] Packer, *Collected Shorter Writings*, I:148.

Furthermore, he writes,

> In the gospel, too, is revealed the love that Christ has to the
> Father, and the wonderful fruits of that love, particularly in
> his doing such great things, and suffering such great things in
> obedience to the Father's will, and for the honour of his justice,
> and law, and authority, as the great moral governor.[20]

Mutual delight characterizes their relationship. As John Murray
says, 'There was an infinitude of reciprocal love' between the Father
and the Son—and, we may add, the Spirit—'love not constrained by
ignorance nor quenched by knowledge, but love drawn out by exclusive
and exhaustive knowledge'.[21]

Affection for good

According to Richard Muller, the classic Reformed definition of the
love of God is his 'propensity for the good'.[22] He cites Benedict Pictet
(1655–1724), who defined God's love as that 'by which God is inclined
towards the creature and delights to do it good, and as it were, to
unite himself with it'.[23] The love of God, according to Charles Hodge,
'includes complacency, desire, and delight, and has rational beings as
its objects'.[24]

Further, God loves what he sees of himself in what he has made. He
loves his image, as reflected by the created order. He loves humanity.
'He loves in them himself,' says Berkhof, 'his virtues, his work, and
his gifts.'[25] He loves even the fallen 'world' and fallen humanity (John
3:16), 'since he recognizes that even the sinner is his image-bearer'.[26]
So also there is a particular love for his redeemed people, in whom his
image is restored, Berkhof continues, as 'he communicates himself [to
them] in the fullest and richest sense'.[27]

---

[20] Jonathan Edwards, *Charity and Its Fruits: Christian Love as Manifested in the
Heart and Life* (1852; London: Banner of Truth Trust, 1969), p. 19.

[21] Murray, *Collected Writings*, III:216.

[22] Muller, *Post-Reformation Reformed Dogmatics*, III:565.

[23] *Ibid.*

[24] Hodge, *Systematic Theology*, III:427.

[25] Berkhof, *Systematic Theology*, p. 71.

[26] *Ibid.*

[27] *Ibid.*

We may say in summary that God's love is his affection for the good as he sees it in himself, in creation, in humanity, and especially in redeemed humanity.

Love and God's love

We need to elaborate on this and clarify it.

First, *God is love, yet he is more than love.* Hopefully by this point in our studies we have understood that God is not only love. When the Bible says that 'God is love', it does not mean that God is love to the exclusion of his other attributes. The apostle does not write that 'love is God'. The equation cannot be reversed. God is more than love. The Bible also says that 'God is light' (1 John 1:5) and that 'God is a consuming fire' (Heb. 12:29). The same grammatical construction is used in both these cases. The God who is love is also truth, holiness, and justice. 'Though God is infinitely benevolent,' says J. W. Alexander, 'infinite benevolence is not all of God.' [28] God's love is a just love, and his justice is a loving justice. We must not allow one attribute to overwhelm and nullify the rest. Justice is exercised lovingly, and love never compromises his justice.[29] Spurgeon puts it this way: 'God is love, but God is also just—as severely just as if he had no love, and yet as intensely loving as if he had no justice. To gain a just view of the character of God you must perceive all his attributes as infinitely developed. Justice must have its infinity acknowledged as much as mercy.'[30]

Second, *the Bible must be allowed to define love.* Not infrequently the love of God has been understood in such a way as to deny God's moral qualities. 'I believe in a God of love', someone will say, as they go on to abolish judgment day and to quench the fires of hell. Or they will affirm the divine acceptance of any and every lifestyle choice. Or they will toss out moral categories altogether, in the name of love. 'It is assumed,' says Packer of modern people, 'that God's love, if real, would

[28] Alexander, *God Is Love*, p. 17.

[29] 'We do wrong to exalt the love of God as his supreme feature just because it is more congenial to our thinking' (I. H. Marshall, *The Epistles of John*, New International Commentary on the New Testament [Grand Rapids, MI: Eerdmans, 1982], p. 212).

[30] Spurgeon, 'A Message from God for Thee', *Metropolitan Tabernacle Pulpit*, VIII:638.

itself take the form of unprincipled indulgence of our whims.'[31] 'A loving God would *never* …'—and then follows a list of moral distinctions, or moral demands that God, it is alleged, would never make. He never would condemn me, or want me to be unhappy, or disapprove of my conduct. At the heart of today's confusion is the contemporary use of the word 'love'. The Bible does not mean by 'love' what Hollywood does. God is love: *agapē*, not *eros*; *caritas*, not *amor*; self-giving and sacrificial love, not romantic or erotic love. One problem faced in Bible translation is that there are five Greek words for 'love', whereas the English language has but one.[32] This contributes to the confusion.

Neither does the Bible mean by 'love' what the moral relativists say it means when they identify it with 'acceptance'. To love, we are told, is to accept everyone and every lifestyle. Conversely, to hate, we are told, is not to accept certain types of people. 'God is love' means that God accepts everyone without reference to moral conduct, many maintain. This is to read into the Bible's affirmation of God's love content that it does not have. When the Bible teaches that 'God is love', it does not imply that God abandons moral distinctions.

All human language must be carefully redefined when it moves from its normal realm among the finite and is applied to the infinite. The core meaning of terms will remain the same, yet, as Packer points out, 'all associations or implications that suggest human finitude and fallenness must be eliminated'. That core meaning must then 'be set in the frame of God's perfection and purity'. This means that the love of God 'is not identical with, but analogous to, what is noblest in human love'.[33] God is love. Yet God remains holy. 'Behold the goodness *and* severity of God,' says the apostle Paul (Rom. 11:22 KJV). Stott says, 'Far from condoning sin'—which the modern view of God's love would have him do—'his love has found a way to expose it (because he is light) and to consume it (because he is fire) without destroying the sinner, but rather saving him.'[34] Hamilton adds helpfully, 'His love is

---

[31] Packer, 'Love of God', *Collected Shorter Writings*, I:146.

[32] Morris, *Testaments of Love*, devotes a chapter to the exposition of *storgē*, family or natural love; *philia*, friendship love; *epithumia*, passion; *eros*, romantic love; and *agapē*, sacrificial love (pp. 114-28).

[33] Packer, 'Love of God', *Collected Shorter Writings*, I:148.

[34] Stott, *Epistles of John*, p. 161.

not and cannot be blind and indulgent, just as his justice and holiness are not, and cannot be, cold and arbitrary.'[35]

Most of our contemporaries assume universalism. They assume that God loves everyone and in the same way. They assume that divine favour is everyone's birthright, everyone's from the womb, an abiding reality that cannot be forfeited. 'Nothing seems quite so self-evident to us today as the love of God', David Wells asserts.[36] Yet in previous eras God seemed to most people to be indifferent, remote, or even hostile. The gods of the ancients were arbitrary and capricious. People lived in terror of their gods for millennia. Costly sacrifices, often of human life, were made in order to placate them. Dread of the next irrational, destructive whim of their gods filled their lives. Not so today. The love of God for all is assumed. The problem, says Wells, is that 'God's love has been universalized and then unhitched from his holiness.'[37]

Most of our contemporaries are religious relativists. They believe that essentially all religions are the same and that everyone, in the end, will wind up in heaven. This outlook, when embraced, not only dilutes the particular love of God for sinners in Christ, but it also undermines Christian mission, and the gospel itself. If all are children of God and loved by God already, then why evangelize? Indeed, why did Christ come, and why did he die?

'We cannot assume,' says Morris, 'that the way we use the word *love* in a modern Western community is the way it was used in the Bible.'[38] 'Our understanding of the love of God must be limited by what the Bible's homiletical flowings of thought actually yield', Packer urges.[39] God is light, and because he is, says Packer,

> Sentimental ideas of his love as an indulgent, benevolent softness, divorced from moral standards and concerns, must therefore be ruled out from the start. God's love is holy love. The God whom Jesus made known is not a God who is indifferent to moral distinctions, but a God who loves righteousness and hates

---

[35] Hamilton, *Letters of John*, p. 59.
[36] Wells, *God in the Whirlwind*, p. 77.
[37] *Ibid.*, p. 86.
[38] Morris, *Testaments of Love*, p. 3.
[39] Packer, 'Love of God', *Collected Shorter Writings*, I:149.

iniquity, a God whose ideal for his children is that they should be 'perfect, even as your Father in heaven is perfect' (Matt. 5:48).[40]

Third, *God is biased towards love.* While we should not allow love to overshadow all God's other attributes, yet we can say that love, in a sense, is more 'natural' to God than his wrath. He prefers to express love over and against his more severe attributes. We are stretching language at this point because God's attributes are a harmonious unity. Love and justice are not warring against each other in God's nature of consciousness. Yet the Bible teaches us that God 'delights in steadfast [or 'unchanging', NASB] love' (Mic. 7:18), but it never teaches that he 'delights to show wrath'. 'God is more inclinable to mercy than wrath,' said the Puritan Thomas Watson. 'Acts of severity are rather forced from him.'[41] The Bible teaches that 'he does not willingly afflict', yet he does willingly and eagerly love (Lam. 3:33; Deut. 6:6-7). He is 'slow to anger' yet 'abounding in steadfast love [loving-kindness]' (Psa. 103:8; cf. Exod. 34:6). Isaiah calls God's judgment his 'strange work' (Isa. 28:21 KJV), or what theologians call his *opera aliena*, his alien task. He is a reluctant judge. It is as though the expression of just wrath were foreign to him. God is more inclined to love, to show kindness, grace, and mercy, than he is to show anger, wrath, and judgment. Charles Hodge points out that 'there are no devices in nature for the promotion of pain for its own sake; whereas the manifestations of design for the production of happiness are beyond computation'.[42] Perhaps we can say that the expression of love is more fundamental to who God is—more comprehensive, more revealing of his inclination or the direction of his nature, more a manifestation of his preference—than is the expression of his wrath. Indeed, God's love, says Gurnall, 'sets all his other attributes on work'.[43]

'God loves,' Morris repeats, 'not because he finds objects worthy of his love, but because it is his nature to love.'[44] When God's glory passed before Moses, that glory was identified with his goodness, as we have seen (Exod. 33:18-19). God revealed himself in this way: 'The

---

[40] Packer, *Knowing God*, p. 110.
[41] Watson, *Body of Divinity*, p. 93.
[42] Hodge, *Systematic Theology*, I:427.
[43] Gurnall, *Christian in Complete Armour*, I:29.
[44] Morris, '1 John', *New Bible Commentary*, p. 1406.

Lord passed before him and proclaimed, "The Lord, the Lord, a God merciful and gracious, slow to anger, and abounding in steadfast love and faithfulness, keeping steadfast love for thousands, forgiving iniquity and transgression and sin'" (Exod. 34:6-7). Words are 'heaped up', says Henry, 'to convince us of God's goodness'.[45] Only after this review of his 'softer' attributes does God say, 'who will by no means clear the guilty, visiting the iniquity of the fathers on the children and the children's children, to the third and the fourth generation' (Exod. 34:7).

These more severe attributes are but the 'last letter in God's name', says Trapp.[46] God's mercies are primary; his judgments clearly are secondary. God is in himself all that love is and does. He is good, kind, patient, generous, giving, sacrificial, and serving. He is also the source of all these qualities in others. 'Love is from God', says the apostle (1 John 4:7). God is the source of all love. Love is 'rooted in God'.[47] All love, including even pagan love, is ultimately a gift which he gives. Wherever, then, I see genuine love, I may trace it back to its source in God.

Consequently, human love, though flawed, impure, and corrupt, provides a glimpse of the depth of divine love and gives us reason for delighting in him.[48] Think of the strength of the love of a mother for her child. Her love is proverbial for its readiness to face danger, to protect at all costs, to provide no matter what. It is persistent, relentless, all-conquering. Isaiah asks, 'Can a woman forget her nursing child, that she should have no compassion on the son of her womb?' (Isa. 49:15). The expected answer is 'No, a woman cannot forget her nursing child.' The bond between mother and child—especially between mother and her *nursing* child—is so strong that she could never forget or neglect that child. Think of the depth, the warmth, and the strength of her affection. Yet even if she could forget that child, God cannot forget his people. God's love for his people exceeds that of the mother

[45] Henry, *Commentary*, on Exod. 34:6-7.
[46] Trapp, *Commentary*, I:226.
[47] Morris, *Testaments of Love*, p. 136.
[48] J. W. Alexander puts it this way: 'Things heavenly take earthly types; and infinite throbbings of Divine love are translated into terms of domestic affection' (*God Is Love*, p. 38).

for her infant: 'Even these may forget, yet I will not forget you' (Isa. 49:15). William Cowper incorporated these sentiments in his wonderful hymn 'Hark, My Soul! It Is the Lord!'

> Can a woman's tender care
>   Cease toward the child she bare?
> Yes, she may forgetful be,
>   Yet will I remember thee.

Cowper then interprets God's meaning further:

> Mine is an unchanging love,
>   Higher than the heights above,
> Deeper than the depths beneath,
>   Free and faithful, strong as death.[49]

The bond between God and his people—the commitment, the strength, and the warmth of his affection—exceeds that between mother and child. It is unchanging and infinite.

Do fathers love their children? The bond between a good father and his children is powerful. He is determined to protect them and provide for them. Nothing pains him like their suffering. A thousand times he would rather that he suffer than they. So David tells us, 'As a father shows compassion to his children, so the LORD shows compassion to those who fear him' (Psa. 103:13). He 'pities' (KJV), as a father does his children. This is meant to warm our hearts, to encourage us, and to strengthen our faith. Taking father love and mother love together, Jeremiah Burroughs, in his classic exposition of the Beatitudes, *The Saints' Happiness*, insists that 'all the love that ever was in any parents towards children, is but as one drop of the infinite ocean of fatherly love that there is in God unto his people'.[50]

Then think of the love of a groom for his bride, and of the bride for her groom. Consider its power and passion. Think of the ardour with which bride and groom contemplate each other. Their delight and affection are boundless. This is the love which the apostle Paul uses to describe Christ's love for his church (Eph. 5:25ff.), and, if the older

---

[49] William Cowper, 'Hark, My Soul! It Is The Lord!'
[50] Jeremiah Burroughs, *The Saints' Happiness* (1660, 1867; Ligonier, PA: Soli Deo Gloria, 1988), p. 194.

writers are correct, is this also the meaning of the Song of Solomon? The church is Christ's bride (Rev. 19:6-8).[51]

A parent rocking his or her child, a child secure in the arms of his or her parent, a groom holding the hand of his bride: these kinds of images, the strongest ones we know, are invoked in Scripture to portray the love of God. They are the deepest affections, the deepest joys, the greatest delights in life, and they point beyond themselves to their source in the love of God, of which they are but a dim reflection. God's love for his people—for us—is deep and strong; it is warm and affectionate; it is persistent and relentless; it is all-determining and all-conquering. We sing with Horatius Bonar (1808–89),

> O love of God, how strong and true:
>   Eternal, and yet ever new;
> Uncomprehended and unbought,
>   Beyond all knowledge and all thought.
>
> O wide-embracing, wondrous love!
>   We read thee in the sky above,
> We read thee in the earth below,
>   In seas that swell, and streams that flow.[52]

Love revealed

How does God reveal his love? Though God reveals his love in creation and providence (as we have seen in our study of 'The Goodness of God'; see Psa. 145:9, 15-16; 104:21; Matt. 5:45; 6:26; Acts 14:17), the supreme revelation of the love of God is in redemption. 'The work of redemption which the gospel makes known,' says Jonathan Edwards, 'above all things affords motives to love; for that work was *the most glorious and wonderful exhibition of love that ever was seen or heard of.*'[53] The apostle John writes, 'In this the love of God was made manifest among us, that God sent his only Son into the world, so that we might live through him' (1 John 4:9).

---

[51] This was a common interpretation of the Song of Solomon among the ancient and medieval authors, as well as among Puritans such as John Owen, Jonathan Edwards, Matthew Henry, and James Durham.

[52] Horatius Bonar, 'O Love Of God, How Strong And True'.

[53] Edwards, *Charity and Its Fruits*, p. 19 (emphasis added).

Incarnation

The apostle might have directed us to the beauty of creation to see the evidence of God's love. There is so much to admire. He might have reminded us of the blessings of God in providence, his protection and his provision. However, these were not the proofs that the apostle John sought. It was 'in this': by God's sending his 'only Son', his one and only Son, his unique Son,[54] that the love of God was 'made manifest'— a word which means to 'make known' or to 'make clear'. God's love was not revealed in a corner.[55] That God 'sent' or 'has sent' (NASB) implies Christ's pre-existence (John 16:28). The sending of his only Son into the world on our behalf is unmistakable evidence, even proof, of the love of God. 'While the origin of love is in the being of God,' says Stott, 'the manifestation of love is in the coming of Christ.'[56] This is what we celebrate each Christmas. The incarnation was a demonstration of the love of God. That God the Son should unite himself to human nature and become a man was a profound act of condescension which demonstrated his love. John's emphasis is upon the love of the Father. He sent his 'one and only Son', his 'only begotten Son', consequently one especially valued and especially dear to his heart. Great sacrifice was involved in the incarnation as the eternal Son relinquished his equality with God to take the form of a bondservant (Phil. 2:5ff.).

Atonement

But his love went further than this. For, second, we see God's love even more emphatically in the atonement. 'In this is love, not that we have loved God but that he loved us and sent his Son to be the propitiation for our sins (1 John 4:10).

'In this is love'. Here is the *demonstration* and *definition* of love. It was 'not that we have loved God'—we did not. All the initiative

---

[54] Since *monogenēs*, 'only begotten', is used of the widow of Nain's son (Luke 7:12) and Jairus' daughter (Luke 8:42), 'only' (ESV) or 'one and only' is probably the best translation (cf. Heb. 11:17; Luke 9:38).

[55] 'The showing of God's love was a public affair' (Colin G. Kruse, *The Letters of John* [Grand Rapids, MI: Eerdmans, 2000], p. 157).

[56] Stott, *Epistles of John*, p. 161.

was with God. 'He loved us.' How? He 'sent his Son'. Why? To be the 'propitiation' (*hilasmos*), that is, the sacrifice that removes the guilt of sin and thereby averts the wrath of God.[57] That God gave his Son, says J. W. Alexander, 'affords the greatest possible manifestation of his uncaused love'.[58] 'The atoning death of Jesus Christ is the supreme achievement and demonstration of God's love', Packer agrees.[59] The apostle is helping us to understand the magnitude of the love of God. God did not just send his Son; he sent his only Son. He did not just send his only Son, but he sent him to die. He did not even just send him to die, but to die a death that involved him in satisfying the infinite, just wrath of God against sin. Calvin calls the cross the 'chief example' of the love of God.[60] 'Propitiation proves love, and love to sinners', says J. W. Alexander. 'Propitiatory love is the chief outshining of supreme splendour.'[61]

How great is the love of God? 'He … did not spare his own Son but gave him up' (Rom. 8:32). The Father did not limit or reduce the suffering inflicted upon his Son for the sins of the world. 'He did not withhold one whit of the full toll of judgment,' says Murray. 'The strokes fell upon him in unrelieved intensity with all the weight due to the sins he bore.'[62] Murray calls the cross 'the supreme exhibition' of the love of both the Father and the Son.[63] God 'so loved the world', says the most memorable of verses, 'that he gave his only Son' (John 3:16).

As a young father I pondered what it meant to sacrifice one's only son for another. It is to give up that which is most precious, that which is most valued, that which is most dear and costly. This is what God did. This is how we are to understand the cross. This is what we are to understand about love. God subjected his one and only Son to the cross, with all the cost that such a sacrifice entailed, for our sakes. That is the measure of his love. At the cross God 'shows his love for us'—for

---

[57] See LXX Lev. 25:9; Num. 5:8; Psa. 130:4; Ezek. 44:27; Amos 8:14; also see Chapter 9 above, '"The Engines of Divine Dignity": The Justice and Righteousness of God'.

[58] Alexander, *God Is Love*, p. 41.

[59] Packer, 'Love of God', *Collected Shorter Writings*, I:155.

[60] Calvin, *First Epistle of John*, p. 290.

[61] Alexander, *God Is Love*, p. 14.

[62] Murray, 'The Father's Love', in *Collected Writings*, III:216-17.

[63] *Ibid.*, p. 215.

the 'weak', the 'ungodly', 'sinners', even his 'enemies' (Rom. 5:6-10), those who were 'hostile' (8:7). The love of God is revealed as a costly, sacrificial love. God so loved the world that he *gave*.

We can also see the love of God from the perspective of the Son. Jesus is the Good Shepherd who '[laid] down his life for the sheep' (John 10:11). Moreover, 'For this reason the Father loves me, because I lay down my life that I may take it up again. No one takes it from me, but I lay it down of my own accord. I have authority to lay it down, and I have authority to take it up again. This charge I have received from my Father' (John 10:17-18). Jesus' death was voluntary. He is emphatic on this point. He need not have died. Because he died willingly, his death was 'a most singular proof of his love to us', Spurgeon preached.[64] 'Greater love has no one than this,' says Jesus, 'that someone lay down his life for his friends' (John 15:13).

Characteristics of God's love

What are the distinctive qualities of God's love? What are its characteristics?'

Just

First, God's love is *just*.[65] Recourse must be sought in propitiation (1 John 4:9). The cross is proof that God is love *and*, as we have been saying, that he is more than love. Why did God not merely wave his magic wand and forgive everybody? Why not decree a universal pardon? Because of his justice. Because he is light. Love is shown in the costliness of the cross, but costliness is a result of the justice of God which he refused to compromise. There is a just penalty for *all* sin and even for *one* sin. 'The wages of sin is death' (Rom. 6:23). Without the shedding of blood, without an atoning death, there can be no forgiveness of sin (Heb. 9:22). Yet justice could never be satisfied by the blood of bulls and goats (Heb. 10:4). Ultimately, animal sacrifices cannot pay the debt of human sin. They are inadequate. The payment is not equal to the crime because animal life is not equivalent in value to human life. Exchanging animal death for human death would be like fining a thief

---

[64] Spurgeon, 'God's Love to the Saints', *Treasury of the New Testament*, IV:541.
[65] See Chapter 10 above, '"Just and Justifier": Righteousness Satisfied and Conferred'.

who stole one million dollars a single dollar as punishment or restitution. The punishment would be inadequate and inequitable; it would be unjust. The cross is proof of God's unyielding determination to see justice done. Sin requires death. Infinite guilt required infinite payment.

Am I lacking certainty of judgment day and the wrath of God against sin? I must look at the cross. Am I looking for the ultimate argument against the false conception of God's love that reduces it to an amorphous indifference to evil? I must look at the cross. There the 'great exchange' took place: our guilt for Christ's righteousness. 'He summed up the debts of man, charged them upon the score of Christ, imputing to him the guilt and inflicting upon him the penalty,' says Charnock. Commenting on Isaiah 53:6 ('the LORD has laid on him the iniquity of us all') and 2 Corinthians 5:21 ('he made him to be sin [for us]'), Charnock writes, 'A punishment for sin ... could not be righteously inflicted, had not sin been first righteously imputed.'[66] Through the cross, God is both 'just and justifier'. The atonement demonstrates both his righteousness *and* his love (Rom. 3:25-26; 5:8-10). We have discussed this at length in our study of the justice of God.

Yet the apostle John's main point is that the cross is proof that God is love. How? Because *God himself paid the costly price required by his justice.* The 'world', says Warfield of John 3:16, 'is not here a term of extension so much as the term of intensity'. It does not, he says, 'suggest that the world is *so big* that it takes a great deal of love to embrace it all, but that the world is *so bad* that it takes a great kind of love to love it at all, and much more to love it as God has loved it when he gave his Son for it'. What is the measure, then, of the love of God? 'It is not that it is so great that it is able to extend over a big world: it is so great that it is able to prevail over the holy God's hatred and abhorrence of sin.'[67] God saved out of his own determination to do that which arises out of his own nature, which is love. As John 'Rabbi' Duncan said during his lecture on Jesus' cry of dereliction (as it has been called) from Psalm 22 ('My God, my God, ...'), 'D'ye know what it was? It was *damnation*—and he took it *lovingly*.'[68]

[66] Charnock, *Existence and Attributes*, II:459; 'every favour from creatures is but a smile from God' (II:489).

[67] Warfield, *Saviour of the World*, pp. 120, 121 (emphasis added).

[68] Cited in A. Moody Stuart, *The Life of John Duncan* (1872; Edinburgh: Banner of Truth Trust, 1991), p. 105.

Sovereign

Second, God's love is *sovereign*.[69] We continue our examination of 1 John 4:10: 'In this is love, not that we have loved God but that he loved us and sent his Son to be the propitiation for our sins.' It was 'not that we loved God'. 'We will never find out what this love is if we start from the human end', Morris insists.[70] The 'we' is emphatic. God did not respond to our prior love. He did not foresee our love. Our love had nothing to do with it. It was not what 'we' did. That is to say, God's love is sovereign and self-determining. It is 'uninfluenced'.[71] It is, says Spurgeon, 'spontaneous [and] self-originating'.[72]

Why are God's people his people? Because God chose Abraham and his descendants. Why was Abraham chosen out of all the people in the world? Were not he and his ancestors idolaters (Deut. 26:5)? Why was Israel chosen from among all the nations? Were the Israelites not of 'one blood' with the rest (Acts 17:26 KJV)? Were they not serving other gods in Egypt when God rescued them from slavery (Josh. 24:14)? No other reason can be found than what Charnock calls God's 'unaccountable sovereignty', that is, 'his love to them'.[73] His determination to choose them and love them was 'an act of God's free pleasure'.[74] Moses explains this:

> For you are a people holy to the LORD your God. The LORD your God has chosen you to be a people for his treasured possession, out of all the peoples who are on the face of the earth. It was not because you were more in number than any other people that the LORD set his love on you and chose you, for you were the fewest of all peoples, but it is because the LORD loves you and is keeping the oath that he swore to your fathers, that the LORD has brought you out with a mighty hand and redeemed you from the house of slavery, from the hand of Pharaoh king of Egypt (Deut. 7:6-8).

Out of all the people on the earth God chose Israel to be his 'treasured possession'. Was it because of a particular virtue he saw in the Hebrew

---

[69] See Chapter 12 above, 'God's Victorious Goodness'.

[70] Morris, '1 John', *New Bible Commentary*, p. 1406.

[71] Pink, *Attributes*, p. 77.

[72] Spurgeon, 'Love's Logic', *Treasury of the New Testament*, IV:564.

[73] Charnock, *Existence and Attributes*, II:442

[74] *Ibid.*

people that he determined to have and love them? No, they were not 'more in number' than others, indeed, they were 'the fewest of all peoples'. Nor was it because of their righteousness, as Moses goes on to explain: 'For you are a stubborn people' and 'rebellious against the LORD' (Deut. 9:4-27). No, God 'set his love on you and chose you … because the LORD loves you'. He loves us because he loves us. He loves us because he willed to love us. 'He fetched the reason of it purely from himself', says Henry.[75] We cannot penetrate beyond this. The apostle Paul writes, 'In love he predestined us for adoption as sons through Jesus Christ, according to the purpose of his will' (Eph. 1:4-5). Love was behind God's predestinating purposes. The 'purpose of his will' provides the reason.

We may also speak of God's sovereign love as *eternal*. 'I have loved you with an everlasting love' (Jer. 31:3). God's decision to love Israel (and us) was not a recent one; it was rooted in his eternal purposes. This is affirmed despite the fact that Judah had been unfaithful, her idolatry likened to adultery and harlotry (Jer. 3:2, 6-10; 5:7; 9:2; 13:27; 23:10, 14; cf. 3:20; 5:11). 'He chose us in [Christ] before the foundation of the world' (Eph. 1:4). There was never a time when his love for us was not (cf. 1 Thess. 1:4; 2 Thess. 2:13; 2 Tim. 1:9).

Much the same is taught again by the apostle Paul in Romans 8. Having affirmed that 'all things work together for good' for believers, he writes, 'For those whom he foreknew he also predestined to be conformed to the image of his Son, in order that he might be the firstborn among many brothers. And those whom he predestined he also called, and those whom he called he also justified, and those whom he justified he also glorified' (Rom. 8:29-30). As many commentators have pointed out, 'foreknew' does not mean to 'know information ahead of time'. Its root meaning is 'to know' in the sense of relational knowledge, as in 'to love'. John Murray notes, 'It is used in a sense practically synonymous with "love", "to set regard upon, to know with peculiar interest, delight, affection, and action".'[76] It means, he

---

[75] Henry, *Commentary*, on Deut. 7:6-8.

[76] Murray, *Romans*, p. 317. Murray cites Gen. 18:19; Exod. 2:25; Psa. 1:6; 144:3; Jer. 1:5; Amos 3:2; Hos. 13:5; Matt. 7:23; 1 Cor. 8:3; Gal. 4:9; 2 Tim. 2:19; 1 John 3:1. He continues, 'It is not the foresight of difference but the foreknowledge that makes difference to exist, not a foresight that recognizes existence but the foreknowledge that determines existence. It is sovereign distinguishing love.'

says, 'whom he knew from eternity with distinguishing affection and delight', and it is virtually equivalent to 'whom he foreloved'.[77] The apostle connects 'foreknew' to 'predestined': 'Those whom he *foreknew* he also *predestined*.' To foreknow is to forelove is to predestine. The point is that God set his love upon us by his own determination to love us, before we were born, before time, in eternity. He determined to love us not because of any virtue or accomplishment seen or foreseen. His is a 'sovereign distinguishing love', says Murray.[78] Spurgeon applies this truth with his usual clarity and wit:

> I believe the doctrine of election because I am quite certain that, if God had not chosen me, I should never have chosen him; and I am sure he chose me before I was born, or else he never would have chosen me afterwards; and he must have elected me for reasons unknown to me, for I never could find any reason in myself why he should have looked upon me with special love.[79]

Furthermore, God's sovereign, 'special' love will not rest until his people are 'conformed to the image of his Son' (Rom. 8:29). His love ensures not a partial but a complete salvation. Again, we cite Murray:

> When we consider the high destiny defined, 'to be conformed to the image of his Son', there is exhibited not only the dignity of this ordination but also the greatness of the lover from which the appointment flows. God's love is not passive emotion; it is active volition and it moves determinatively to nothing less than the highest goal conceivable for his adopted children, conformity to the image of the only begotten Son.[80]

If sovereign love is saving love, and if our salvation is not partial or incomplete, his love must be *unchanging*. God loves us immutably. He will not quit loving us. He will not grow tired of us, lose patience with

[77] *Ibid.* C. E. B. Cranfield argues in his magisterial study of Romans that *proegnō*, 'foreknowledge', denotes 'God's gracious election' (Cranfield, *Romans*, I:432).

[78] Murray, *Romans*, p. 318.

[79] C. H. Spurgeon, *Autobiography*, Vol. 1: *The Early Years, 1834–1859* (London: Banner of Truth Trust, 1962), p. 166. He says elsewhere, 'Divine love is its own cause, and does not derive its streams from anything in us whatsoever' ('Love's Logic', *Treasury of the New Testament*, IV:571).

[80] Murray, *Romans*, p. 318.

us, or abandon us. He will perfect or complete the good work he has begun in us (Phil. 1:6).

'It is not that love is in God, but that God himself is love,' Spurgeon reminds us, leading to the conclusion, 'Can there be a more concise and more positive way of saying that the love of God is *infinite*?'[81] Spurgeon speaks of 'the great rolling ocean of the love of God, without bottom and without shore'.[82] His love is as strong as death, and many waters cannot quench it (Song of Sol. 8:6-7). We are saved by God's sovereign determination to have us and to do us the greatest good. We are saved by his eternal, unchanging decision. We are saved by his boundless, limitless love. Hence the question of the apostle as he takes us to what Hodge calls 'the very summit of the mount of confidence': 'Who shall separate us from the *love* of Christ?' Then follows a list of possible enemies that might separate us but cannot:

> Who shall separate us from the love of Christ? Shall tribulation, or distress, or persecution, or famine, or nakedness, or danger, or sword? ... No, in all these things we are more than conquerors through him who loved us. For I am sure that neither death nor life, nor angels nor rulers, nor things present nor things to come, nor powers, nor height nor depth, nor anything else in all creation, will be able to separate us from the love of God in Christ Jesus our Lord (Rom. 8:35, 37-39).

'How wonderful, how glorious, how secure is the gospel!' exclaims Hodge.[83] We are safe. We are secure. Why? Because God's love in Christ Jesus is sovereign. It is eternal, unchanging, and infinite. 'The love of God in itself is the eternal purpose and act of his will. This is no more changeable than God himself,' says Owen.[84] 'There is no measuring the love he bears toward you,' Spurgeon adds. 'He has loved you from before the foundation of the world, and he will love you

---

[81] Spurgeon, 'Bread Enough, and to Spare', *Treasury of the New Testament*, II:16 (emphasis added).

[82] Spurgeon, 'God's Love to the Saints', *Treasury of the New Testament*, IV:555.

[83] Hodge, *Romans*, pp. 290, 293.

[84] Owen, *Communion with God*, *Works*, II:30.

when time shall be no more.'[85] His is a love that 'wilt not let me go'.[86]
He will preserve us. We are 'kept by the power of God' (1 Pet. 1:5 KJV).
He will hold on to us. He will not let us slip away, having determined
in eternity to have us. 'The love of God,' says Packer, 'is sovereign love,
and must always be acknowledged as such.'[87] We celebrate that love
with Augustus Toplady:

> The work which his goodness began,
>   The arm of his strength will complete;
> His promise is Yea and Amen,
>   And never was forfeited yet.
> Things future, nor things that are now,
>   Not all things below nor above,
> Can make him his purpose forgo,
>   Or sever my soul from his love.[88]

Initiating

Third, the love of God is an *initiating* love. We are building now on a
previous point. God's love *initiates* love.[89] He 'loved' and he 'sent'
(1 John 4:10). His love was active. He took the first step with us. '*Agapē*
does not wait to be courted,' says Packer, 'but takes the initiative in
giving help where help is required.'[90] God sent his Son to die while we
were still rebels. This is the scale of God's love. Nothing outside God
nor within us sparked his saving action. Nothing in us prompted his
love or awakened it.

God's love is not a *responsive* love, as human love so often is. We
love those who love us. Not so with God. He did not see or foresee
our faith; he gave faith as a gift (Eph. 2:8-9). He did not respond to
our choice; he chose us first (John 15:16). He did not respond to our

[85] Spurgeon, 'Prodigal Love for the Prodigal Son', *Treasury of the New Testament*, II:27.
[86] George Matheson, 'O Love That Wilt Not Let Me Go'.
[87] Packer, 'Love of God', *Collected Shorter Writings*, I:147.
[88] Augustus M. Toplady, 'A Debtor to Mercy Alone'.
[89] New Testament scholar Stephen Smalley says, 'John emphasizes'—not merely affirms—'the biblical truth that the divine initiative is central to the plan of salvation' (Stephen S. Smalley, *1, 2, 3 John*, *Word Biblical Commentary*, vol. 51 [Waco, TX: Word Books, 1984], p. 243).
[90] Packer, 'Love of God', *Collected Shorter Writings*, I:146.

wisdom, strength, or noble birth; rather, he chose the foolish, the weak, the base, the despised (1 Cor. 1:26-31). He did not respond to our love, as seen or foreseen; the love of God came first, not second. 'We love because he first loved us' (1 John 4:19). His love came before our seeking, before our repentance, before our faith. God's love 'goes not only before our love" says Owen, 'but also [before] anything in us that is lovely'.[91] It was 'while we were still sinners'—sin representing all that is undesirable, repugnant, and distasteful—that 'Christ died for us' (Rom. 5:8). It was while we were still 'in [our] blood', as the prophet Ezekiel so vividly describes it, that God set his love upon us (Ezek. 16:1-14). 'When we had not as yet one throb of spiritual feeling, one pulse of hope, or breathing of desire, the Lord loved us even then', says Spurgeon. 'The fact is,' he continues, God's love 'had no reason derived from us upon which to ground itself'.[92] God's love is 'free, uncaused and spontaneous', says Stott, 'and all our love is but a reflection of his and a response to it'.[93] The God who is love demonstrated his love at the cross by allowing his only Son to be set upon by men who were full of hate, 'that we might live through him' (1 John 4:9).

We see God further initiating love in drawing us to himself. 'Calvinism holds that divine love does not stop short at graciously inviting,' says Packer, 'but that the triune God takes action to ensure that the elect respond.'[94] Isaac Watts, in his beautiful communion hymn,[95] has us sing:

'Twas the same love that spread the feast
That sweetly drew us in;
Else we had still refused to taste,
And perished in our sin.

The Father has given a people to the Son, and they 'will come to me', says Jesus (John 6:37). Divine power ensures the human response. The Father 'draws' the unbelieving to the Son (6:44).[96] Those who

---

[91] Owen, *Communion with God*, *Works*, II:29.

[92] Spurgeon, 'Love's Birth and Parentage', *Treasury of the New Testament*, IV:571.

[93] Stott, *Epistles of John*, p. 162.

[94] Packer, 'Love of God', *Collected Shorter Writings*, I:153.

[95] Isaac Watts, 'How Sweet and Awful Is the Place'.

[96] Jesus uses a strong word, *elkō*, which means 'to compel', even 'to drag', as in James 2:6.

come to Christ do so only as they are 'granted' by the Father (6:65). He enables and ensures our saving response. So also we only know the Father as the Son is pleased to 'reveal' him to us (Matt. 11:27). Faith is a 'gift of God' (Eph. 2:8-9). God not only sent Christ for us, but he also sends his Spirit to us and in us to draw us to Christ.

We experience the redemptive love of God, from top to bottom, start to finish, entirely at God's own initiative. His initiating love is both regenerating and enabling love. 'But God,' says the apostle Paul, 'because of the great love with which he loved us, even when we were dead in our trespasses, made us alive together with Christ' (Eph. 2:4-5). Who made us alive? God did. Why? Because of his 'great love'. Similarly, James writes, 'Of his own will he brought us forth by the word of truth, that we should be a kind of firstfruits of his creatures' (James 1:18). It was by God's 'own will' that we were 'brought forth' by the agency of his 'word of truth'.

This is a good point at which to note that the love of God is trinitarian.[97] All of the above passages demonstrate this to be true. The idea that in procuring our salvation Jesus twisted the arm of a reluctant Father is refuted. Commenting on John 3:16 Morris says, 'Notice that the cross is not said to show us the love of the Son (as in Gal. 2:20), *but that of the Father.'* 'The atonement proceeds from the loving heart of God. It is not something wrung from him.'[98] The Father *planned* redemption, the Son *accomplished* redemption, and the Spirit *applies* redemption. God the Father 'so loved the world' that he sent his Son; God the Son is the embodiment of that 'greater love' which lays down his life for his friends (John 15:13); and it is by the Holy Spirit that the love of God is 'shed abroad' (KJV) or 'poured into our hearts' (Rom. 5:5; cf. 15:30). The love of God is a Trinitarian love, which Charles Wesley (1707–88) leads us to celebrate, first of the Son, then of the Spirit, and finally of the Almighty Father:

> Love divine, all loves excelling,
> Joy of heaven to earth come down;

[97] See Chapter 2 above, 'Our Triune God'.
[98] Leon Morris, *The Gospel According to John*, New International Commentary on the New Testament (Grand Rapids, MI: Wm. B. Eerdmans Pub., 1971), p. 229 (emphasis added).

Fix in us thy humble dwelling;
  All thy faithful mercies crown!
Jesus, thou art all compassion;
  Pure, unbounded love thou art;
Visit us with thy salvation;
  Enter every trembling heart.

Breathe, O breathe thy loving Spirit
  Into every troubled breast!
Let us all in thee inherit;
  Let us find thy promised rest.
Take away the love of sinning;
  Alpha and Omega be;
End of faith, as its Beginning,
  Set our hearts at liberty.

Come, Almighty, to deliver,
  Let us all thy grace receive;
Suddenly return and never,
  Never more thy temples leave.
Thee we would be always blessing,
  Serve thee as thy hosts above,
Pray and praise thee without ceasing,
  Glory in thy perfect love.[99]

Personal

Fourth, the love of God is *personal* and *particular*. 'Agapē is precise about its objects', says Packer; '[it] focuses on particular people with particular needs'.[100] The love of Christ is personal, not impersonal; and particular, not general. J. Gresham Machen speaks of 'the warm and tender individualism of our Reformed Faith'.[101] Christ 'loved *me*, and gave himself for *me*', says the apostle Paul (Gal. 2:20). The personal pronouns are vital. God's love is no mere general goodwill. It is 'an immeasurably richer reality' of individualizing sovereign grace, says Packer.[102]

---

[99] Charles Wesley, 'Love Divine, All Loves Excelling'.
[100] Packer, 'Love of God', *Collected Shorter Writings*, I:146.
[101] Machen, *God Transcendent*, p. 148.
[102] Packer, 'Love of God', *Collected Shorter Writings*, I:159.

It is true that God loves the whole world of John 3:16. He loves, says Warfield, 'not merely some individuals out of the world', and 'not one here and there only in the world', but 'the world in its organic completeness'.[103] Some overzealous Calvinists have tried to restrict the meaning of *cosmos* to the 'world of the elect'. However, to use 'world' in this restricted way would be unprecedented and unnatural. 'World' denotes fallen, sinful humanity. 'World' means not just Jews, Romans, or Africans, but everybody. God's love is for all humanity, and is not, says Morris, 'confined to any national group or any spiritual elite'.[104] That God loves the world does not mean that God is pleased with the fallen, sinful world. Neither does it mean that every individual will be saved. The natural question then is: What kind of love is it (and what good is it) if it does not save?

Our answer is that it is a love that shows benevolence to all people, causing the rain to fall and the sun to shine 'on the just and on the unjust' (Matt. 5:45). Jesus is the light of the *world* (John 8:12). All the world benefits from the light of moral and religious truth found in him. He is 'the true light', John announces in the prologue to his Gospel, 'which enlightens everyone' (John 1:9). Indeed, 'the light shines in the darkness', though the darkness fails to receive it (1:5). 'The light has come into the world', to be a blessing to the world, but 'people loved the darkness rather than the light' (3:19). It is a love that makes salvation available to all and offers it to all. 'Everyone' who believes will be saved (Rom. 10:11). This is true without exception. Heaven is offered to all and is certain for all who believe.

Furthermore, it is love that motivates God to save some from out of the world. Believers 'are not something other than the "world" when the gospel first comes to them', D. A. Carson reminds us. 'They would not have become true disciples apart from the love of God for the world.'[105] Why was there a cross at all? Because God cared about the plight of fallen, sinful humanity. God had compassion on our race of rebels.

Yet the benefits of God's universal redemptive love, as opposed to his universal goodwill (that we have seen in Matt. 5:45-48; Acts

---

[103] Warfield, *Savior of the World*, pp. 128-29.
[104] Morris, '1 John', *New Bible Commentary*, p. 229.
[105] D. A. Carson, *The Gospel According to John* (Grand Rapids, MI: Eerdmans, 1991), p. 205.

14:16-17; 17:25-27, 30), are *particular*. 'He loved us,' says Machen, 'not as infinitesimal particles in the mass of the human race, but he loved us every one.'[106] Jesus laid down his life for his sheep. Who are the sheep? Those whom he knows and calls by name, who hear and know his voice and who follow his lead (John 10:3-5, 11-16). Jesus says the sheep whom he knows, calls, leads, and for whom he died are 'all that the Father gives me' (6:37). They are a definite body of people. With his blood Jesus purchased 'the church of God' (Acts 20:28). Jesus prays not for the world but 'for those whom you have given me, for they are yours' (John 17:9). Both his intercessory love and his atoning love are particular. Jesus went to the cross with our names in mind, knowing the very 'sheep' for whom he was dying. His love is not only personal and particular, but it was also effectual. 'Christ did not die there on Calvary merely to make possible our salvation,' says Machen; 'he died to save us.'[107]

This particular and personal love of God is that which is so often celebrated by our hymn-writers, especially Isaac Watts and Charles Wesley. This love for us, for me personally, is the occasion of ceaseless wonder. Charles Wesley asks:

> And can it be that *I* should gain
>   An interest in the Saviour's blood?
> Died he for *me*, who caused his pain—
>   For *me*, who him to death pursued?
> Amazing love! How can it be
>   That thou, my God, shouldst die for *me*?
>
> He left his Father's throne above,
>   So free, so infinite his grace;
> Emptied himself of all but love,
>   And bled for Adam's helpless race:
> 'Tis mercy all, immense and free,
>   For O my God, it found out *me*![108]

---

[106] Machen, *God Transcendent*, p. 147.
[107] *Ibid.*
[108] Charles Wesley, 'And Can It Be That I Should Gain?'

Watts joins him:

> Alas! and did my Saviour bleed?
> And did my Sovereign die?
> Would he devote that sacred head
> For such a worm as *I*?
>
> Was it for crimes that *I* had done,
> He groaned upon the tree?
> Amazing pity! Grace unknown!
> And love beyond degree![109]

When we grasp the particular and personal characteristics of God's love, we can hardly contain ourselves. Amazing love! Love beyond degree! 'What wondrous love is this, O my soul!'[110]

Transformative

Fifth, the love of God is *transformative*. It changes us. It designs to take us from the depths of degradation to the heights of redemption. We have seen that 'in love' we were 'predestined'. To what end? 'For adoption as sons through Jesus Christ' (Eph. 1:4-5). We were chosen in Christ 'before the foundation of the world'. To what end? 'That we should be holy and blameless before him' (1:4). 'Conformity to God, in purity, is the fruit of electing love', says Charnock, commenting on Ephesians 1:4.[111] We were foreknown and predestined for what purpose? 'To be conformed to the image of his Son' (Rom. 8:29). The love of God does not 'accept' us just as we are. True love leaves only perfection untouched. True love aims to deliver, save, improve, and perfect all that is imperfect, removing its flaws and purifying its virtues.

Follow the train of thought in Ephesians 2:4-6:

> But God, being rich in mercy, because of the great love with which he loved us, even when we were dead in our trespasses, made us alive together with Christ—by grace you have been saved—and raised us up with him and seated us with him in the heavenly places in Christ Jesus.

[109] Isaac Watts, 'Alas! And Did My Saviour Bleed'.
[110] American folk hymn, 'What Wondrous Love Is This!'
[111] Charnock, *Existence and Attributes*, II:271.

Because of 'the great love with which he loved us', and because he is 'rich in mercy', even though we were 'dead in our trespasses', God 'made us alive together with Christ' and 'by grace … raised us up with him' and 'seated us with him in the heavenly places in Christ Jesus'. He takes us from the depths of spiritual death and raises us to the heights of heavenly glory. From death to life; from darkness to light. Love raises us up from death that we 'might walk in newness of life' (Rom. 6:4). We are now 'dead to sin' but 'alive to God in Christ Jesus' (Rom. 6:11). Sin may no longer have 'dominion' over us (6:14). The apostle Paul continues in Ephesians 2 to write not only of salvation (2:8-9) but transformation: 'For we are his workmanship, created in Christ Jesus for good works, which God prepared beforehand, that we should walk in them (2:10). Why were we created anew in Christ Jesus? 'For good works,' says the apostle, 'that we should walk in them.' We are new creatures in Christ, the old having passed away and all things having become new (2 Cor. 5:17).

In his High Priestly Prayer Jesus prayed 'that the love with which you have loved me may be in them, and I in them' (John 17:26). This prayer was fulfilled at Pentecost with the outpouring of the Holy Spirit, who, the apostle says, 'shed abroad' or 'poured into our hearts' the love of God (Rom. 5:5). God's love is transformative. He fills us with his love, thereby enabling us to love. 'Love does not leave us as we were,' says Morris; 'it demands that we live in the spirit of selfless love.'[112] Indeed, 'the love of Christ controls us'. Consequently, we live no longer for ourselves but for Christ (2 Cor. 5:15). We are now 'rooted and grounded in love' (Eph. 3:17) and we 'walk in love' (5:2). We are new people, growing, improving, increasingly holy, and increasingly characterized by love. This is to say that the love of God is a *persevering* love and a *triumphant* love. God will not be deterred. We are not stuck with an old selfishness, pride, anger, lust, and envy. Where flaws persist in those whom he loves, he exercises discipline that his flawed people might share in his holiness and yield the 'peaceful fruit of righteousness' (Heb. 12:5-11). He will not quit on us. He will not grow tired of our failures. We repeat: 'He who began a good work in you will bring it to completion [or 'perfect it' NASB] at the day of Jesus Christ' (Phil. 1:6). His love guarantees it.

[112] Morris, *Testaments of Love*, p. 162.

Dynamic

Sixth, God's love is *dynamic*. It grows in response to goodness. According to first-generation Reformer Wolfgang Musculus (1497–1563), 'he who of his infinite goodness loves us without cause', loves us still more 'when we are godly'.[113] So it is that Jesus says, 'If you keep my commandments, you will abide in my love, just as I have kept my Father's commandments and abide in his love' (John 15:10). We 'abide' or 'continue' in Jesus' love *if* we keep his commandments. Abiding in Christ's love is conditional upon obedience. We can never lose his preserving love. However, we can diminish or increase our sense of his love and the strength of his love. 'God loves a cheerful giver' (2 Cor. 9:7). The apostle Paul wrote those words in the context of begrudged giving. Did God no longer love his less-than-cheerful givers? Of course not. Yet he can and does love with greater love the good manifest in giving that is cheerful. Love is dynamic. It grows. Think of a human analogy. We love our children, no matter what. Nothing they do can forfeit our love for them. Yet that love can fluctuate. Sometimes our love grows, as when we beam with godly pride at their acts of selfless love or sacrifice. We might even say, 'I've never loved you more than right now.' At other times our love is diminished, as when they rebel, disobey, or behave in ungodly ways. We still love them, yet our love can ebb and flow according to their virtues and deeds. Jesus said of the Father's love of him: 'For this reason the Father loves me, because I lay down my life that I may take it up again' (John 10:17). The Father loved the Son from 'before the foundation of the world' (17:24). Yet that love grew in response to Jesus' redemptive sacrifice.

This view runs contrary to considerable popular teaching today. Nevertheless, is it not the case that it is to be our 'ambition' to be 'pleasing' to God rather than displeasing (2 Cor. 5:9 NASB)? Is God not delighted when we serve him, obey him, and honour him, whereas when we fail to do so there is an absence of delight? As we 'do good', says David, the God who does not delight in flawed sacrifices will 'delight in right sacrifices' (Psa. 51:16-19). So it is that upon a foundation of unchanging love God's pleasure in us, his delight in us, his affection for us, increases or decreases as the goodness he sees in us increases or decreases.

[113] Cited in Muller, *Post-Reformation Reformed Dogmatics*, III:564.

This divine love of the good in us, Musculus maintains, ought to motivate believers to be 'studious in goodness, godliness, and righteousness', and to be grateful for God's wisdom.[114] Let us then express our gratitude for the love of God—his sovereign, eternal, unchanging, infinite, boundless love for us in Christ Jesus our Lord:

> O the deep, deep love of Jesus!
>   Vast, unmeasured, boundless, free;
> Rolling as a mighty ocean
>   In its fullness over me.
> Underneath me, all around me,
>   Is the current of thy love;
> Leading onward, leading homeward
>   To thy glorious rest above.
>
> O the deep, deep love of Jesus!
>   Spread his praise from shore to shore;
> How he loveth, ever loveth,
>   Changeth never, nevermore;
> How he watches o'er his loved ones,
>   Died to call them all his own;
> How for them he intercedeth,
>   Watcheth o'er them from the throne.[115]

---

[114] Cited in Muller, *Post-Reformation Reformed Dogmatics*, III:564.
[115] Samuel Trevor Francis, 'O The Deep, Deep Love Of Jesus!'

FOURTEEN

God's Transforming Love

Beloved, let us love one another, for love is from God, and whoever loves has been born of God and knows God. Anyone who does not love does not know God, because God is love. In this the love of God was made manifest among us, that God sent his only Son into the world, so that we might live through him. In this is love, not that we have loved God but that he loved us and sent his Son to be the propitiation for our sins. Beloved, if God so loved us, we also ought to love one another. No one has ever seen God; if we love one another, God abides in us and his love is perfected in us.—1 John 4:7-12

HOW then are we to respond to the love of God? 'It is impossible to experience this love and remain unchanged,' Leon Morris insists.[1] This love is transformative, and those who receive it in Christ respond with an *answering* love. 'When we open our hearts to God's love we discover that love is creative. It takes us, loveless and selfish as we are, and remakes us.'[2] Here is how Jonathan Edwards expressed the same insight over 200 years before:

> Divine knowledge and divine love go together. A spiritual view of divine things always excites love in the soul, and draws forth the heart in love to every proper object. ... When persons have a true discovery of the excellency and sufficiency of Christ ... when they experience a right belief of the truth of the gospel, such a belief is accompanied by love.[3]

[1] Morris, *Testaments of Love*, p. 165.
[2] *Ibid.*
[3] Edwards, *Charity and Its Fruits*, p. 21.

God inspires and imparts divine love to the beloved. 'Christ's love is fuel to ours. It is both mother and nurse to our love.'[4] Again, 'love will kindle love'.[5] God's love 'produces its like in believers', explains Morris.[6] We are new creatures in Christ (2 Cor. 5:17), with new lives (Rom. 6:4), new hearts (Ezek. 11:19), and new loves. We once loved the darkness and hated the light (John 3:19-20). Now we love Jesus who is the light (3:21; 8:12), and all that is connected with him—his word, truth, people, cause, and mission. He creates in us a capacity for true love. Those who are 'born of God'—that is, those who are born again and 'know God'—love. Their love is 'from God' (1 John 4:7) and is an expression of their new nature. 'We have now a divine *faculty* of loving', says Scottish theologian Robert S. Candlish (1806–73), and a *desire* to love.[7] This love is of a heavenly, not earthly, origin. It is 'not that we have loved God' (1 John 4:10); we have no natural capacity to generate love. Rather, God both imparts this love to us and inspires this love in us. 'Beloved,' Spurgeon reminds us, 'if you love God, it is with no love of yours, but with the love which he has planted in your bosoms.'[8]

Love then becomes the powerful motive behind all that we do. Love 'de-centres' the self. The one who loves finds the centre of himself outside of himself, focused on the one loved. Paul's epistle to the Ephesians, which anchors our salvation in the love which predestined us (Eph. 1:5), celebrates the 'great love with which he loved us' (2:4), and admires 'the love of Christ that surpasses knowledge' (3:19), would have us be 'rooted and grounded in love' (3:17) and 'walk in love, as Christ loved us' (5:2).[9] Our entire 'walk', or course of life, is to be characterized by love. 'Let all that you do be done in love' (1 Cor. 16:15). 'And above all these,' says Paul to the Colossian believers, having just outlined a long list of Christian virtues, 'put on love, which binds everything together in perfect harmony' (Col. 3:14). Love is regularly

---

[4] Gurnall, *Christian in Complete Armour*, I:108.

[5] *Ibid.*, I:120.

[6] Morris, *Testaments of Love*, p. 174.

[7] Robert S. Candlish, cited in Morris, *Testaments of Love*, p. 174, n. 17 (emphasis added).

[8] Spurgeon, 'Love's Birth and Parentage', *Treasury of the New Testament*, IV:572.

[9] 'Love is both soil and rock, the root from which everything grows, the foundation on which everything is built' (Morris, *Testaments of Love*, p. 183).

the virtue for which the apostle prays for the churches. For the Ephesians he prays that they might be 'rooted and grounded in love'; for the Philippians, that their 'love may abound more and more, with knowledge and all discernment' (Phil. 1:9); and for the Thessalonians, that the Lord might make them 'increase and abound in love for one another and for all' (1 Thess. 3:12).

The aim of Paul's instruction is 'love that issues from a pure heart and a good conscience and a sincere faith' (1 Tim. 1:5). Love can be the aim because it is the comprehensive Christian virtue. Love, says Edwards, is 'the very sum of all Christian virtue'.[10] It is the greatest of all virtues. It is greater than the greatest speaking gifts; greater than the greatest knowledge gifts; greater than a faith which can move mountains; greater than the martyr's ultimate sacrifice. Faith, hope, and love are essential, 'but the greatest of these is love' (1 Cor. 13:1-3, 13). Divine love is the essence of all Christianity.[11] Indeed, Edwards continues, love is 'the very quintessence of all religion, the very thing wherein lies summarily the sincerity, spirituality and divinity of religion'.[12] In practice that means we are to reciprocate and replicate the love of God.

Reciprocate

Earlier we observed that Jesus prayed to the Father for his disciples 'that the love with which you have loved me may be in them, and I in them' (John 17:26). His prayer was fulfilled at Pentecost, and ever since then, through the Holy Spirit by whom the Father's love is 'poured into' our hearts (Rom. 5:5). Love is the 'fruit' of the Holy Spirit's work within us (Gal. 5:22; cf. 2 Tim. 1:7). 'The presence in us of the Holy Spirit,' says Augustine, 'means that we love God "through God".'[13] The love of God for us in Christ Jesus imparts and inspires a love for God from us in return. 'The Christian's love to Christ takes fire at Christ's

---

[10] Edwards, *Charity and Its Fruits*, p. 24. Love 'comprehends all holy virtues and exercises'; it is 'the source and sum of all graces' (Jonathan Edwards, 'Treatise on Grace', in *Selections from the Unpublished Writings of Jonathan Edwards*, ed. Rev. Alexander B. Grosart [1865; Ligonier, PA: Soli Deo Gloria, 1992], p. 34).

[11] Edwards, 'Treatise on Grace', p. 32.

[12] *Ibid.*, p. 33.

[13] Cited in Morris, *Testaments of Love*, p. 185, n. 45.

love to him', Gurnall maintains.[14] This new capacity makes it possible for us to begin to fulfil the primary ethical demand of the Bible: that we should love God. Jesus cited Deuteronomy 6:5 when he taught that the 'great and first commandment' is to love God: 'And he said to him, "You shall love the Lord your God with all your heart and with all your soul and with all your mind"' (Matt. 22:37-38).

The love of Christ enables and motivates a genuine (albeit imperfect) love for God in return. We love God not merely with our lips (Mark 7:6), but from the heart. 'If anyone loves God,' says Paul, assuming that all believers do, 'he is known by God', which is to say, he is loved by God (1 Cor. 8:3). We love God because of God's prior love for and knowledge of us. The apostle's use of the word 'known' in 1 Corinthians 8:3 indicates not a bare knowledge, but, says the Dutch theologian Herman Ridderbos (1909–2007), 'the gracious and loving electing act of God'.[15] Simply stated, we love him because he first loved us (1 John 4:19). Our love for God is his gift to us. 'The saints' love for God is the fruit of God's love to them, as it is the gift of that love.'[16]

Reticence

Love for God in believers is expected by the biblical writers, yet they rarely elaborate on the theme or claim it for themselves (John 14:21; Rom. 8:28; Eph. 6:24; 1 Cor. 2:9; James 1:12; Heb. 6:10; 1 Pet. 1:8).[17] We do not hear them describing how much they love God, or referring to the greatness of their love for Christ. Recall that it was regarding this very thing that the risen Lord challenged Peter three times ('Do you love me?' John 21:15-17). The reason behind this reticence is a matter of conjecture. Perhaps it is humility. Highlighting our paltry love for God seems unwarranted given the incalculable magnitude of God's love for us; what is our thimble-full in comparison with his mighty ocean! Typically, the people of God have recognized the relative absence of their love for God. So it is that Isaac Watts leads us to sing,

---

[14] Gurnall, *Christian in Complete Armour*, I:584.

[15] Cited in Morris, *Testaments of Love*, p. 170. Ridderbos continues: '"to be known" by him in this way means the same as to have been chosen by him and loved by him' (p. 170).

[16] Edwards, *Religious Affections*, p. 175.

[17] 'It is interesting that Paul rarely speaks of man's love for God' (Morris, *Testaments of Love*, p. 170).

> Come, Holy Spirit, heavenly Dove,
> With all thy quick'ning powers;
> Kindle a flame of sacred love
> In these cold hearts of ours!

His lamentation is this:

> Dear Lord, shall we for ever live
> At this poor dying rate?
> Our love, so faint, so cold to thee,
> And thine to us so great!

Note the contrast: God's love for us is 'so great', yet our love is 'so faint, so cold'. He pleads,

> Come, Holy Spirit, heavenly Dove,
> With all thy quick'ning powers;
> Come, shed abroad a Saviour's love,
> And that shall kindle ours![18]

William Cowper expresses much the same:

> Lord, it is my chief complaint
> That my love is weak and faint;
> Yet I love thee and adore;
> O for grace to love thee more.[19]

Similarly, Spurgeon, when commenting on the phrase 'Love is strong as death' (Song of Sol. 8:6), asks: 'Would it not sound like satire if it were applied to my poor, weak, and scarcely living love to Jesus my Lord?'[20] Normally the people of God have been slow to trumpet their 'poor, weak, and scarcely living love'. Instead, the soul that enjoys a true knowledge of God, Edwards maintains, 'is astonished at its ignorance and that it knows so little' and 'loves so little'.[21] Hence Watts' prayer that the Holy Spirit might exercise his 'quick'ning powers' to 'kindle a flame of sacred love' in our hearts by shedding abroad the Saviour's love. Our 'weak and faint' love shall only grow strong by God's gracious enabling.

---

[18] Isaac Watts, 'Come, Holy Spirit, Heavenly Dove'.
[19] William Cowper, 'Hark My Soul! It Is The Lord'.
[20] Spurgeon, *Morning and Evening*, 13 October.
[21] Edwards, *Religious Affections*, p. 250.

Desire and delight

Nevertheless, ardent affection for God is expected. The apostle Peter writes of those who have received the apostolic witness to Jesus: 'Though you have not seen him, you love him. Though you do not now see him, you believe in him and rejoice with joy that is inexpressible and filled with glory' (1 Pet. 1:8). 'It is the character of every true disciple of Christ that they do love their Lord and Master', says Hutcheson.[22] Loving Christ engages all the affections. We 'rejoice with joy that is inexpressible and filled with glory'. 'It is not impossible for a child of God', Nisbet maintains, despite trials and afflictions, 'to have his heart now and then filled with such joy *as hardly can be kept within doors.*'[23] 'Love,' says George Swinnock, '[is] the top, the cream of our affections.'[24] Since what is good is the object of love, God, who is the greatest good, will be the object of our greatest love.

A recent sermon on election mined Dan Fogelberg's song 'Longer' for language with which to describe the unchanging and eternal love of God:

> Longer than there've been fishes in the ocean
> Higher than any bird ever flew
> Longer than there've been stars up in the heavens
> I've been in love with you.

There are multiple problems with associating God's love, biblical love, with the love celebrated in a popular love song. Is God 'in love' with us? The word 'in' restricts the meaning of love to romantic love. Does God have romantic affections for his people? This is confusing at best. We must remind ourselves that God's love in the Bible is not *eros* (sensual love), but *agapē* or *philia* (self-giving, sacrificial love). In Latin translation it is *caritas*, not *amor*.[25] The same is true of our love for God. Gordon MacDonald, former pastor of Grace Chapel in Lexington, Massachusetts, and editor-at-large of *Leadership Journal*, recognizes the

---

[22] Hutcheson, *Gospel of John*, p. 302.
[23] Nisbet, *1 and 2 Peter*, p. 26 (emphasis added).
[24] Swinnock, *Incomparableness of God*, *Works*, IV:474.
[25] Morris, *Testaments of Love*, repeats the well-known fact that *eros* is never used in the New Testament. Similarly, the church fathers avoided using the word *amor* in translating the concept of divine or Christian love into Latin.

problem when he speaks about the reasons why he is inclined to use the word 'devotion' rather than 'love' with respect to our relationship with Jesus. 'It is difficult to escape the sentimental flavouring in the word love,' he explains. 'I do not find sentimental love in that follow-me relationship initiated with his disciples.'[26]

The older theologians (e.g. Swinnock, Edwards) identified love with desire and delight: desire when the loved one is absent; delight when present. The incomparable God evokes incomparable desire, like that of the deer that pants for the waterbrook (Psa. 42:1), and like one's thirst in a dry and weary land (63:1). When truly known, God is desired above all else. The 'one thing' that the psalmist 'asked of the LORD' and would 'seek after' was this: 'that I may dwell in the house of the LORD all the days of my life, to gaze upon the beauty of the LORD and to enquire in his temple' (Psa. 27:4). 'Whom have I in heaven but you? And there is nothing on earth that I desire besides you' (73:25). God is to be desired above all else. We are to delight ourselves in the Lord (37:4), to feast on the abundance of his house and drink from the river of his delights (36:8). 'He that knoweth God aright is fully satisfied in him', says Swinnock.[27] The true knowledge of God 'diffuseth into the soul a sweet tranquillity, silent peace, secret settled calmness, besides a ravishing prevision, and blessed fore-fruition of its fuller acquaintance in the other life'.[28]

Arguably, no one has written with more insight on our love for God than Jonathan Edwards. Edwards, like Swinnock before him, identified love with desire and delight. In his *Personal Narrative* he recalls a moment of spiritual breakthrough while meditating on 1 Timothy 1:17. He experienced a new sense of 'inward, sweet delight in God and divine things'. This delight became a theme throughout his ministry, culminating in his brilliant *Treatise Concerning the Religious Affections* (1746), which is an extended exposition of 1 Peter 1:8. Those regenerated by the Spirit of God acquire a taste, desire, and delight in divine things. Edwards draws parallels between our love for those who are near to us and our love for God. Those whom we love we will aim to honour and

[26] Gordon MacDonald, 'How to Spot a Transformed Christian', in *Leadership Journal*, Vol. 33, Number 3, Summer 2012, p. 37.
[27] Swinnock, *Incomparableness of God*, *Works*, IV:486.
[28] *Ibid*., IV:487.

please; we desire their company and delight in their presence. So it is with love for God: it 'causes a man to *delight* in the thoughts of God, and to *delight* in the presence of God, and to *desire* conformity to God, and the enjoyment of God'.[29]

Genuine Christianity is characterized by love for God and the things of God. This is its distinguishing mark, and perhaps the only characteristic of Christianity that cannot be counterfeited. 'The Scriptures do represent true religion, as being summarily comprehended in love, the chief of the affections and fountain of all other affections.'[30]

This love for God is based upon the knowledge of God (1 John 4:7). Unlike Friedrich Schleiermacher (1768–1834), Edwards does not make the mistake of subsuming the whole of the Christian religion under the category of religious feelings. The affections are evoked by that knowledge of God which arises out of the biblical text as it is illuminated and applied by the Holy Spirit.[31] For Edwards, the affections are anchored in the historic truths of God as revealed in creation, providence, and redemption, and which are recorded in Scripture. Grace is mediated through the understanding, as the old Puritans taught. The truth fires the heart. One comes to delight in God's character and his works. By way of knowledge one comes to desire more understanding of his infinite, eternal, and immutable goodness, power, and wisdom. One grows in one's desire to experience his presence. For example, Paul prays that the Philippians' 'love may abound more and more'. In what manner? 'With knowledge and all discernment' (Phil. 1:9). The knowledge of God and of his works sparks love. The 'new self' is 'renewed in knowledge' (Col. 3:10). This is not a speculative knowledge, says John Davenant (c. 1576–1641), but 'a lively, efficacious, and operative knowledge', wrought by the Holy Spirit.[32] This spiritual

---

[29] Edwards, *Religious Affections*, p. 136 (emphasis added).

[30] *Ibid*., p. 35.

[31] 'For Schleiermacher, the words of Scripture weren't God-given but took shape as human beings reflected on their religious experience … Edwards' theology took on a different character because he believed that objective revelation has been given to us in history and the words of scripture' (Michael J. McClymond and Gerald R. McDermott, *The Theology of Jonathan Edwards* [New York: Oxford University Press, 2012], pp. 671-72).

[32] John Davenant, *Colossians* (1627; Edinburgh: Banner of Truth Trust, 2005), II:87.

knowledge transforms. 'Send out your light and your truth,' prays the psalmist; 'let them lead me; let them bring me to your holy hill and to your dwelling!' (Psa. 43:3). The result of increased light and truth is fellowship with God and transformed affections: 'Then I will go to the altar of God, to God my exceeding joy' (43:4). 'When God sends his light and truth into our hearts,' says Henry, 'these will guide us to the upper world in all our devotions.'[33]

It was as Jesus 'opened' the Scriptures to the disciples on the road to Emmaus that their eyes were opened and their 'hearts burn[ed] within' (Luke 24:31-32). Their affections, their passions, were powerfully engaged as they heard Jesus expound the Scriptures. Jesus' sermon 'brought a divine heat with a divine light into their souls, such as put their hearts into a glow, and kindled a holy fire of pious and devout affections in them'.[34] Jesus said, 'It is written in the Prophets, "And they will all be taught by God." Everyone who has heard and learned from the Father comes to me' (John 6:45). Edwards concludes from these and other passages that 'knowledge is the way that first opens the hard heart, and enlarges the affections, and so opens the way for man into the kingdom of heaven'.[35]

By way of contrast, the problem with the Pharisees was that they had 'taken away the key of knowledge' (Luke 11:52). Although the Jews who opposed Paul had 'a zeal for God', it was 'not according to knowledge' (Rom. 10:2). The false believers at Corinth had no knowledge of God. The evidence for this was an absence of transformation: they 'go on sinning' (1 Cor. 15:34).

'Truly spiritual and gracious affections'—that is, love for God, as well as joy and delight in him—'arise from the enlightening of true understanding to understand the things that are taught of God and Christ', Edwards maintains.[36] One comes to grasp what Edwards calls 'the loveliness of divine things'. One acquires 'the sense of the moral beauty of divine things', such as the excellency of Christ and of the word of God, and the beauty of holiness and of God's moral

---

[33] Henry, *Commentary*, on Psa. 43:3-4.
[34] *Ibid.*
[35] Edwards, *Religious Affections*, p. 192.
[36] *Ibid.*, p. 193.

perfections.[37] Love for God may be defined as 'the saint's relish of the supreme excellency of the divine nature inclining the heart to God as the chief good'. The transformed heart comes 'to relish or taste the sweetness of the divine relation'. The soul 'is brought to relish the excellency of the divine nature' and, as a natural result, to 'incline to God in every way'.

Again, the first effect of regeneration 'is to give the heart a divine taste or sense; to cause it to have a relish of the sweetness of the supreme excellency of the divine nature'.[38] The believer now hates sin and desires to do what is right (Rom. 7:15, 18). In his inner being he delights in the law of God. He serves the law of God with his mind and is 'obedient from the heart to the standard of teaching' to which he was committed (Rom. 7:22, 25; 6:17). 'Oh how I love your law!' the child of God is taught to say. 'It is my meditation all the day' (Psa. 119:97; cf. verses 113, 127, 140, 159, 163, 167). Indeed, 'your law is my delight' (119:174). Love for God, joy in God, delight in God, desire for God, a relish of the things of God: these are the marks of authentic Christianity.[39]

Obedience and service

Thomas Chalmers (1780–1847) spoke of 'the expulsive power of a new affection'.[40] Jerome (AD 347–420) appealed to the same principle: 'one love extinguishes another'.[41] The once seductive, enticing, compulsive love for the world is expelled and replaced by love for God, resulting in obedience and service. Jesus and the apostles expect that our love for God will be manifested concretely in an obedience and service that arise out of what J. Gresham Machen called 'the deep affection of

[37] Edwards, *Religious Affections*, pp. 195, 199.

[38] Edwards, *Treatise on Grace*, pp. 36-37.

[39] Edwards, *Religious Affections*. This is especially true of God's holiness. Holy persons, says Edwards, 'love God, in the first place, for the beauty of his holiness or moral perfection, as being supremely amiable in itself'. Love of God for his holiness 'is what is most fundamental and essential in their love' (p. 182). Further, 'A true love for God must begin with a delight in his holiness' (p. 183). The love which God imparts results in true affection for, love for, delight in, and desire for the triune God, Father, Son, and Holy Spirit.

[40] Thomas Chalmers, *The Expulsive Power of a New Affection* (1855: Edinburgh: Thomas Constable & Co., 2012).

[41] Latin: *unus amor extinguit alium*. Cited in Gurnall, *Christian in Complete Armour*, I:120.

the heart'. 'True service,' he continued, is not a substitute for love but the expression of love.'[42] Love for God will result in a love for holiness and the disciplines that sustain the Christian life. The believer will come to sing:

> O Love that casts out fear,
> O Love that casts out sin,
> Tarry no more without,
> But come and dwell within.[43]

Love's 'surest' evidence, says Henry, is to be confirmed by devoted service.[44] Jesus says, 'If you love me, you will keep my commandments' (John 14:15). True love for Christ, Hutcheson adds, 'will break forth in proofs and evidences of itself'. Moreover, 'the true touchstone and evidence of love to Christ' is 'obedience to the commandments':[45]

> Whoever has my commandments and keeps them, he it is who loves me. And he who loves me will be loved by my Father, and I will love him and manifest myself to him. ... If anyone loves me, he will keep my word, and my Father will love him, and we will come to him and make our home with him (John 14:21; 14:23; cf. 15:10; 1 John 5:3).

If we love Christ, we will obey his commands and 'keep' his word. We will want to serve, honour, obey, and please him. 'Love is the root,' says Henry, 'obedience the fruit.'[46] It is only in those who keep his word that the love of God is perfected (1 John 2:3-5).

Jesus makes emphatic the connection between love and faithful service in his threefold questioning of Peter at the end of John's Gospel:

> 'Simon, son of John, do you love [*agapaō*] me more than these?'

> 'Yes, Lord; you know that I love [*phileō*] you.'

This is repeated a second and third time (perhaps corresponding to Peter's threefold denial of Christ), with Jesus responding respectively, 'Feed my lambs', 'Tend my sheep', 'Feed my sheep' (John 21:15-17).

---

[42] Machen, *God Transcendent*, p. 68.
[43] Horatius Bonar, 'O Love That Casts Out Fear'.
[44] Henry, *Commentary*, on John 14:21.
[45] Hutcheson, *Gospel of John*, p. 302.
[46] Henry, *Commentary*, on John 14:23.

Feeding and tending the sheep is designated by Jesus as 'notable proof' of Peter's profession of love for Christ.[47] What is the sign of Peter's love? Devotion to Christ and his church; faithfulness to his apostolic and pastoral task of caring for the flock by feeding and leading it; and unwavering commitment to discipleship, even to death. 'Follow me', says Jesus (John 21:18-19).

This, then, is what it means to love Christ. If we love him, the evidence will be courageous devotion, not sentimental emotion. Those who love Christ take up their cross and follow a crucified Master (Matt. 16:24-25).

These are the same motivations to which Jesus points in the Sermon on the Mount. Why give alms in secret instead of announcing it by blowing one's own trumpet? Why pray in secret instead of openly on street corners? Why fast in secret instead of putting on a gloomy face for all to see? In order to please our Father in heaven (Matt. 6:1-6, 16-18)!

'The love of Christ controls us' (2 Cor. 5:14). Consequently, 'we make it our aim to please him' (5:9). Consequently, we 'no longer live for [ourselves] but for him who for [our sakes] died and was raised' (5:15). Machen says of those who share the apostle's conviction:

> Once they are convinced that Christ's death was a death for them, this gratitude to the one who died hems them in, restrains them from evil, more effectively than they could have been restrained by prison bars.[48]

Love for God is the motive of motives for obedience and service. Christ's love for us enables and inspires the whole direction of our lives. Christ did not die for us on the cross in order that we might live with impunity in sin or live for ourselves. No, he died that we might live for him

Again, our hymn-writers, none more so than Isaac Watts, help us to understand how God's redemptive love inspires our answering love:

> Were the whole realm of nature mine,
> That were an offering far too small;

---

[47] Hutcheson, *Gospel of John*, p. 435.
[48] Machen, *God Transcendent*, p. 143.

> Love so amazing, so divine,
>> Demands my soul, my life, my all.[49]

Christ's love inspires my service:

>> But drops of grief can ne'er repay
>> The debt of love I owe.
>> Here, Lord, I give myself away;
>> 'Tis all that I can do.[50]

Of course, this responsive love cannot but have an emotional or affective component. The heart swells with gratitude. A desire to know, please, and honour him who has so loved us grows. This is *agapē*, sacrificial love, infused with adoration, devotion, desire, and delight.

Richard Baxter, in his classic work *The Saints' Everlasting Rest*, gives extensive directions for stirring up love for God in our hearts:

Contemplate God's goodness

> Let thy faith, as it were, take thy heart by the hand, and show it the sumptuous buildings of thy eternal habitation, and the glorious ornaments of thy Father's house; show it those mansions which Christ is preparing, and display before it the honours of the kingdom. Let faith lead thy heart into the presence of God, and draw as near as possible thou canst, and say to it, Behold the Ancient of days; the Lord Jehovah, whose name is, I AM. This is he who made the worlds with his word: this is the Cause of all causes, the Spring of action, the Fountain of life, the First Principle of the creature's motions, who upholds the earth, who ruleth the nations, who disposeth of events, and subdueth his foes; who governeth the depths of the great waters, and bounded the rage of her swelling waves; who ruleth the winds, and moved the orbs, and causeth the sun to run its race, and the several planets to know their courses.[51]

---

[49] Watts, 'When I Survey The Wondrous Cross'.
[50] Watts, 'Alas! And Did My Saviour Bleed?'.
[51] Richard Baxter, *The Saints' Everlasting Rest* (Fearn, Ross-shire: Christian Focus, 1998), p. 579.

Contemplate his loving work in creation and providence

This is he that loved thee from everlasting, that formed thee in the womb, and gave thee this soul; who brought thee forth, and showed thee the light, and ranked thee with the chiefest of his earthly creatures; who endued thee with thy understanding, and beautified thee with his gifts; who maintaineth thee with life, and health, and comforts; who gave thee thy preferments, and dignified thee with thy honours, and differenced thee from the most miserable and vilest of men. Here, O here, is an object, now, worthy thy love; here shouldst thou even put out thy soul in love; here thou mayst be sure thou canst not love too much. This is the Lord that hath blessed thee with his benefits; that hath spread thy table in the sight of thine enemies, and caused thy cup to overflow (Psa. 23).[52]

These contemplations will awaken love

Thus do thou expatiate in the praises of God, and open his excellences to thine own heart, till thou feel the life begin to stir, and the fire in thy breast begin to kindle; as gazing upon the dusty beauty of flesh doth kindle the fire of carnal love; so this gazing on the glory and goodness of the Lord will kindle this spiritual love in thy soul.[53]

Does love still languish? If so, 'show it yet more'. Lead your heart to Christ:

show it the Son of the living God, whose name is Wonderful, Counsellor, the mighty God, the everlasting Father, the Prince of peace (Isa. 9:6): show it the King of saints on the throne of his glory, who is the First and the Last, who is, and was, and is to come; who liveth and was dead, and behold, he lives for evermore; who hath made thy peace by the blood of his cross, and hath prepared thee, with himself, a habitation of peace; his office is to be the great peacemaker; his kingdom is a kingdom of peace; his gospel is the tidings of peace; his voice to thee now

---

[52] Baxter, *Saints' Everlasting Rest*, pp. 579-80.
[53] *Ibid.*, p. 580.

is the voice of peace. Draw near and behold him; dost thou not hear his voice?[54]

Contemplate his suffering and our benefits

Why, it is he that brought thee up from the pit of hell: it is he that reversed the sentence of thy damnation; that bore the curse which thou shouldst have borne, and restored thee to the blessing that thou hast forfeited and lost, and purchased the advancement which thou must inherit for ever: and yet dost thou not know him? Why, his hands were pierced, his head was pierced, his sides were pierced, his heart was pierced, with the sting of thy sins, that by these marks thou mightest always know him. Dost thou not remember when he found thee lying in thy blood, and took pity on thee, and dressed thy wounds, and brought thee home, and said unto thee, 'Live'? (Ezek. 16:6-9; Luke 10:30, etc.) Hast thou forgotten since he wounded himself to cure thy wounds, and let out his own blood to stop thy bleeding? Is not the passage to his heart yet standing open? If thou know him not by the face, the voice, the hands, if thou know him not by the tears and bloody sweat, yet look nearer, thou mayest know him by the heart; that broken-healed heart is his; that dead-revived heart is his; that soul-pitying, melting heart is his; doubtless, it can be none's but his. Love and compassion are its certain signature; this is he, even this is he, who would rather die than thou shouldst die, who chose thy life before his own, who pleads his blood before his Father, and makes continual intercession for thee. If he had not suffered, oh what hadst thou suffered! What hadst thou been, if he had not redeemed thee! Whither hadst thou gone, if he had not recalled thee! There was but a step between thee and hell, when he stepped in, and bore the stroke; he slew the bear, and rescued the prey, he delivered thy soul from the roaring lion. And is not here yet fuel enough for love to feed on? Doth not this loadstone snatch thy heart unto it, and almost draw it forth of thy breast?[55]

---

[54] Baxter, *Saints' Everlasting Rest*, p. 580.
[55] *Ibid.*, pp. 580-81.

'What depth of love in the Christian's heart is called forth by that story of the dying love of Christ!' Machen exclaims, 'and as we think of that story our hearts melt within us and we are ashamed to offend against such love.'[56]

Replicate

We not only are to reciprocate the love of God, we are to replicate it. As is the case for our love for God, this love for others is *agapē* and *philia*, sacrificial love, not romantic or sensual love.[57] It is not even *storgē*, family or natural love. It is supernatural love that moves one to give of oneself. 'Beloved, let us love one another, for love is from God, and whoever loves has been born of God and knows God' (1 John 4:7).

Imparted love

'Beloved' (*agapētos*, 'loved one') is a favourite way of the apostles to refer to fellow believers (so used fifty-two times in the New Testament).[58] 'Beloved', that is, those who have already received love, 'let us love [*agapaō*] one another,' the apostle John directs. Love is 'from God', imparted to those 'born of God' and who 'know God'. The indicatives of redemption are followed by the imperative—'Let us love one another'. This is the third time that the apostle John has urged us in his first epistle to love one another (2:8-10; 3:11-18).[59] Because God is love, we must love (1 John 4:8). The apostle's point is ethical: 'Let us love one another.' Love for others is to be our response to God's love. 'Whoever loves has been born of God and knows God.' We love because we have been 'born of God'. Since God's nature is love, a true encounter with God through Christ involves the implanting of the divine love into the soul. The one who is born of God takes on his attribute of love which is

---

[56] Machen, *God Transcendent*, pp. 152-53.

[57] *Agapē* and *philia* typically are used interchangeably in the New Testament, as Morris, *Testaments of Love* (pp. 125ff., 180) and others have pointed out (e.g. D. A. Carson, *Exegetical Fallacies* [Grand Rapids, MI: Baker, 1984], pp. 30, 51-54).

[58] Rom. 16:5, 8, 9; 1 Cor 4:14, 17; 10:14; 15:58; Phil. 2:12; 4:1; 2 Tim. 1:2; James 1:16, 19; 2:5; cf. Rom. 1:7; 12:19; 16:12; 2 Cor. 7:1; 12:19; Eph. 5:1; 6:21; Col. 1:7; 4:7, 9, 14; 1 Thess. 2:8; 1 Tim. 6:2; Philem. 1, 2, 16; Heb. 6:9.

[59] His is not a 'lesson about the love of God for its own sake', as Kruse points out (Kruse, *Letters of John*, p. 161).

expressed towards others. Love enters into his or her ethical DNA. The birth of which the apostle John speaks is a supernatural birth. It means to be 'born from above', or 'born of the Spirit' (John 3:2ff.). Through this new birth God imparts his nature to his children. We become new creatures. The old hatreds and the old angers pass away. All things become new (2 Cor. 5:17). We become like our heavenly Father. 'Our love then to one another,' says Spurgeon, 'is simply God's love to us, flowing into us, and flowing out again.'[60] The corollary is that 'Anyone who does not love does not know God.' Why? Because 'God is love' (1 John 4:8). 'Nothing [is] more evidential of relations and alliance to God,' says Poole, 'than a duly regulated love, which is of him.'[61]

The apostle John repeats his teaching: 'Everyone who believes that Jesus is the Christ has been born of God, and everyone who loves the Father loves whoever has been born of him' (1 John 5:1). Notice the connections: those who believe that Jesus is the Christ are 'born of God'. They have a new, divinely given nature. They in turn 'love the Father' and all those who have been 'born of him'. God imparts his love (Rom. 5:5), resulting in love for God and love for the people of God. Everyone who 'knows' God—that is, who has an ongoing personal experience of God in Christ—is transformed by the experience. Our knowledge of the love of God is far more than information. As we have seen, it is transformation.[62] 'To speak of knowing God without knowing love is clearly ridiculous', Morris insists.[63] A genuine knowledge of God results in love. Love, says Spurgeon, is 'the distinguishing mark of the people of God'.[64] Francis Schaeffer influenced a whole generation of young Christians when in the 1970s he identified love as 'the mark of the Christian'.[65]

---

[60] Spurgeon, 'God's Love to the Saints', *Treasury of the New Testament*, IV:558.

[61] Poole, *Commentary*, III:937.

[62] 'A person cannot come into a real relationship with a loving God without being transformed into a loving person,' as I. Howard Marshall rightly maintains (Marshall, *Epistles of John*, p. 212).

[63] Morris, *Testaments of Love*, p. 137.

[64] Spurgeon, 'Herein Is Love', *Treasury of the New Testament*, IV:554.

[65] Francis A. Schaeffer, *The Mark of the Christian* (Downers Grove, IL: Inter-Varsity Press, 1970).

Inspired love

We can also say that God's love is infectious. One cannot truly know God without being infected—or, better, influenced and inspired. One is inspired to become like him and to love as he loves. The Bible leaves no room for a religion or an experience of God that does not result in love. If we truly know the God who is love, that knowledge will motivate within us a love for others. However, if we are merely 'religious' and have not experienced a personal knowledge of God through Jesus Christ, then it is possible to remain unloving though professing to be followers of Christ. But an experiential knowledge of the God who is love must impact the character and nature of the person concerned: that person will begin to love, and in so doing will reflect the image and likeness of the one who is love.[66] Those who know God will wish to be like him.

John reminds his readers: 'Beloved, if God so loved us, we also ought to love one another' (1 John 4:11). His point is that God's love provides the model, the influence, the inspiration, and the power for how we are to love. God loved us with initiating, costly, sacrificial love; we are to love in the same manner.

In Ephesians 4 and 5 Paul teaches that we have an 'old self' which belonged to our 'former manner of life'. It is 'corrupt through deceitful desires' and it is to be 'put off'. In its place we are to 'put on' a 'new self' in Christ which is 'created after the likeness of God in true righteousness and holiness' (4:22-24). Our speech, temper, labour, indeed every aspect of our whole life is to be characterized by holy love (4:25-32). We are to 'be imitators of God, as beloved children'. We are to 'walk in love, as Christ loved us and gave himself up for us' (5:1-2). Because we are 'beloved [*agapetoi*] children', we bear the family image of love and thus imitate our Father by walking in love.

Both the Father and the Son are examples of the love that we are to imitate. We are to love as Christ loved. We are to 'follow in his steps' (1 Pet. 2:21). We are to have the same attitude as Christ Jesus. What attitude was that? It was the attitude of considering others more important than ourselves, and looking out not merely for our own

---

[66] 'There can be no real knowledge of God which is not expressed in love for fellow believers' (Kruse, *Letters of John*, p. 157).

interests but also for the interests of others (Phil. 2:3ff.). And just as God took the initiative with the undeserving, so should we. How often conflicts with our neighbours, in our schools, in the workplace, and in our families remain unresolved because no one will take the first step towards resolution! Pride gets in the way. We will not budge. 'They'll have to come to me', we say. This is not the love of God. For God took the initiative, and so must we. His love is 'the only unerring pattern to be absolutely followed, and without any reserve or limitation', Hutcheson insists.[67]

Many questions with respect to duty are answered by focusing our eyes on the cross. What are we to do with a rebellious teenager? We are to love him or her with a love that costs us something. What are we to do with a hateful, cruel, hurtful neighbour, church member, or fellow worker? We are to remind ourselves of the cross and love that person with sacrificial love. What are we to do with needy fellow believers? Love them with the love which God has imparted to us. 'True love cannot long be dormant', says Spurgeon. It is 'of an active nature; it must be at work. Love longs for expression.'[68]

How important is it that we love one another? Think of the place 'love' occupies in Jesus' 'farewell sermon', the Upper Room Discourse of John 13–16. Three times he gives his disciples the 'new commandment' to love one another (13:34; 15:12, 17). Gurnall points out how 'large a room in his thoughts' this command occupied 'at that time, when he had so little time left in which he was to crowd and sum up *all the heavenly counsel and comfort that he desired to have with them before his departure*'. 'This is *my* commandment', Jesus said, indicating, Gurnall continues, that if he should have 'a darling commandment, in which he takes some singular delight … *this should be it*'.[69]

'Love' was not only the theme of his teaching to his disciples; it was also the subject matter of his intercession on their behalf in his High Priestly Prayer of John 17. 'Christ went out from preaching up peace to pulling down peace from heaven by prayer … what he insisted on most in preaching he enlargeth most upon in prayer.'[70] His heart's desire was

---

[67] Hutcheson, *Gospel of John*, p. 224.
[68] Spurgeon, 'God's Love to the Saints', *Treasury of the New Testament*, IV:539.
[69] Gurnall, *Christian in Complete Armour*, I:551 (emphasis added).
[70] *Ibid.*, I:552.

'that they may become perfectly one, so that the world may know that you sent me and loved them even as you loved me' (John 17:21, 23).

FIFTEEN

God's Love and Ours

You have heard that it was said, 'You shall love your neighbour and hate your enemy.' But I say to you, Love your enemies and pray for those who persecute you, so that you may be sons of your Father who is in heaven. For he makes his sun rise on the evil and on the good, and sends rain on the just and on the unjust. For if you love those who love you, what reward do you have? Do not even the tax collectors do the same? And if you greet only your brothers, what more are you doing than others? Do not even the Gentiles do the same? You therefore must be perfect, as your heavenly Father is perfect.—Matthew 5:43-48

WE have seen that we are to reciprocate God's love by loving him and we are to replicate his love by loving others. Who are these others that we are to love? We are to replicate the love of God in our relationships with three different groups.

The objects of Christian love

Our enemies

First, let us love our enemies. This duty is rooted in the command to love our neighbour, which itself is anchored in the nature of God. You are to love your enemies, Jesus tells his disciples, 'so that you may be sons of your Father who is in heaven. For he makes his sun rise on the evil and on the good, and sends rain on the just and on the unjust' (Matt. 5:45). We are to love our enemies because God loves his enemies and we are to live as sons of our heavenly Father, bearing the family image and replicating his love. Otherwise we are doing no more than the unbelieving. Even they manage to love those who love them (Matt. 5:46-48).

'Imitate your Father in those things that are his brightest perfection', says Henry.[1] This means that we are to love even those who hate, curse, and abuse us (Luke 6:27-28). When we love those who love us, we merely 'consult our own advantage'. When we render good for evil, we 'speak a nobler principle' and act according to a 'higher rule'. We are to find even in our enemies that which 'is amiable and commendable'.[2] Because God is 'kind to the ungrateful and the evil', so also must we be. Because God is merciful, so must we (Luke 6:36). We are to go the extra mile, turn the other cheek, and give the coat from off our backs (Matt. 5:38-42).

Could there be a more difficult command to fulfil? We have been wronged: we want to see our enemies crushed; we want to see them pay for their evil; we want to be the ones who make them pay. But Jesus says we are to love (*agapaō*) our enemies with sacrificial, costly, caring love—a love that does them good and offers prayer for them. Enemies are no more, and no less, than fellow sinners who need the saving grace of God in Christ. It may be that our loving them is the means by which they are introduced to the God of love.

Louis Zamperini, the great American athlete and war hero, struggled intensely with his hatred of the Japanese prison guards who tormented him, beating, confining, and starving him day after day for eighteen months during the Second World War. After his conversion to Christ his hatred was conquered by the love of God. He went back to Japan in 1950 to forgive those very guards and to tell them of the love of God and the cross of Christ. He went not to avenge but to win, not to destroy but to save. He was able personally to forgive many of his tormentors, though he failed in his attempts to contact Matsuhiro Watanabe, a man who had beaten him mercilessly on a near-daily basis, clubbing him nearly to death. Remarkably, Zamperini wrote to him in 1984: 'I committed my life to Christ. Love replaced the hate I had for you. Christ said, "Forgive your enemies and pray for them."'[3]

[1] Henry, *Commentary*, on Luke 6:36.
[2] *Ibid.*, on Matt. 5:43-48.
[3] The story is told in Zamperini's autobiography, *Devil at My Heels* (New York:

Corrie ten Boom tells a similar story in *The Hiding Place*. Her saintly sister, Betsie, died in a German concentration camp just before the end of the war. Corrie seethed with anger. She hated the Germans, and particularly the merciless guards who had brutalized them. When later she encountered an SS guard who had humiliated them at the Ravensbrück camp, her initial vengeful thoughts gave way to what she called an overwhelming love. 'When he tells us to love our enemies,' she said, '*he gives, along with the command, the love itself.*'[4] As with Zamperini, the love of God in Christ conquered her hatred, and she too went to her former tormentors as an ambassador for Christ and forgave them. The love of God in Christ imparts a capacity to love our enemies.

Our neighbours

Second, we are to love our neighbours. The parable of the Good Samaritan defines 'neighbour' for us. Jesus taught the parable within the context of the question, 'Who is my neighbour?' (Luke 10:29; cf. Lev. 19:18). His answer is all-encompassing: my neighbour is everyone with whom I come into contact, including a total stranger who is in need of my neighbourly help (Luke 10:30-37). Love is not to be restricted to a tribe, a race, or a family. The question should not be 'Who is my neighbour?' but rather, 'Who proved to be a neighbour to the one in need?' (10:36). We are to love whoever crosses our path. 'We should regard ... the whole race of mankind as our neighbours', J. C. Ryle insists.[5] Who, then, can I love at work? Who can I love in my community? Who can I love in my school? The love of neighbour, like the love of enemies, is anchored in the nature of God (Matt. 5:45-48). To whom may I show this God-like, sacrificial, costly love?

E. P. Dutton & Co., 1956), and most recently by Laura Hillenbrand in *Unbroken: A World War II Story of Survival, Resilience, and Redemption* (New York: Random House, 2010), p. 397.

[4] Corrie ten Boom, *The Hiding Place* (Washington Depot, CT: Chosen Books, 1971), emphasis added.

[5] J. C. Ryle, *Expository Thoughts on the Gospels: Luke* (1858; Edinburgh: Banner of Truth Trust, 2012), I:287.

The brotherhood of the church

Third, we are to love the brothers. Love of the brotherhood is a primary concern of the New Testament. Often this covenantal concern is applied wrongly to the whole world. Yes, we are to love the lost. However, our primary obligation is to the brethren. 'Beloved, let us love *one another*'—that is, let us love our Christian brothers (1 John 4:7). Again, 'If God so loved us, we also ought to love *one another*'— that is, our Christian brothers (4:11). Though our love is not exclusive, it is yet to be ordered by a covenantal priority. We are to 'do good to everyone, and *especially to those who are of the household of faith*' (Gal. 6:10). Jesus loves his church. He 'nourishes and cherishes it' (Eph. 5:29). So, likewise, must we.

John relentlessly expounded this theme in his first epistle. The command to love the brothers is the 'new commandment' that is really the 'old commandment' (1 John 2:7-8). Only those who love the brothers abide in the light of God (2:9-11). The children of God are 'evident', he says; they may be identified by their covenantal love. Those who do not love the brothers cannot be his children (3:10). They are not born of God (3:9). The love of the Father is not in them (2:15).

The love of Jesus is the pattern of our love for the brethren. 'By this we know love, that he laid down his life for us, and we ought to lay down our lives for the brothers' (3:16; 2:7-11). This means we cannot ignore the needs of our fellow believers. 'But if anyone has the world's goods and sees his brother in need, yet closes his heart against him, how does God's love abide in him?' (3:17). To close one's heart to needy brethren is to give evidence that the love of God is not in us. 'It is a poor and untrue religion which leaves the hungry in distress', says J. Gresham Machen.[6] Wherever the love of God has been imparted, loving deeds on behalf of the brethren follow: 'Little children, let us not love in word or talk but in deed and in truth' (3:18).

We may provide another example. How was the church at Corinth to 'prove' that its love for the brothers, particularly the brothers found in needy sister churches, was 'genuine' (2 Cor. 8:8)? By following the example of the churches in Macedonia (e.g. Philippi and Thessalonica) by giving sacrificially even out of their 'extreme poverty'; by allowing

---

[6] Machen, *God Transcendent*, pp. 69-70.

their joy to overflow in a wealth of generosity (8:2); by giving 'according to their means' and even 'beyond their means' (8:3). They were to 'give proof before the churches' of their love (8:24). Love is shown to be authentic through costly acts of service.

What is love, that is, true love, divine love? It is sacrifice, service; it is selflessness. Love embraces the unworthy and assists the needy. This New Testament love 'involves a consuming passion for the well-being of others, and this love has its wellspring in God', says F. F. Bruce.[7]

'That person who wronged me,' we may say, 'doesn't deserve my love.' Yes, but is the same not true of us? God did not love us because he found us appealing and worthy. He did not say, 'Oh, they are wonderful people! They are so kind, obedient, and loving that I think I will save them. They deserve it.' The idea is preposterous. Christ died for the ungodly, 'while we were still sinners', 'while we were enemies' (Rom. 5:8ff.)! Have we been on the receiving end of such love? Has the love of Christ been 'shed abroad in our hearts' (5:5 KJV)? If so, we can do no less than love others in the same way. We are to see in those we find difficult to love the image of ourselves, those upon whom Christ set his love.

Why is John so concerned that we love one another in this way? Because he treats love as a sign of Christian authenticity. He is concerned not only for the health of the church, but that through the love Christians exercise towards others the world might see the love of God: 'No one has ever seen God; if we love one another, God abides in us and his love is perfected in us' (1 John 4:12). No one has 'seen' God. So how are we to know that he loves us? When 'we love one another', God is present; he 'abides in us', and his love is 'perfected' or 'completed'. John Stott explains:

> The unseen God, who was once revealed in his Son, is now revealed in his people if and when they love one another … God's love which originates in himself (1 John 4:7-8) and was manifested in his Son (verses 9-10) is perfected in his people (verse 12).[8]

As Christians love each other, the world sees the love of God. Indeed, 'the love of God displayed in his people is the strongest

---

[7] F. F. Bruce, *Epistles of John* (Grand Rapids, MI: Eerdmans, 1970), p. 107.
[8] Stott, *Epistles of John*, p. 164.

apologetic that God has in the world'.[9] This is why we cannot allow ourselves to refuse to love our fellow Christians. We cannot be indifferent, aloof, uninvolved, or detached from our brothers. We cannot resolve to ignore, shun, or be unkind to a fellow believer, especially a fellow church member, without injuring the message of the gospel. To do so is to obscure the love of God which is manifested at the cross and perfected in our fellowship with one another. Jesus said, 'By this all people will know that you are my disciples, if you have love for one another' (John 13:35; cf. 15:12). 'Mutual love', says Hutcheson, is appointed by Christ 'to be the badge whereby his followers may be discerned'.[10] This is 'the principal note of the true church', Henry maintains, and 'the distinguishing character of his disciples'. 'Nothing will be more effectual than this to recommend them to the esteem and respect of others.'[11]

Contemplate this when thinking of how to respond to another Christian! If an unbeliever were watching us interact, would he see the love of God? Would he see the image of God's love, sacrifice, care, and compassion? What does the world see in us? When the world looks at the church, does it see the love of God manifested in the love we have for one another? It is beyond tragic that some churches are well known for turmoil and conflict. We have known of churches where actual fist-fights have broken out in their meetings. The absence of love undermines the credibility of the gospel. When we indulge in loveless behaviour, or the pursuit of petty personal concerns at the expense of others, we suffocate the message.

See a need? Then meet it. Aware of a wound? Help to heal it. Take the initiative. Keep the cross at the centre of your thinking. Let it inspire your actions. The consequences are eternal. God is love. He demonstrated it at the crucified Jesus. He continues to demonstrate it in the love that believers in the cross show for one another. Let us then love one another 'earnestly', or 'fervently', and let love 'cover a multitude of sins' (1 Pet. 4:8).

[9] Bruce, *Epistles of John*, p. 109.
[10] Hutcheson, *Gospel of John*, p. 289.
[11] Henry, *Commentary*, on John 13:35.

The character of Christian love

Can we elaborate on what this love from God looks like? Can we flesh out its qualities and provide specific details? Thankfully, the apostle Paul has already done that for us. The newly converted Corinthians, living in a sensuous and perverse civilization, needed instruction on what true love looks like. 'They were impatient, discontented, envious, inflated, selfish, indecorous, unmindful of the feelings or interests of others,—suspicious, resentful, censorious.'[12] Consequently, in chapter 13 of 1 Corinthians the apostle 'gives thirteen notes of a charitable person'.[13] By way of contrast with the Corinthians' unlovely behaviour, Paul commends the love that 'never ends' (1 Cor. 13:8). How does this divine love express itself in human relationships?

Patient

It is 'patient' (1 Cor. 13:4; long-tempered). Love is 'slow to be raised to resentment', says Hodge; it 'patiently bears with provocation and is not quick to assert its rights or resent an injury'.[14] It is tolerant of people in their weakness, ignorance, and lack of progress. It accommodates their limitations. It takes their disadvantages into consideration. It is not short-tempered or easily provoked.

God is patient, and we are to be the same (1 Pet. 3:20). In the New Testament, patience is connected with 'bearing with one another' (Eph. 4:2; Col. 3:13), 'endurance' (Col. 1:11), encouraging the 'faint-hearted', and helping the 'weak' (1 Thess. 5:14). To be patient is to look not with frustration or irritation but with sympathy on the limitations and failings of others.

Kind

Love is 'kind', 'good natured', 'disposed to do good'.[15] Since God 'is kind to the ungrateful and the evil', so we are to be the same (Luke 6:35). Jesus associates kindness with love and lending, with goodness and mercy (Luke 6:27ff.). Paul associates it with compassion, humility,

---

[12] Hodge, *1 and 2 Corinthians*, p. 269.
[13] Poole, *Commentary*, III:586.
[14] Hodge, *1 and 2 Corinthians*, p. 269.
[15] *Ibid.*

gentleness, and patience (Col. 3:12-13). It is contrasted with severity in Romans 11:22. Kindness is love taken a step beyond patience. Patience is enduring the foolishness and failures of others; kindness is doing good to those who are foolish and who fail. Patience is tolerating the weaknesses of others; kindness is returning their irritating habits, idiosyncrasies, slights, and offences with acts of love. Kindness is love turning the other cheek, going the extra mile, and giving the coat from off one's back even to those who curse, hate, mistreat us (Luke 6:27-36). It is dealing gently and generously with others.

Be kind to one another, for the Saviour 'knows no such true Christians, as are of a sordid, selfish, cross and contentious spirit', Edwards insist. Nothing is a greater absurdity than a morose, hard, spiteful, true Christian.[16]

Does not envy

Love does not 'envy'. It is not 'jealous' (NASB), which has been defined as 'any wrong feeling excited in view of the good of others'.[17] The Greek philosopher Xenophon defined the envious as 'those who are annoyed only at their friends' successes'. When another person gets the job, relationship, or recognition which I sought; when my neighbour's children score the touchdowns, win the academic awards, or receive the prizes in art or music—how easy it is to become resentful, embittered, or even accusatory. They are undeserving; the system is rigged; they must have cheated, we say. Or they have lobbied hard for the position; they know all the right people; they bribed their way to the top; I would never do that! Soon bitterness and resentment take root, and eat away at the soul with destructive consequences. Thomas Brooks warns:

> Envy is as pernicious a wickedness, as it is a foolish and a groundless wickedness. Envy is a scourge to scourge the soul; it is a serpent to sting the soul; it is a poison to swell the soul; it is a saw to saw the soul; it is a moth that corrupts the soul, and it is a canker that eats up the soul; and therefore fly from it as you would fly from the most cruel and destroying adversary.[18]

[16] Edwards, *Religious Affections*, p. 284.
[17] Hodge, *1 and 2 Corinthians*, p. 269.
[18] Brooks, 'An Ark for All God's Noahs', *Works*, II:47.

The foundation of envy, says Charnock insightfully, 'is a quarrel with God'. It challenges God's 'right of disposal, and consequently, the propriety of his own goods'. It is to charge him 'with a blind or unjust distribution', and so it bespatters 'his wisdom and righteousness'.[19] Similarly, Brooks warns further that to be 'angry, because God is bountiful to others; to frown, because God smiles upon others; to be bitter, because God is sweet in his dealings with others; and to sigh, because God multiplies favours and blessings upon others; what is this but to turn others' good into our own hurt, others' glory and mercy into our own punishment and torment?' It creates a hell in our own hearts.[20]

This is not how the people of God ought to be. Rather, we are told to 'rejoice with those who rejoice' (Rom. 12:15). Love is not embittered by the success of others. Love does not resent their accomplishments.

Does not boast

Love does not 'boast'; it does not 'show off',[21] vaunt itself, or brag. A believer is not a braggart nor a windbag.[22] 'Love does not seek to win admiration and applause', says Hodge;[23] it is not self-promoting.

A major cultural shift occurred in this respect in the early 1960s. Until then, boasting was seen as bad form. The athletes of that era rarely spoke of their own achievements and typically credited their teammates for their success while speaking admiringly of their opponents. This was true in baseball (Willie Mays and Sandy Koufax), in football (Johnny Unitas and Jim Brown), in basketball (Jerry West and Oscar Robertson), and in boxing (Jack Dempsey and Joe Louis). That generation of athletes was succeeded by the likes of Muhammad Ali and Joe Namath, who

---

[19] Charnock, *Existence and Attributes*, II:468.

[20] Brooks, *An Ark for All God's Noahs, Works*, II:47.

[21] Max Zerwick and Mary Grosvenor, *A Grammatical Analysis of the Greek New Testament*, Vol. 2: *Epistles–Apocalypse* (Rome: Biblical Institute Press, 1979), p. 524.

[22] According to Morris, a possible meaning of the term (*Testaments of Love*, p. 245).

[23] Hodge, *1 and 2 Corinthians*, p. 269. Lenski adds, 'Behind boastful bragging there lies conceit, an overestimation of one's own importance, ability, or achievements' (R. C. H. Lenski, *The Interpretation of St Paul's First and Second Epistles to the Corinthians* [1937; Minneapolis, MN: Augsburg Publishing House, 1963], p. 556.

were followed by the trash-talking, chest-thumping, self-glorifying athletes of today. 'It ain't bragging if you can do it', they say. Oh, but it is!

Love is content to let one's accomplishments speak for themselves. 'If you've got it, flaunt it', we are told. No, love does not flaunt its assets. If you have got it, there is no need to put it on display. Love does not boast, because love knows that apart from Christ the true vine we can do nothing (John 15:5). 'What do you have that you did not receive?' the apostle asks the vainglorious Corinthians. 'If then you received it, why do you boast as if you did not receive it?' (1 Cor. 4:7). Consequently, we should direct all the credit, honour, and glory to God alone. Love never designs to draw attention to oneself. Love is modest and reserved.

Not arrogant

Similarly, love is not 'arrogant'. It is not 'puffed up' (KJV). It does not have an inflated (and unwarranted) opinion or 'high conceits' of oneself.[24] Love is not 'full of one's own importance'.[25] We are not to think of ourselves 'more highly than [we] ought'; rather, we are to exercise 'sober judgment' (Rom. 12:3). '"Knowledge" puffs up', filling one with a sense of superiority to others (1 Cor. 8:1; cf. Col. 2:18). Knowledge, in all its forms, can have this effect. Normally we associate 'knowledge' with the academic 'smart Alec' who has more 'book-learning' than anyone else and so thinks he is always the smartest person in the room. Yet there is also the technology whizz, who swells with pride over his expertise and regards with contempt those who are behind the times. There is also the pop-culture groupie, who thinks that those who are not up on the latest songs, the latest shows, and the latest styles and fashions are hopelessly naïve and out of touch. Then there is the health fanatic, who looks disdainfully at those who are not into the latest diet and exercise fads. There is also the avid follower of politics, and the armchair theologian, whose views lead them to scorn the unenlightened. Then there are those who just know better, who simply smile and roll their eyes whenever they hear anything that contradicts the 'received truth' as they know it. '"Knowledge" puffs up, but love builds

[24] Poole, *Commentary*, III:586.
[25] Zerwick and Grosvenor, *Grammatical Analysis*, II:524.

up' (1 Cor. 8:1). Be warned: 'If anyone imagines that he knows something, he does not yet know as he ought to know' (8:2).

Pride in these various forms leads to distance and separation between people. Humility brings people together. 'Love,' says Hodge, is modest and humble; modest because humble.'[26] 'Do not be haughty, but associate with the lowly' (Rom. 12:16). See the connection. We ought to regard ourselves as 'the very least of all the saints', better than no one else, superior to no one else, the servant of all (Eph. 3:8).

Not rude

Love is not 'rude' (verse 5). It does not 'behave itself unseemly' (KJV) or 'act unbecomingly' (NASB). It does not 'behave dishonourably or indecently'.[27] It 'does nothing of which one ought to be ashamed', says Hodge.[28] It is not 'ill-mannered' (TEV). Love is tactful, courteous, polite, gracious, and mannerly.

Consider the apostle Paul before Porcius Festus: 'most excellent Festus' is how he addressed the pagan Roman governor (Acts 26:25). He was not rude. He gave honour to whom honour was due (Rom. 13:7). He was not unnecessarily discourteous. He observed the social conventions of the day.[29]

Good manners, properly understood, are simply a way in which we say to others, 'You first, me second.' Opening the door for another, saying 'please' and 'thank you', chewing with your mouth closed, dressing up for a funeral or wedding, and scores of other social niceties are expressions of love, of putting others before ourselves, of considering their comfort and ease above our own. Love is not rude. It does not indulge in profanity. It is not crude or vulgar. Love does nothing, says Poole, 'which in the opinion of men shall be a filthy or indecent

[26] Hodge, *1 and 2 Corinthians*, p. 269.

[27] Zerwick and Grosvenor, *Grammatical Analysis*, II:524.

[28] Hodge, *1 and 2 Corinthians*, p. 270. It is not contrary to 'form, fashion, or manner that is proper' (Lenski, *First and Second Epistles to the Corinthians*), p. 557.

[29] Love, says Calvin 'does not delight in meaningless ostentation, or does not make a great fuss, but always acts in a moderate and seemly way' (John Calvin, *The First Epistle of Paul the Apostle to the Corinthians* [Grand Rapids, MI: Eerdmans, 1960], p. 277).

action'.[30] It gives 'thought to do what is honourable in the sight of all' (Rom. 12:17).

Does not seek its own

Love 'does not insist on its own way' or 'seek its own' (NASB), literally, 'the things of itself'. It does not seek its own advantage, its own position, its own limelight, or its own pleasure. It is not selfish; it is not out for itself. Take heed of these apostolic exhortations: 'Let no one seek his own good, but the good of his neighbour' (1 Cor. 10:24). 'Let each of us please his neighbour for his good, to build him up' (Rom. 15:2). Paul lamented that some 'seek their own interests, not those of Jesus Christ' (Phil. 2:21). He noted that even preachers may 'preach Christ from envy and rivalry' or 'out of selfish ambition' and 'pretence' (Phil. 1:15-17 NASB). He warned that in the last days there would be 'lovers of self', and 'lovers of pleasure rather than lovers of God' (2 Tim. 3:2, 4).

There is, of course, a proper self-regard, a valid concern for one's own safety and health, and a valid ambition to fully utilize one's gifts and abilities. But the problem being addressed by the apostle is excessive self-interest which consists in 'neglecting others through thinking about ourselves, or being distracted by concern for our own interests from that consideration, which God commands us to have for our neighbours'.[31] Instead of pursuing self-interest we are to 'seek first the kingdom of God' (Matt. 6:33). True love seeks first the good of others. 'Let each of us please his neighbour for his good, to build him up.' Why? 'For Christ did not please himself' (Rom. 15:2-3). Jesus is our pattern.

Not irritable

Love is not 'irritable', or 'provoked' (NASB) or 'hot-tempered'.[32] It is 'not touchy' (J. B. Phillips). One does not have to 'walk on eggshells' in the presence of love. Love does not blow up. It 'does not suffer itself to be raised to resentment', says Hodge.[33] George Sweeting, former President

---

[30] Poole, *Commentary*, III:586.
[31] Calvin, *First Corinthians*, p. 277.
[32] Zerwick and Grosvenor, *Grammatical Analysis*, II:524.
[33] Hodge, *1 and 2 Corinthians*, p. 270. Other definitions include 'never flies into a temper' (William Barclay, *The Letters to the Corinthians*, *The Daily Study Bible*

and Chancellor of Moody Bible Institute, quotes a student who said, 'I lose my temper, but it's all over in a minute'; to whom Sweeting responded: 'So is the hydrogen bomb. But think of the damage it produces.'[34]

There is such a thing as 'righteous indignation'. However, 'the anger of man does not produce the righteousness of God' (James 1:20). Consequently, we are to 'put … away' anger (Col. 3:8) and 'all bitterness and wrath and anger and clamour and slander … with all malice' (Eph. 4:31). The person who is not irritable 'is not without his passions,' says Poole, but 'he is not governed … and overruled by them'.[35]

Being 'hurt' is another form of irritability. Some of us do not get angry, but we get our feelings hurt too easily, and over the slightest setback. We are overly and selfishly sensitive. We pout and sulk. We nurse our wounds, punishing our transgressors with silence or aloofness. We withhold love. Both anger and hurt are weapons that we wield in order to control others. Because love does not 'seek its own', it is not 'irritable', whether in the form of easily provoked anger or thin-skinned sensitivity.

Not resentful

Love is not 'resentful'; it 'does not take into account a wrong suffered' (NASB). The apostle here employs an accounting term. One enters items in a ledger so as not to forget them. However, love does not consciously labour to remember wrongs committed against it, reliving hurts, nursing resentment, brooding over offences, keeping score. Love does not maintain a list of enemies.[36] There is a certain sordid pleasure we get

[Edinburgh: Saint Andrew Press, 1954], p. 135). 'Christian love never becomes exasperated with people,' he says. 'Exasperation is always a sign of defeat' (p. 136). It means 'not merely, "does not fly into a rage", but "does not yield to provocation": it is not embittered by injuries, whether real or supposed' (Archibald Robertson and Alfred Plummer, *A Critical and Exegetical Commentary on the First Epistle of St Paul to the Corinthians* [Edinburgh: T & T Clark, 1914], p. 294).

[34] George Sweeting, *Catch the Spirit of Love* (Colorado Springs, CO: Victor Books, 1983), p. 59.

[35] Poole, *Commentary*, III:586.

[36] 'So many people nurse their wrath to keep it warm; they brood over their wrongs until it is impossible to forget them. Christian love has learned the great lesson of forgetting' (Barclay, *Letters to the Corinthians*, p. 136).

from keeping resentment alive—a twisted enjoyment, an air of superiority, perhaps, over the offending party.

At the end of May 2014, Red Sox slugger David Ortiz came to bat against Tampa Bay's David Price for the first time that season. Price fired a high, hard fastball square into Ortiz's back. 'Ortiz was not amused', observed Charles Krauthammer in an article entitled 'Plotting Revenge, American-Style'. Both benches emptied. Angry shouting and shoving ensued. 'Everyone knew this was not an accident.'[37] The background was 5 October 2013. Ortiz had hit two home runs off Price. After the second, he stood at home plate and admired his accomplishment, and then trotted very slowly around the bases. Major league baseball pitchers do not tolerate grandstanding at their expense. Price yelled at him to stop showboating, but to no avail. All through the fall, the long winter, the spring, and the first third of the season, Price seethed. For eight months he nursed his grudge. At the first opportunity, he took his revenge at 94 miles per hour.

Keeping a record of wrongs is typical of human nature. Quebec license plates read, '*Je me souviens*,' I remember. Remember what? The Battle of the Plains of Abraham, when Quebec fell to the British in 1759. The Serbs fought with fury in the 1990s to avenge the fall of Kosovo to the Turkish Muslims. When did that occur? In 1389. The Islamists invoke Andalusia on the Iberian Peninsula as their battle cry, lost to Christian Spain in 1492. Love does not store up grievances. Love does not recall and rehearse every cross word. Love lets it go. Love forgets. Love moves on, love restores the offender. Love does not harbour resentment.

Does not rejoice at wrongdoing

Love 'does not rejoice at wrongdoing, but rejoices with the truth' (verse 6). Love does not indulge the malicious pleasure we often take in hearing of the downfall of another, a pleasure that drives the news and gossip industries. Love is not indifferent to moral considerations, laughing at evil, winking at sin, being entertained by blasphemy, idolatry, and perversion.

[37] Charles Krauthammer, 'Plotting Revenge, American-Style', *Savannah Morning News*, 14 June 2014.

Rather, love 'rejoices with the truth'. It delights in the truth, the truth as it is in Jesus (Eph. 4:21), who is Truth itself (John 14:6). We have been given the 'truth about God' (Rom. 1:25; 3:7), 'the truth of the gospel' (Gal. 2:5), the 'word of truth' (2 Tim. 2:15). Love rejoices in the clear expression of moral and religious truth, and in the spread of the knowledge of the truth.

Love is never to be pitted against truth. Truth is never to be compromised in the name of love. Love does not mean 'accepting' lifestyle choices with the consequence that truth is silenced. Rather, we '[speak] the truth in love' (Eph. 4:15). Indeed, because we know the truth—the truth that corresponds with ultimate reality, with God himself—it would be unloving to withhold the truth. To withhold the information that God has given us in his word about the human condition, the law of God, the judgment of God, and the way of salvation would be cruel. Love rejoices in the truth and proclaims it.

Bears all

Paul now sums up his description of love with four verbs, each qualified by 'all things'. Love 'bears all things' (verse 7), probably meaning that it endures the offences, insults, slanders, false accusations, and hardships that result for the sake of the greater cause of the gospel. Paul would 'endure anything rather than put an obstacle in the way of the gospel of Christ' (1 Cor. 9:12). We are to walk 'with all humility and gentleness, with patience, bearing with [or 'putting up with'] one another in love' (Eph. 4:2). Instead of complaining, gossiping, or counter-attacking, one quietly bears the offences and moves on. Love knows when to keep one's mouth shut. 'Love covers a multitude of sins' (1 Pet. 4:8). If love covers a multitude of sins, what does it do with mere annoyances, petty differences, misunderstandings, perceived social slights, and unexplained behaviour? How much latitude we ought to give each other, and how much grace we ought to extend! How quick we ought to be to say in our hearts, 'I'm sure harm wasn't meant; I'm certain nothing untoward was intended; I'm sure they didn't mean to hurt us'! 'Love,' says Watson, 'puts the fairest and most candid gloss upon the actions of a friend: love covers evil. … Love takes everything in the best sense.'[38]

[38] Watson, *Art of Divine Contentment*, pp. 115-16.

Love even conceals the faults of others. It 'covereth faults with her large mantle', Trapp maintains.[39] Love does not expose the worst about its neighbours. Love quietly endures wrongs for the sake of the kingdom of God. Repeatedly in the Christian ministry we have to swallow hard in the face of even gross wrongs and leave justice in God's hands, for God's time. False accusations have to be ignored because answering them would only perpetuate controversy and undermine the proclamation of the gospel.

Believes all

Love 'believes all things'. Believes what? The best about others. Love interprets all the actions of a friend 'with so much sweetness and simplicity', Gurnall insists, that, even when that friend's behaviour seems contrary or suspicious, love 'ever puts the most favourable sense upon all he doth that is possible'.[40] Love 'takes the kindest view possible of people and circumstances'.[41] To believe all things, says Morris, is 'that quality which is always ready to allow for circumstances, and to see the best in others'.[42]

Love walks that fine line between gullibility (falling for the slick presentation of the dishonest salesman) and cynicism (distrusting everyone, thinking everyone else is dishonest or stupid). Because we are naturally malicious, we are also suspicious, and take the wrong meaning out of nearly everything. Yet love calls us back to humanity so that we may think of others in a kindly and sincere way.[43]

Our scepticism about other people's intentions and motives may be a by-product of wrongly construing the doctrine of original sin. After all, our adversaries are 'totally depraved'. So of course they meant the worst! Of course they intended to harm us! They are sinners, are they not? Yes, they are, but so are we. Our ability to discern the motives

[39] Trapp, *Commentary*, V:545.

[40] Gurnall, *Christian in Complete Armour*, II:98.

[41] Sweeting, *Catch the Spirit*, p. 75.

[42] Leon Morris, *The First Epistle of Paul to the Corinthians* (Grand Rapids, MI: Eerdmans, 1958), p. 185.

[43] 'In doubtful cases he will prefer being too generous in his conclusions to suspecting another unjustly' (Robertson and Plummer, *First Epistle of St Paul to the Corinthians*, p. 295); see also, Calvin, *First Corinthians*, p. 278.

of even our own hearts, mixed, layered, and confused as they are, is extremely limited, never mind those of the hearts of others! When we pretend to voice the motives of others, it is often so that we might rob their good deeds of their virtue: 'He was kind because he is hoping to get …' We not only accuse our adversaries of bad deeds, but we discredit their good deeds by attributing to them corrupt or self-serving motives.

Often we are tempted to create poisoned narratives for others that explain everything. 'She looked away from me because she is angry over what my child did to her child, even though my child didn't mean anything by it'; 'He drove off and didn't wait for me, even though he knew I needed a ride, because he didn't want to be seen with me by his high-society friends.' We may even go Freudian: 'He has this subconscious need for affirmation, and because we didn't lavish praise on him, he snubbed us.' The truth is, she may have looked away because she had just got word that her husband had cancer. He may have driven off because he did not know you needed a ride; he would have been more than happy to have provided one. We attribute the worst motives and the worst intentions on the skimpiest of evidence, with the resulting alienation and distance. Do not do it!

God's judgment will be universal; no one will be exempt. 'For we will all stand before the judgment seat of God,' the apostle teaches us. 'Each of us will give an account of himself to God' (Rom. 14:10-12). So the point is this: 'Let us not pass judgment on one another any longer' (14:13). Wait for the day of judgment. Leave the task of judging in God's hands. Take seriously the apostle's words to the Corinthian Christians: 'Therefore do not pronounce judgment before the time, before the Lord comes, who will bring to light the things now hidden in darkness and will disclose the purposes of the heart. Then each one will receive his commendation from God' (1 Cor. 4:5). We should not 'pronounce judgment' because we lack the necessary knowledge to make a fair judgment. We should 'neither assume [God's] prerogative, nor anticipate his decision', says Hodge.[44] However, God will 'bring to light the things now hidden in darkness'. He, and he alone, is able to 'disclose the purposes of the heart'. There is too much that we do not know and cannot know.

[44] Hodge, *1 and 2 Corinthians*, p. 67.

In the meantime, believe the best. Take people at their word until they prove themselves to be untrustworthy. Do not pretend that we can know the reasons why people act as they do and say what they do. Calvin identifies the balance:

> Not that a Christian knowingly and intentionally allows himself to be imposed upon; not that he strips himself of wisdom and discernment so as to let people find it easier to cheat him; not that he has forgotten how to distinguish black from white! What then? As I have already said, what Paul is asking for here is sincerity and humanity in forming judgments; and here he affirms that these two virtues constantly go hand in hand with love. What that will mean in practice is that a Christian will consider it better to be taken in through his own kindness and good nature than to cause harm to his brother through ill-founded suspicion.[45]

Love 'neither wishes evil to, nor suspects evil of, another'.[46]

Hopes all

Love 'hopes all things'. This quality may have particular application to the context of failure or betrayal. Love hopes for recovery. Love hopes for restoration. Love believes in the final victory of the gospel. It is, says Morris, 'a refusal to take failure as final',[47] and it confidently looks to the ultimate triumph of the grace of God. It 'hopes for the best with regard to all men'.[48]

Let us imagine a situation in which a failed loyalty has been confirmed, where deliberate harm was indeed intended. We believed the best, and our confidence was betrayed. What now? Love holds out hope that the offender will see his sin, will recognize the mistake, and will admit the fault; and that full reconciliation will take place.

The church as a whole will hold out hope that its prodigals will return home, that its backsliders will see the error of their ways, that the alienated will be reconciled to Christ and his church. Our attitude is *hopeful*. We long to see restoration and believe that the gospel,

---

[45] Calvin, *First Corinthians*, p. 278.
[46] Gurnall, *Christian in Complete Armour*, II:181.
[47] Morris, *First Corinthians*, p. 186.
[48] Hodge, *1 and 2 Corinthians*, p. 271.

because it is the power of God, may yet bring about restoration in the most discouraging of circumstances. We hold out hope that the rebellious will 'come to [their] senses' and be reconciled to the Father and to the church (Luke 15:17 NASB). We believe the best about them and hope for the best for them.[49]

Endures all

Love 'endures all things'. 'Bears' and 'endures' are close synonyms. The difference may be that the former has reference to annoyances and troubles, while the latter has reference to persecutions and the suffering that ensues. Or, perhaps more likely, the distinction may be between passive bearing and active endurance. To endure is to be thought not so much as 'patient, resigned acquiescence' but as 'an active, positive fortitude'. Love 'is not overwhelmed, but manfully plays its part whatever the difficulty'.[50] It is able, in hardship, to 'sustain the assault of an enemy'.[51] It pushes on; it perseveres. It overcomes all obstacles and is undeterred by difficulties. Because it bears, believes, and hopes, it also endures. It believes in final victory and so presses on towards it. It never quits (cf. 1 Cor. 15:58; Rom. 8:37).

Never ends

Finally, love 'never ends' (verse 8). Love will never fail. It will never collapse under pressure. Love conquers all. It overcomes evil with good (Rom. 12:21). 'Many waters cannot quench love, neither can floods drown it' (Song of Sol. 8:7). It persists through all. It is permanent. It is eternal. Indeed, says Poole, 'it shall go with us into another world'.[52] Hence it is the greatest of virtues (1 Cor. 13:13).

---

[49] 'When love has no evidence, it believes the best. When the evidence is adverse, it hopes for the best' (Robertson and Plummer, *First Epistle of St Paul to the Corinthians*, p. 295).

[50] Morris, *First Corinthians*, p. 186.

[51] Hodge, *1 and 2 Corinthians*, p. 271. He notes the word's military origins.

[52] Poole, *Commentary*, III:586.

The example of Christian love

The apostle has described divine love as it is expressed in the life of man: infinite love in finite relations. Nowhere can this more clearly be seen than in the person and life of the Lord Jesus Christ, when the infinite was joined to the finite. As imitators of God, we are to 'walk in love, as Christ loved us and gave himself up for us' (Eph. 5:1-2; cf. 5:25-30). We are to love one another just as Jesus has loved us (John 13:34). We are to have the 'attitude … which was also in Christ Jesus' (Phil. 2:5 NASB). What attitude was that? One that did 'nothing from selfish ambition or empty conceit'. One that in humility of mind counted others more significant or more important than himself. One that looked not only to his own interests, but also to the interests of others (Phil. 2:3-4 NASB).

What did Jesus do? Though he was in 'the form of God', he 'did not count equality with God a thing to be grasped, but emptied himself, taking the form of a servant, being born in the likeness of men. And being found in human form, he humbled himself by becoming obedient to the point of death, even death on a cross' (Phil. 2:6-8 NASB).

What is this but sacrifice? What is sacrifice but love? He 'emptied himself', not by divesting himself of his divine nature, but by taking on servanthood and human nature. Both the incarnation and atonement were acts of love that we are to imitate. We are to 'have this mind among [ourselves]', the apostle says. This is the love that bears, believes, hopes, and endures all things, the love that never fails. This is the love that seeks not its own. He left us an 'example' of sacrificial love. We are to 'follow in his steps' (1 Pet. 2:21). B. B. Warfield beautifully summarizes what it means for us to imitate the incarnation:

> He was led by his love for others into the world, to forget himself in the needs of others, to sacrifice self once for all upon the altar of sympathy. Self-sacrifice brought Christ into the world. And self-sacrifice will lead us, his followers, not away from but into the midst of men. Wherever men suffer, there will we be to comfort. Wherever men strive, there will we be to help. Wherever men fail, there will we be to uplift. Wherever men succeed, there will we be to rejoice. Self-sacrifice means not indifference to our

times and our fellows: it means absorption in them. It means forgetfulness of self in others. It means entering into every man's hopes and fears, longings and despairs: it means manysidedness of spirit, multiform activity, multiplicity of sympathies.[53]

We can be certain that most of this teaching on love is redundant. We have heard it all before. Indeed, it was redundant for the first-century believers. The apostle Paul told the Thessalonians: 'Now concerning brotherly love you have no need for anyone to write to you, for you yourselves have been taught by God to love one another' (1 Thess. 4:9; cf. 2 Thess. 3:25). Yes, we know these things already. God has filled our hearts with divine love. But now it is our turn to express that love towards others. I leave the last word on this subject to Jonathan Edwards: 'Consider that as a principle of love is the main principle in the heart of a real Christian, so the labour of love is the main business of the Christian life.'[54]

---

[53] Warfield, 'Imitating the Incarnation', *The Savior of the World*, p. 269.
[54] Edwards, *Charity and Its Fruits*, p. 25.

Bibliography

Aczel, Amir D., *Why Science Does Not Disprove God* (New York: William Morrow, 2014).

Alexander, J. W., *God is Love* (1860; Edinburgh: Banner of Truth Trust, 1985).

Barclay, William, *The Letters to the Corinthians, The Daily Study Bible.* (Edinburgh: Saint Andrew Press, 1954).

Barth, Karl, *Epistle to the Romans,* (1922; London: Bloomsbury T & T Clark, 2016).

Bavinck, Herman, *Our Reasonable Faith,* (1907; Grand Rapids, MI: Baker Book House, 1977).

—*The Doctrine of God,* (Grand Rapids, MI: Wm. B. Eerdmans Publishing Co., 1951).

Baxter, Richard, 'The Divine Life', in *Practical Works of Richard Baxter,* Vol. III, (1664, 1838; Ligonier, PA: Soli Deo Gloria, 1990).

—*The Saints' Everlasting Rest,* (1649; Fearn, Ross-shire: Christian Focus Publications, 1998).

Bayly, Lewis, *The Practice of Piety: Directing a Christian How to Walk that He May Please God,* (1611, 1842; Morgan, PA: Soli Deo Gloria, n.d.)

Beeke, Joel R. and Mark Jones, *A Puritan Theology: Doctrine for Life,* (Grand Rapids, MI: Reformation Heritage Books, 2012).

Berkhof, Louis, *Systematic Theology,* (1939; London: Banner of Truth Trust, 1958).

Blackwell, Sarah, *At the Existentialist Café* (New York: Other Press, 2016).

Boom, Corrie ten, *The Hiding Place* (Washington Depot, CT: Chosen Books, 1971).

Boston, Thomas, 'An Illustration of the Doctrines of Christian Religion' in *Complete Works of the Late Thomas Boston*, Vol. I (1853; Wheaton, IL: Richard Owen Roberts Publishers, 1980).

à Brakel, Wilhelmus, *The Christian's Reasonable Service*, Vol. I (1701; Grand Rapids. MI: Reformation Heritage Books, 1992).

Brand, Dr Paul and Philip Yancey, *Fearfully and Wonderfully Made* (Grand Rapids, MI: Zondervan Publishing House, 1980).

Bridges, Charles, *A Commentary on Proverbs* (1846; London: Banner of Truth Trust, 1968).

   —*A Commentary on Ecclesiastes* (1860; London: Banner of Truth Trust, 1961).

Bridges, Jerry, *The Pursuit of Holiness* (Colorado Springs, CO: NavPress, 1978).

Brooks, Thomas, 'An Ark for All God's Noahs', *Works of Thomas Brooks*, Vol. II (1866; Edinburgh: Banner of Truth Trust, 1980).

Brown, David, *The Four Gospels: A Commentary, Critical, Experimental and Practical* (London: Banner of Truth Trust, 1970).

Bruce, F. F., *Epistles of John* (Grand Rapids, MI: Wm. B. Eerdmans Publishing Co., 1970).

Burroughs, Jeremiah, *An Exposition of the Prophesy of Hosea* (1643, 1863; Beaver Falls, PA: Soli Deo Gloria Publications, n.d).

   —*The Saints' Happiness* (1660, 1867; Ligonier, PA: Soli Deo Gloria Publishing, 1988).

Calvin, John, *A Harmony of the Gospels, Matthew, Mark, and Luke*, Vols I-III (1555; Grand Rapids, MI: Wm. B. Eerdmans Publishing Co., 1972).

   —*Commentaries on the Twelve Minor Prophets: Hosea*, Vol. First, translated by John Owen (Grand Rapids, MI: Baker Book House, 1979).

—*Commentaries on the Twelve Minor Prophets: Zechariah and Malachi*, Vol. Fifth, Translated by John Owen (Grand Rapids, MI: Baker Book House, 1979).

—*Institutes of the Christian Religion,* John T. McNeill, ed. (Philadelphia, PA: The Westminster Press, 1960).

—*The First Epistle of John, John Calvin's New Testament Commentaries*, David W. Torrance and Thomas F. Torrance, eds. (Grand Rapids, MI: Wm. B. Eerdmans Publishing Co., 1959).

—*The First Epistle of Paul the Apostle to the Corinthians, Calvin's Commentaries*; David W. Torrance and Thomas F. Torrance, eds. (Grand Rapids, MI: Wm. B. Eerdmans Publishing Co., 1960).

—*The Epistles of Paul the Apostle to the Galatians, Ephesians, Philippians and Colossians, Calvin's Commentaries.* David W. Torrance and Thomas F. Torrance, eds. (Grand Rapids, MI: Wm B. Eerdmans Publishing Co., 1965).

—*The Gospel According to St. John, Part One, Calvin's Commentaries*, (Grand Rapids, MI: Wm. B. Eerdmans Publishing Co., 1961).

—*The Second Epistle of Paul the Apostle to the Corinthians and the Epistles to Timothy, Titus and Philemon, Calvin's Commentaries* (Grand Rapids, MI: Wm. B. Eerdmans Publishing Co., 1964).

Carson, D. A. *Exegetical Fallacies* (Grand Rapids, MI: Baker Book Co., 1984).

—*The Gospel According to John* (Grand Rapids, MI: Wm. B. Eerdmans Publishing Co., 1991).

Chalmers, Thomas, *The Expulsive Power of a New Affection* (1855; Edinburgh: Thomas Constable and Co., 2012).

Charnock, Stephen. *The Existence and Attributes of God.* Vols. I & II (1681–82; Grand Rapids, MI: Baker Book House, 1979).

—'The Voluntariness of Christ's Death' in *Christ Crucified* (Fearn, Ross-shire: Christian Focus Publications, 1996).

Cotton, John, *An Exposition of First John* (1657; Lafayette, IN: Sovereign Grace Publishers, 2001).

Cranfield, C. E. B, *A Critical and Exegetical Commentary on the Epistle to the Romans*, Vol. 1, *The International Critical Commentary*, ed. J. A. Emerton and C. E. B. Cranfield (Edinburgh: T & T Clark Limited, 1975).

Denney, James, *The Second Epistle to the Corinthians, The Expositor's Bible* (London: Hodder and Stoughton, 1894).

Durham, James, *A Commentary on the Book of Revelation* (1658; Willow Street, PA: Old Paths Publications, 2000).

——*The Song of Solomon* (1688, 1840; Edinburgh: Banner of Truth Trust, 1982).

Eadie, John, *A Commentary on the Greek Text of the Epistle of Paul to the Ephesians* (1883; Eugene, OR: Wipf and Stock Publishers, 1998).

Edwards, Jonathan, 'A Careful and Strict Inquiry into the Prevailing Notion of the Freedom of the Will', *Works of Jonathan Edwards*, Vol. II (1834; Edinburgh: Banner of Truth Trust, 1974).

——'Christian Knowledge: or The Importance and Advantage of a Thorough Knowledge of Divine Truth', *Works of Jonathan Edwards*, Vol. II (1834; Edinburgh: Banner of Truth Trust, 1974).

——*Charity and Its Fruits: Christian love as manifested in the heart and life* (1852; Edinburgh: Banner of Truth Trust, 1969).

——'Men Naturally Are God's Enemies', *Works of Jonathan Edwards*, Vol. II (1834; Edinburgh: Banner of Truth Trust, 1974).

——*On Knowing Christ, Select Works of Jonathan Edwards* (Edinburgh: Banner of Truth Trust, 1990).

——*Our Great and Glorious God*, ed. Don Kistler (Morgan, PA: Soli Deo Gloria Publications, 2003).

——*Selections from the Unpublished Writings of Jonathan Edwards: Treatise on Grace*, Alexander B. Grosart, ed. (1865: Ligonier, PA: Soli Deo Gloria, 1992).

——'Sinners in the Hands of an Angry God', *Works of Jonathan Edwards*, II (1834; Edinburgh: Banner of Truth Trust, 1974).

——*Treatise Concerning the Religious Affections, Select Works of Jonathan Edwards*, Vol. III (London: Banner of Truth Trust, 1961).

Emerson, Matt, 'At Its Heart, Science Is Faith-Based Too', *Wall Street Journal*, March 3, 2016.

Fairbairn, Patrick, *Exposition of Ezekiel* (1851; Minneapolis, MN: Klock & Klock Publishers, 1979).

—*The Pastoral Epistles* (1874; Minneapolis, MN: James and Klock Publishing Co., 1976).

Ferguson, Sinclair B., *John Owen on the Christian Life* (Edinburgh: Banner of Truth Trust, 1987).

—'The Reformed Doctrine of Sonship', Nigel M. de S. Cameron and Sinclair B. Ferguson, eds. *Pulpit and People: Essays in Honour of William Still on His 75th Birthday* (Edinburgh: Rutherford House Books, 1986).

—*The Trinitarian Devotion of John Owen* (Sanford, FL: Reformation Trust, 2014).

Flavel, John, 'An Exposition of the Assembly's Shorter Catechism', *Works of John Flavel*, Vol. VI (1820; Edinburgh: Banner of Truth Trust, 1968).

—*The Mystery of Providence* (1678; Edinburgh: Banner of Truth Trust, 1963).

—'Navigation Spiritualized', *Works of John Flavel*, Vol. V (1820; Edinburgh: Banner of Truth Trust, 1968).

Frame, John M., *The Doctrine of God* (Phillipsburg, NJ: P&R Publishing, 2002).

Franklin, James, 'What's in the Details', review article of *What Science Knows: And How It Knows It, Wall Street Journal*, April 30, 2014.

Gay, Jason, 'Caitlyn Jenner and What Courage Means', *Wall Street Journal*. June 20, 2015.

Gerstner, John H., *The Rational Biblical Theology of Jonathan Edwards*, Vol. II (Orlando, FL: Ligonier Ministries, 1992).

Green, Joel B., *The Gospel of Luke: The New International Commentary on the New Testament* (Grand Rapids, MI: Wm. B. Eerdmans Publishing Co., 1997).

Greenhill, William, *An Exposition of Ezekiel* (1645-67, 1863; Edinburgh: Banner of Truth Trust, 1994).

Gundry, Stanley N., *Love Them In: the Proclamation Theology of D. L. Moody* (Chicago, IL: Moody Press, 1976).

Gurnall, William, *The Christian in Complete Armour* (1662, 1665; London: Banner of Truth Trust, 1964).

Haldane, Robert, *Exposition of the Epistle to the Romans* (London: William Oliphant & Company, 1874).

Hamilton, Ian, *Let's Study the Letters of John* (Edinburgh: Banner of Truth Trust, 2008).

Hawking, Stephen, *A Brief History of Time* (New York, NY: Bantom Books, 1998).

Henry, Matthew, *Exposition of the Old and New Testaments*, Vols. I-VI (1708-10; various editions).

—*The Pleasantness of a Religious Life* (Fearn, Ross-shire: Christian Focus Publications, 1998).

Hillenbrand, Laura, *Unbroken: A World War II Story of Survival, Resilience, and Redemption* (New York: Random House, 2010).

Hodge, Charles, *A Commentary on 1 & 2 Corinthians* (1857, 1859; Edinburgh: Banner of Truth Trust, 1974).

—*A Commentary on Romans* (1864: London: Banner of Truth Trust, 1972.

—*Systematic Theology*, Vol. I (1871; Grand Rapids, MI: Wm. B. Eerdmans Publishing Co., 1981).

Howe, John, *The Redeemer's Tears Wept Over Lost Souls* (1684; Grand Rapids, MI: Baker Book House, 1978).

—'The Blessedness of the Righteous', *Works of John Howe*, Vol. II (1848; Ligonier, PA: Soli Deo Gloria Publications, 1990).

Hughes, P. E., *Paul's Second Epistle to the Corinthians, The New International Commentary on the New Testament* (Grand Rapids, MI: Wm. B. Eerdmans Publishing Co., 1962).

Hutcheson, George, *The Gospel of John* (1657, 1841; London: Banner of Truth Trust, 1972).

Jamieson, Robert; Fausset A. R.; Brown, David; *Commentary: Practical and Explanatory on the Whole Bible* (1864; Grand Rapids, MI: Zondervan Publishing House, 1961).

Jenkyn, William, *An Exposition upon the Epistle of Jude* (1653; Beaver Falls, PA: Soli Deo Gloria, n.d.).

Johnson, Marcus Peter. *The Incarnation of God: The Mystery of the Gospel as the Foundation of Evangelical Thinking* (Wheaton, IL: Crossway Books, 2015).

Johnson, Terry L. *When Grace Comes Alive: Living Through the Lord's Prayer* (Fearn, Ross-shire: Christian Focus Publications, 2003).

Jones, David H. ed., *The Hymnbook* (Richmond, VA: Presbyterian Church in the United States, 1955).

Kapic, Kelly M., *Communion With God: The Divine and the Human in the Theology of John Owen* (Grand Rapids, MI: Baker Academic, 2007).

Kelly, Douglas F., *Systematic Theology*, Vol. II (Fearn, Ross-shire: Christian Focus Publications, 2014).

—*Creation and Change: Gen 1.1 – 2.4 in the Light of Changing Scientific Paradigms* (1997; Fearn, Ross-shire: Mentor, 2008).

Kerr, Philip, *Prayer* (New York: Putnam, 2014).

Krauthammer, Charles, 'The Myth of "Settled Science"', *Savannah Morning News*, February 22, 2014.

—'Plotting Revenge, American-style', *Savannah Morning News*, June 14, 2014.

Kruse, Colin G., *The Letters of John* (Grand Rapids, MI: Wm. B. Eerdmans Publishing Co., 2000).

Lenski, Richard C. H. *Lenski's Commentary on the New Testament*: *The Interpretation of 1 Corinthians,* Richard C.H. Lenski and Patrick H. Alexander (Peabody, MA: Hendrickson Publishers, August 1998).

Lewis, C. S. *The Abolition of Man* (1944, 1947; C. S. Lewis Pte. Ltd., 1974).

Lewis, Peter, *The Genius of Puritanism* (Sussex: Carey Publications, 1977).

Lloyd-Jones, D. Martyn, *God's Way of Reconciliation: An Exposition of Ephesians 2* (London: Evangelical Press, 1972).

MacDonald, Gordon, 'How to Spot a Transformed Christian', *Leadership Journal*, Summer 2012.

Machen, J. Gresham, *God Transcendent* (1949; Edinburgh: Banner of Truth Trust, 1982).

Manton, Thomas, *Commentary on James*, (1693; London: Banner of Truth Trust, 1962).

—*Complete Works of Thomas Manton*, Vol. V, 'A Practical Commentary or An Exposition with Notes of the Epistle of John'''(1870; Worthington, PA: Maranatha Publications, n.d.)

—*Psalm 119*, Vol. II (1680; Edinburgh: Banner of Truth Trust, 1990).

Marshall, I. H., *The Epistles of John, The New International Commentary of the New Testament* (Grand Rapids, IL: Wm. B. Eerdmans Publishing Co., 1982).

McClymond, Michael J. and McDermott, Gerald R., *The Theology of Jonathan Edwards* (New York: Oxford University Press, 2012).

McDermott, Gerald R., 'Guided By the Great Cloud: Why Tradition is Vital for Understanding Scripture', *Christianity Today*, November 2014, Vol. 58, No. 9.

McHugh, Paul, 'Transgender Surgery Isn't the Solution', *Wall Street Journal*, June 12, 2014, A13.

Moore, T. V., *Commentary on Zechariah* (1856; London: Banner of Truth Trust, 1959).

—*Commentary on Haggai and Malachi* (1856; London: Banner of Truth Trust, 1960).

Morris, Leon, *Testaments of Love: A Study of Love in the Bible* (Grand Rapids, MI: Wm. B. Eerdmans Publishing Co., 1981).

—*The Apostolic Preaching of the Cross* (1955; Grand Rapids, MI: Wm. B. Eerdmans Publishing Co., 1965).

—*The First Epistle of Paul to the Corinthians, Tyndale New Testament Contemporaries* (Grand Rapids, MI: Wm. B. Eerdmans Publishing Co., 1958).

Motyer, J. A., Class Notes, Trinity College, 1977–79.

—*Look to the Rock: An Old Testament Background to Our Understanding of Christ* (Leicester, England: InterVarsity Press, 1966).

—*The Message of Exodus: The Days of Our Pilgrimage, The Bible Speaks Today: Old Testament* (Downers Grove, IL: InterVarstiy Press, 2005).

—*The Prophecy of Isaiah: An Introduction & Commentary* (Downers Grove, IL: InterVarsity Press, 1993).

Muller, Richard A., *Post-Reformation Reformed Dogmatics: The Rise and Development of Reformed Orthodoxy, ca. 1520 to ca. 1725, Vol. III The Divine Essence and Attributes* (Grand Rapids, MI: Baker Academic, 2003).

Murray, John, *Collected Writings of John Murray, Vol. Two: Select Lectures in Systematic Theology* (Edinburgh: Banner of Truth Trust, 1977).

—*The Epistle to the Romans, The New International Commentary to New Testament*, ed. F. F. Bruce (Grand Rapids, MI: Wm. B. Eerdmans Publishing Co., 1968).

Nisbet, Alexander, *Exposition of 1 & 2 Peter* (1658; Edinburgh: Banner of Truth Trust, 1982).

Nolan, Tom, 'Romantics But Not Rebels', *Wall Street Journal*, March 17-18, 2014.

Noll, Mark A., *The Scandal of the Evangelical Mind* (Grand Rapids, MI: Wm. B. Eerdmans Publishing Co., 1994).

Owen, John, 'Of Communion with God the Father, Son, and Holy Ghost', *Works of John Owen*, Vol. II (1850–53; London: Banner of Truth Trust, 1965).

—'On the Mortification of Sin in Believers', *Works of John Owen*, Vol. VI (1850–53; London: Banner of Truth Trust, 1967).

—'Vindiciae Evangalicae', *Works of John Owen*, Vol. XII (1850–53; London: Banner of Truth Trust; 1966).

Pink, A. W., *The Attributes of God* (Grand Rapids, MI: Baker Book House Company, 1975).

Packer, J. I., Class notes, Trinity College, Bristol England, Fall 1977.

—'God' in *New Dictionary of Theology*, Ferguson Sinclair B. & David F. Wright, eds. (Downers Grove, IL: InterVarsity Press, 1988).

—'God is Light: Divine Holiness and Justice', *The Reformation Study Bible*, R. C. Sproul, Gen. Ed. (Orlando, FL: Ligonier Ministries, 2005).

—*Knowing God* (Downers Grove, IL: InterVarsity Press, 1973).

—'Providence', *The Reformation Study Bible*, R. C. Sproul, Gen. Ed. (Orlando, FL: Ligonier Ministries, 2005).

—'The Love of God: Universal and Particular' in *Celebrating the Saving Work of God: The Collected Shorter Writings of J. I. Packer*, Vol. I (Carlisle: Paternoster Press, 1998).

—'The Spirituality of John Owen', *A Quest for Godliness*. Wheaton, IL: Crossway Books, 1998).

—'The Trinity and the Gospel', *Celebrating the Saving Work of God, The Collected Writings of J. I. Packer*, Vol. I (Carlisle: Paternoster Press, 1998).

—'Theism for Our Time', *God Who is Rich in Mercy*, Peter T. O'Brien and David G. Peterson, eds. (Grand Rapids, MI: Baker Books, 1986).

Phillips, J. B., *Your God Is Too Small* (1952; New York: The Macmillan Company, 1953).

Polkinghorne, John C., *One World* (Philadelphia, PA: Temple Foundation Pres, 2007).

Poole, Matthew, *Commentary on the Holy Bible*, Vols. I-III (1683–85, 1865; London: Banner of Truth Trust, 1963).

Robertson, Archibald and Alfred Plummer, *A Critical Exigetical Commentary on the First Epistle of Paul to the Corinthians: The International Critical Commentary* (Edinburgh: T & T Clark, 1914).

Ross, Hugh, *The Creator and the Cosmos: How the Greatest Scientific Discoveries of the Century Reveal God* (Colorado Springs, CO: NavPress Publishing Co., 1994).

Ryle, J. C., *Expository Thoughts on the Gospels: Luke, Vols I & II* (1858; Edinburgh: Banner of Truth Trust, 2012).

—*Holiness: Its Nature, Hindrances, Difficulties, & Roots* (1877, 1879; Edinburgh: Banner of Truth Trust, 2014).

Schaefer, Henry F., *Science & Christianity: Conflict or Coherence* (Watkinsville, GA: Apollos Trust, 2003).

Schaeffer, Francis A., *Escape from Reason* (Downers Grove, IL: InterVarsity Press, 1968).

—*The God Who Is There* (Downers Grove, IL: InterVarsity Press, 1968).

—*The Mark of the Christian* (Downers, Grove, IL: InterVarsity Press, 1975).

—*The New Super-Spirituality* (Downers Grove, IL: InterVarsity Press, 1972).

Schreiner, Susan E., *The Theater of His Glory: Nature & the Natural Order in the Thought of John Calvin* (Grand Rapids, MI: Baker Academic, 1991).

Shedd, William G. T., *Dogmatic Theology*, Vol. I (1888; Grand Rapids, MI: Zondervan Publishing House, nd).

Sibbes, Richard, 'The Bruised Reed and Smoking Flax', *Works of Richard Sibbes*, Vol. I. 1862; Edinburgh: Banner of Truth Trust, 1973).

—'The Danger of Backsliding', *Works of Richard Sibbes*, Vol. VII (1862–64; Edinburgh: Banner of Truth Trust, 1982).

Smalley, Stephen S., *1, 2, 3 John: Word Biblical Commentary*, Vol. 51 (Waco, TX: Word Books, 1984).

Smith, Christian and Denton, Melinda Lundquist, *Soul Searching: The Religious and Spiritual Lives of American Teenagers* (2005; New York: Oxford University Press, 2009).

Sproul, R. C., *The Holiness of God* (Wheaton, IL: Tyndale House Publishers, 1985).

Spurgeon, C. H., *Autobiography. Revised Edition, Vol. 1: The Early Years, 1834–1859* (1897–1900; London: Banner of Truth Trust, 1967).

—'A Message From God for Thee', Metropolitan Tabernacle Pulpit, Vol. VIII (London: Passmore & Alabaster, 1862).

—'Bread Enough, and to Spare', *Treasury of the New Testament*, Vol. II (London: Marshall, Morgan, and Scott, 1934).

—'Fellowship with God', *Treasury of the New Testament*, Vol. IV (London: Marshall, Morgan and Scott, 1934).

—'God's Love to the Saints', in *Treasury of the New Testament*, Vol. IV (London: Marshall, Morgan and Scott, 1934).

—'Herein is Love', *Treasury of the New Testament*, Vol. IV (London: Marshall, Morgan and Scott, 1934).

—'Love's Birth and Parentage', *Treasury of the New Testament*, Vol. IV. (London: Marshall, Morgan and Scott, 1934).

—'Love's Logic', *Treasury of the New Testament*, Vol. IV (London: Marshall, Morgan and Scott, 1934).

—*Morning and Evening* (1866; Grand Rapids, MI: Zondervan Publishing House, 1980).

—'Prodigal Love for the Prodigal Son', *Treasury of the New Testament*, Vol. II (London: Marshall, Morgan, and Scott, 1934).

—*The Treasury of David* (1892; Grand Rapids, MI: Zondervan Publishing House, 1950).

—'Zealots', in *Metropolitan Tabernacle Pulpit*, Vol. XI (1865; Cleveland, OH: Pilgrim Press, 1973).

Steinmetz, Katy, 'The Transgender Tipping Point: America's Next Civil Rights Frontier', *Time*, May 29, 2014.

Stott, John R. W., *The Epistles of John: An Introduction and Commentary, Tyndale New Testament Commentaries* (1964, Grand Rapids, MI: Wm. B. Eerdmans Publishing Co., 1975).

—*The Message of Ephesians: God's New Society, The Bible Speaks Today* (Leicester, England: InterVarsity Press, 1979).

—*Your Mind Matters* (1972. Downers Grove, IL: InterVarsity Press, 2006).

Stuart, A. Moody, *The Life of John Duncan* (1872; Edinburgh: Banner of Truth Trust, 1991).

Sweeting, George, *Catch the Spirit of Love* (Colorado Springs, CO: Victor Books, 1983).

Swinnock, George, 'The Incomparableness of God', *Works of George Swinnock*, Vol. IV (1868: Edinburgh: Banner of Truth Trust, 1992).

The Presbyterian Hymnal (1927; Richmond, Virginia: John Knox Press, 1952).

Thornwell, James Henley, *The Collected Writings of James Henley Thornwell, Vol. I – Theological* (1875; Edinburgh: Banner of Truth Trust, 1974).

Tozer, A. W., *The Knowledge of the Holy* (New York: Harper & Row Publishers, 1961).

Trapp, John, *Commentary on the Old and New Testaments*, Vols. I-V (1647; 1865–68; Eureka, CA: Tansky Publications, 1997).

Trinity Hymnal (1984; Norcross, GA: Great Commission Publications, Inc., 1990).

Turretin, Francis, *Institutes of Elenctic Theology*, Volume 1, ed. James T. Dennison, Jr., tr. George Musgrave Giger (1679; Phillipsburg, NJ: P&R, 1992).

Vanauken, Sheldon. *A Severe Mercy* (1977; London: Hodder and Stoughton; 1979).

Vos, Geerhardus, *Biblical Theology: Old & New Testaments* (Grand Rapids, MI: Wm. B. Eerdmans Publishing Co., 1948).

Warfield, B. B., 'God's Immeasurable Love', *The Saviour of the World* (New York: Hodder and Stoughton, 1913).

—'Imitating the Incarnation', *The Saviour of the World* (New York: Hodder and Stoughton, 1913).

—*Selected Shorter Writings*, Vol. 2, John E. Meeter, ed. (Phillipsburg, NJ: Presbyterian and Reformed Publishing Co., 1973).

—'The Biblical Doctrine of the Trinity', *Biblical & Theological Studies*, Samuel G. Craig, ed. (Philadelphia, PA: Presbyterian Reformed Publishing Co., 1968).

Watson, Thomas, *A Body of Divinity* (1692; London: Banner of Truth Trust, 1958).

—*The Art of Divine Contentment* (1653; Morgan, PA: Soli Deo Gloria Publications, 2001).

—*The Lord's Prayer* (1692; London: Banner of Truth Trust, 1960).

Wells, David F., *God in the Wasteland* (Grand Rapids, MI: Wm. B. Eerdmans Publishing Co., 1994).

—*God in the Whirlwind: How the Holy-love of God Reorients Our World* (Wheaton, IL: Crossway, 2014).

Wenham, G. J.; Motyer, J. A.; Carson, D. A.; France, R. T.; eds. *The New Bible Commentary: 21st Century Edition* (1953; Downers Grove, IL: InterVarsity Press, 1994).

Zamperini, Louis, *Devil at My Heels* (New York: E. P. Dutton and Co., Inc., 1956).

Zerwick, Max and Grosvenor, Mary, *A Grammatical Analysis of the Greek New Testament, Vol. II, Epistles to Apocalypse* (Rome: Biblical Institute Press, 1979).

Index of Scripture References

MATTHEW (CONT'D)

EPHESIANS (CONT'D)

EPHESIANS (CONT'D)

PHILIPPIANS

COLOSSIANS

General Index

241-42, 243, 245-53, 259, 261, 264, 265, 266-80, 298, 299, 309 n111
cheap grace, 229
children of wrath, 230, 266
Chisholm, Thomas, 118
Christian life
  as example to others, 182-83
  false expectations of, 49
  as good fight and race, 168
  as imitation of communicable attributes of God, 22
  as lived in the Spirit, 45
  and love for God, 318-322
Christology, 14
Chrysostom, 12
circumstances, 129, 135, 177-78, 279
Clark, John C., 20 n48
Comăneci, Nadia, 93
'Come, Holy Spirit, Heavenly Dove', 317
communicable attributes of God, 49
  governed by incommunicable attributes, 85
communion with God, 39-41
complaining, 279
comprehensiveness, 74
conquest of promised land, 196
Constantine, 37
contemplation, of goodness of God, 325-27
contentment, 140, 279-81
Cotton, John, xii, 284
Council of Chalcedon, 12
Council of Constantinople, 12, 37-38
Council of Ephesus, 12

Council of Nicea, 12
Cowper, William, 138, 293, 317
Cranfield, C. E. B., 219-20, 301 n77
creation, 19, 87-111
  enjoyment of, 103-5
  ex nihilo, 90-91
  God's power in, 64
  goodness of, 243-47
  observation of, 106
  original and subsequent, 90 n20
  our response to, 99-111
Creator-creature distinction, 49-50, 88
Creator-creature relation, 88
credibility of ministry, 182
Crieff Fellowship, 131
Cromwell, Oliver, 102
cross, 21-22
  fleeing to, 224-25
  and holiness of God, 158-59
  and love of the Father, 305
  meets mercy and justice of God, 218-21
  as supreme exhibition of love of Father and Son, 296
crucifixion, and providential governance of God, 125-26
cultural relativism, 170
curse of death, 266
cynicism, 348
Cyril of Jerusalem, 84
Cyrus, 122
Dabney, Robert L., 12
Daniel, prayer of, 172
dark night of the soul, 137
Davenant, John, xii, 320
David, sin of, 196